ELEMENTS OF GRAMMAR

Kluwer International Handbooks of Linguistics

VOLUME 1

The titles published in this series are listed at the end of this volume.

Elements of Grammar

Handbook in Generative Syntax

Edited by

LILIANE HAEGEMAN

KLUWER ACADEMIC PUBLISHERS
DORDRECHT / BOSTON / LONDON

Library of Congress Cataloging-in-Publication Data

Elements of grammar : handbook in generative syntax / edited by
Liliane Haegeman.
p. cm.
Includes index.
ISBN 0-7923-4297-6 (alk. paper)
1. Grammar, Comparative and general--Syntax. 2. Generative
grammar. I. Haegeman, Liliane.M. V.
P291.E45 1997
415--dc20 96-43878

ISBN 0-7923-4297-6;

Published by Kluwer Academic Publishers,
P.O. Box 17, 3300 AA Dordrecht, The Netherlands.

Kluwer Academic Publishers incorporates
the publishing programmes of
D. Reidel, Martinus Nijhoff, Dr W. Junk and MTP Press.

Sold and distributed in the U.S.A. and Canada
by Kluwer Academic Publishers,
101 Philip Drive, Norwell, MA 02061, U.S.A.

In all other countries, sold and distributed
by Kluwer Academic Publishers Group,
P.O. Box 322, 3300 AH Dordrecht, The Netherlands.

02-0799-150 ts

Printed in the Netherlands (on acid-free paper)

To Nelson

TABLE OF CONTENTS

LILIANE HAEGEMAN

ELEMENTS OF GRAMMAR*

1. INTRODUCTION

The aim of this handbook is to provide a forum in which some of the generative syntacticians whose work has had an impact on theoretical syntax over the past 20 years are invited to present their views on one or more aspects of current syntactic theory. The handbook is destined for an audience of linguists working in the generative framework. A general background knowledge of generative syntax is essential for the understanding of this book, but I hope that the introduction below will make the book accessible not only to a specialized audience but also to advanced students who are relatively new to the field.

During the last five years, the views on theoretical syntax have undergone a number of changes which have a direct bearing on the analyses proposed for empirical data. This situation is mainly due to the developments in the theory referred to as the Minimalist Program (Chomsky 1991, 1993, 1995). While the Minimalist Program adopts, reinterprets and elaborates some of the principles and formalisms of the classical "Government and Binding" ("GB") framework (see Chomsky 1995: 1–11 for discussion), it also departs significantly from many of the standard assumptions of the classical GB approach. To mention but one telling example: the structural configuration "government", which had become central in many respects (Case assignment, ECP, definition of domain for binding etc.) in the traditional GB framework, does not play any role in Minimalism. The literature written in the Minimalist paradigm does not as yet offer a fully fledged theoretical framework: Minimalism is a research program which is being explored and developed and which has already undergone considerable modifications since the first publications appeared in the early nineties.[1] The developments in the Minimalist theory have had a fruitful impact on a more classical "GB"-type approach to theory; Minimalism leads syntacticians to re-examine the concepts standardly assumed in work in syntax, and to explore ways in which "Minimalist" concepts (checking theory, for instance, as discussed in section 2.2.2) can be incorporated in a more classical approach.

The chapters in this volume each focus on one specific aspect of the grammar. As a general theme, the papers are all concerned with the question of the composition of the clause, i.e. what kind of components the clause is made up of, and how these components are put together in the clause. The questions raised concerning the structure of the clause can equally be

Liliane Haegeman (ed.), Elements of Grammar, 1–71.

raised for the structure of other projections, notably the DP. See for instance Abney (1987), Szabolcsi (1989), Taraldsen (1990), Giorgi and Longobardi (1990), Cinque (1994), etc. Pollock's and Rizzi's contributions to this volume deal with the question of the functional structure of the clause, the former concentrating on the IP domain, the latter on the CP domain. Baker's and Grimshaw's papers deal with the insertion of lexical material in the structure. The former focuses on the insertion of arguments in the clause, i.e. constituents having a thematic relation to the predicate; the latter deals with problem of clitic combinations in Romance. McCloskey's paper concerns the traditional notion "subject". He shows that what once was thought of as a unitary concept has gradually become "deconstructed" in the course of the development of generative grammar. Brody, finally, examines the relation between various components of the clause as expressed in the form of chain-relations.

All the contributors to this volume refer more or less intensively to notions introduced by Minimalism and all the papers address questions which every syntactic theory, Minimalist or classical, eventually has to address. Michal Brody espouses his own radically representational version of Minimalism (see section 2.3 below); Jane Grimshaw adopts Optimality Theory as the theoretical basis for her work (see section 5).

In my own introduction I do not attempt to provide a complete survey of the state of the art in generative syntax or of the current developments. Such types of surveys would be the subject matter of a book. What I will do is highlight some of the developments that have occurred in theoretical syntax in the last ten years. My choice of topics is admittedly highly subjective: I have selected those components of the theory that seem to me to be of ongoing interest both for classical GB approaches and for Minimalist approaches, and which are also relevant to the papers in this volume. I will also point out some relations between proposals in the literature which have been made independently and which had, so far, not been brought to bear on each other. Occasionally I will add more speculative remarks, suggesting possible further developments and ramifications.

An introductory textbook to syntactic theory will characteristically try to outline the basic building blocks of a theory and to provide the stable stepping stones for the novice. My introduction to the current handbook may appear rather to be doing the opposite. All work in generative syntax shares the basic methodological assumptions concerning, for instance, what constitutes the type of evidence admitted in linguistic analysis, or how a syntactic argument is formulated. There is also a clear convergence on many specific issues. For instance, nowadays, no one will dispute the need to distinguish functional projections from lexical projections. However, general theoretical issues (say, the issue of locality) or individual empirical phenomena (say, verb movement) may often receive different analyses, depending on the specific assumptions of the researcher, and the different analyses proposed each have their advantages and disadvantages. I will illustrate some of these different types of analyses in the course of this introduction. I hope that this will not discourage the student away from theoretical syntax. Rather, I hope that my introduction and the papers in this book will show clearly that research in generative linguistics is part of an ongoing debate, that a lot of progress has been made in generative syntax, and also that there is a lot of work yet to be done. Many questions, theoretical and empirical, remain unanswered and even the clear and definite analyses which we thought we had arrived at for a certain range of phenomena should be regularly re-submitted to a critical evaluation.

The introduction to the handbook is organized as follows. In section 2 I discuss the levels of representation postulated in the classical GB framework, and I introduce some Minimalist variants: classical Minimalism (Chomsky 1993, 1995), which is strongly derivational, and Brody's (1995a) radically representational approach. In this section we shall consider the general notion of "movement" as it is currently used in generative syntax. Sections 3 and 4 deal with elements of the structure of the clause. In section 3 I discuss the thematic layer of the clause, introducing the notions of thematic hierarchy, Uniformity of Theta Assignment, and the hypothesis that the base position of the subject is VP-internal. In section 4 I discuss the decomposition of the IP layer and the CP layer and the questions raised both for Minimalist and for classical approaches. In section 5 I introduce optimality theory and the question of lexical insertion.

2. LEVELS OF REPRESENTATION

2.1. *The Government and Binding Model*

The classical format of the Government and Binding model of syntactic representation is the so-called T-model, with its different levels of representation as summarized in (1):[2]

(1)

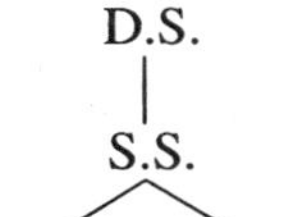

Assuming the theory as presented, for instance, in introductory textbooks such as my own *Introduction to Government and Binding Theory* (Haegeman 1994b), the English sentence (2a) would have the D-structure representation in (2b), the S-structure representation in (2c) and the LF representation in (2d). The representations in (2) are partial and will serve as the basis for discussion. For expository reasons many details are omitted.

(2) a. John eats chocolate.
b. [$_{CP}$ [$_{C^\circ}$-WH] [$_{IP}$ e [$_{I^\circ}$-s] [$_{VP}$ [$_{DP}$ John] eat [$_{DP}$ chocolate]]]]
c. [$_{CP}$ [$_{C^\circ}$-WH] [$_{IP}$ [$_{DP}$ John$_j$] [$_{I^\circ}$t$_i$] [$_{VP}$ [$_{DP}$ t$_j$] eat-s$_i$ [$_{DP}$ chocolate]]]]
d. [$_{CP}$ [$_{C^\circ}$-WH] [$_{IP}$ [$_{DP}$ John$_j$] [$_{I^\circ}$ eat-s$_i$-t$_i$] [$_{VP}$ [$_{DP}$ t$_j$] t$_i$ [$_{DP}$ chocolate]]]]

French (3a) has the D-structure (3b), the S-structure (3c) and the LF (3d):

(3) a. Jean mangeait du chocolat.
Jean ate of chocolate
"Jean ate chocolate."
b. [$_{CP}$ [$_{C^\circ}$-WH] [$_{IP}$ e [$_{I^\circ}$-ait] [$_{VP}$ [$_{DP}$ Jean [$_{I^\circ}$ mange-] [$_{DP}$ du chocolat]]]]
c. [$_{CP}$ [$_{C^\circ}$-WH] [$_{IP}$ [$_{DP}$ Jean$_j$] [$_{I^\circ}$ mange$_i$-ait] [$_{VP}$ [$_{DP}$ t$_j$] t$_i$ [$_{DP}$ du chocolat]]]]
d. [$_{CP}$ [$_{C^\circ}$-WH] [$_{IP}$ [$_{DP}$ Jean$_j$] [$_{I^\circ}$ mange$_i$-ait] [$_{VP}$ [$_{DP}$ t$_j$] t$_i$ [$_{DP}$ du chocolat]]]]

The classical conception of the multi-level approach to sentence structure is relatively static: at each level, the clause is projected in full. The modifications between the levels are instantiations of movement, i.e. move-α, where α may be a head or a maximal projection. The levels of PF and of LF are what have come to be called "interface" levels in the Minimalist Program: they are the interface of the language module with the articulatory-perceptive modules, on the one hand, and with the conceptual-cognitive systems, on the other hand. D-Structure and S-structure are internal to the syntactic computational system.

2.1.1. *D-structure*

In the D-structure, (2b), the lexical items are base-generated in their thematic positions: the transitive verb, *eat*, projects a VP which contains the two theta-marked arguments, namely the AGENT *John* and the THEME *chocolate* (for the base position of the subject, cf. the discussion in section 3.3 and also in McCloskey's paper). Thus, D-structure respects the theta criterion, the requirement that (i) each argument be assigned one and only one theta role and, conversely, (ii) that each theta role associated with a lexical head be assigned to one and only one argument.[3] D-structure respects other selectional requirements: VP is the complement of, i.e. selected by, a functional head, I°, which contains the tense and agreement morphology, here *-s*. IP, in turn, is then selected by C. That C selects IP is suggested by the fact that in English, for instance, the complementizer *that* introduces a finite clause and the complementizer *for* introduces a non-finite clause. CP itself may be embedded or independent. C serves to encode the illocutionary force of clause: declarative, interrogative, relative, etc. Anticipating the discussion in section 4.2, observe that C has a dual function: it selects the clausal complement (finite/non-finite) and it also encodes the illocutionary force of the clause.

Schematically, the clause structure decomposes into three layers, each associated with a specific type of information: (i) the VP layer, or the thematic layer, (ii) the IP layer, which contains the functional morphology, and (iii) the CP layer, which establishes the force of the clause.

(4)
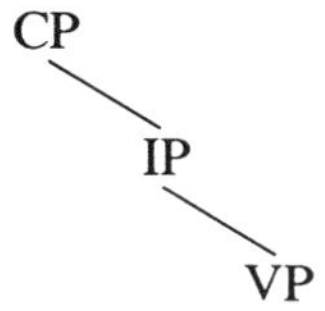

We will return to these layers in sections 3 and 4. We will see that the simple structure in (4) has to be decomposed into a more articulated structure, where each of the layers decomposes into a set of discrete projections.

As can be seen from (3b), the D-structure of French (3a) is analogous to English (2b): again the verb is inserted under V°, and its arguments are projected in their thematic positions. The differences between English (2a) and French (3a) emerge at S-structure.

2.1.2. *S-structure*

2.1.2.1. *Movement Dependencies.* S-structure is relevant for the licensing of the morphological properties of the constituents of the clause. It is standardly assumed that a constituent base-generated at one particular position in the structure need not necessarily be found at that point throughout the derivation and that it may be moved to another (c-commanding) position at S-structure. The movement-relation reflects a dependency between two positions in a clause. Consider, for instance, the position of the direct objects in the sentences in (5):

(5) a. John will buy this book.
b. Which book will John buy?

In (5a) the direct object DP *this book* is adjacent to the verb *buy*. This position corresponds to the thematic properties of the object, which is assigned its thematic role ("theme") by the verb *buy*. On the other hand, in (5b) the object *which book* does not occupy the position adjacent to the verb. Rather it occurs clause-initially, a position which is required by virtue of the presence of the *wh*-element *which*, which encodes illocutionary force, here interrogative. However, at the same time, in (5b) *which book* is the object of *buy* just as in (5a) *this book* is the object of *buy*. The thematic properties of *which book* in (5b) require it to be part of the VP; the presence of the *wh*-word *which* requires it to be clause-initial. To capture the dual relation of *which book* in sentence (5b) – object of *buy* and encoder of illocutionary force – we can say that in (5b) *which book* is base-generated in the object position, and that it moves leftward to the higher position at S-structure. This dependency between the sentence-initial position and the VP-internal base position of *which book* can be represented as in (5c), where t encodes the thematic or base position of the moved object. Dependency relations such as those in (5c) can be expressed in terms of chains. In (5c) there is a chain formed by the preposed *which book* and its trace (5d).

(5) c. Which $book_i$ will John buy t_i?
d. ⟨which $book_i$, t_i⟩

The existence of dependencies such as that between the sentential initial constituent *which book* and the postverbal position signalled by t in (5c) is relatively uncontroversial, although there is no full agreement as to whether the dependency must be expressed derivationally via movement of a constituent, or whether the notion of movement is a metaphor to express a representational dependency. We return to this point in section 2.2.3. Brody's contribution to this volume considers the conditions which govern chain formation, against a background of Minimalist – and Radically Minimalist – assumptions. See also section 2.3 for an introduction to Radical Minimalism.

Two types of dependencies – i.e. of chains – are traditionally distinguished: (i) dependencies between head positions, which could be expressed in terms of X°-movement, and (ii) dependencies between positions hosting maximal projections, expressed by XP-movement. We will briefly look at both types in the following sections.

2.1.2.2. *Head Movement.* The classical GB approach assumes that at S-structure the verb merges with its verbal morphology by a process of morphological incorporation (Baker 1988). According to assumptions current up until the late eighties (see Pollock 1989 and also Pollock's contribution to this volume for references), the finite verb is created derivationally. In (3a) above, for instance, the form *mangeait* ("ate"), which is inflected for past tense and for third person singular, is not base-generated as such. Rather the root of the verb *mange-* is base-generated under V°, the inflectional morpheme *-ait*, an affix, is base-generated under I°, and the root *mange-* incorporates into the finite inflectional morphology, *-ait*, forming the new complex head *mangeait*. The incorporation of the verb to the affix is obligatory: it satisfies the morphological subcategorization frame of the affix. In English, similarly, roots are generated under V°, inflectional morphemes are generated under I°. In English, contrary to French, the root of the lexical verb does not move to I°. Rather, it is proposed that the inflection lowers onto the verb. Evidence for the difference between French and English verb positions is provided by (6): in

French, the finite verb precedes the negative marker *pas* ("not") (6a′) and the frequency adverb *souvent* ("often") (6b′). In English, on the other hand, the finite lexical verb cannot precede the negation marker *not* (cf. (6a)/(6c)) or the adverb *often* ((6b)/(6d)).

(6) a. *John eats not chocolate

a′. Jean ne mange pas de chocolate
Jean *ne* eats not of chocolate
"Jean does not eat any chocolate."

b. *John eats often chocolate

b′. Jean mange souvent du chocolat
Jean eats often of chocolate
"Jean eats often chocolate"

c. Jean does not eat chocolate

d. Jean often eats chocolate

Lowering operations, such as lowering the inflection to the verb postulated for English (2) above, are problematic, however, since the traces of the lowered constituents will violate the ECP, the condition that traces have to be properly governed and identified by an antecedent. The question arises, for instance, how the trace of the lowered inflection, t_i, in (2c) could satisfy the ECP, since the inflection *-s* is lower in the structure and hence cannot c-command its trace. We discuss a first solution to the lowering problem in the next section.

2.1.2.3. *XP Movement and Pied Piping.* In addition to dependencies between head positions, there are also dependencies between XP positions. Both in English and in French the subject DP *John/Jean* in (2) and (3), for instance, cannot remain VP-internally, as its case cannot be licensed there. The DP will undergo leftward A-movement to the specifier of IP, where it will be assigned nominative case (2c, 3c). Thus there is a dependency relation between the specifier position of IP, which hosts the moved subject DP, and the VP-internal base position in which the thematic role of the subject is licensed.

Let us for a moment return to our example (5b), in which movement affects the object phrase *which book*. We assume that the DP *which book* is required to move because of the presence of the *wh*-feature associated with *which*, witness the fact that in (5a), *this book* does not undergo movement. *Which* is a *wh*-element which signals the interrogative force of the clause. Strictly speaking, then, the component of *which book* which triggers the movement of the phrase is the element *which*. Observe, though, that we cannot move the marker of illocutionary force, *which*, all by itself:

(5) c. *Which will you buy book?

So, even though it is *which* alone which triggers the movement, *which* moves with its nominal complement (*book*). We say that *which* pied pipes *book*. *Book* in (5c) appears where it does, not by virtue of its own intrinsic features, but rather because it is associated with an element, *which*, which has this distributional requirement.

Other, perhaps better known, cases of Pied Piping concern examples with PPs containing *wh*-complements such as those in (7):

(7) a. Who did you talk to?
b. To whom did you talk?

In (7a) only the complement of the preposition (*who*) is moved, stranding the preposition *to* in a lower position. In (7b) the preposition *to* is pied piped by the *wh*-movement.

If the surface position of a constituent may be linked to one or more lower positions, the question arises at which of these related positions the various properties of the constituent get evaluated. It is clear, for instance, that although *which book* in (5b) occupies the specifier position of CP (see Rizzi's contribution to the volume for a more precise account), its thematic properties get evaluated at the VP-internal base position. We return to this problem in section 2.1.3.2.

2.1.3. *Logical Form (LF)*

In (2) and in (3) the difference between the S-Structure and the LF representation is minimal. For English (2d) the LF representation will undo the potential ECP violation created by I-lowering (cf. the discussion of (2c) above): the verb-inflection complex created by the S-structure lowering moves up and adjoins to the offending trace, t_i (Chomsky 1991). Other effects of LF movement concern interpretation. I briefly illustrate two cases here: *wh*-raising (1.1.3.1) and reconstruction (1.1.3.2).

2.1.3.1. Wh-*Raising*. Consider English (8):

(8) a. *John will meet whom?
b. Whom will John meet?

In the interrogative sentence (8b) the *wh*-phrase *whom* is fronted. This is the only option in English: (8a), in which *whom* remains in the base position, is ungrammatical. (8b) has the D-structure (8c), S-structure (8d) and LF (8e):[4]

(8) c. $[_{CP}$ [C°+WH] $[_{IP}$ e $[_{I°}$ will] $[_{VP}$ $[_{DP}$ John] meet $[_{DP}$ whom]]]]
d. $[_{CP}$ $[_{DP}$ $whom_k]$ $[_{C°}$ $will_i$ $_{+WH}]$ $[_{IP}$ $[_{DP}$ $John_j]$ $[_{I°}$ $t_i]$ $[_{VP}$ $[_{DP}$ $t_j]$ $meet_j$ $[_{DP}$ $t_k]]]]$
e. $[_{CP}$ $[_{DP}$ $whom_k]$ $[_{C°}$ $will_{i+WH}]$ $[_{IP}$ $[_{DP}$ $John_j]$ $[_{I°}$ t_j $t_i]$ $[_{VP}$ $[_{DP}$ $t_j]$ meet $[_{DP}$ $t_k]]]]$

Wh-movement moves the *wh*-phrase to the specifier of CP at S-structure. As mentioned already in the discussion of (5b), this movement serves to license the interrogative force of the clause.[5] In (8d) the moved *wh*-constituent occupies [Spec, CP], its scope domain is the domain which it c-commands, i.e. the clause.

S-structure movement of *wh*-phrases is not a property of all languages. In the following examples from Chinese the italicized *wh*-constituent does not occupy a scope position (Huang 1995: 149, ex 97).

(9) a. Zhangsan yiwei Lisi mai-le shenme?
Zhangsan think Lisi bought what
"What does Zhansan think Lisi bought?"

b. Zhangsan xiang-zhidao Lisi mai-le shenme.
Zhangsan wonder Lisi bought what
"Zhangsan wonders what Lisi bought."

The *wh*-constituent *shenme* ("what") occupies the same position in (9a) as in (9b), in spite of the fact that its scope differs. In (9a) *shenme* has matrix scope – the sentence is a direct question – and in (9b) it has embedded scope. The difference in interpretation of the *wh*-phrases in (9a) and (9b) is not reflected by S-structure movement. Since LF is the level encoding interpretive matters, one would expect the LF representations of (9a) and (9b) to encode the fact that the question word *shenme* in (9a) has matrix scope and that in (9b) has embedded scope. The standard proposal (see May 1985) is that at LF the *wh*-constituent *shenme* will raise to the relevant scope position. The LF representation of (9a) is (9c), that of (9b) is (9d) (Huang 1995: 149: his (100a) and (101b)):

(9) c. [$shenme_i$ [Zhansan yiwei [[Lisi mai-le t_i]]]]
d. [[Zhangsan xiang-zhidao [$shenme_i$ [Lisi mai-le t_i]]]]

LF representations are not expected to differ cross-linguistically. The cross-linguistic variation between Chinese interrogatives and their English counterparts rests in the availability of overt movement; it is a matter of S-structure and PF representations, not of LF.

2.1.3.2. *Reconstruction.* Another operation standardly postulated for LF is reconstruction. Reconstruction can be seen as the counterpart of Pied Piping. While Pied Piping means that extra material is moved along with the target of movement (as seen above in the discussion of (5b) and of (7b) in section 2.1.2.3), reconstruction as it were returns the pied piped material to a lower position. The effect of reconstruction operations is to undo Pied Piping.

In our discussion of Pied Piping we said that a moved constituent does not necessarily get evaluated exhaustively in its surface position. Specifically, in (5b), the thematic role of the constituent *which book* is determined in the base position. With respect to pied piped material, the question arises at which point in the dependency relation the properties of a constituent get evaluated. Reconstruction is in a sense an answer to this question. Let us illustrate this problem with examples showing the relation between Pied Piping and binding relations, i.e referential dependency relations between DPs.

Consider, for instance, the sentences in (10). Each sentence contains the reflexive *himself*, i.e. an anaphoric element which, following Principle A of the Binding Theory, must be bound by a coindexed constituent in an A-position. In each of the examples, the DP *which pictures of himself* has moved leftward. Following the reasoning in section 2.2.2.3, we can say that the target of movement in these examples is the interrogative element *which*, which must move to a left peripheral position where it can encode illocutionary force. In each of the examples, though, *which* has pied piped its complement, *pictures of himself.*

(10) a. John wondered which pictures of himself Mary liked.
b. Which pictures of himself_i will John_i sell?
c. Which pictures of himself_i does John_i think that Jane will sell?

Let us consider the interpretation of *himself* in the above examples, in terms of the requirements of the Binding Theory. (10a) is unproblematic: *himself*, the anaphor, is bound by the matrix subject *John*. In this example, the Binding Theory can apply to the S-structure representation. (10b) is grammatical, even though the reflexive *himself* is not c-commanded by the antecedent *John*. One might account for this by proposing that the Binding Theory, or at least Principle A, applies at D-structure: at D-structure, the *wh*-phrase *which pictures of himself* will occupy its base position and the reflexive can be bound by the subject DP:

(11) $[_{IP}$ ec will $[_{VP}$ John sell which pictures of himself?]][6]

But even though it provides a means of accounting for the grammaticality of (10b), a D-structure approach to binding fails to predict the grammaticality of (10c). The antecedent of *himself* must be a DP with the features [masculine; singular], i.e. *John* rather than *Jane*. As was the case in (10a) and (10b), the antecedent *John* does not c-command *himself* at S-structure. In this example, though, the D-structure will not provide us with the adequate representation either:

(12) a. D-structure
$[_{CP}$ $[_{IP}$ ec $[_{VP}$ John$_i$ does think $[_{CP}$ that $[_{IP}$ ec will $[_{VP}$ Jane sell which pictures of himself$_i$]]]]]]?

At D-structure the only potential binder for the reflexive is *Jane*, in [Spec,VP]. How can we then account for the grammaticality of this example? Consider, again, the S-structure of (10c):

(12) b. [Which pictures of himself$_i$ does [John$_i$ think $[_{CP}$ t'_i that $[_{IP}$ Jane will sell t_i?]]]]

Following standard assumptions, the *wh*-phrase *which pictures of himself* moves successive cyclically via the embedded [Spec, CP] to the matrix [Spec, CP]. In (10c) the reflexive is bound by *John*, but neither the S-structure position nor the D-structure position of the *wh*-phrase can ensure this kind of binding in an obvious way. We need a configuration in which there is a c-command relation between *John* and *himself*, but we need to ensure that in such a configuration the potential antecedent *Jane* does not intervene as a c-commanding subject. The relevant position is the one signalled by the intermediate trace, t′ in (12). It is proposed in the literature that the binding configuration required for this sentence is achieved by reconstruction. The *wh*-phrase in our example has moved through the embedded [Spec, CP] and is reconstructed there at LF. As a first approximation let us propose that it be reconstructed there.

(12) c. does John$_i$ think $[_{CP}$ [which pictures of himself$_i$]$_j$ that $[_{IP}$ Jane will sell t_j]]

While (12c) provides the configuration to allow *himself* to be bound by *John*, it is not an adequate LF representation for (10c) either. Recall that (10c) is a question and that we assume that the *wh*-constituent (*which* in this example) licenses the interrogative force of the clause at the CP level. English *wh*-phrases move to [Spec, CP] at S-structure; we assume that analogously Chinese *wh*-constituents move to [Spec, CP] at LF (cf. 1.3.2.1). But in (12c) the *wh*-phrase is reconstructed in full, thus undoing the licensing of the interrogative force and destroying the parallel between English and Chinese LF representations. A more complex type of reconstruction is needed, which does lower the argument but preserves the LF position of *which*, the interrogative operator. (12d) is a rough representation. We decompose the *wh*-phrase into its component parts, with the constituent carrying the *wh*-feature in the scope position and the reflexive in a lower position, where it can be interpreted.

(12) d. $[_{CP}$ [which$_k$] does $[_{IP}$ John$_i$ think
$[_{CP}$ [t_k pictures of himself$_i$]$_j$ that $[_{IP}$ Jane will sell t_j]]]]

In (12d) *pictures of himself*, which was pied piped by *which*, is reconstructed now to a lower position.

2.2. *Some Notes on the Minimalist Program*

Over the last 5 years, and keeping within the main tenets of the Principles and Parameters framework, Chomsky (1995) has been developing a novel approach to syntax referred to as the Minimalist Program. It is not feasible, at this stage, to provide a complete introduction to this program, which is in the process of being elaborated. In the present discussion I will briefly present some of the concepts developed in the Minimalist approach. It seems to me that for many of these issues discussed in the Minimalist literature a polarization of the two approaches, which we might refer to as the "classical GB approach" and the "Minimalist approach", is not necessarily the optimal way of looking at things and that many of the concepts which were introduced in the Minimalist Program can be integrated into the classical model. The points introduced below are related to the papers in this volume. The issues discussed in sections 3, 4 and 5 below are of relevance both to a Minimalist and a "classical" generative approach.

2.2.1. *Merge and Move: A Dynamic Approach to Clause Structure*

Chomsky (1993, 1995) proposes that the linguistic computational model links two levels of representation, "LF" and "PF", the so-called interface levels. Chomsky no longer postulates the language-internal levels of representation S-structure and D-structure. The static multi level approach to syntactic representations is replaced by a more dynamic conception of the build up of clauses. I will give a rather intuitive outline of the Minimalist approach to clause structure, simplifying the technical complexities and leaving out of the discussion the differences between the successive concrete implementations of the core ideas.

In Minimalist theory, the construction of a clause consists of picking items from the lexicon, the inventory of morphemes of the language, and building up structure by combining these items or their projections. Let us assume that we start from the following array of elementary units, the lexical items, taken from the lexicon.

(13) *John, left*, I[+Tense, +AGR][7]

The array of items in (13) constitutes what Chomsky (1995: 225–227) refers to as the Numeration; these components will be the building blocks for a sentence. Roughly, the construction of the sentence *John left* will proceed as follows (see Collins 1994, Fujita 1996 for accessible discussions). First, we select the elements *John* and *left* from the Numeration (13).

(14) a. Select *John*
b. Select *left*

We then combine these two elements or their projections into one phrase marker. The verb *left* merges with *John*:

(14) c. Merge (*John, left*)

Merge gives rise to a structure in which the projection of *John* (say a DP) is inserted into an empty position of the projection of *left* (a VP) (see Collins 1994, Chomsky 1995).

(14) d.

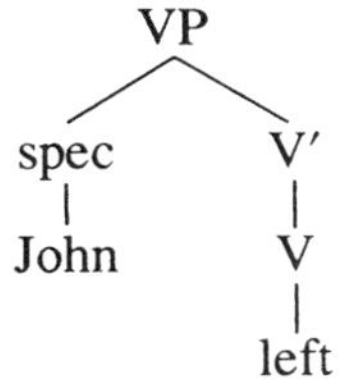

One of the important innovations of the Minimalist approach and one which has also been gaining ground in most non-minimalist work, is the idea that the inflected forms of the lexical elements are not created by the derivation. Lexical items are inserted ("base-generated" in the classical terminology) *with* their inflection. So, rather than inserting the verb *leave* under V° and then inserting the past morphology under I°, we insert the inflected form *left*. Similarly, NPs (or DPs) are inserted with their case morphology (abstract or overt). Thus in the Numeration *John* will already be associated with case, in our example, the nominative case. We return to this point in sections 2.2.2 and 2.2.3 (see also Pollock, this volume).

Proceeding with the derivation, we then select the functional head I° from the Numeration, and we merge I° and the phrase marker created above (14f), yielding (14g).

(14) e. Select I

f. Merge (I, VP)

g.

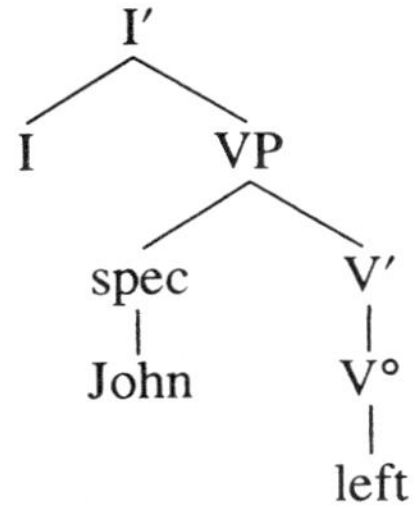

The subject DP *John* has to license its nominative case. Let us assume that this is done in the specifier position of I° (see section 4). *John* will have to move to reach a specifier head relation with I°, giving rise to the structure (14h). In order to allow the licensing of nominative case, an empty slot is created in the specifier position of IP and *John* moves into that slot.

(14) h. Move *John*

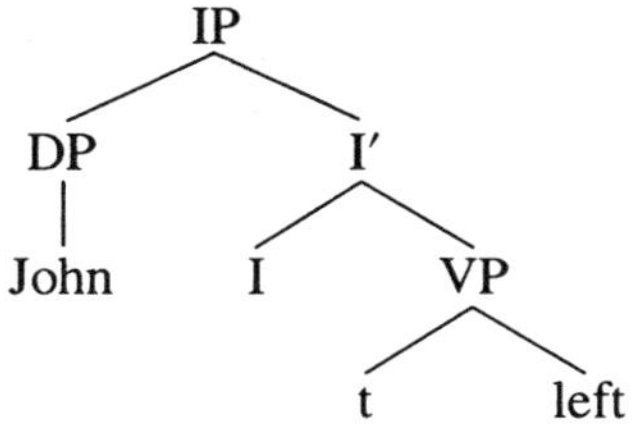

As is shown by the simplified representations above, the Minimalist approach to clause structure is dynamic: there is not a single static layer of D-structure in which all items of the clause are inserted at one go; rather, structures are built up step by step, integrating new elements into the structure by a merger operation ("Merge") or by the rearranging of elements already in the structure ("Move"). Merge and Move are the elementary operations which will eventually generate the clausal structure.

The computational system generates structures which will, at some point, be submitted to Spell out, i.e. they will be given an overt form. Spell out feeds the PF interface, the overt shape of the sentence. Syntactic structures are also interpreted, i.e. they are assigned a semantic representation, corresponding to the level of LF. With respect to our previous example, the sentence *John left* will be spelt out at point (14h). For the Full Interpretation of the sentence, though, we have the further requirement that the verb *left*, associated with past tense morphology, be related to the abstract past tense of the functional node I. This will be achieved by LF – i.e. covert – movement of V° to I°.

(14) i.

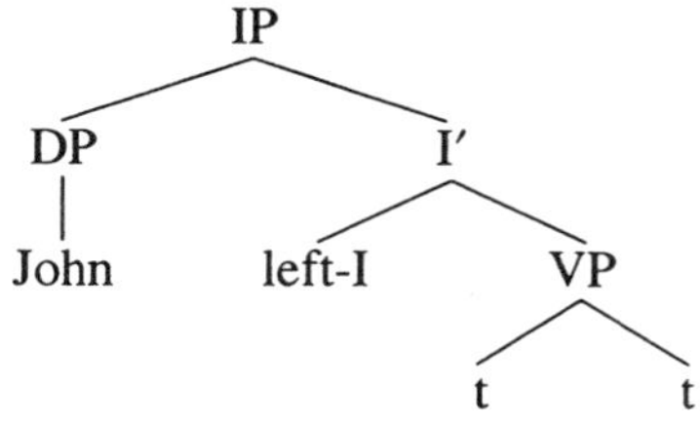

The covert movement of V° to I° in (14i) does not feed Spell out, it is input to LF. (15) summarizes the organization of the grammar in the Minimalist Program.

(15) a.
Lexicon
|
Numeration
|
Select
Merge & Move
|
Spell out (14h) = PF
|
Move (covert)
|
LF (14i)

If movement is triggered by an attraction from a head, then we might propose that Attract is the fundamental step in the derivation. Replacing the concept of Move, as triggered by a feature of the moved constituent, by Attract, as triggered by a feature of the landing site, has many repercussions. I will not go into these here since they are not directly relevant for the papers in this volume (see Chomsky 1995, Fujita 1996).

(15) b.
Lexicon
|
Numeration
|
Select
Merge
Attract
|
Spell out (14h) = PF
|
Attract (covert)
|
LF (14i)

Observe that Minimalist Spell out, unlike classical S-structure, is not conceived of as a static level of representation. Rather, Spell out is the point at which the structure that has been formed is rendered overt. Beyond Spell out, lexical insertion of items drawn from the lexicon is no longer available (but see Chomsky 1995 for some discussion).

The Minimalist Program assumes that operations in the derivation of clauses are subject to a principle of Economy. The link between the interface levels, PF and LF, has to be established as economically as possible. Economy, in this system, is instantiated in a number of respects. We focus on just a few. Again, the Minimalist program is in a state of flux which would not allow me to give a definitive account of the role of economy (see for instance Fujita (1996) on the role of Economy).

One instantiation of the Economy Principle is that movement should only take place when necessary, i.e. “Movement as a last resort”. This interpretation of economy is already present in Chomsky (1991). According to “Movement as a last resort” approaches, there should be no optional movement in the grammar (see also Rizzi, this volume). This is a consequence which poses a challenge to current work in syntax.[8] As seen above, movement may be overt, “in the syntax”, or covert, “at LF”. Movement which takes place before the Spell out point is overt; movement which occurs after Spell out, i.e. which feeds LF but not PF, is non-overt. The latter type of movement is input to the semantic representation (“LF”) of the sentence only, it has no bearing on the spelt out form. Chomsky (1991, 1993, 1995) proposes that overt movement is a more costly operation than covert movement. For reasons of Economy, then, covert movement is preferred, or to put it differently: movement is delayed as late as possible (“Procrastinate”).

2.2.2. *Checking Theory*

Up until the late eighties, the standard assumption was that verbs are base-generated as stems under the lexical heads, and their inflectional morphology, person, number and Tense endings, is base-generated separately under inflectional heads. This view was illustrated in the discussion of (2) and in (3), repeated here for the reader’s convenience as (16) and (17):

(16) a. John eats chocolate
b. [$_{CP}$ [$_{C^\circ}$-WH] [$_{IP}$ e [$_{I^\circ}$-s] [$_{VP}$ [$_{DP}$ John] eat [$_{DP}$ chocolate]]]]
c. [$_{CP}$ [$_{C^\circ}$-WH] [$_{IP}$ [$_{DP}$ John$_j$] [$_{I^\circ}$ t_i] [$_{VP}$ [$_{DP}$ t_j] eat-s$_i$ [$_{DP}$ chocolate]]]]
d. [$_{CP}$ [$_{C^\circ}$-WH] [$_{IP}$ [$_{DP}$ John$_j$] [$_{I^\circ}$ eat-s$_i$-t$_i$] [$_{VP}$ [$_{DP}$ t_j] t_i [$_{DP}$ chocolate]]]]

(17) a. Jean mangeait du chocolat
b. [$_{CP}$ [$_{C^\circ}$-WH] [$_{IP}$ e [$_{I^\circ}$-ait] [$_{VP}$ [$_{DP}$ Jean [$_{I^\circ}$ mange-] [$_{DP}$ du chocolat]]]]
c. [$_{CP}$ [$_{C^\circ}$-WH] [$_{IP}$ [$_{DP}$ Jean$_j$] [$_{I^\circ}$ mange$_i$-ait] [$_{VP}$ [$_{DP}$ t_j] t_i [$_{DP}$ du chocolat]]]]
d. [$_{CP}$ [$_{C^\circ}$-WH] [$_{IP}$ [$_{DP}$ Jean$_j$] [$_{I^\circ}$ mange$_i$-ait] [$_{VP}$ [$_{DP}$ t_j] t_i [$_{DP}$ du chocolat]]]]

In French the verb moves to the inflectional head; in English the inflection is lowered on the verb. These operations which unite the verb-stem and the inflection are required to meet the morphological subcategorization frame of I°, an affix (see Lasnik 1980: 162).

In the Minimalist program, lexical items are selected from the lexicon with their inflectional endings. In (14), for instance, we selected *left*, the past tense form of *leave*, as an item. Functional heads such as I° do not dominate inflectional morphology which is to be associated to lexical heads by incorporation: rather, they dominate bundles of abstract features whose role is to check the morphological features of the lexical items.

As already mentioned above, the location of the trigger for movement has also been reconsidered. In the earlier versions of Minimalism (Chomsky 1993), the trigger for movement was conceived of as residing within the moved constituent. In (14), *John*, for instance, has to move in order to license its Case (or agreement) features. In the more recent developments of the Minimalist program (Chomsky 1995), the trigger for movement does not reside within the moved constituent. Rather, the trigger for movement is a feature of its landing site. A head will have an array of features and when these features are strong they attract elements with matching features (see section 2.2.2). Move is replaced by Attract (Chomsky 1995, Fujita 1996).

Assume that in our example above, I° dominates the features Agr (3sg) and T (past) (but see below for discussion). The features on the abstract head will attract the features associated with the overt lexical items. Thus, the Tense and agreement morphology associated with the V-stem check the abstract features (AGR, T) on the functional head. Feature checking is a matching of the features and is done by adjoining the inflected V to the relevant functional head. When the abstract feature on a functional head is strong, it will attract the lexical item with the associated features before Spell out, and attraction is the trigger for overt movement.

In the derivation of (14) the English verb does not move before Spell out. Translated in terms of attraction, this means that the features of I° are not strong. In French, on the other hand, features of I° are strong and the strong features of I° attract the verb *parlait*. As a consequence the verb will move to I° before Spell out. Roughly, and again omitting many important aspects of the derivation, sentence (18a) will have the Numeration (18b) and the derivation (19):

(18) a. Jean parlait
Jean talked

b. *Jean, parlait,* I[+Tense, +AGR]

(19) a. Select *Jean*

b. Select *parlait*

c. Merge (*Jean, parlait*)

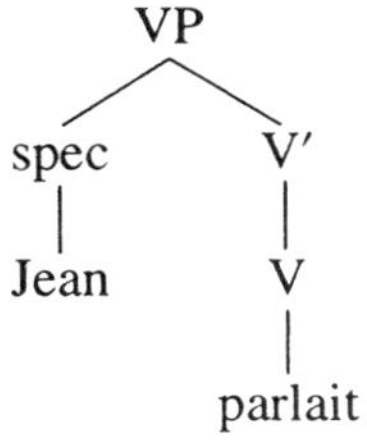

d. Select I

e. Merge (I, VP)

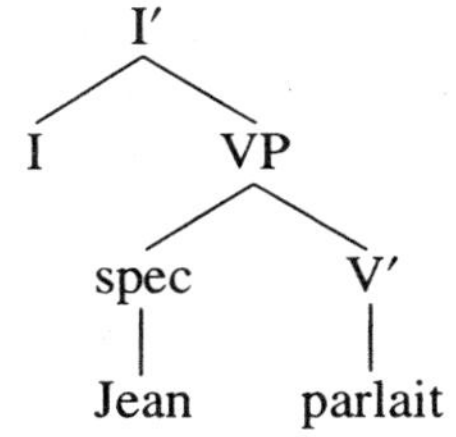

f. Attract/Move *parlait*

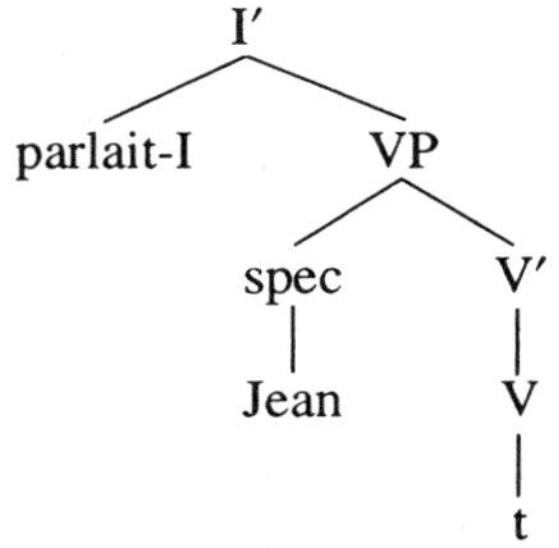

g. Attract/Move *Jean*

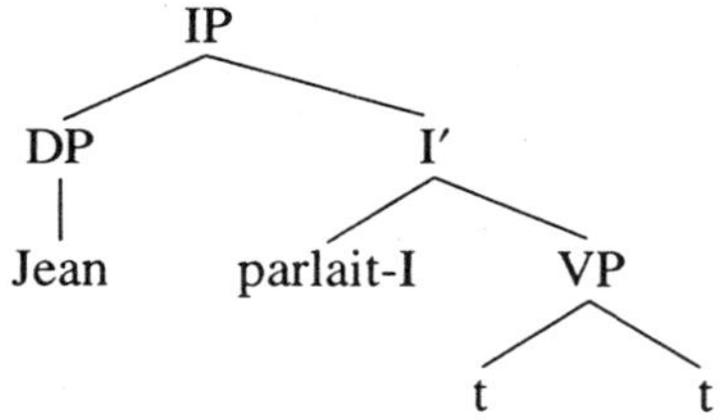

According to checking theory, English verb movement does not take place before Spell Out. After VP has merged with the I projection, *John* moves to check its features (case, Agr). It is only after spell out (at LF) that *left* will move to I.

Observe that though checking theory finds its origins in the Minimalist literature it is not as such incompatible with the more classical approach to generative syntax. Many authors whose work is not strictly speaking "Minimalist" have adopted the model of checking theory for their analyses.

Chomsky (1995) refines the notion feature attraction. Take for instance the attraction of the DP *John* by I in our example (14). Simplifying for reasons of space the following is proposed, suppose I has a D-feature which has to be checked. This means that I has to have a DP-specifier: which would capture the extended projection principle. Now it is proposed that the attraction only affects specific features: I in (14) attracts the D-feature of

John. But pure feature movement is not admitted before Spell out, because of phonological principles: words cannot be broken up across the structure. Hence *John*, the full constituent, is pied piped by the D-feature movement. Movement of categories is then seen as some form of generalized Pied Piping. After Spell out, though, in the covert syntax, what we think of as LF movement is movement of features and Pied Piping is not needed.

2.2.3. *Inflectional Heads: Bound Morphemes vs. Free Morphemes*

Let us pursue the idea that verb movement is due to the attraction by a higher inflectional head. An alternative way of interpreting the notion of attraction is suggested in Pollock's contribution to this volume. Let us pursue this idea for a moment. In section 4.2.3 of his contribution to this volume, Pollock (this volume, 258) says:

> We would then claim that languages like Japanese and Korean, in which, contrary to Navajo, the morphological ordering of affixes does seem to directly mirror their syntactic scope, have "real" head-to-head incorporation, à la Baker, not checking, as argued for Korean . . . If so one might go one step further and claim that checking and real head-to-head incorporation can co-exist in certain languages.

In what follows I briefly speculate on a possible elaboration of this idea beyond the proposal made by Pollock.

One might argue that functional heads are of two types: either they are affixes, i.e. bound morphemes (cf. Pollock, this volume, Chomsky 1995, chapter 4, 238, Roberts 1996), or, alternatively, they are free morphemes. By definition, affixes will require that V-movement take place in order to satisfy their morphological subcategorization frame. If the functional head is a free morpheme, it will not trigger head movement. In other words, verb movement to the inflectional head would not be triggered by "strong" features of a functional head, rather it would be triggered by a morphological property ("affixhood") of the inflectional head.

The affixal nature of the functional heads could be stated in the terms of Pollock's (1989) original analysis of V-movement by saying either that in French, for instance, the functional heads (say I) dominate the bound morphemes, or, alternatively, that functional heads are always abstract, and some such abstract heads are affixal in nature.[9]

In checking approaches, parametric variation in verb movement is related to feature strength: in French, for instance, AGR is said to be strong, while in English it is weak. In the alternative view entertained here, where it is the affixal nature of the head which triggers V-movement to I, parametric variation in verb movement will be expressed in terms of the affixal nature of functional heads (cf. Chomsky 1995: p. 382 note 20, Lasnik 1994, Roberts 1996). To differentiate between French (in which the finite verb moves to a higher functional head) and English (where it does not) one could say that in French I is an affix – hence it attracts the verb stem – while in English it is not – hence there is no attraction of V.

This view of inflection, though inspired by the passage from Pollock cited above, is not developed as such in Pollock's paper and remains at this point highly speculative. The proposal above potentially has far-reaching ramifications, though, about which I can at this point only offer some speculative remarks. As one consequence, the above proposal may, for instance, lead us to dispense with covert V-movement. In English (20a) the functional head designated as I would not be an affix, hence it does not attract the verb.

(20) a. John $[_I]$ often talks about you

However, given that I represents verbal inflectional features (Tense, for instance) it would be reasonable to assume that V (*talks*) and I have a dependency relation. This relation can be established representationally. Consider the representation (20b):

(20) b. $[_{IP}$ John$_i$ $[_{Ii}]$ $[_{VP}$ often $[_{VP}$ t_i $[_V$ talks$_i]$ about you]]]]

John$_i$ originates VP-internally (see section 3.2) and it moves to the specifier of I. Given that *John* and I attain a specifier head relation we propose that they are co-indexed. If we furthermore assume that the base position of *John* is the specifier of VP, and that there too the specifier head relation is expressed in terms of co-indexation, then in fact V and I will be coindexed in spite of the absence of V-movement to I; because they share a specifier. The shared specifier creates a dependency between the two heads. As this dependency between I_i and V_i is not created by movement, it is a representational chain $\langle I_i, V_i \rangle$ (see also Rizzi 1996, and Rizzi's contribution to this volume (317–318) for the use of representational head chains created by shared specifiers).

As mentioned, a consequence of the admittedly very sketchy approach outlined above would be that it allows one to dispense with covert verb movement. In languages where inflectional heads are affixes, V moves overtly (at S-structure in traditional terms, before Spell out in Minimalist terms (see above)), and in languages where the inflectional head is not an affix, the shared specifiers due to subject movement give rise to a representational head chain. At this point the alternative outlined here has not been worked out in detail, so we leave it on this rather speculative note.

2.2.4. *Copy Theory of Movement*

In the Minimalist program, traces are interpreted as copies of the moved constituents.[10] At PF and at LF a deletion process eliminates redundant copies of the moved constituent. In Chomsky (1993), copy theory is developed in relation to the reconstruction effects discussed in Section 2.1.3.2.

Consider (21), where the *wh*-phrase *which pictures of himself* has been preposed to the [Spec,CP] position (from Broekhuis and Den Dikken 1993):

(21) a. John does not know which picture of himself Bill saw.

The sentence is ambiguous: *himself* may either be bound by the matrix subject *John* or by the embedded subject *Bill. Which pictures of himself* occupies the embedded [Spec, CP]. In the first reading, where *John* is the antecedent of *himself*, the surface position of the *wh*-phrase in [Spec, CP] will allow for the binding of *himself* by *John.* In the second reading, where *Bill* is the antecedent, though, *Bill* does not c-command *himself.* In the standard approach of GB theory outlined above, reconstruction will return (part of) the moved constituent back into its base position in order to create the second configuration.

In the Minimalist approach, another line of enquiry is pursued. Movement is not interpreted as the displacement of a constituent to a higher position, leaving an empty category ("trace") in the extraction site. Rather, when the constituent is moved to a higher position, it leaves a copy in the extraction site. Thus, movement of *which pictures of himself* in (21a) creates the following structure:

(21) b. John does not know
[[which picture of himself] Bill saw [which picture of himself]]

Movement of the *wh*-phrase creates the chain of copies of the moved constituent: ⟨*which pictures of himself, which pictures of himself*⟩. At the interface levels redundant copies are eliminated. At the level of Phonetic Form, the lower member of the chain is deleted. On the other hand, at LF, the interpretive level, deletion proceeds differently. *Which* is the marker of interrogative force and hence must be retained at the CP level. Moreover, *himself* must be bound. Following Chomsky's (1993) proposals as elaborated in detail in Broekhuis and den Dikken (1993), let us propose the following LF derivation. At both points in the chain ⟨*which pictures of himself, which pictures of himself*⟩, created in (21b), we extract the marker of illocutionary force and adjoin it to the member of the chain from which it is extracted. This adjunction may take place in two fashions. As a first option we extract only the element *which*:

(21) c. John does not know
[[which] [t picture of himself]] Bill saw [[which] [t picture of himself]]

The traces left by extraction are interpreted as variables (21d). Then, LF deletion will take place: we delete the variable at the top of the chain and we retain the top copy of *which*, the operator. Conversely, at the lower end of the chain, we delete the operator and we retain the variable, resulting in a representation as in (21e):

(21) d. John does not know
[[which x] [x picture of himself]] Bill saw [[which x] [x picture of himself]]

e. John does not know
[[which x] Bill saw [x picture of himself]]

In representation (21e) *himself* can be bound by the embedded subject *Bill*.

For the second reading, the complete *wh*-phrase is pied piped by the extraction and adjoined:

(22) a. John does not know
[which picture of himself [t]] Bill saw [which pictures of himself [t]]

Operator variable structures are created in each of the copies:

(22) b. John does not know
[which x, x a picture of himself [x]]
Bill saw [which x, x a picture of himself [x]]

LF deletion takes place, deleting the adjoined operator in the lower copy of the chain:

(22) c. John does not know
[which x, x a picture of himself]
Bill saw [[x]]

In (22c) *himself* is bound by the matrix subject *John*.

Chains created by movement consist of copies with all the properties of the moved element. Copy theory of movement entails that the entire derivation of the clause can be traced back by inspecting the structure of the clause: copies of moved constituents will appear at the base position of the constituent, at the final landing site and at intermediate landing sites. Moreover, given copy theory of movement, each chain member encodes all the features of the moved constituent. This strict and systematic implementation of a copy approach to movement leads to an important question. Using traces of movement, and more specifically traces interpreted as (iterated) copies of the chain members, we can systematically read off the derivational history of the clause simply by inspecting the syntactic representation of the clause. The structure formed will also serve as input to both interface levels, PF and LF, which will be created by the selective deletion processes outlined above. Since we can read off the entire record of the derivation simply on the basis of a single representation, the question arises whether we could not just as well create one level of representation in which we insert not simply lexical items but also chains consisting of a sequence of (coindexed) copies of the same constituent. Chains would result from repeatedly selecting the same item from the numeration. Thus the copy theory of movement may lead to a strongly representational view of the structure.

The opposition between the derivational and the representational view is part of a long-standing debate (see Rizzi 1986, Koster 1993, for instance). One current trend in the Minimalist program is to opt for a strongly derivational approach to syntax. This is illustrated in Chomsky (1995) and the references cited there. On the other hand, keeping in line with the main goals of Minimalism, Brody (1995, the paper in this volume) has developed a strongly representational approach.

2.3. *Radical Minimalism*

Instead of the multi-level approaches of the traditional GB model (DS, SS, LF, PF) or of the Minimalist program (LF, PF), Brody (1995a) proposes a model using one enriched syntactic representation from which both morpho-phonological Spell out ("PF") and semantic representation ("LF") are read off simultaneously (cf. Koster 1993). This one level theory dispenses with movement and encodes all effects of displacement in terms of chains. In (23a), for instance, the *wh*-operator *when* heads an operator-variable chain; the sentential scope of the *wh*-phrase *in situ* is represented by an expletive scope marker which is adjoined to the overt operator. I will represent the expletive scope marker as OP.[11]

(23) a. When did you see whom?

b.

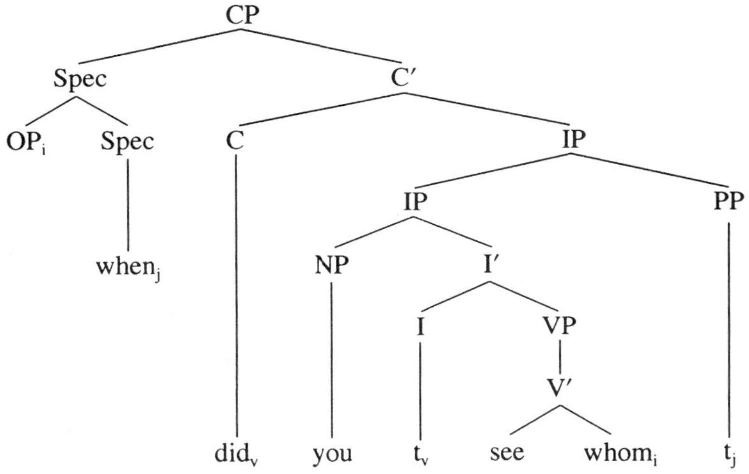

The scope of *whom* is determined by the non-overt OP with which *whom* will form a chain.

Following Brody's approach, the scope of *wh*-phrases can be determined by two kinds of chains: one option is that the *wh*-phrase is spelt out as the head of a chain. This is the case for the chain headed by *when* in (23b). Alternatively the operator is spelt out in a lower position and the CHAIN is headed by an expletive scope marker. This is the case for the chain of *whom* in (23b). The parametric variation between languages with multiple *wh*-movement and those without can be expressed in terms of the Spell out conditions on *wh*-chains. Brody (1995a) postulates that there is a transparency condition on the spell out of chains:

(24) Transparency
The contentive category in the chain must be in the highest position licensed by morphology.

In languages with multiple movement (Rudin 1988, Puskas 1992, 1995) the heads of all the *wh*-chains must be spelt out as overt operators; in English only one chain allows for the head to be spelt out as an overt operator; an *in situ* operator must become part of a CHAIN headed by a non-overt scope marker. In (23b), the *wh*-phrase *when* is spelt out as the head of a chain, while the phrase *whom* cannot be spelt out as the head of a chain.

In his contribution to this volume, Brody further explores the role of chains in the grammar, examining in detail the approach to chain formation in the Minimalist Program and in Radical Minimalism.

3. THE THEMATIC LAYER

In the early generative tradition (Chomsky 1965) the clause structure proposed for configurational languages was that in (25a):[12]

(25) a.

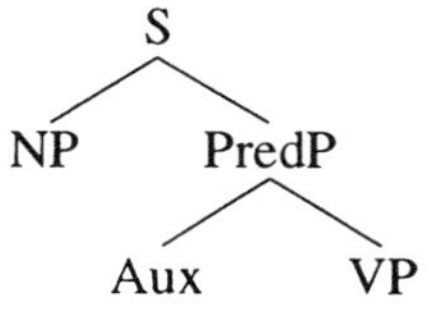

S has two immediate constituents, NP and PredP, the Predicate Phrase. The NP immediately dominated by the node S is the subject. While categories such as VP and NP were clearly endocentric, i.e. projections of a head (V, N), the relation of S to PredP or to VP was not immediately clear. In fact, (25a) suggests strongly that the clause, S, is an exocentric constituent, composed of two projections.

One important step in the generative approach was the development of X-bar theory and the generalization of the endocentric approach to clause structure: all constituents, including S, are projections of a head (among others, Chomsky 1970, Jackendoff 1977, Stowell 1981, Chomsky 1986a). The structure (25a) became re-interpreted as in (25b):

(25) b.

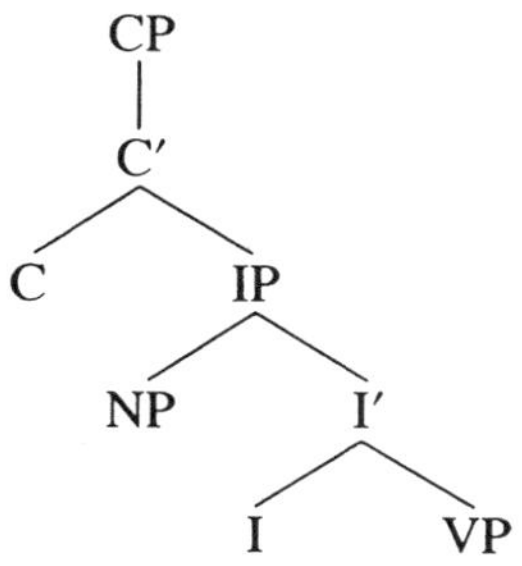

A further constraint which was also imposed on syntactic structure is that all structure be binary branching (see Kayne 1984), ruling out structures such as (25c).

(25) c.

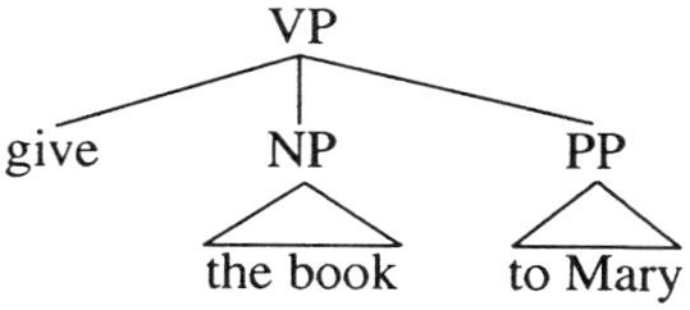

We return to ditransitive structures briefly in the next section. For a detailed discussion the reader is referred to Kayne (1984), Larson (1988), Baker (this volume). See also note 14.

Clauses consist of three layers of projections: CP, IP, VP, each with a specialized function. The projection of V, VP, is the lexical or the thematic layer. This projection contains the thematic information of the clause, the lexical head which assigns the thematic roles and the arguments to which these roles are assigned. The projection of I, IP, is the domain for the licensing of inflectional morphology, such as tense and agreement. The canonical subject position is the specifier position of IP. At the CP level the illocutionary force of the clause is encoded. In a root clause, the CP level is the interface between the clause and the discourse.

Up until the mid-eighties, it was also assumed that the thematic position of the subject (at least in the case of intransitive and transitive sentences) was the specifier of IP: the subject was the "external" argument of the verb, i.e. the argument realized outside the VP (cf. Marantz 1984 for arguments that set apart the external argument from the other arguments, see also the discussion in Baker's and McCloskey's contributions to this volume). One of the important modifications that took place over the past ten years is the proposal that all thematic roles are assigned within the projection of the lexical head and thus that subjects originate in a VP-internal position. This point is discussed briefly in section 3.3 and in greater detail in McCloskey's contribution to this volume. McCloskey also provides an extensive bibliography.

3.1. *Lexical Heads and The Assignment of Theta Roles*

One principle that determines the build-up of clause structure in the classical GB theory is the Projection Principle, the principle which requires that clause structure be projected on the basis of lexical information. Notably, thematic roles, as encoded in the theta grid of a predicate, had to be associated with arguments.

In terms of the Minimalist framework, the thematic requirements of a head are satisfied by merging an argument with the lexical head which assigns the theta role. For instance the merger of *John* and *left* in (14) will satisfy the thematic properties of the verb. Pursuing the role of Economy in the Minimalist framework, Fujita (1996) tries to unify Merge and Attract. The following scenario could be envisaged: we could propose that thematic roles are encoded by a feature F of the verb. We might then say that thematic features are always strong. If we project a phrase marker headed by the predicate *left*, the thematic feature F will be satisfied by merging V with an argument, selected from the Numeration. In an attempt to simplify the computational model, Fujita (1996) goes on to suggest that in fact the Merge operation (i.e. lexical insertion of an argument in a projection of the predicate) can be viewed as a form of Attract: the thematic feature on the lexical head attracts the argument which will satisfy this feature directly from the Numeration.

One important question which has dominated the study of thematic structure in the literature concerns the realization of thematic roles. Consider (26):

(26) a. Eng. John has bought some books.
b. Fr. Jean a acheté des livres.
c. It. Gianni ha comprato libri.
d. Du. Jan heeft boeken gekocht.
e. Ge. Hans hat Bücher gekauft.

In all of the above examples, the AGENT theta role of the verb (*buy*, *acheter*, *comprare*, *kopen*, *kaufen*) is an external theta role in the sense that it is realized by the subject and the THEME role is an internal role, realized by means of the direct object. That the AGENT is the subject in each of the sentences above is shown, for instance, by the fact that it is associated with nominative case (cf. (27)).

(27) a. Eng. He has bought them
b. Fr. Il les a achetés
c. It. Egli li ha comprati
d. Du. Hij heeft ze gekocht
e. Ge. Er hat sie gekauft

It is also the AGENT DP which agrees in number with the finite verb:

(28) a. Eng. John and Mary have bought some books
b. Fr. Jean et Marie ont acheté des livres
c. It. Gianni e Maria hanno comprato libri
d. Du. Jan en Marie hebben boeken gekocht
e. Ge. Hans und Maria haben Bücher gekauft

The pattern above can be generalized across many long ways: transitive verbs distribute their thematic roles systematically in the same way: the AGENT is realized as the subject, the THEME is realized as the object. In other words we do not find, nor do we expect to find, a language in which (26a) is expressed as (29a), or where (27c) is expressed as (29b):

(29) a. *Some books have bought John
meaning: "John has bought some books"

b. *They have bought him
meaning: "He has bought them."

Similarly, in ditransitive sentences, where the verb has three arguments, AGENT, GOAL and THEME, it is the AGENT which realizes the subject of the sentence, and there is also a hierarchical relation between indirect object and direct object (see Baker (this volume) for apparent counter-examples).[13] The regularities in the linking of thematic roles and syntactic positions is expressed in the following principle (Baker 1988).

(30) The Uniformity of Theta Assignment Hypothesis (UTAH)
Identical thematic relationships between items are represented by identical structural relationships between those items at the level of D-structure.

The relationships between thematic roles and the structural positions which realize them are expressed in terms of hierarchical ranking: thematic roles are ranked according to a thematic hierarchy and that hierarchy determines phrase structure. For early discussion of the relevance of the thematic hierarchy for syntactic structure see Jackendoff (1972); for a discussion of argument structure see also Grimshaw (1991a). If the theta role of an argument X is ranked higher than the theta role of a second argument, Y, then X c-commands Y at the level of D-structure. For instance, AGENTS are higher on the thematic hierarchy than THEMES, hence in transitive sentences AGENTS will be chosen as subjects. Where other internal arguments are concerned (GOAL, BENEFACTIVE, EXPERIENCER, LOCATION) there is some controversy in the literature over the relative ranking of the specific theta roles. For instance Baker (1996) shows that all of the following three rankings have been advocated in the literature:

(31) a. AGENT > BENEFACTIVE/GOAL > THEME > LOCATION
b. AGENT > GOAL/EXPERIENCER/LOCATION > THEME
c. AGENT > THEME > GOAL/EXPERIENCER/LOCATION

If one adopts the ranking (31a) or (31b), then the GOAL argument should c-command the THEME argument at D-structure, while according to (31c) the THEME should c-command the GOAL. As discussed by Baker, the controversy over the relative ranking of THEME with respect to the other internal arguments is due to a number of points. I mention just some here.

One problem that arises with three argument verbs is that, for instance, in English such verbs sometimes are realized in alternating structures. In (32a) the THEME appears as the direct object, in (32b) the GOAL seems to be the direct object. In (33a) the THEME of the action is the direct object, in (33b) it is the LOCATION which is the direct object. In his contribution to this volume Baker examines three-argument verbs such as those illustrated in (32) and (33).

(32) a. I gave the candy to the children.
b. I gave the children the candy.

(33) a. I loaded the hay onto the truck.
b. I loaded the truck with hay.

The alternation found in (32) and (33) is also found, for instance, in Dutch:

(34) a. Ik gaf het snoep aan de kinderen.
I gave the candy to the children

b. Ik gaf de kinderen het snoep.
I gave the children the candy

(35) a. Ik laadde hooi op de wagen.
I loaded the hay onto the truck

b. Ik laadde de wagen met hooi.
I loaded the truck with hay.

A related problem is that even when there is no alternation in structures, the choice of the object argument seems not to be rigidly fixed. Baker mentions the case of *donate* which always appears in the frame (32a), with the THEME as the object and the GOAL realized as a PP, and *owe*, which appears only in the configuration (32b), with both THEME and GOAL realized as DPs.

Other languages do not have the alternations displayed in English and in Dutch, but they choose one of the two patterns illustrated above. In French, ditransitive verbs always are used in sentences with the pattern in (32a), while Sesotho has only the equivalent of (32b) (see discussion in Baker's contribution to this volume). For early discussion of ditransitive verbs and verbs with multiple arguments the reader is referred to Kayne (1984).

Baker (1996 and this volume) proposes that the DP-PP patterns in the (a) examples above are closer to the underlying structure; THEMES are ranked higher than GOALS or LOCATIONS in the thematic hierarchy. English (32b), for instance, is argued to be derived from a structure where the verb takes a PP complement with a non-overt preposition (cf. Kayne 1984). The derivation is illustrated in (36). Following Larson (1988) (see also Hale and Keyser 1991, 1993), Baker assumes a layered VP structure,[14] with a functional projection AspP intervening between the VP-layers or VP-shells (see Travis 1992, also section 4.1.2 below). The AGENT argument is the specifier of the higher VP-shell.

(36)

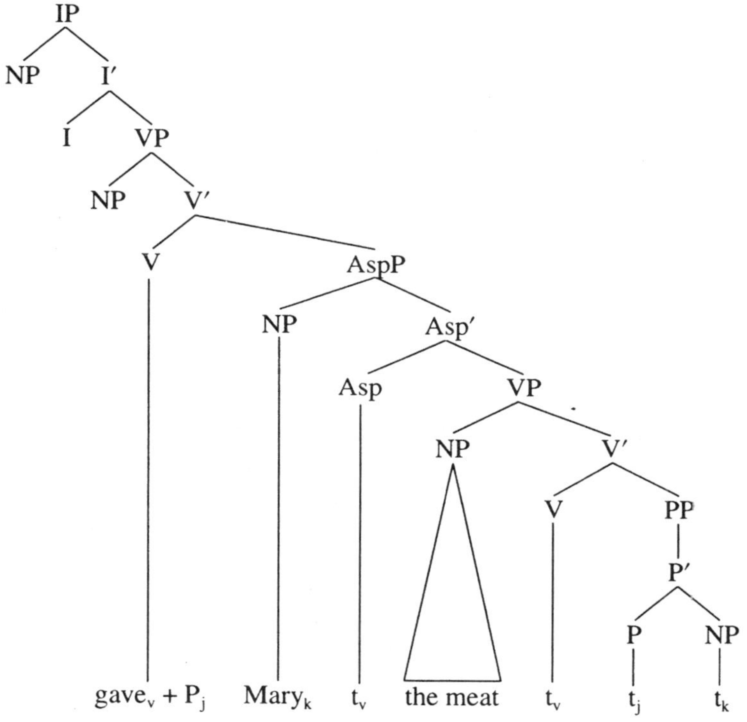

The verb, *give*, incorporates the empty preposition; the complement of the preposition, *Mary*, undergoes rightward movement to the specifier of a functional projection AspP. (32b) thus has the structure in (36). I refer the reader to Baker's own discussion for details.

The UTAH plays an important role in the syntactic enquiry. In a classical GB approach, the UTAH will allow one to derive the D-structure position of the arguments from the lexical information, more specifically the thematic structure of the predicate. In the Minimalist approach to clause structure, the UTAH may determine that the argument which is ranked lower on the thematic hierarchy merges with (or is attracted by) the predicate (say, V) before a higher argument.

In his contribution to this volume Mark Baker reconsiders and evaluates the UTAH on the basis a number of examples, some of which at first sight might seem to be problematic. He provides evidence that the AGENT is universally external to the other theta roles, and he also argues for the universal ranking of internal arguments. After discussing some controversies over the detailed formulation of the UTAH (what is the thematic hierarchy? is the UTAH relativized? etc.) he also considers the place of the UTAH in grammar, notably in Minimalist type approaches.

3.2. *The Subject*

We have repeatedly referred to the notion subject. This notion is central in traditional thinking about philology and grammar, and it is also used in models of grammar elaborated in the generative tradition. We have associated with the subject a number of diverse properties: the subject is the highest nominal position of the clause, the subject realizes the external argument, the subject has nominative case, the subject agrees with the finite verb, the subject serves as the prototypical antecedent for anaphor binding, etc.

McCloskey's contribution to this volume focuses on the notion subject and its role in generative syntax. He gives a survey of the properties which are commonly associated with the subject (see especially the introduction to his paper). As McCloskey points out, the properties commonly attributed to the subject are not homogeneous but they bear on a range of different types of information, including categorial information (the subject is nominal), information concerning the realization of thematic roles (the subject is the prototypical bearer of the AGENT role), hierarchical information (the prominence of the subject in the clause is reflected in terms of binding of reflexives or licensing of polarity items), morphological information (the subject bears nominative case and agrees with the inflected verb). Following the modular approach advocated in generative grammar, McCloskey points out that it is surprising that these heterogeneous types of information should all be related to one single component of the grammar. It would seem more in keeping with the modularity view that properties which are of quite a distinct nature should be related to distinct components in the grammar. Pursuing a modular view of grammar, one might expect that the notion subject will be decomposed. And McCloskey shows that this is indeed what has happened. Over the past ten years especially, we have witnessed a gradual deconstruction of the traditional notion subject. In his paper, McCloskey discusses this development and examines in detail some recent proposals about the syntax of subjecthood.

Probably the most important development in our conception of the notion subject is what is referred to as the Internal Subject Hypothesis (cf. Sportiche 1988, Koopman and Sportiche 1991, and many others, cf. McCloskey's references) the idea that the thematic or base position of the subject is

VP-internal. From the earliest work in generative syntax (cf. (25a)) up until the mid eighties (25b), the subject was identified as the highest NP (or DP) of the clause – i.e. [NP, S] in (25a), or [NP, IP], in (25b). It was generally assumed that the canonical subject position was the base position of the subject of transitive and intransitive verbs. The theta role assigned to the subject was "external" in that it was assigned outside of the VP.

The association of the external theta role and the highest nominal position in the clause, however, has become challenged on the basis of empirical and theoretical considerations. Apart from the fact that the traditional notion "subject" associates a number of heterogeneous properties to one position, as discussed above, there are also empirical considerations which challenge the view that the thematic role of the subject is assigned in [Spec, IP]. McCloskey, for instance, cites the following example (his (4a)):

(38) a. The girls will write a book and be awarded a prize for it.

If it might be possible to argue that the external theta role of the verb *write* in the left-hand conjunct of (38) is assigned to the DP *the girls*, in the specifier position of IP, the same reasoning cannot apply to the right conjunct. It is uncontroversial that the thematic position of the subject of the passive verb such as *be awarded* is VP-internal. If (38a) involves VP coordination, it will constitute a violation of the coordinate structure constraint (cf. Burton and Grimshaw 1992). In (38b) *the girls* is extracted only from one of the two conjuncts:

(38) b. The $girls_i$ will $[_{VP}$ write a book] and $[_{VP}$ be awarded t_i a prize for it].

According to the Internal Subject Hypothesis, the canonical subject position, [Spec, IP], is no longer the position to which the thematic role of the subject is assigned. It is assumed that the subject originates VP-internally, i.e. that its thematic role is assigned by the verb itself within the V-projection. This assumption makes theta role assignment more uniform in that one can propose that all thematic roles are assigned in the domain of the theta role assigner. In those languages where the subject occupies the specifier position of IP, the surface position of the subject is a derived position: it is the result of NP-movement, i.e. A-movement to [Spec, IP]. The motivation for the A-movement of the subject will be the same as that for other types of A-movement: the subject moves to the specifier of IP for case reasons. (38a) now receives a straightforward analysis:

(38) c. $[_{IP}$ The $girls_i$ will $[_{VP}$ t_i write a book] and $[_{VP}$ t_i be awarded t_i a prize for it]]

Following the Internal subject Hypothesis, (38c) is an instantiation of an Across the Board application of NP-movement.

McCloskey surveys some of the empirical arguments which have been put forward for the Internal Subject Hypothesis. These arguments are of two kinds (i) "lower origin arguments", which provide evidence for a dependency between the subject and a lower position, and (ii) "lower position arguments", based on data in which a subject occupies a VP-internal position in the syntax. I illustrate the two kinds of arguments briefly here.

Consider the French sentences in (39):

(39) a. Toutes les filles ont gagné le prix.
all the girls have won the prize

b. Les filles ont toutes gagné le prix.
the girls have all won the prize

In (39a) the subject of the clause *toutes les filles* ("all the girls") consists of the quantifier *toutes* ("all") and the DP *les filles* ("the girls"). In (39b) the DP *les filles* is separated from the quantifier *toutes*, which occurs lower in the structure. It is assumed that in (39b) too, the quantifier and the DP originally belong together. According to the Internal Subject Hypothesis *toutes les filles* originates in the VP-internal thematic position of the subject in both (39a) and (39b). In (39a) *toutes les filles* moves as one constituent, and in (39b) the DP *les filles* moves away, stranding the associated quantifier (see Sportiche 1988, Koopman and Sportiche 1991). In (39b) the lower position of the quantifier is thus evidence for the lower origin of the subject DP *les filles*.

Lower position arguments for the Internal Subject hypothesis are arguments which explore the observation that in certain types of sentences the DP which functions as the grammatical subject of a clause does not occupy the [Spec, IP] position, but is actually found in a lower position of the structure. So called transitive expletive constructions are sometimes advanced as evidence for the lower base position of the subject. Let us consider this construction, which has also received a lot of attention in the Minimalist literature, in some detail.

In the standard case (40a) the link between the VP-internal base position of the subject and its surface position is created by means of NP movement of the subject:

(40) a. Toutes les filles ont t gagné.
all the girls have won

b. Trois filles ont t gagné.
three girls have won

However, as McCloskey points out, the dependency between the canonical subject position and the lower VP-internal base position of the internal argument is expressed either by movement (41a) or, alternatively, by an expletive-argument chain (41b).

(41) a. Trois filles ont été tuées t hier
three girls have been killed yesterday

b. Il a été tué trois filles hier
there have been killed three girls yesterday

In (41a) the subject *trois filles* ("three girls") originates as the object of *tuées* ("killed"), and moves to the [Spec, IP] position for case licensing. In (41b) the DP remains in its base position and is related to the [Spec, IP] via an expletive-argument chain ⟨*il, trois filles*⟩. If the external argument of the verb originates in a lower position and has to undergo A-movement to reach [Spec, IP], then we would expect that the A-movement relation also co-exists with an expletive-argument relation. This expectation is borne out as illustrated in (42):

(42) a. Someone has eaten an apple

b. það hefur einhver borðað epli
there has someone eaten an-apple

In English (42a) the subject has undergone A-movement. In the parallel Icelandic example (42b) the indefinite subject *einhver* ("someone") remains lower in the structure and is in construction with an expletive in a higher nominal position. Sentences which contain a transitive verb and in which the subject is part of an expletive-argument chain are referred to as transitive expletive constructions (see Vikner 1991, 1995, Jonas and Bobaljik 1993, Bobaljik and Jonas 1996, etc.). In (42b) the subject remains in a lower position. It could be argued (but see below for complications) that the position occupied by *einhver* in (42b) is the base position of the subject, [Spec, VP].

McCloskey's paper surveys developments of the concept "subject" in the generative literature and evaluates the arguments presented for the Internal Subject hypothesis. As we will see section 4.2.1.4., these arguments have become harder to evaluate given the phrase structural articulation of IP in work of the late 1980's and early 1990's to which we turn in section 4.1.

4. THE STRUCTURE OF THE CLAUSE

In the middle of the 80's the clause structure (25b), repeated here for the reader's convenience as (43), was generally adopted in syntactic description (Chomsky 1986a):

(43)

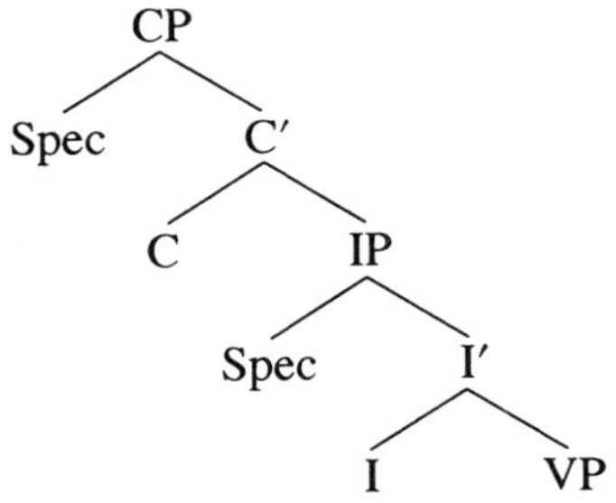

Clauses are projections of V extended with projections of functional heads, the relevant functional heads being I(nflection), C(omplementizer). The reader is referred to Grimshaw (1991b) for the notion of extended projection. This conception of the clause has not changed, but the inventory of functional heads has increased rather dramatically, with VP, IP and CP being decomposed into a number of discrete projections. At the basis of the proliferation of functional heads in the structure of the clause is work by Pollock (1989).[15] In the next sections I will discuss the decomposition of IP (section 4.1) and of CP (section 4.2).

4.1. *The Structure of The Functional Layer of The Clause: IP*

4.1.1. *Verb Movement and The Split IP*

The empirical starting point of Pollock's (1989) work is the contrast in (44) between the position of the verb in French and in English:

(44) a. Jean embrasse souvent Marie.
Jean kisses often Marie
"Jean often kisses Marie"

a′. John often kisses Marie.

b. Jean n'embrasse pas Marie
Jean kisses not Marie
"Jean does not kiss Marie"

b′. John does not kiss Mary.

Following Emonds (1978) and many others, we can characterize the difference between French and English finite verbs in terms of the availability of movement of the finite lexical verb at S-structure (before Spell out in Minimalist terms). In (44) the finite verb *embrasse* precedes the adverb *souvent* (44a) or the negation marker *pas* (44b). Assuming that these adverbs have a fixed position in the clause (see also Cinque 1995 and section 4.1.2.2), and assuming that the verb is base-generated in a position adjacent to its object, then the pre-adverbial position of the verb indicates that there must be a landing site for the verb to the left of the adverb. In the classical approach to phrase structure in (43), this landing site is identified as I. English finite lexical verbs do not move to I, but English finite auxiliaries do. In (45a)–(45c) the auxiliaries *have* and *be* appear to the right of the adverbs of frequency, in (45d)–(45f) they precede *not*, the marker of negation:

(45) a. John has often mentioned you
b. John is always working
c. John was always invited
d. John has not mentioned you
e. John is not working
f. John was not invited

However, pursuing this type of procedure Pollock (1989) shows that we are led to the conclusion that more than one landing site is available in the clausal structure and that the simple structure in (43) is insufficient for an adequate representation of the clause. The crucial data are given in (46):

(46) a. Souvent manger du chocolat c'est mauvais pour la peau.
often eat of chocolate it is bad for the skin
"To often eat chocolate is bad for the skin."

b. Manger souvent du chocolat c'est mauvais pour la peau.

c. Ne pas manger de chocolat c'est mauvais pour la peau.
ne not eat of chocolate it is bad for the skin
"Not to eat chocolate is bad for the skin."

d.*Ne manger pas de chocolat c'est mauvais pour la peau.

In (46a) the lexical infinitive *manger* follows the adverb *souvent* and is adjacent to its complement *du chocolat*. Arguably, the verb occupies the base position. In (46b) the infinitive precedes the adverb, hence it must have moved to a functional head. However, while the infinitive may precede the adverb *souvent*, the landing site to the left of the negative marker *pas* is NOT available for the infinitive. This suggests that the landing site of the verb in (46b) is distinct from the landing site which we identified above and which is to the left of the negation marker. That the relevant head is projected in infinitival clauses is shown in (46e) where the non-finite auxiliary *être* ("be") precedes *pas*:

(46) e. N'être pas invité à la fête, c'est triste.
ne be not invited to the party, it is sad.

This leads Pollock to postulate a more articulated structure of the clause where the original unitary I node is split into two nodes ("Split INFL"). Pollock proposes that the higher instantiation of the I node is a functional node with the tense feature, while the lower head contains the AGR features. The canonical subject position (cf. 2.2 above), i.e. the highest nominal position of the clause, is now reinterpreted as [Spec, TP].

(47) a.

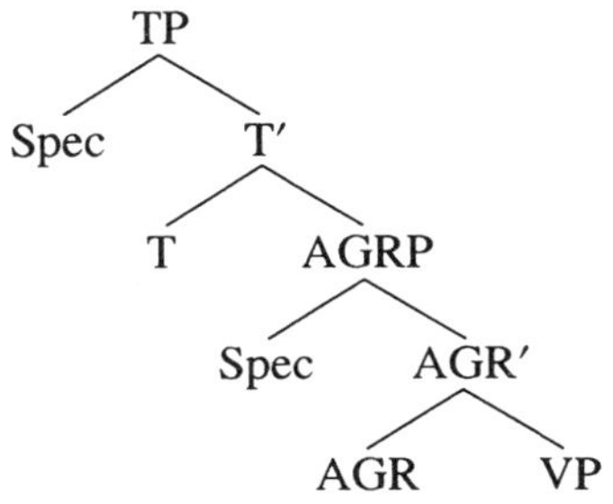

A number of objections were raised to Pollock's original analysis, and he addresses them in the paper included in this volume.[16] One type of objection (Iatridou 1990) concerns the empirical motivation for the split INFL proposal. Iatridou's objections are examined and discussed in detail in Pollock's contribution to this volume. Another type of objection does not challenge the need for more than one functional head in a clause, but it concerns the hierarchy of these heads (Ouhalla 1990, Belletti 1990).

Consider the overt sequencing of inflectional morphology in French (48):

(48) a. Ils travaill-ai-ent
they work-past-3plural

b. Il travaill-ai-t
he work-past-3singular

The AGR morphology *-ent/-t* is outside the T morphology *-ai*. Observe that the sequencing illustrated for French (48a) is also found in other languages. (49) illustrates Dutch.

(49) a. ze werk-t-en
they work-past-3plural

b. ze werk-t-e
she work-past-3singular

Again, in (49) the agreement morphology is external to the past Tense morphology.

Belletti (1990) proposes that the sequence of the inflectional morphemes reflects the hierarchical ordering of the functional nodes (cf. the Mirror

Principle, Baker 1986) and that since the Agreement morphology occurs outside the Tense morphology, the former must be attached after the latter. If inflectional affixes are generated separately in functional heads, AGRP must dominate TP. The bare V first moves to T to pick up the Tense morphology, then to AGR to pick up the Agreement morphology. The sequencing of the AGR and T morphemes reflects the derivational history of their attachment. The canonical subject position will now be [Spec, AgrP]. See also Chomsky (1991).

(47) b.

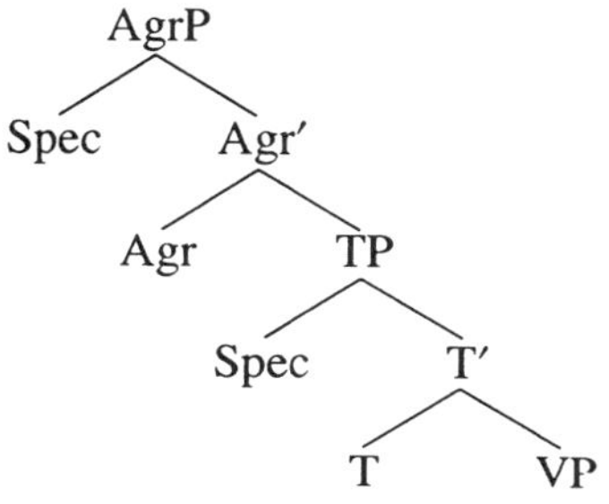

In his contribution to this volume, Pollock admits that (47b) follows from the classical derivational approach to verb morphology in which inflectional endings are generated separately on functional heads and are combined with the verb as a result of head-to-head movement. He stresses that a hierarchy such as that in (47b) is not necessarily the preferred one when one adopts the checking approach of Chomsky's Minimalist Program (1993), described in section 2.2. According to this approach, lexical heads such as V or N are selected and inserted in the phrase marker with their inflectional morphology. Pollock argues that given checking theory (47a) is preferable. I refer the reader to his paper for the discussion.

Recall that in section 2.2.3. we speculated on an alternative to checking theory which relied heavily on the morphological nature of the inflectional heads.

4.1.2. *Functional Projections in The IP Domain*

As a consequence of Pollock's seminal work further evidence has been put forward for a further decomposition the IP domain. In addition to the projection for subject agreement (AgrSP), it is proposed that there is also a projection for object agreement (Chomsky 1991, see section 4.1.2.1), that there is a functional projection for the expression of sentential negation, labelled NegP (Pollock 1989, Kayne 1989, 1991) or SigmaP (Laka 1990), that the category Aspect heads its own projection (cf. Hendrick 1991, Travis 1992, see also (36) above and Baker's contribution to this volume), that there is a projection for mood, MoodP (Rivero 1994, Rivero and Terzi 1995, Pollock this volume), that adverbials are generated in the specifier position of specialized functional projections (Cinque 1995, see section 4.1.2.2), that clitics head their own projections (Sportiche 1996), that specific subjects move to a specialized projection (RefP) (Kiss 1996), that even in English there is some form of short V-movement (Pesetsky 1989, Johnson 1991, Costa 1996, etc.). Postulating additional projections – and the related movements – obviously has many ramifications in the grammar. I will examine some cases more closely. In section 4.1.3 I will discuss some general questions concerning the functional structure.

4.1.2.1. *AgrP and The Split VP.* One point of controversy in current syntactic theory concerns the relation between VP and the functional projections. Analogously to the proposal that there is an agreement projection which will license the agreement feature(s) (and/or the nominative case) of the subject, labelled AgrSP, it is also proposed that there is an agreement projection responsible for checking the agreement features (and/or the accusative case) of the object, AgrOP. In Chomsky (1991) it is proposed that transitive sentences have the structure in (47c):

(47) c.

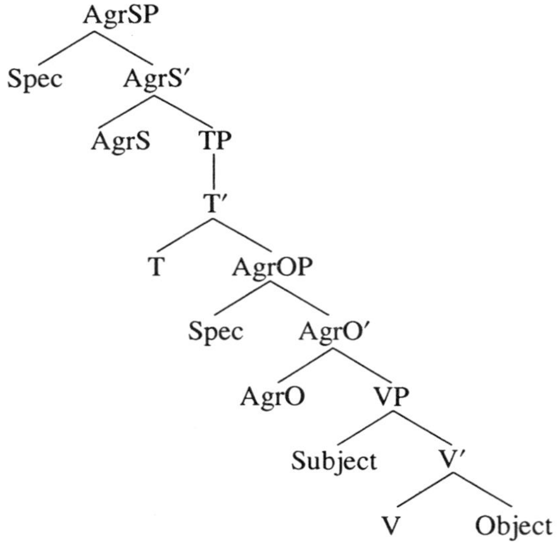

In English, subjects move to the specifier of AgrSP at S-structure. The agreement features of objects are licensed at LF, when the object moves to [Spec, AgrOP] (but see Pesetsky 1989 and Johnson 1991 for arguments that objects also move in English). In other languages, it is proposed, objects move to [Spec, AgrOP] at S-structure (before Spell out): this movement is referred to as Object shift. The Mainland Scandinavian languages are a case in point:

(50) a. Peter kobte$_v$ den$_i$ [$_{VP}$ ikke [$_{VP}$ t_v t_i]]
Peter bought it not

"Peter didn't buy it." (Danish: Vikner 1991: 300)

b. A barnum drakk$_v$ stúdentinn bjórinn$_i$ [$_{VP}$ stundun [$_{VP}$ t_v t_i]]
in bar-the drank student-the beer-the sometimes

"In the bar, the student sometimes drank the beer." (Icelandic: Bobaljik 1995: 118)

Object shift depends on the movement of V (cf. Holmberg 1986: 184): in (50a) *kobte* has moved out of the VP, in (50b) *drakk* has also moved out of the VP. The dependency of object shift and verb movement is known as Holmberg's generalization.

In (47c) functional layers and thematic layers are kept separate. In such a structure, the object movement to [Spec, AgrOP] will have to cross the base position of the subject. In the Minimalist approach this kind of move is problematic as it seems to violate the principle of Shortest Move (whose main function is to capture Rizzi's Relativized Minimality effects (Rizzi 1990b)). Chomsky (1993) proposes to deal with this in terms of "equidistance": it is proposed that the head to head movement of V to AgrO creates a configuration in which the specifier of VP and the specifier of AgrOP are equidistant.

An alternative proposal to avoid the crossing of the base position of the subject by object shift is represented in (51) (see Collins and Thrainsson 1993, Koizumi 1993, Bobaljik 1995):

(51)

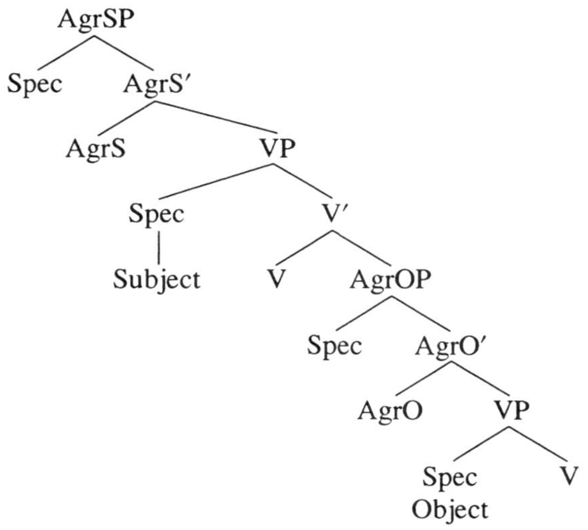

In (51) the base position of the object is within a lower VP, the base position of the subject is in a higher VP. An AgrOP layer is sandwiched between the two VP layers. This proposal is sometimes referred to as the Split VP. In the Split VP hypothesis, lexical layers which are responsible for theta role assignment – i.e. VPs – are now interrupted by functional layers which are responsible for feature checking. In other words, theta role assignment is discontinuous and alternates with feature checking operations. In (51) the base position of the subject, the specifier of the higher VP, is higher than the derived position of the object, [Spec, AgrOP].

In his discussion McCloskey evaluates the two types of structures and discusses evidence in favour of (47c), where the base position of the subject is lower than the derived position of the object.

McCloskey traces what he calls the deconstruction of the subject. In the earlier theory the subject was considered to be the highest nominal position in the clause, in more recent theories subjecthood is decomposed: the subject originates in a lower position and in many languages (though not all: see McCloskey's paper) it moves to the highest nominal position. Observe that the developments outlined above imply a deconstruction process of the object analogous to the deconstruction of the subject. In the earlier stages of the framework the object was the lowest nominal position in the clause, the NP position dominated by V′. In current approaches, the object originates in [NP, V′] but it moves overtly or covertly to the specifier position of AgrOP. Both subject and object thus are associated with a lower thematic position and a higher checking position.

4.1.2.2. *Adverbial Projections.* In generative studies of adverbials,[17] it is often proposed that adverbials are modifiers which are adjoined to the projections they modify (see Zubizarreta 1987; Sportiche 1988 for instance). Cinque (1995) examines the syntax of adverbs and he proposes that "AdvPs are only found in the unique Spec positions of different maximal projections." (1995).

Cinque says:

> within each portion of the clause, there is a rigidly fixed sequence of AdvPs . . . there is evidence for the existence of one head position to the immediate left, and one head position to the immediate right, of each such AdvP. For example, in Italian, the past participle can be found to the left of MICA and in between any of the other AdvPs . . .

Pursuing this line, the clause will have the following structure, the relevant functional heads are signalled as X.

(52)

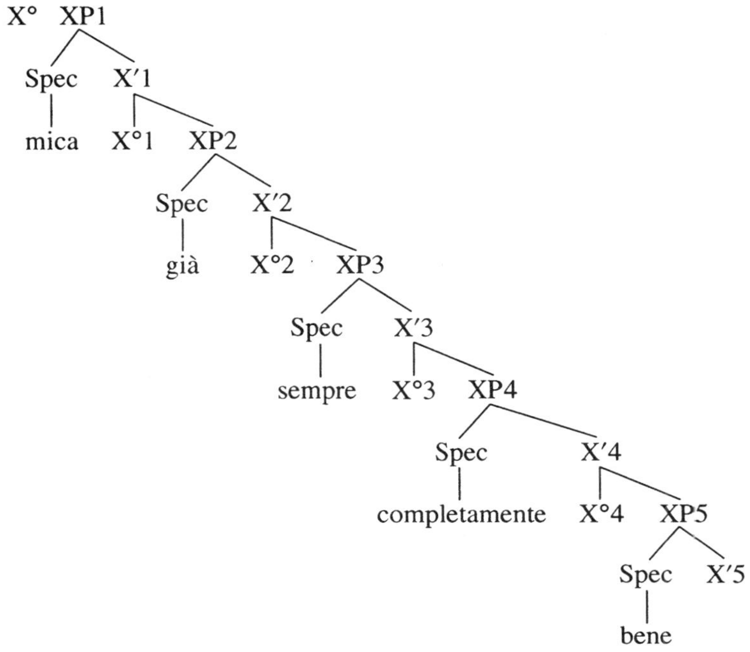

In his contribution to this volume, Rizzi also shows that preposed adverbials cannot be argued to be simply adjoined to the clausal projection but must be associated with specific projections. I refer the reader to his paper for extensive discussion.[18]

4.1.2.3. *NegP.* Among the functional projections which, at one point, received a lot of attention in the literature I mention the projection NegP, which encodes sentential negation (cf. Laka 1990, Zanuttini 1991). The relative position of NegP in the hierarchy of functional projections was – and still is – a matter of debate (cf. Laka 1990, Ouhalla 1990, Zanuttini 1991, Pollock 1989 and Pollock this volume etc.). As empirical studies of the distribution of markers of sentential negation develop, other questions are beginning to be asked. Originally it was assumed that NegP was the locus of sentential negation and it also seemed to be a tacit assumption in much work on negation that there was one (and only one) NegP per negative clause. This view has come under scrutiny recently on two grounds.

On the one hand, since the 1960s, the syntax of negative clauses has often been aligned with that of interrogative clauses (Klima 1964, Rizzi 1996, Haegeman 1995a). It is assumed that interrogative clauses are marked by the presence of an interrogative feature on a functional head. This feature is encoded as *wh* (Klima 1964, May 1985, Rizzi 1990a, Rizzi 1996) or Q (Katz and Postal 1964, Chomsky 1995). In the literature, it is usually assumed that the relevant interrogative feature does not project its own functional projection but rather that it is instantiated on a functional head which is independently postulated. Rizzi (1990a, 1996, this volume), for instance, assumes that *wh* is instantiated on T° in root clauses, and that it is associated with C° in embedded clauses. In other words, there is no projection which is labelled "WHP". An analogous line of reasoning could be pursued for the marker of sentential negation. In his contribution to this volume, Rizzi suggests that the feature NEG is base-generated on T° in English (his section 10). If *not* is the specifier of NegP in (53a), then NegP is projected. However, as such, the NEG feature, which encodes sentential negation on a functional head, is not necessarily associated with Neg° but may also be associated with T°. This raises the question whether sentences such as (53b) and (53c), which are arguably negative sentences (see Klima 1964, Haegeman 1995a for arguments), but in which there is no constituent which is necessarily associated with NegP, contain a specialized projection NegP (see Haegeman 1995a for a brief discussion).

(53) a. John has not talked
b. John said nothing
c. Never in my life will I talk to her again.

A second challenge for postulating a one-to-one relation between negative clauses and the specialized projection NegP is put forward in work by Zanuttini (1991, 1995, 1997). On the basis of a detailed comparative study of Romance languages and their dialects, and pursuing Cinque's (1995) proposals for the clause structure discussed in the previous section, Zanuttini (1995, 1997) shows that in certain languages not one but several projections of Neg° may occur in a clause, each of which may be associated with specialized semantic functions.

Consider, for instance, the Piedmontese examples in (54) from Zanuttini (1995):

(54) a. Gianni a l'ha nen capì tut (Piedmontese)
Gianni cl cl'has neg understood everything.'
"Gianni didn't understand everything."

b. Gianni a l'ha pa capì tut! (Piedmontese)
Gianni cl cl'has neg understood everything
"Gianni didn't understand everything (though you thought he would)"

In (54a) sentential negation is expressed by *nen*, in (54b) it is expressed by *pa*. While *nen* simply negates the sentence, *pa* in (54b) is presuppositional: it negates a proposition which the speaker had believed was true (cf. Zanuttini 1995: 2). Zanuttini shows that Piedmontese *pa* does not occupy the same position as *nen*. While *nen* cannot precede *già* ("already"), *pa* can precede *già*:

(55)	a.	A	l'ha	pa	già	ciamò,	che	mi	i	sapia!
		s-cl	cl'has	neg	already	called,	that	I	cl	know

"He hasn't already called, that I know!"

b.*	A	l'e	nen	già	andait	a	ca.
	s-cl	cl'is	neg	already	gone	to	home

Similarly, whereas *pa* precedes *pi* ("any more"), *nen* follows *pi*:

(56)	a.	A	l'han	pa	pi	telefuna,	da	ntlura.
		cl	cl'have	neg	more	telephoned,	since	that-time

"They haven't called any more, since then!"

b.	A	l'han	pi	nen	ricevu	gnente.
	cl	cl'have	more	neg	received	nothing

"They have no longer received anything."

Zanuttini proposes that *pa* is generated higher in the structure than *nen*. Pursuing her analysis on the basis of a number of Romance dialects, she arrives at the conclusion that clauses may have more than one functional projection expressing negation. In fact, she identifies at least four in matrix clauses. I refer the reader to her paper for discussion.

4.1.2.4. *The Internal Subject Hypothesis and The Split INFL.* In section 3.2, we discussed the hypothesis that the base position of the subject is not [Spec, IP] but that it originates lower in the structure. One type of argument in support of this view concerned the so called transitive expletive constructions and is discussed in McCloskey's contribution to this volume (repeated from (42b)):

(57)	það	hefur	einhver	borðað	epli.
	there	has	someone	eaten	an-apple

"Someone has eaten an apple"

In (57) an expletive *það* occupies the canonical subject position and the indefinite subject *einhver* ("someone") remains lower in the structure. In a representation such as (25b)/(43), where the functional domain of the clause consists simply of IP, there is only one specifier position lower than [Spec, IP], namely [Spec, VP], hence *einhver* will occupy that position. Thus an example such as (57) might be taken to illustrate a situation where the subject is in its base position, i.e. [Spec, VP].

However, given the explosion of functional categories discussed above, the fact that the subject is lower in the structure in (57) does not entail that it occupies the specifier of VP. Adopting the hierarchy of functional projections in (47b) in which AgrP dominates TP, one might equally assume (see Jonas and Bobaljik 1993, Bobaljik and Jonas 1996) that the subject *einhver* in (57) occupies [Spec, TP] in (57). This means that (57) shows that the subject need not occupy the highest A-position of the IP domain, but it does not necessarily constitute an example of a subject DP in its base position.

As shown by McCloskey in his contribution to this volume, the articulation of IP into a number of functional projections means that it has become extremely difficult to give unambiguous examples in which the subject occupies a lower position which can be identified as [Spec, VP]. Let me illustrated this difficulty in determining the position of the lower subject on the basis of an example from West Flemish (WF), a dialect of Dutch (see Haegeman 1992 for a description of some of the properties of this dialect).

Like Dutch, WF has transitive expletive constructions. The WF construction is less constrained than its Dutch counterpart (for discussion of the constraints in Dutch see McCloskey note 18)

(58) a. da-der nen student under gezien eet
that there a student them seen has
"that a student has seen them."

In (58a) *da* is the complementizer; it is adjacent to the expletive *der* ("there"). If one assumes that WF is an OV language (but see Zwart 1993 for counter-arguments), one might conclude that in (58a) the subject *nen student* occupies the specifier of VP.

(58) b. da-der [$_{VP}$ nen student [$_{V'}$ under gezien]] eet

However, (58b) is probably inadequate: the weak pronoun *under* ("them") does not normally stay VP-internally in WF. At contrasts with the strong pronoun UNDER (cf. Cardinaletti and Starke 1994, Haegeman 1993b, 1994a, 1996b):

(59) a.* da Jan gisteren under gezien eet
that Jan yesterday them seen has

b. da Jan gisteren UNDER gezien eet
that Jan yesterday THEM seen has

If we assume that the weak pronoun *under* always leaves the VP and moves to a higher functional projection, then in (58a) the subject *nen student*, appearing to the left of *under*, cannot be VP-internal and must also have moved up. One possibility is that *nen student* may have moved to the specifier of TP (cf. Jonas and Bobaljik 1993, Bobaljik and Jonas 1996).

(59) c. da der [$_{TP}$ nen student$_i$ [$_{FP}$ under$_j$ [$_{VP}$ t_i t_j gezien]] eet[19]

However, now consider the distribution of the indefinite subject *nen student* in (60):

(60) a. dat der nen student under gisteren allemole gezien
that there a student them yesterday all seen
eet
has
"that a student saw them all yesterday."

b. dat der under nen student gisteren allemole gezien eet

c. dat der under gisteren nen student allemole gezien eet

d. dat der under gisteren allemole nen student gezien eet

(60a) is compatible with the proposal formulated above (59c), in which the expletive is in the canonical subject position [Spec, AgrSP], and in which the indefinite subject might occupy [Spec, TP]. But in (60b) the object *under* precedes the indefinite subject. Observe that the weak pronoun *under* cannot precede a definite subject:

(61) *dat under Valère gisteren gezien eet
that them Valère yesterday seen has

It is not clear what the position of *under* can be in (60b).[20] One option is that the indefinite subject is in [Spec, TP], that the expletive *der* is in [Spec, AgrP], and that there is an additional intermediate position for the object *under*. Observe that this position need not be reserved for pronouns, as seen in (62):

(62) dat der die boeken nen student gisteren allemole
that there those book a student yesterday all
gekocht eet
bought has
"that a students bought those books all yesterday."

Alternatively, the indefinite subject in (60b) occupies a position lower than [Spec, TP]. But observe that the indefinite subject appears to the left of adverbial material which we assume is not VP-internal. If adjuncts are VP-external, then this suggests that the subject in (60b) does not occupy the specifier of VP.

In (60c) the indefinite subject follows the adverbial *gisteren* and precedes a quantifier *allemole* ("all"), floated off the object. The same pattern is found with a full DP object in (63):

(63) da der die boeken gisteren nen student allemole
that there those books yesterday a student all

gekocht eet
bought has

"that a student bought those books all yesterday."

Since Sportiche (1988) it is assumed that quantifiers signal traces of the associated argument DP (see McCloskey, this volume). Let us explore the consequences of this view for a moment.

If one were to assume an underlying OV structure, the floated quantifier *allemole* could be taken to signal the base position of the object. Following this view the subject might be argued to be in the hierarchically higher [Spec, VP] position. However, assuming a VO base-order (cf. Kayne 1994, Zwart 1993, 1997), the question is less easily solved. As it precedes the verb, the floated quantifier *allemole* cannot now be taken to signal the base position of the object. If we continue to assume that floated quantifiers signal intermediate positions of the associated arguments, then the quantifier will be taken to signal an intermediate, VP-external, position through which the object *under allemole* has moved. This position could, for instance, be [Spec, AgrOP]. Under this view, we conclude that the subject may be taken to occupy a VP-external position which is lower than [Spec, TP], as discussed above, but which is also higher than [Spec, AgrOP].

In (60d) the indefinite subject is lower than the quantifier floated off the object. Again the same pattern is available with a lexical DP object:

(64) dat der die boeken gisteren allemole nen student
that there those books yesterday all a student

gekocht eet
bought has

"that a student bought the books all yesterday."

For (60d), various options are open. We might say that the quantifier is stranded higher than in (60c), in which case the subject can again be taken to be VP-external, as in (60c), or, possibly, (60d) IS an example in which the subject remains lower than [Spec, AgrOP], perhaps VP-internally.

The data discussed above do not exhaustively cover the empirical domain of transitive expletives in WF, nor do they give us definitive solutions. The point of my discussion is not to provide an analysis of the transitive expletive construction in this language, but rather to illustrate the complexity of the problem. As the reader can see, the analysis of the data above remains, and has to remain, tentative in many points, and each hypothesis depends on one's specific assumptions for the structure of the articulated IP and VP. Observe, for instance, that not everyone is in agreement that floated quantifiers are associated with intermediate DP positions. Bobaljik (1995), for instance, proposes that floated quantifiers are adverbs (cf. McCloskey, this volume, Doetjes 1992). The tentative nature of the above discussion is due to the general uncertainty as to the functional structure of the IP, concerning which many questions remain without answers.

4.1.3. *General Questions*

Inspired by Pollock's work on the clause structure, we have witnessed over the past decade an explosion of functional categories within the IP domain, each of these being motivated on empirical grounds for at least one language (group). This development leaves a number of important questions, both for classical GB approaches and for Minimalist approaches. I will briefly list some of them here.

In the current literature there is no unanimity concerning the inventory of functional categories. The question has to be raised whether the functional categories postulated on empirical grounds for one language must be universally present in all languages (cf. the discussion in Iatridou 1990, Cinque 1995, Nash and Rouveret 1996). An alternative to postulating the universal instantiation of these functional categories would be to propose that the functional categories are part of the universal inventory but that their instantiation in individual languages is (perhaps to some extent) a matter of parametric variation.

If functional categories are essentially defined by the abstract features which they host, the question also arises whether each abstract feature necessarily projects its own projection, or whether features may jointly project.

On closer inspection of the current literature it turns out that very often bundles of features are taken to head a projection. In both the classical GB literature, and in Minimalist approaches, for instance, AGR is generally taken to be a bundle of Person and Number features, which presumably project jointly (and may also move jointly, cf. Chomsky 1995, Fujita 1996). Shlonsky (1989) proposes that Number and Person may project separately (see also Rouveret 1991).[21] Conversely, as mentioned above, it is conceivable that while NegP is projected in negative sentences with *not* in English, negative sentences in which the negation is expressed by a negative quantifier (53b) or sentences with negative inversion (53c) may well lack the functional projection NegP.

Giorgi and Pianesi (1996) allow for parametric variation in terms of the association of features to morphemes: while some features, say x and y, cluster on one morpheme and jointly project in one language, x and y may each head a single projection in another language. The latter situation, where each feature heads a projection, is referred to as Feature Scattering (Giorgi and Pianesi 1996: 20). Giorgi and Pianesi relate the types of associations of features to morphemes to the traditional distinction between agglutinative or isolating languages on the one hand and flexive languages on the other.

The association [of a feature to a morpheme lh] could be one to one, giving agglutinative or isolating languages, or it could happen that the same morpheme is associated to more features, in this way obtaining the so-called flexive languages, such as Italian. We will call the categories obtained by means of such a multiple association *syncretic* and *hybrid* categories. (1996: 19)

An example of a morpheme to which two features are associated is the *-a* morpheme of Italian *bella* ("beautiful") which realizes both gender (feminine) and number (singular).

In recent work Nash and Rouveret (1996) introduce the concept of "fission", i.e. splitting of functional features of one category, which is similar to Giorgi and Pianesi's feature scattering:

Tense is the only conceptually necessary F-category in simple root clauses. . . . Additional functional heads may be created in the course of the syntactic derivation, which, having no features of their own, are not included in the initial numeration. The identity of these heads, which we will label proxies, is purely morphological, not semantically predictable. . . . The formal features of F-heads can, and if uninterpretable and unchecked, must move in overt syntax. Proxy heads result from the fission an unchecked feature form its original head' (1996).[22]

Once we have established the functional projections of a domain, the question arises whether these functional categories have a universal hierarchy or whether, on the other hand, there may be parametric variation in their hierarchical organization (see Ouhalla 1990, Zanuttini 1991 for early discussions of this issue).

The question concerning the inventory of functional projections available and/or instantiated in a clause and their hierarchy is one that has to be addressed both in traditional and Minimalist approaches. Putting the problem in Minimalist terms, for instance, in order to be able to derive a sentence one has to know which is the inventory of functional heads that one can select from, which functional heads will be part of the Numeration, and which features they host.

4.1.4. *Layered Specifiers*

A recent development in the Minimalist program might signal the return to less articulated conceptions of clause structure. It is proposed (Ura 1994, Chomsky 1995) that the functional projections be reduced to those that are conceptually necessary (cf. Nash and Rouveret 1996). In addition, one head may host more than one feature and hence may have more than one specifier. Constituents which would have been interpreted as specifiers of distinct functional heads in a Pollock-style analysis, are then reinterpreted as part of the layered specifiers to one single head in Chomsky (1995). Let me illustrate this point with two examples.

Since Pollock (1989), the specifier of AgrP and the specifier of TP were distinguished by virtue of the heads they were associated with. In the WF transitive expletive sentence (65), the expletive *der* might be argued to be the specifier of AgrSP and the indefinite subject *drie studenten* ("three students") arguably is the specifier of TP (cf. the discussion in section 4.1.2.4).

(65)	dan	der	drie	studenten	dienen	boek	gekocht	een
	that	there	three	students	that	book	bought	have

"that three students bought that book"

Recent versions of Minimalism (Chomsky 1995: chapter 4, section 10) dispense with the functional head Agr, and reinterpret the constituent structure in terms of layered specifiers of single heads: in (65) *der* and *drie studenten* are now taken both to be specifiers of a single head T (see also Ura 1994).

Observe that if we assume that in French or in English NegP dominates TP and is dominated by AgrP, then in the layered specifier account which collapses Agr and T, *not* and *pas* will no longer be specifiers of a specialized projection NegP, but they will also have to be analysed as specifiers of T. For further complications to this proposal see also Chomsky's own discussion.

Similarly, while in earlier versions of Minimalism it was proposed that the object checks its features in [Spec, AgrOP] more recent views provide the following structure:

(66) a.

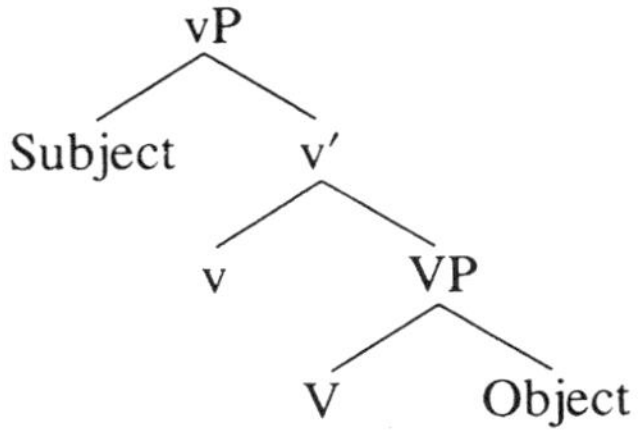

b.

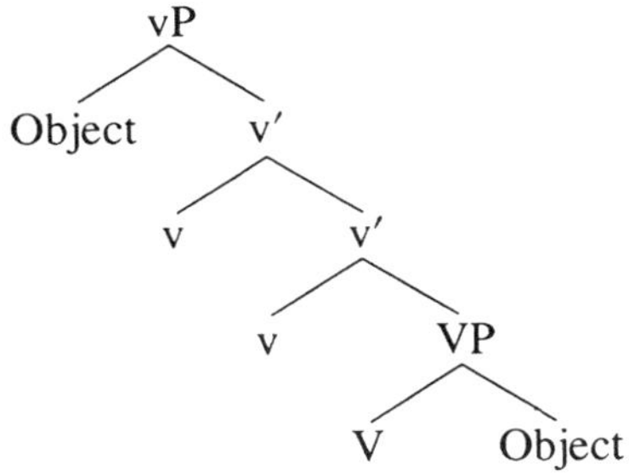

Object and subject are associated with distinct lexical heads, the former being an argument of V, the latter of what is repesented as "v" (a "light verb") (cf. Grimshaw and Mester 1988, Hale and Keyser 1993, Chomsky 1995). vP is then a specialized projection for the external argument (see the discussion in section 3.3 and in McCloskey's contribution). Object shift does not move the object to the specifier of a specialized functional projection; rather it moves the object to an outer specifier position of vP, as in (66b). Analogously to the proposal discussed above, which collapses TP and AgrSP, the proposal in (66) collapses AgrOP and a projection of V.

As before, this proposal raises questions. In the Scandinavian examples of object shift in (50), repeated here for the reader's convenience as (67) the object moves past the negative adverb

(67) a. Peter kobte$_v$ den$_i$ [$_{VP}$ ikke [$_{VP}$ t$_v$ t$_i$]]
Peter bought it not
"Peter didn't buy it."
(Danish: Vikner 1991: 300)

b. A barnum drakk$_v$ stúdentinn bjórinn$_i$ [$_{VP}$ stundun [$_{VP}$ t$_v$ t$_i$]]
in bar-the drank student-the beer-the the sometimes
"In the bar, the student sometimes drank the beer."
(Icelandic: Bobaljik 1995: 118)

If we adopt the layered specifier account for (67) then the marker of sentential negation *ikke* as well as the frequency adverb *stundun* must also be reinterpreted as specifiers of vP, hence we must allow for multiple specifier structures.

Assuming the multiplication of specifiers, the problem will arise how to capture the hierarchical and linear relations between these specifiers. Consider, for instance, the following data from WF.

(67) c. da Valère Marie Jan zeker dienen boek gisteren
that Valère Marie Jan certainly that book yesterday
nie ee zien geven
not has see give
"that yesterday Valère certainly did not see Mary give that book to Jan."

In this example *Valère* is the subject of the matrix perception verb *zien* ("see"). *Marie* is the subject of the lower verb, *geven* ("give"), *Jan* is the lower indirect object and *dienen* boek is the lower direct object. All lower arguments precede the negation marker *nie* ("not") which negates the matrix clause and, we assume, is generated in the matrix domain. Thus in (67c) all lower arguments must have moved into the matrix domain. In an approach in which there are distinct functional projections associated with direct object, indirect object etc., each of the lower arguments may target a specific projection. In an approach with layered specifiers, one might have to argue that the lower subject *Marie*, the lower indirect object *Jan*, the lower direct object *dienen boek*, the higher adverbial *zeker* ("certainly") and the higher negation marker *niet* are all specifiers to v. But at the same time, observe that we have to continue to ensure that the arguments have the order in (67c) since alternative orders are ungrammatical:

(67) d.*da Valère (SU) Jan (IO) dienen boek (DO) zeker Marie (SU) gisteren nie ee zien geven

For further discussion of the problem of the relative order of the arguments see also Haegeman (1993a).

The same problem will arise if we assume that the adverbials discussed in section 4.1.2.2 in terms of specifiers of specialized projections above are reinterpreted as multiple specifiers of one head. In an articulated structure with stacked functional projections hierarchical and linear relations can be captured in terms of selectional restrictions. It is not clear how such restrictions can be reduplicated in a layered specifier approach.[23, 24]

4.2. *The Split CP*

4.2.1. *Focus and Topic*

With respect to the development of the clausal structure we have seen that there is, on the one hand, a trend for identifying functional projections and developing a more articulated IP, and, on the other hand, there is a recent return to simpler structures with multiple specifiers. The same development can be found with respect to the layer usually labelled CP.

In the classical clause structure (25b) the CP level contains one functional projection, headed by the complementizer (cf. (43), Chomsky 1986a). As has been noted in the literature (e.g. Culicover 1991, 1993, Nakajima 1996), this structure is inadequate in view of, for instance, the English data in (68):

(68) I swear that never again will I go there

In (68) the complementizer *that* is separated from the specifier of IP by (i) a maximal projection, *never again*, and (ii) a head, *will*. In order to accommodate sentences such as (68) we need to postulate more structure in the CP layer. In his contribution to this volume, Rizzi considers this problem in detail. Italian data such as (69) lead him to postulating a richly articulated structure of CP:

(69) a. Dicono che IL TUO LIBRO dovremmo dare a
they say that the your book we should give to
Gianni domani.
Gianni tomorrow

b. Dicono che IL TUO LIBRO domani dovremmo dare a Gianni

c. Dicono che domani IL TUO LIBRO dovremmo dare a Gianni,

d. Dicono che domani IL TUO LIBRO a Gianni gli dovremmo dare

e. Dicono che a Gianni IL TUO LIBRO domani gli dovremmo dare

f. Dicono che a Gianni gli dovremmo dare il tuo libro domani

In the Italian sentences (69), one or more constituents appear in the left periphery of the clause. In (69a) *IL TUO LIBRO* ("your book") is focalized. In (69b) the focalized constituent is followed by a topicalized adjunct of time, *domani* ("tomorrow"). In (69c) the topicalized constituent *domani* precedes the focalized constituent. In (69d) and in (69e) one topicalized constituent precedes the focalized constituent, the other one follows. In (69f), finally, there is a topicalized constituent, *a Gianni*, and there is no focalized constituent. (For embedded topicalization see also, among others, Authier 1992, Lasnik and Saito 1984, 1992.)

The question arises if preposed constituents can be created by mere adjunction to IP (Lasnik and Saito 1984) or whether they involve fully-fledged functional projections. The question also has become more prominent in view of recent proposals by Kayne (1994) in which adjunction is ruled out.

The English negative inversion data in (68) provide evidence that at least some cases of preposing involve the activation of a functional projection. For topicalization, Lasnik and Saito (1984), among others, propose an adjunction approach. Rizzi's paper offers a number of arguments against an adjunction approach. On the basis of a range of empirical and theoretical considerations Rizzi proposes that the CP domain may also contain a unique Focus projection, FocP, whose specifier hosts the focalized constituent and whose head hosts an abstract Focus-feature, and a recursive Topic Projection, whose specifier hosts a topicalized constituent and whose head hosts a Top feature.[25, 26] For the projections ForceP and FinP, see the next section.

(70)

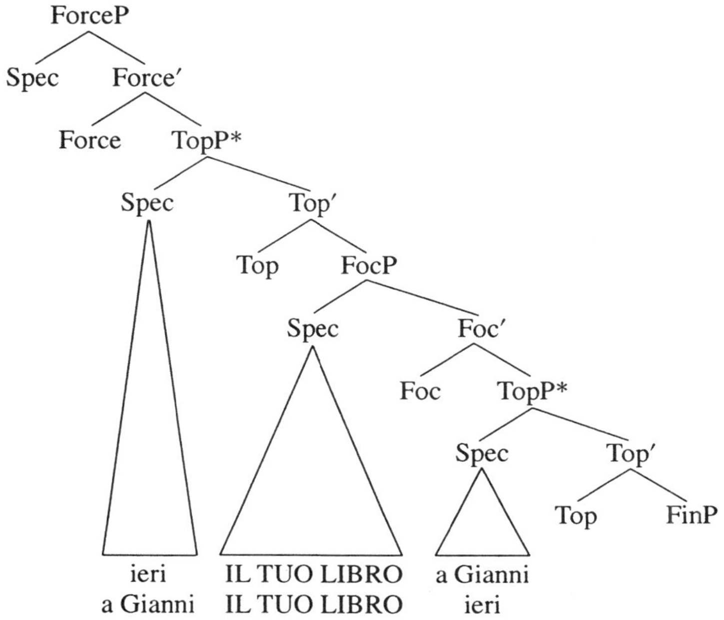

Rizzi's proposal that there is a structural focus position as such is not new. In the literature on Hungarian, for instance, it has often been pointed out that focalized constituents occupy a specialized position (Brody 1990, 1995b, Kiss 1987, Horvath 1985). (71), taken from Puskas (1995), shows how the structure postulated for Italian in Rizzi's paper carries over to Hungarian:

(71) Azt hiszem [hogy ezt a filmet MARIVAL làtta [Janos t]]
that think-1sg that this film -acc mary-instr saw John nom

"I think that Johns saw this film WITH MARY"

In Hungarian, unlike is the case in Italian, focalized constituents trigger subject verb inversion: in (71) the verb *làtta* moves to Foc, [Spec, FocP] being occupied by the focalized constituent *MARIVAL*.[27]

4.2.2. *Force and Finiteness*

In addition to postulating a projection for focalization and a recursive projection for topicalization, Rizzi also proposes that CP be decomposed into two projections. The classical view of clause structure, the embedded CP, registers the illocutionary force of the clause (interrogative, declarative, relative, etc.). Moreover, the complementizer determines the type of IP which it introduces. English *that* selects finite clauses and English *for* selects infinitival clauses. Observing this dual nature of C, Rizzi (this volume) proposes that C contains both a Force feature and a Fin feature. That C contains a finiteness component is suggested, for instance, by the fact that some Germanic dialects have complementizers which inflect for person and number, as illustrated in the WF paradigm in (72), where the complementizer *da* takes different forms depending on the person and number of the subject (see Haegeman 1992).

(72) dan-k ik nor us goan
that I I to house go
"that I go home"

da-j gie nor us goat
da-se zie nor us goat
da-me wunder nor us goan
da-j gunder nor us goat
dan-ze zunder nor us goan

Rizzi proposes that CP be split up into two specialized projections: ForceP and FinP.

The questions raised above concerning the articulated structure of IP also arise here. Let me just discuss one problem. The decomposition of CP into ForceP and FinP may be interpreted in a number of ways. One option is to say that in the absence of FocP and TopP, the features Force and Fin are instantiated on a single head, C. This would be the case, for instance, in an example such as (73a). It might be proposed that the two features project independently only in the presence of topicalized or focalized constituents, as would be the case in (73b):

(73) a. I think [$_{CP}$ that [John will go to Paris tomorrow]]
b. I think [$_{ForceP}$ that [$_{TopP}$ tomorrow [$_{FinP}$ [$_{Fin}$] [John will go to Paris]]]]

Given a certain view of economy, which avoids unnecessary structure (cf. Cardinaletti and Starke's (1994) Avoid Structure), the unitary C in (73a) would be preferable, and the split C as in (73b) would only be licit when required by the presence of focus or topic material. Alternatively, one might adopt the view that Force and Fin always project specialized projections, so that even in examples without preposing both projections are instantiated:

(73) c. I think [$_{ForceP}$ that [$_{FinP}$ [$_{Fin}$] [John will go to Paris tomorrow]]]

The answer to the question above will of course be determined at least in part by the answer to the general question of the status of abstract features and the extent to which they project specialized projections.

4.2.3. *Extensions of The Split CP*

In his paper, Rizzi also shows that the landing site of relative *wh*-elements is high in the C-domain, since they always precede topicalized elements. Bianchi (1995) examines in detail the repercussions for the structure of relative clauses adopting Rizzi's split COMP analysis.

(74) a. un uomo a cui il premio Nobel, lo daranno
a man wo whom the Nobel prize they will give
senz'altro
certainly

b.*un uomo il premio Nobel a cui, lo daranno senz'altro

(75) a.* A chi il premio Nobel lo daranno?
to whom the Nobel prize it they-will-give

b. Il premio Nobel, a chi lo daranno?

An empirical question which arises in the context of Rizzi's paper is how his proposal applies to the Verb Second languages (see Haegeman 1996a, 1997b). In these languages, the finite verb in the root clause is always in second position and it is preceded by one constituent. (76) illustrates Dutch:

(76) a. Ze kocht gisteren een boek
she bought yesterday a book
"She bought a book yesterday."

b. ZIJ kocht gisteren een boek
SHE bought yesterday a book
"SHE bought a book yesterday."

c. EEN BOEK kocht ze gisteren
A BOOK bought she yesterday
"A BOOK, she bought yesterday."

d. Dat boek heeft ze gisteren voor JAN gekocht
this book has she yesterday for Jan bought
"That book she bought for JAN."

e. Gisteren heeft ze dat boek voor Jan gekocht
yesterday has she that book for Jan bought
"Yesterday she bought that book for Jan."

f. Wat heeft ze gisteren gekocht?
what has she yesterday bought
"What did she buy yesterday?"

The first constituent in a V2 pattern may be, among others, a weak pronoun subject (76a), a tonic pronoun subject (76b), a focalized object with focal stress (76c), a topicalized object with contrastive stress (76d), an adverbial with no marked stress (76e), and a *wh*-phrase (76f). It is not clear how these data are to be interpreted in terms of the articulated CP. It is not clear, for instance, if the finite verb occupies the same position in all of the examples in (76) above. Furthermore, the fact that expletive (76g) and quasi-argument (76h) subjects may also occupy the first position suggests, against Branigan (1995), that the position occupied by the first overt constituent need not be an A′ position (a focus position or a topic position):

(76) g. Er zijn gisteren veel studenten gekomen
there are yesterday many students come
"Many students came yesterday."

h. Het heeft gisteren de hele dag geregend.
it has yesterday the whole day rained
"Yesterday, it rained all day."

Based on data such as those above, some authors conclude that there is no unitary landing site for the inflected V° in root clauses of the V2 languages (for various viewpoints, see Shlonsky 1992, Zwart 1993, Muller and Sternefeld 1993, Branigan 1995, Haegeman 1995b, 1997b[28]).

4.2.4. *Layered Specifiers*

In a Minimalist approach to the articulated structure of CP, Koizumi (1995) discusses English topicalization and negative inversion data such as those in (77):

(77) a. Robin says that, the birdseed, he is going to put in the shed
b. Becky said that at no time would she agree to visit Mary

Koizumi (1995: 141) proposes a layered specifier approach to such structures (cf. section 4.1.4 above). The topicalized phrase is an outer specifier of the projection whose inner specifier is the preposed negative constituent. One functional head (Pol) carries several functional features – in the relevant example the features [+top] and [+neg] – and layered specifiers can satisfy the multiple features of the head.

(78)

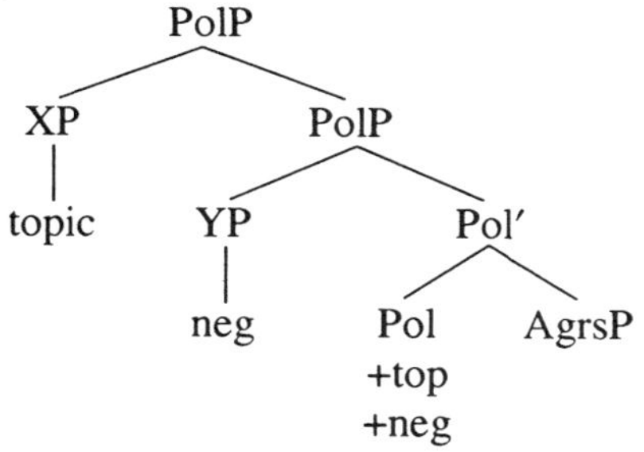

Obviously, the question arises whether the layered specifier account will be able to capture the array of empirical data covered by Rizzi's paper. Browning (1996) also provides a Minimalist analysis for some of the data discussed in Rizzi's paper. See also Nakajima (1995) for discussion of the split CP.

5. OPTIMALITY AND LEXICAL INSERTION

5.1. *The Framework*

Jane Grimshaw's contribution is cast in the framework of Optimality Theory, which was originally developed for phonology (Prince and Smolensky 1993, Grimshaw forthcoming). The core of Optimality Theory resides in the hypothesis that constraints are universal, potentially conflicting, and ranked. Contrary to the standard assumptions in the generative approach, where the violation of constraints leads to ungrammaticality, Optimality Theory admits that constraints can be violated while maintaining a well-formed sentence. Where two constraints conflict on a given input, it is the ranking of the constraints that determines which of the available options is grammatical. Grammars are nothing more than rankings of the set of universal constraints.

In "classical" GB approaches and in Minimalist approaches to syntactic theory, there is a strong tendency to locate the source of parametric variation in the morphology. For instance, verb movement is assumed to be determined by the relative strength/weakness of the AGR/T morphology of the verb. In Optimality Theory, parametric variation is expressed in terms of variation in the ranking of constraints. The interaction of constraints as regulated by Optimality Theory explains a number of otherwise puzzling generalizations.

Consider for instance the notion of the "last resort" use of a certain grammatical device as discussed in section 2.2.1. In terms of Optimality Theory, such a device – let us call it D – will be one that violates a constraint, say C1. Hence there will be some cost associated with D being used, namely that the particular constraint C1 is violated. The form which does not violate this constraint will be ranked higher, except in one specific context. The relevant context is one in which there is an additional constraint, C2, which is ranked higher than constraint C1 and which can only be satisfied by the use of device D. Only in such circumstances will the use of D be grammatical and optimal.

Similarly, Economy (see section 2.2.1) also finds an instantiation in Optimality Theory. Suppose that there is a constraint, C3, against movement, which will be violated every time a trace appears. It follows that movement will only take place when it results in the satisfaction of a constraint higher than C3. In such terms movement will be restricted to what is necessary.

5.2. *Expletive Insertion*

By way of a concrete example of the application of Optimality Theory, let us consider the distribution of expletives in English.[29] Consider the sentences in (79):

(79) a. John bought a house
b. John did not buy a house

In (79b) the auxiliary *do* is inserted, but this auxiliary does not contribute to the semantics of the sentence. It is used as a dummy verb, i.e. an expletive (see also Pollock, this volume: 243).

Following Optimality approaches, the distribution of the English auxiliary *do* can be understood in terms of constraint conflict. The occurrence of *do* violates a constraint of Full Interpretation, because *do* has no semantic analysis. The verb thus occurs only when a higher ranked constraint[30] is satisfied by its presence and violated in its absence. *Do* is possible only when necessary. From this perspective it is not a lexical accident that English has a semantically empty auxiliary. Rather it is a consequence of the grammar of the language, i.e. the ranking of the constraints of Universal Grammar, which forces the verb *do* to appear, but without its meaning. In Optimality terms, the hypothesis is that *do* minimally violates Full Interpretation: any other verb would violate it more, having a more highly specified semantics which is unparsed, or unanalysed, when the verb is meaningless. Every language with the (relevant) constraint rankings must have *do*, no language with crucially different rankings can have it. The appearance of empty *do* is far from being a language particular lexical fact.

Consider now the use of expletive *it* in (80)

(80) a. That John should have talked about this is very strange.
b. It is very strange that John should have talked about this.

If we compare (80a) and (80b) there is no semantic difference between the two. This suggests that *it* again does not contribute to the meaning of the sentence, in violation of Full Interpretation.

In terms of Optimality Theory, the appearance of the expletive *it* in English could be given the same analysis, fundamentally, as that of *do*-insertion. English ranks Full Interpretation below the constraint(s) requiring a filled subject position. Hence the grammar of English prefers using a nominal without its meaning to leaving the subject position unfilled. Italian, with a different constraint ranking, makes the opposite choice. But this is not a fact about the lexicons of English and Italian, it is a fact about their grammars. Here again, the hypothesis is that *it* rather than some other nominal element occurs because it represents minimal violation: stripping the meaningful pronoun *it* of its semantics is a lesser violation than stripping any other nominal of the language.

5.3. *Clitic Sequences and Opaque Clitics*

In her contribution to this volume, Grimshaw examines the distribution of clitics in Romance from the point of view of Optimality Theory. After a general introduction to the principles governing the lexical insertion of clitics, she addresses the problem of the so called "opaque" clitics in Romance (Bonet 1995).

5.3.1. *Romance Clitics*

5.3.1.1. *Clitics as Bundles of Features.* Concerning the feature specifications of clitics, Grimshaw proposes that

> it is unilluminating at best to characterize each clitic as a fully specified set of morphosyntactic features . . . Alternatively, we can treat clitics as potentially underspecified bundles of morphosyntactic features. In a situation where a clitic with a given specification is called for, an output clitic with exactly that specification will be the best realization, but if there is no such clitic available, an underspecified clitic which best matches the input may suffice. (section 4)

Grimshaw assumes that clitics vary according to how much morphosyntactic information they encode. For instance, she proposes that the Italian clitic *si* is underspecified for the features reflexive, person, plural, gender, case. Or, to cite Grimshaw, "it is a clitic which has no properties" (see also Bonet 1995). Because of this underspecification *si* can be used as a reflexive, third person, plural, feminine, accusative clitic in a given context because no clitic with a better specification is available. But, being underspecified, *si* can also be used as an impersonal subject.

Given a choice of clitics in a given language, the clitic must be selected which best matches the input. In other words, Grimshaw proposes that there is a faithfulness constraint on the selection of clitics, which requires the clitic which best analyzes (is most faithful to) the input to be selected.[31]

5.3.1.2. *Opaque Clitics (Bonet 1995).* Opaque clitics are cases where the clitic occurring in a sequence of clitics is not the one to be expected on the basis of the clitics as they occur in isolation, i.e. where the faithfulness constraint is violated. Grimshaw re-interprets the opaque clitics phenomenon in terms of Optimality Theory.

The basic idea is that there is a constraint against adjacent occurrences of identical forms (see her section 2.2):

(81) *X X

Constraint (81) applies, for instance to the duplication of clitics. This constraint may conflict with the faithfulness constraint discussed above. If (81) ranks higher than the faithfulness constraints, then a sequence of identical clitics will have to be avoided. If (81) ranks lower than the faithfulness constraint then a duplication of clitics is allowed. I will illustrate this point with some examples taken from Grimshaw's paper.

Consider first the distribution of the clitic *si* in Italian, which Grimshaw considers to be underspecified. In Italian, the impersonal subject is expressed by the clitic *si* (82a); given its underspecification, this clitic is also used for the 3rd person reflexive (82b). When both uses of *si* would have to occur in a single sentence (82c), we would end up with the sequence *si si*, violating (81). Instead of the ungrammatical sequence *si si*, we actually find *ci si* (82d), where the impersonal subject is not realized as it would be in isolation.

(82) a. Lo si sveglia
him/it impers wake-up (3sg)
"one wakes him/it up"

b. Se lo compra
refl him/it buys
"she/he buys it for her/himself"

c.* Si si lava
Imp-refl washes

d. Ci si lava
ci si washes
"one washes oneself" (adapted from Bonet 1995: 609, her (2))

The "perfect" clitic, namely *si*, which best respects the faithfulness constraint, is not available in (82c/d), because of (81), which ranks higher than the faithfulness constraint. The sequence *ci si* represents the best the language can do in the situation. According to Optimality Theory, the chosen clitic involves minimal violation of the morphological faithfulness constraints.

In Italian (82) *ci* replaces *si* in order to avoid the duplication of the clitic. There is more than one way to resolve the problem posed by clitic duplication. For instance, rather than change one of the clitics (as is done in (82)), one of the clitics might actually delete. This is the case in Spanish, where, at least in some dialects, the reduplication *se se* is replaced by *se*:

(83) a.* Se se lava
"One washes oneself."

b. Se lava (see Grimshaw's (19))

Grimshaw also discusses the Italian dialect of Cornegliano (see Bonet 1995) where the *si si* sequence is possible, i.e. where (82c) is grammatical. She proposes that in this particular dialect, the faithfulness constraint ranks higher than (81): the sequence *si si* is the best sequence. Constraint reranking thus accounts for cross-linguistic and cross-dialectal variation.

5.3.2. *Duplication in Dutch*

Grimshaw's paper deals with the duplication of clitics in Romance. Obviously, constraint (81) also applies to other languages. Let me just illustrate the same type of phenomenon in Dutch. The data are taken from Bennis (1986), see also van Riemsdijk (1978).

Dutch has a clitic element *er* ("there") which appears in four different constructions (examples from Bennis 1986, 174–178): existential *er* as illustrated in (84a), *er* as the complement of a preposition, illustrated in (84b), quantitative *er* in (84c) and locative *er* in (84d). For detailed discussion I refer to Bennis (1986).

(84) a. Er loopt een jongen in de tuin.
there walks a boy in the garden
"There is a boy walking in the garden."

b. Ik heb er_i met hem over t_i gesproken.
I have there with him about talked
"I have talked to him about it"

c. Ik heb er_i gisteren twee t_i gekocht.
I have there yesterday two bought
"I bought two yesterday."

d. Jan koopt er een boek.
Jan buys there a book
"Jan is buying a book there."

Bennis (1986: 178, 1980) signals that "a peculiar property of *er* is that one surface realization may have more than one syntactic function."

Consider, for instance, the combination of existential *er* and prepositional *er*, in (85a):

(85) a.*	dat	er	er$_i$	twee	jongens	op t$_i$	zaten
	that	there	there	two	boys	on	sat

"that two boys were sitting on it."

(85a), with the sequence *er er*, violates (81) and is replaced by (85b):

(85) b.	dat	er	twee	jongens	op	zaten
	that	there	two	boys	on	sat

In (85b) *er* seems to function both as expletive and as complement of the preposition *op*.

5.3.3. *Conclusion*

Grimshaw's paper illustrates the application of Optimality Theory to the domain of morphosyntax, based on a strictly delineated set of data. The situation which is illustrated is that in which two clitics co-occur and where there is a conflict between two goals: one goal is to utilize the very best clitic, the one which would occur in isolation, and the other goal is to avoid duplication. Grimshaw shows that variation among languages and dialects can be explained partly in terms of the ranking of these two goals. If the goal of avoiding duplication ranks higher than the goal of using the best clitic, then various strategies are available to solve the conflict. For instance, one clitic can delete (as in Spanish (83) and in Dutch (85)); or, alternatively, one clitic can be replaced by another one (as in the Italian examples (82)). These strategies are the result of alternative rankings of constraints in the clitic system, as expected in the light of Optimality Theory. In dialects where the goal of using the best clitic ranks higher than that of avoiding duplication, the duplication will be tolerated. Constraint re-ranking thus is used to account for the existence of considerable cross-dialectal and cross-linguistic variation in the clitic system.

University of Geneva

NOTES

* Thanks to Kleanthes Grohmann and to Michal Starke for their comments on a first version of this introduction. Needless to say, all remaining inadequacies and errors are my own.

[1] Chomsky (1991) was written against the classical GB background. With its emphasis on economy, it is a precursor of the Minimalist literature.

[2] For a different view see Riemsdijk and Williams (1981).

[3] For the notion of adjunct theta role see Zubizarreta (1987) and Pollock (1989).

[4] These structures are approximate. I assume that the modal auxiliary *will* originates under

I (see Lightfoot 1979). Contrary to our representation (7a), it is argued, for instance (Rizzi 1990a, 1996), that the *wh*-feature originates on the I-node in root clauses. See also note 5.

[5] May (1985) and Rizzi (1990a, 1996) propose that *wh*-constituents are subject to the *wh*-criterion, a well formedness condition which requires that a *wh*-constituent be in a specifier head relation with a head carrying the *wh*-feature. Such a well formedness condition can be extended to negative constituents (Rizzi (1996), Haegeman (1995a)), focalized constituents, topicalized constituents. See Rizzi's contribution to this volume for discussion.

[6] For arguments that the subject *John* originates VP-internally, see section 3.3 and especially McCloskey's contribution to this volume.

[7] In section 4.1.1 we turn to the decomposition of the functional head I into two functional heads reflecting its feature composition: AGR and T.

[8] The following examples from French, for instance, suggest that infinitives of lexical verbs may optionally move past adverbs such as *souvent* ("often"). See also section 4.1.1.

(i) a. Souvent manger du chocolat, c'est mauvais.
often eat chocolate, it is bad

b. Manger souvent du chocolat, c'est mauvais

In the literature, there is a trend to try to reinterpret what appears to be optional movement in terms of obligatory movement. Thus, for instance, the alternation between (iia) and (iib) is not an optional movement. Rather in (iib) *this book* preposes because it has to check a topic feature (cf. Rizzi's contribution):

(ii) a. I like this book
b. This book, I like.

[9] Cf. Chomsky (1995: 269), for instance, who says: "In any case v must enter into a checking relation with the affixal feature [-v] ("takes verbal affix") of T". See also.his note 20.

[10] This idea was present also in the classical approach, where traces were often taken to have internal structure (cf. the so called "layered traces"). However, the copy theory of traces has been exploited maximally in the Minimalist framework. Again, as was the case for checking theory, the copy theory of traces is also compatible with a more traditional approach to syntax.

For the status of intermediate traces (i.e. "copies") with respect to Attract, the reader is referred to work by Fujita (1996).

[11] The following German sentence, from McDaniel, Chiu and Maxfield (1995: 711) is an example where a lower *wh*-phrase, *mit wem*, is bound by an overt scope marker, *was*:

(i) Was glaub-st du mit wem Daniel spricht?
what think you with whom Daniel talks

"With whom do you think that Daniel is talking?"

See also McDaniel (1989).

[12] In the literature a dichotomy is often proposed between configurational languages and non-configurational languages. The former are assigned hierarchically organized structures, the latter have "flat" structures. I will not discuss the syntax of so-called non-configurational languages. For some discussion of the configurationality issue I refer the reader to the literature (Hale 1973, 1980, 1983, 1985; Speas 1990: 138–145, the papers in Maràcz and Muysken 1989, Kiss 1987, Horrocks 1994 and Baker, this volume: 84–86).

[13] The same hierarchy will also determine the distribution of arguments in other projection such as DP, AP etc. For a discussion of DPs see, among others, Grimshaw (1991a), Baker (1988, this volume), Giorgi and Longobardi (1990), Cinque (1994).

[14] The proposal that a simple verb like *give* is decomposed into a number of component parts dates back to the generative semantics tradition (Shibatani 1976, see also Fodor 1970). For instance, it has been argued that *open* in (ia) is to be interpreted as "cause to become open".

(i) a. Calvin opened the door again.

Evidence for the decomposition comes from the interpretation of adverbs. In (ia), *again* may either be taken to modify Calvin's action ("causing") or the change in state of the door ("becoming open") (see Stechow 1995):

(i) b. Calvin opened the door, which he had done in the past
c. Calvin opened the door, which had been open before.

Similarly, various authors (Guéron 1995, Kayne 1993, Noonan 1993) propose that *have* be interpreted as *be* + preposition. Evidence for this type of analysis comes from pairs such as (ii):

(ii) a. There are many skyscrapers in New York
b. New York has many skyscrapers

Harley (1995) proposes that ditransitive verbs such as *give* in English, which appear both in the double object construction and with the DP + PP pattern, can be decomposed in two different ways, roughly as in (iii).

(iii) a. John gave the book to Mary
= John caused the book to be LOC Mary

b. John gave Mary the book
= John caused Mary to have the book

She proposes that the existence of (iiib) in a particular language depends on the language having the construction with possessive *have*. For more discussion see Harley's own work (1995).

For further discussion of the various approaches to the decomposition of V see also Hale and Keyser (1991, 1993), Larson (1988), Miyagawa (forthcoming), Pesetsky (1994).

15 For the proposal that the VP projection be decomposed in a number of VP shells. i.e. component parts each headed by a V head, the reader is referred to Larson (1988) and Hale and Keyser (1993) for discussion. See also note 14 above, and the discussion in section 4.1.2.

16 Pollock's contribution to this volume was written in 1992, but had remained unpublished. It is included in this volume because it addresses issues which are of relevance to current grammatical theory.

17 See also: Ernst (1984), Jackendoff (1972), McConnel-Ginet (1982).

18 In fact Rizzi's approach implies a position somewhat intermediate between a pure adjunction approach to adverbials and Cinque's approach in which adverbials are specifiers of projections. This position is motivated, among others, on the data in (i). (ia) and (ib) illustrate the well known *que/qui* alternation in French. It is generally assumed that the complementizer *qui* is required in order to govern the subject trace. In order to account for the contrast between French (ic) and (id), Rizzi proposes that while preposed adjuncts adjoin to such a projection, topicalized arguments move to the specifier of a Topic Projection:

(i) a. *Voici l'homme que je crois que t pourra nous aider
this is the man that I think that will be able to help us

b. Voici l'homme que je crois qui[AGR] t pourra nous aider
this is the man that I think that will be able to help us

c. Voici l'homme que je crois qui l'année prochaine t pourra
this is the man who next year will be able to
nous aider
help us

d.?*Voici l'homme que je crois qui, ton livre, pourra l'acheter
this is the man that I think that your book will be able to buy

I refer to Rizzi's own paper for detailed discussion of this issue.

Conceivably, one might follow Cinque's approach in arguing that adverbials are associated with specialized projections, while proposing that, rather than occupying the specifier of these projections, they are adjoined to them. This is not the place to pursue this issue. For an alternative analysis of the contrast between preposed adjunct and preposed argument in (ic/id) see also Browning (1996). See also note 27.

19 The analysis would also be compatible with a VO account.

20 For discussion of the WF clitics, see Haegeman (1993b, 1994a, 1997b), Grohmann (1996).

21 In later versions of Minimalism the AGR node and its projection is abandoned in favour of the notion of layered specifiers. See section 4.1.4.

22 In fact, Rizzi's contribution to this volume will suggest an approach to structure in which agreement projections can be interpreted as proxies, projections dependent on substantive functional projections. See notes 24 and 27 for some further comments.

23 Exactly the same question arises, of course, for the sequencing of adjectives in DPs (see Cinque 1994: 95–97)

24 The reader will observe that while Chomsky's recent proposals involve the elimination of Agreement projections, Rizzi's contribution to this volume, which postulates that any substantive functional projection may be associated with AGR-features and with a dominating AgrP, in fact would lead to an increase in Agreement projections. (See notes 18, 22, and 27.) However, if there seems to be a conflict between the two proposals, note that what they have in common is that projections of agreement are no longer conceived of as independently motivated projections.

25 We assume that focalized constituents must attain a specifier-head relation with a head carrying the feature Foc. In Italian this feature is base generated on Foc. For some speakers there is an adjacency requirement, suggesting that focalization implies V-movement, which brings Italian close to Hungarian as far as focalization is concerned (see Brody 1990, 1995b, Horvath 1985, Kiss 1987, Puskas 1992).

26 See also Rizzi's own contribution for additional references to other work in which an articulated structure of CP is proposed.

27 Rizzi also suggests that the CP domain may contain projections of agreement. As mentioned in notes 18 and 24 above, Rizzi's AGR-projections could be conceived of as proxies in the terminology of Nash and Rouveret (1996), since they are parasitic on substantive projections. Thus, for instance, Rizzi proposes that the head Top may be associated with AGR-features which can then be relevant for the licensing of subject traces. I refer to his paper for discussion. For a recent alternative analysis of the contrast between preposed adjuncts and preposed arguments see Browning (1996).

28 In Haegeman (1997b) I propose, following Koster (1978), that topicalization structures such as (ia) are not instances of strict V2, but rather involve a non overt operator in FinP:

(i) a. Jan, ken ik
Jan can I

b. $[_{ForceP}\ [_{TopP}$ Jan $[_{FinP}$ OP ken $[_{IP}$ ik]]]

29 This section is based on a presentation given by Jane Grimshaw at the Conference on Grammar and Knowledge, at Keio University, in March 1996. Obviously, my summary cannot do justice to the problem of expletive insertion, but hopefully it gives the reader an idea of how Optimality Theory would account for the problem.

30 The relevant constraint would be "Obligatory heads".

[31] In her paper (section 2.2.) Grimshaw formulates the faithfulness constraint in terms of two feature matching requirements between input and output:

(i)	FILL FEATURE:	Only features in the input can appear in the output
(ii)	PARSE FEATURE	All features in the input must appear in the output

REFERENCES

Abney, S. (1987) *The English Noun Phrase in its Sentential Aspects*. MIT diss.

Authier, M. (1992) 'Iterated CPs and embedded topicalization', *Linguistic Inquiry* **23**, 329–336.

Baker, M. (1985). 'The Mirror Principle and Morphosyntactic Explanation', *Linguistic Inquiry* **16**, 373–415.

Baker, M. (1988) *Incorporation: A Theory of Grammatical Function Changing*. Chicago University Press, Chicago.

Baker, M. (1996) 'On the structural position of themes and goals', in: J. Rooryck and L. Zaring (eds.) (1996), *Phrase Structure and The Lexicon. Studies in Natural Language and Linguistic Theory*. Kluwer Academic Publishers, Dordrecht, Boston and London, pp. 7–34.

Baker, C. L. (1991) 'The syntax of English *Not:* the limits of core Grammar', *Linguistic Inquiry* **22**, 387–429.

Barss, A. (1986a) *Chains and Anaphoric Dependence*. MIT diss.

Barss, A. (1988) 'Paths, connectivity and featureless empty categories', in: Cardinaletti, Cinque and Giusti (eds.), *Constituent Structure*. Foris, Dordrecht, pp. 9–34.

Belletti, A. (1990) *Generalized Verb Movement*. Rosenberg and Sellier, Turin.

Bennis, H. (1980) '*Er*-deletion in a modular grammar', in: S. Daalder and M. Gerritsen (eds.), *Linguistics in the Netherlands, 1980*. North-Holland, Amsterdam, pp. 58–68.

Bennis, H. (1986) *Gaps and Dummies*. Foris, Dordrecht.

Bernstein, J. (1991) 'DPs in French and Walloon: Evidence for parametric variation in nominal head movement', *Probus* **3**, 1–26.

Bernstein, J. (1993) *Topics in the Syntax of Nominal Structure across Romance*. Ph.D. diss CUNY.

Bianchi, V. (1995) *Consequences of Antisymmetry for the Structure of Headed Relative Clauses*. Ph.D. Diss. Scuola Normale Superiore, Pisa.

Bobaljik, J. (1995) *Morphosyntax: The Syntax of Verbal Inflection*. MIT diss.

Bobaljik, J. and D. Jonas (1996) 'Subject positions and the role of TP', *Linguistic Inquiry* **27**, 195–236.

Bonet, E. (1995) 'Feature structure of Romance clitics', *Natural Language and Linguistic Theory* **13**, 607–647.

Branigan, P. (1995) *Verb Second and A-bar Syntax of Subjects*. Ms. Memorial University of Newfoundland.

Brody, M. (1995a) *Lexico-Logical Form – A Radically Minimalist Theory*. MIT Monograph: Cambridge.

Brody, M. (1995b) 'Focus and checking theory', in: I. Kenesei (ed.), *Levels and Structures (Approaches to Hungarian, Vol 5)*. JATE, Szeged, pp. 30–43.

Broekhuis, H. and M. den Dikken (1993) *Chomsky's Minimalistische Programma*. Ms. University of Amsterdam.

Browning, M. (1996) 'CP recursion and *that*-t effects', *Linguistic Inquiry* **27**, 237–256.

Burton, S. and J. Grimshaw (1992) 'Coordination and VP-internal subjects', *Linguistic Inquiry* **23**, 305–313.

Cardinaletti, A. and M. Starke (1994) *The Typology of Structural Deficiency*. Ms. University of Geneva, University of Venice.

Chomsky, N. (1965) *Aspects of the Theory of Syntax.* MIT Press, Cambridge.
Chomsky, N. (1970) 'Remarks on nominalizations', in: R. Jacobs and P. Rosenbaum (eds.), *Readings in English Transformational Grammar.* Ginn & Co, Waltham, Mass., pp. 184–221.
Chomsky, N. (1986a) *Barriers.* MIT Press, Cambridge.
Chomsky, N. (1986b) *Knowledge of Language: Its Nature, Origin and Use.* Praeger, New York.
Chomsky, N. (1991) 'Some notes on the economy of derivation', in: R. Freidin (ed.), *Principles and Parameters in Comparative Grammar*, pp. 417–454. Reprinted in Chomsky (1995).
Chomsky, N. (1993) 'A minimalist program for linguistic theory', in: K. Hale and S. J. Keyser (eds.), *The View from Building 20.* MIT Press, Cambridge. pp. 1–52. Reprinted in Chomsky (1995).
Chomsky, N. (1995) *The Minimalist Program.* MIT Press, Cambridge.
Cinque, G. (1994) 'On the evidence for partial N-movement in the Romance DP', in: G. Cinque, J. Koster, J.-Y. Pollock, L. Rizzi and R. Zanuttini (eds.), (1995) *Paths Towards Universal Grammar. Studies in Honour of Richard Kayne.* Georgetown University Press, pp. 85–110.
Cinque, G. (1995) *Adverbs and the Universal Hierarchy of Functional Projections.* GLOW abstract.
Collins, C. (1994) *Merge and Greed.* Ms. Cornell University
Collins, C. and H. Thrainsson (1993) 'Object shift in double object constructions and the Theory of Case', in Phillips (ed.), *MIT Working Papers in Linguistics, 19. Papers on Case and Agreement II.* pp. 131–147.
Costa, J. (1996) 'Adverb positioning and V-movement in English: Some more evidence', *Studia Linguistica* **50**, 22–34.
Culicover, P. (1991). 'Topicalization, inversion and complementizers in English', in: D. Delfitto, M. Everaert, A. Evers and F. Stuurman (eds.), *OTS Working Papers. Going Romance and Beyond.* Department of Linguistics, University of Utrecht, pp. 1–45.
Culicover, P. (1993) 'Evidence against ECP accounts of the that-t effects', *Linguistic Inquiry* **24**, 557–561.
Doetjes, J. (1992) 'Rightward floating quantifiers float to the left', *The Linguistic Review* **9**, 313–332.
Ernst, T. (1984) *Towards an Integrated Theory of Adverb Positions in English.* Ph.D. Indiana.
Emonds, J. (1978) 'The verbal complex V′-V in French', *Linguistic Inquiry* **9**, 151–175.
Fodor, J. (1970) 'Three reasons for not deriving "kill" from "cause to die"', *Linguistic Inquiry* **1**, 429–438.
Fujita, K. (1996) *Generalized Attract and Economy of Derivation.* Ms.
Giorgi, A. and G. Longobardi (1990) *The Syntax of Noun Phrases: Configuration, Parameters and Empty Categories.* CUP, Cambridge.
Giorgi, A. and F. Pianesi (1995) 'Extraction from subjunctive clauses and clausal architecture', Paper presented in the research seminar, University of Geneva.
Giorgi, A. and F. Pianesi (1996) *Tense and Aspect: From Semantics to Morphosyntax.* Ms. University of Bergamo and IRST, Trento.
Grimshaw, J. and A. Mester (1988) 'Light verbs and theta-marking', *Linguistic Inquiry* **19**, 205–232.
Grimshaw, J. (1991a) *Argument Structure.* MIT Press
Grimshaw, J. (1991b) *Extended Projections.* Ms. Brandeis University.
Grimshaw, J. (forthcoming) 'Minimal projections, heads and optimality', *Linguistic Inquiry.*
Grohmann, K. (1996) *Some Remarks on the West Germanic Mittelfeld: Scrambling, Case and Pronominalization.* BA Honours diss. University of Bangor.
Guéron, J. (1995) 'On *have* and *be*', in: J. Beckman (ed.), *Proceedings of NELS 25. Amherst,* GLSA.

Haegeman, L. (1992) *Theory and Description in Generative Grammar: A Case Study of West Flemish*. CUP, Cambridge.
Haegeman, L. (1993a) 'Some speculations on argument shift, clitics and crossing in West Flemish', in: J. Bayer and W. Abraham (eds.), *Linguistische Berichte*, Special issue on Dialektsyntax, pp. 131–160.
Haegeman, L. (1993b) 'The morphology and distribution of object clitics in West Flemish', *Studia Linguistica* **47**, 57–79.
Haegeman, L. (1994a) 'The typology of syntactic positions: L-relatedness and the A/A'-distinction', *Groninger Arbeiten zur Germanistischen Linguistik* **37**, 115–157.
Haegeman, L. (1994b) *Introduction to Government and Binding Theory*. Blackwells, Oxford.
Haegeman, L. (1995a). *The Syntax of Negation*. CUP, Cambridge.
Haegeman, L. (1995b) *Root Null Subjects and Root Infinitives in Early Dutch*. Paper presented at the GALA conference and at the BU conference. Ms. University of Geneva.
Haegeman, L. (1996a) 'Root null subjects and root infinitives in Early Dutch', in: C. Koster and F. Wijnen (eds.), *Proceedings of the Groningen Assembly on Language Acquisition*, pp. 239–250.
Haegeman, L. (1996b) 'Object clitics in West Flemish', in: A. Halpern and A. Zwicky (eds.), *Second Position Clitics*, CSLI Publications, Stanford, pp. 135–136.
Haegeman, L. (ed.) (1997a) *The New Comparative Syntax*. Longman, London.
Haegeman, L. (1997b) 'Verb second, the split CP and null subjects, in Early Dutch Finite Clauses', *GenGenP* **4**(2), 133–175.
Hale, K. (1973) 'Person marking in Warlpiri', in: S. R. Anderson and P. Kiparsky (eds.), *Festschrift for Morris Halle*. Hold, Rinehart and Winston, New York, pp. 308–344.
Hale, K. (1980) *The Position of Warlpiri in a Typology of The Base*. Indiana University Linguistics Club.
Hale, K. (1983) 'Warlpiri and the grammar of non-configurational languages', *Natural Language and Linguistic Theory* **1**, 5–47.
Hale, K. (1985) *On Non-Configurational Structures*. Ms. MIT
Hale, K. and S. J. Keyser (1991) 'On the syntax of argument structure', *Lexicon Project Working Paper 34*. MIT Center for Cognitive Studies.
Hale, K. and S. J. Keyser (1993) 'On argument structure and the lexical expression of syntactic relations', in: K. Hale and S. J. Keyser (eds.), *The View from Building 20*. MIT Press, Cambridge.
Harley, H. (1995) *If You Have, You Can Give*. Ms. University of Lille: France.
Hendrick, R. (1991) 'The morphosyntax of aspect', *Lingua* **85**, 171–210.
Holmberg, A. (1986) *Word Order and Syntactic Features in The Scandinavian Languages and English*. Ph.D. diss, University of Stockholm.
Horrocks, G. (1994) 'Subjects and configurationality: Modern Greek Clause Structure', *Journal of Linguistics* **30**, 81–109.
Horvath, J. (1985) *Focus in The Theory of Grammar and the Syntax of Hungarian*. Foris, Dordrecht.
Huang, J. (1993) 'Reconstruction and the structure of VP: Some theoretical consequences', *Linguistic Inquiry* **24**, 69–102.
Huang, J. (1995) 'Logical form', in: Webelhuth (ed.), pp. 125–175.
Iatridou, S. (1990) 'About AGR(P)', *Linguistic Inquiry* **21**, 551–117.
Jackendoff, R. (1972) *Semantic Interpretation in Generative Grammar*. MIT Press, Cambridge.
Jackendoff, R. (1977) *X-bar Syntax*. MIT Press, Cambridge.
Johnson, Kyle (1991) 'Object positions', *Natural Language and Linguistic Theory* **9**, 577–636.
Jonas, D. and J. Bobaljik (1993) 'Specs for subjects: the role of TP in Icelandic', in: J. Bobaljik and C. Phillips (eds.), *Papers on Case and Agreement, I*. MIT working papers in linguistics, pp. 59–98.
Katz, J. J. and P. Postal (1964) *An Integrated Theory of Linguistic Descriptions*. MIT Press.

Kayne, R. (1984) *Connectedness and Binary Branching*. Foris, Dordrecht.
Kayne, R. (1989) 'Null subjects and clitic climbing', in: Jaeggli and Safir (eds.), *The Null Subject Parameter*. Kluwer, Dordrecht, pp. 239–261.
Kayne, R. (1991) 'Romance clitics, verb movement and PRO', *Linguistic Inquiry* **22**, 647–686.
Kayne, R. (1993) 'Towards a modular theory of auxiliary selection', *Studia Linguistica* **47**.
Kayne, R. (1994) *The Antisymmetry of Syntax*. MIT Press, Cambridge.
Kiss, K. (1987) *Configurationality*. Reidel: Dordrecht.
Kiss, K. (1996) 'Two subject positions in English', *The Linguistic Review* **13**, 119–142.
Klima, E. (1964) 'Negation in English', in: J. Fodor and J. Katz (eds.), *The Structure of Language*. Prentice Hall, New Jersey, pp. 246–232.
Koizumi, M. (1993) 'Object agreement and the split VP hypothesis', in: J. D. Bobaljik and C. Phillips (eds.), *Papers on Case and Agreement I*. MIT Working papers in Linguistics **18**, 99–148.
Koizumi, M. (1995) *Phrase Structure in Minimalist Syntax*. Ph.D. diss. MIT.
Koopman, H. and D. Sportiche (1991). 'The position of subjects', *Lingua* **85**, 211–258.
Koster, J. (1978) *Locality Principles in Syntax*. Kluwer, Dordrecht.
Koster, J. (1993). *Structure Preservingness and The End of Transformationalism*. Ms. Groningen.
Laka, I. (1990) *Negation in Syntax: On The Nature of Functional Categories and Projections*. Ph.D. thesis. MIT.
Larson, R. K. (1988) 'On the double object construction', *Linguistic Inquiry* **19**, 335–391.
Lasnik, H. (1980) 'Restricting the theory of transformations. A case study', in: N. Hornstein and D. Lightfoot (eds.), *Explanations in Linguistics. The Logical Problem of Language Acquisition*. Longman, London, pp. 152–173.
Lasnik, H. and M. Saito (1984) 'On the nature of proper government', *Linguistic Inquiry* **15**, 235–289.
Lasnik, H. and M. Saito (1992). *Move Alpha*. MIT Press, Cambridge.
Lasnik, H. (1994) *Verbal Morphology: Syntactic Structures Meets the Minimalist Program*. Ms. University of Connecticut.
Lightfoot, D. (1979) *Principles of Diachronic Syntax*. Cambridge University Press, Cambridge.
Marantz, A. (1984) *On The Nature of Grammatical Relations*. MIT Press, Cambridge.
Marécz, L. and P. Muysken (eds.) (1989) *Configurationality: The Typology of Asymmetries*. Foris, Dordrecht.
May, R. (1985) *Logical Form*. MIT Press, Cambridge.
McConnell-Ginet S. (1982) 'Adverbs and logical form', *Language* **58**, 144–184.
McDaniel, D. (1989) 'Partial and multiple *wh*-movement', *Natural Language and Linguistic Theory* **7**, 565–604.
McDaniel, D., B. Chiu and T. L. Maxfield (1995) 'Parameters for *wh*-movement types: Evidence from child English', *Natural Language and Linguistic Theory* **13**, 709–753.
Miyagawa, S. (Forthcoming) 'Against optional scrambling', *Linguistic Inquiry*.
Muller, G. and W. Sternefeld (1993) 'Improper movement and unambiguous binding', *Linguistic Inquiry* **24**, 461–507.
Nakajima, H. (1996) 'Complementizer selection', *The Linguistic Review* **13**, 143–164.
Nash, L. and A. Rouveret (1996) *Functional Heads and Proxies: An Asymmetric Set*. GLOW abstract 1996.
Noonan, M. (1993) 'Statives, Perfectives and Accusativity: The importance of being have', in J. Mead (ed.), *Proceedings of the West Coast Conference on Formal Linguistics* **11**, 354–370.
Ouhalla, J. (1990) 'Sentential negation, relativized minimality, and the aspectual status of auxiliaries,' *The Linguistic Review* **7**, 183–213.
Pesetsky, D. (1989) *Language Particular Processes and the Earliness Principle*. MIT ms.
Pesetsky, D. (1994) *Zero Syntax*. MIT Press, Cambridge.

Pollock, J. Y. (1989). 'Verb movement, UG and the structure of IP', *Linguistic Inquiry* **20**, 365–424.
Prince, A. and P. Smolensky (1993) *Optimality Theory: Constraint Interaction in Generative Grammar.* Ms. Rutgers University. To appear: MIT Press, Cambridge.
Puskas, G. (1992) 'The *wh*-criterion in Hungarian', *Rivista di Grammatica Generativa* **17**, 141–186.
Puskas, G. (1995) 'A split CP approach: Evidence from Hungarian', *GenGenP* **3**(2), 1–12.
Riemsdijk, H. van (1978) *A Case Study in Syntactic Markedness.* Foris, Dordrecht.
Riemsdijk, H. van and E. Williams (1981) 'NP structure', *The Linguistic Review* **1**, 171–217.
Ritter, E. (1991) 'Two functional categories in noun phrases: Evidence from Modern Hebrew', *Syntax and Semantics* **25**, 37–62.
Rivero, M.-L. (1994) 'Clause structure and V-movement in the languages of the Balkan', *Natural Language and Linguistic Theory* **12**, 63–120.
Rivero, M.-L. and A. Terzi (1995) 'Imperatives, V-movement and logical mood', *Journal of Linguistics* **31**, 301–332.
Rizzi, L. (1986) 'On chain formation', in: Borer (ed.), *Syntax and Semantics, 19: The Grammar of Pronominal Clitics.* Academic Press, New York.
Rizzi, L. (1990a). 'Speculation on verb second', in: Mascaro and Nespor (eds.), *Grammar in Progress*, pp. 375–386.
Rizzi, L. (1990b) *Relativized Minimality.* MIT Press, Cambridge.
Rizzi, L. (1996) 'Residual verb second and the *wh*-criterion', to appear in: A. Belleti and L. Rizzi (eds.), *Parameters and Functional Heads. Essays in Comparative Syntax.* Oxford University Press, Oxford and New York.
Roberts, I. (1996) *L'accord, l'anti accord et la théorie de vérification.* Paper presented at the Linguistics Research Seminar in Geneva.
Rooryck, J. and L. Zaring (1996) *Phrase Structure and The Lexicon. Studies in Natural Language and Linguistic Theory.* Kluwer Academic Publishers, Dordrecht, Boston and London.
Rouveret, A. (1991) 'Functional categories and agreement', *The Linguistic Review* **8**, 353–387.
Rudin, C. (1988) 'On Multiple questions and multiple *wh*-fronting', *Natural Language and Linguistic Theory* **6**, 445–501.
Shibatani, M. (1976) 'The grammar of causative constructions. A consectus', in: M. Shibatani (ed.), *Syntax and Semantics 6: The grammar of Causative Constructions.* Academic Press, New York.
Shlonsky, U. (1989) *The Hierarchical Representation of Subject Verb Agreement.* Ms.
Shlonsky, U. (1992) 'The representation of agreement in COMP', *GenGenP* **0**(0), 39–52.
Speas, M. J. (1990) *Phrase Structure in Natural Language.* Kluwer Academic Publishers, Dordrecht, Boston and London.
Sportiche, D. (1988) 'A theory of floating quantifiers and its corollaries for constituent structure', *Linguistic Inquiry* **19**, 425–449.
Sportiche, S. (1996) 'Clitic constructions', in: J. Rooryck and A. Zaring (eds.), *Phrase Structure and the Lexicon. Studies in Natural Language and Linguistic Theory.* Kluwer Academic Publishers, Dordrecht, Boston and London.
Stechow, A. von (1995) 'Lexical decomposition in syntax', in Egli et al. (eds.), *Lexical Knowledge in The Arganization of Language.* John Benjamins, Amsterdam and Philadelphia.
Stowell, T. (1981) *Origins of Phrase Structure.* MIT diss.
Szabolczi, A. (1989) 'Noun phrases and clauses: Is DP analogous to CP?', in: J. Payne (ed.), *The Structure of Noun Phrases.* Mouton.
Taraldsen, T. (1990) 'D-Projections and N-Projections in Norwegian', in: J. Mascaro and M. Nespor (eds.), *Grammar in Progress.* Foris, Dordrecht, pp. 419–431.
Travis, L. (1992) 'Inner aspect and the structure of VP', *NELS* **23**.

Ura, H. (1994) *Varieties of Raising and The Feature-Based Bare Phrase Structure Theory.* MIT dissertation.

Vikner, S. (1991) *Verb Movement and the Licensing of NP Positions in The Germanic Languages.* Doctoral Dissertation, University of Geneva.

Vikner, S. (1995) *Verb Movement and Expletive Subjects in The Germanic Languages.* Oxford University Press, New York, Oxford.

Webelhuth, G. (1995) *Government and Binding Theory and the Minimalist Program.* Blackwells, Oxford.

Zanuttini, R. (1991) *Syntactic Properties of Sentential Negation. A Comparative Study of Romance Languages.* Ph.D. Thesis, University of Pennsylvania.

Zanuttini, R. (1995) *Dialectal Variation as an Insight into The Structure of Grammar.* Ms.

Zanuttini, R. (1997) 'Negation and V-movement', in: Haegeman (ed.) (1997a), *The New Comparative Syntax.* Longman.

Zubizarreta, M.-L. (1987) *Levels of Representation in The Lexicon and in The Syntax.* Foris, Dordrecht.

Zwart, J. W. (1993) *Dutch Syntax.* Ph.D. diss University of Groningen.

Zwart, J. W. (1997) 'The Germanic SOV languages and the Universal Base Hypothesis', in: L. Haegeman (ed.) (1997a), *The New Comparative Syntax.* Longman.

MARK C. BAKER

THEMATIC ROLES AND SYNTACTIC STRUCTURE*

1. INTRODUCTION: THE LINKING PROBLEM

One central task for any theory of grammar is to solve the so-called "linking problem": the problem of discovering regularities in how the participants of an event are expressed in surface grammatical forms and explaining those regularities.

Suppose that one adopts a broadly Chomskyan perspective, in which there is a distinction between the language faculty and other cognitive faculties, including what Chomsky has recently called the "Conceptual-Intensional system". Then there must in principle be at least three stages in this association that need to be understood. First, there is the nonlinguistic stage of conceptualizing a particular event.[1] For example, while all of the participants in an event may be affected by the event in some way or another, human cognizers typically focus on one or the other of those changes as being particularly salient or relevant to their interests. This participant is taken to be the "theme" or "patient" of the event, perhaps in some kind of nonlinguistic conceptual representation, such as the one developed by Jackendoff (1983, 1990b). Second, this conceptual/thematic representation is associated with a linguistic representation in which the entity seen as the patient of the event is represented as (say) an NP that is the direct object of the verb that expresses what kind of an event it was. This is the interface between language and the conceptual system. Finally, there is the possibility of adjusting this representation internally to the language system, by way of movements, chain formations, Case assignment processes, or whatever other purely syntactic processes there may be. For example, the NP that represents the theme and starts out as the direct object of the verb may become the subject if there is no other subject in the linguistic representation, either because there was no agent in the conceptual representation (as with an unaccusative verb), or because it was suppressed (as with a passive verb).

Since there are at least these three stages between an event and a surface-linguistic description of it, there is room for a good deal of complexity in theory and analysis. Therefore, most syntactic theorists assume that at least one step in the association is relatively trivial. In part, this is a tactical move, an effort to cut down the number of analytic choices that a theory must make in order to develop an analysis of any particular phenomena. However, the need for restrictions also seems to be empirically motivated by the fact that there are in fact important linking regularities both within

Liliane Haegeman (ed.), Elements of Grammar, 73–137.

and across languages. How extensive these regularities are is a matter of debate, but to the extent that they exist, there must be a fair amount of rigidity in the system.

Outside of Chomsky's Principles and Parameters (P&P) framework, the most popular way to constrain the linking problem is at the third stage: to say that there is essentially no difference between the initial grammatical representation and the surface grammatical representation. This choice leads to the various "monostratal" theories of grammar, including Lexical Functional Grammar, the various Phrase Structure Grammars, Role and Reference Grammar, and others. Since the syntax proper is so tightly constrained, these approaches tend to take on a rather asyntactic flavor, with much of the explanatory burden being carried by the lexicon and/or the semantics rather than syntax. As such, they shade into functionalist approaches, which downplay the existence of syntax as something distinct from semantics, discourse, pragmatics, and diachrony.

The opposite choice has been predominant within the P&P approach. This approach allows nontrivial syntactic derivations internal to the language faculty, and instead attempts to constrain the interface between conceptual representations and syntactic representations in a particularly tight way. One widely-cited expression of this leading idea is the following, from Baker (1988a: 46):

(1) *The Uniformity of Theta Assignment Hypothesis* (UTAH)
Identical thematic relationships between items are represented by identical structural relationships between those items at the level of D-structure.

Part of Baker's motivation for introducing this principle was to put teeth into the generative theory of that time (the early 1980s). Generative theory then as now aspired to achieve explanatory adequacy by having a very tightly constrained view of what syntax could do. However, in practice the result of this approach was often not deeper analyses of interesting phenomena, but rather a banishing of those phenomena from the domain of syntax – typically into the realm of the lexicon. Within the terms of the theory, this seemed regrettable: if one is going to have a nontrivial syntax at all, then that syntax should be required to pull its own weight. The UTAH, then, was an attempt to identify a domain in which the answer to analytic questions must be a syntactic one.

This being said, the UTAH was clearly a working hypothesis, not a full-fledged principle. Baker (1985, 1988a) purposely left it vague and flexible in at least three important respects. First, it was presented without an explicit theory of thematic roles that could define when two NPs count as having the same thematic role. Thus, even holding the UTAH constant, a fine-grained thematic theory that distinguishes many thematic roles would have different implications for syntactic structure than a coarse-grained thematic theory that distinguishes only two or three "macroroles" (see Pesetsky (1995: ch. 2, 3)). Similarly, I did not present an explicit theory of syntactic positions that defined what was meant by "identical structural relationships." Strict identity of position sounds like a very strong condition, but one can replace the word "identical" in (1) with the word "equivalent" and it then becomes clear that one must define which syntactic positions count as equivalent (see Larson (1990: 600–602)).[2] Finally, no explicit rule was given to match thematic roles to structural positions beyond a few simple and relatively clear-cut cases. As a result of this vagueness, the UTAH has become something of an inkblot test, into which its various proponents (and opponents) can read what they wish. As a result, the UTAH exists in a variety of different versions, the advantages of which have not been systematically investigated.

With this background in mind, the current article has a threefold goal. First, it reviews some of the evidence that something like the UTAH is correct, both for English and for other, superficially very different languages. Second, it seeks to give more specific content to the UTAH, clarifying certain points left unresolved previously and discussing differences between alternative versions of the UTAH. In particular, I consider which thematic role distinctions the UTAH is sensitive to, whether an "absolute" or "relative" interpretation of the UTAH is appropriate, and whether linking is primarily sensitive to thematic role distinctions or aspectual distinctions. Finally, I discuss how the UTAH fits into Chomsky's (1993, 1994) Minimalist Program for linguistic research, an issue that has not received much explicit attention. I argue that inasmuch as the UTAH calls for a simple correspondence between a linguistic representation and a Conceptual-Intentional one, it fits well with the Minimalist tenet that there should be "optimal" interfaces between language and other cognitive systems. Indeed, once the UTAH is recast so as to fit into this somewhat different theoretical environment, it reduces to a matter of "virtual conceptual necessity."

2. EXTERNAL AND INTERNAL ARGUMENTS

Let us begin with the vague UTAH in (1) and see how one could evaluate its validity. To do this, it is helpful to break the linking problem down into two parts: first, there is the matter of deciding which of the participants in a given event is to be expressed as the subject of the sentence; second, there is the matter of deciding which of the remaining participants is to be expressed as the direct object (if any). Any remaining participants are then typically expressed as oblique NPs that appear with adpositions or Case markers that express their thematic role rather directly.[3] In this section, then, I begin by considering the matter of subject choice in two-place verbs. This is the least controversial aspect of linking theory:

there is wide agreement that agents rather than themes are chosen as subjects in most languages. However, there is still some disagreement as to whether this rule of thumb is valid for all clauses and all languages. Moreover, looking at this issue with some care will also give us a valuable model of how to proceed when we come to the much more controversial question of how internal arguments are linked.

2.1. *English*

Consider morphologically simple (i.e., nonpassive) verbs in English that describe simple two-participant events involving an agent and a patient (or theme). Virtually every such verb expresses the agent of the event as its subject as shown in (2a); there are no verbs that follow the pattern in (2b), where the theme of the event is expressed as the subject.

(2) a. John hit/built/found/pushed/bought/cleaned/broke/described the table.
b.*The table plit/puilt/vound/fushed/pought/bleaned/proke/tescribed John.

Furthermore, a structural relationship holds between the patient-object and the verb in English that does not hold of the subject and the verb. In simple sentences, the object but not the subject must be (right-)adjacent to the verb. Moreover, the object and the verb constitute a unit to the exclusion of the subject for processes like VP-deletion, VP-pronominalization, and VP-fronting.

(3) a. John [$_{VP}$ hit the table] and Bill did [$_{VP}$ (so)] too.
John said he would hit the table, and [$_{VP}$ hit the table] I guess he did –.
b.*[$_{XP}$ John hit] the table and [$_{XP}$ (so)] did the chair.
*John said he would hit the table, [$_{XP}$ John hit] I guess – did it.

Finally, the agent-subject "has prominence" over the patient-object in a variety of ways involving anaphora, coreference, and quantification. Thus, pronouns and anaphors contained in the object can be referentially dependent on the subject, but not vice versa.

(4) a. John$_i$ washed himself$_i$
John$_i$ washed pictures of himself$_i$
Every man$_i$ washed his$_i$ car.
*He$_i$ washed John's$_i$ car. (out by Condition C)
b.*Heself$_i$ washed John$_i$. (out by Condition A)
*Friends of himself$_i$ washed John$_i$. (out by Condition A)
*His$_i$ friends washed every man$_i$. (out by Weak Crossover)
John's$_i$ friends washed him$_i$.

Facts like these from English and similar languages motivate the twin claims of P&P linking theory built into the UTAH: (i) that agents are always (underlying) subjects, and (ii) "subject" is a structural notion – it is a position in phrase structure that is outside the VP (see (3)) and hence "higher than" (c-commanding) the position of the patient/object (see (4)).

The one area of controversy regarding subject selection in English concerns predicates describing psychological states. In this particular semantic domain, there do seem to be (nearly-)synonymous verbs that have opposite linking patterns, as shown in (5).

(5) a. John likes long novels.
John fears dogs
John worries about the ozone layer

b. Long novels please John.
Dogs frighten John.
The ozone layer worries John.

The general Chomskian framework allows for three possible interpretations of this fact: (i) the data in (5) shows that the UTAH is false, and different predicates require different linking patterns as an idiosyncratic lexical property; (ii) the (a) and (b) sentences have similar underlying configurations, but at least one of them (probably (b)) involves a nontrivial syntactic derivation; (iii) the thematic roles in the (b) sentences are actually different from those in the (a) sentences.

In fact, no one has advocated option (i) in the recent literature, as far as I know. It seems wrong to infer from the fact that a restricted class of predicates appear to be idiosyncratic that all predicates are idiosyncratic. On this view it would be hard to explain the observation that most verbs work predictably, apart from this semantically coherent domain.

Option (ii) is advocated in Belletti and Rizzi's well-known article (1988), as well as much work in the Relational Grammar tradition. Indeed, there are some important things to be said in its favor: Belletti and Rizzi show that sentences like (5b) have a number of syntactic peculiarities in Italian (and also English) that can be explained if they are derived by moving the "theme" argument into the subject position syntactically. Moreover, their analysis is compatible with a somewhat weakened version of the UTAH, as they point out. I return to a brief discussion of Belletti and Rizzi's theory in section 4.2.1 below.

However, the correct option seems to be option (iii): denying that *long novels* and *John* have the same θ-roles in both (5a) and (5b). This nonsyntactic approach to the problem of psych verbs is defended by Pesetsky (1987, 1995) and Dowty (1991: 579–580, 586–587). Dowty in particular sketches an explanation for why only this class of verbs seems to be so variable in its linking properties: neither participant in the event is an obvious choice for an agent or a patient. John is an animate and sentient being, which would tend to make him like an agent; on the other hand, the long novels cause an emotional reaction in John, making them like an agent. This ambivalence as to what is really the agent underlies the alternative linkings. Moreover, Dowty points out (citing William Croft) that the (b) examples can have an inchoative change-of-state reading, but the (a) examples cannot. Pesetsky (1987, 1995) points out another subtle difference between the two, that comes out particularly clearly in examples like (6).

(6) a. John is angry at the article.
    b. The article angered John.

Whereas (6a) clearly asserts that the article is the target of John's anger, (6b) does not: here the article is the cause of John's (change of) emotion but not necessarily the target of it. According to (6b), the article could in fact be a brilliant exposé of government corruption that makes John angry at the authorities, even though he likes the article very much. Putting together these pieces, we find that John is seen as undergoing a change of state and hence is a patient in (6b), while the article is seen as a cause in (6b) and is in this respect like an agent. Indeed, Pesetsky points out that verbs like *please*, *frighten*, and *anger* are morphologically causative forms in many languages, including Japanese. If this is the correct thematic analysis, the linking patterns are expected: the cause of the event maps onto the subject position in (2), (5b), and (6b), and the patient/theme of the event uniformly maps onto the object position. Thus, these sentences are consistent with the UTAH even without any syntactic derivation. The apparent problem for the UTAH with psych verbs is largely attributable to the fact that the thematic roles have been misdiagnosed.

While this approach works well for the *frighten*-class psych verbs, something more must be said about subject selection in *fear*-class psych verbs. While it is true that there is no reason to say that *John* refers to a patient/theme or *long novels* refers to a causer in these sentences, at first glance there is not much reason to say the opposite either. The standard view has been to say that *John* is an experiencer, where that is a thematic role distinct from agent/causer (Belletti and Rizzi 1988, Grimshaw 1990). There would then be a linking rule stating that experiencers can be expressed as subjects when there is no causer/agent. This idea could be made compatible with a weakened version of the UTAH under certain conditions (see section 4.2.1), but it would mean that syntactic structure is coarser-grained than thematic structure. Because of this, I tentatively adopt a slightly different approach, inspired by Dowty (1991). Dowty suggests that because John is sentient (an experiencer), he is in that respect like a canonical agent; indeed he is more like a canonical agent than any other participant in the event.[4] For this reason, *John* is the subject of a predicate like *fear* by the usual agent-to-subject rule, but the term "agent" is now understood as a fuzzy, prototype notion rather than a categorical one. (In fact, "agent" is not a very felicitous term; a more accurate one would be Levin and Rappaport-Hovav's (1995) "internal cause", which includes agency as a special case.) Indeed, it is a property of John's psychological make-up – though not necessarily his will – that causes him to respond in a particular way to dogs; indeed, we might be tempted to consider him a coward. If these remarks are correct, then *fear* and *frighten* are both agent-theme verbs, once these notions are understood in a broad enough way. The apparent alternation comes from the fact that there are two ways these notions can sensibly apply to describe a certain eventuality, although what exactly is expressed is subtly different depending on the choice. Finally, it is a consequence of this approach that *fear* should behave like an ordinary transitive verb in most respects, and this seems to be true (Belletti and Rizzi 1988, Grimshaw 1990).[5]

2.2. *Ergativity*

Next, let us consider to what degree the principles of subject choice seen in English are universal. Suppose, contrary to the UTAH, that the association between thematic roles and syntactic positions were arbitrary and variable, either because agents are not necessarily subjects, or because subjects are not necessarily "external" positions. Then one would expect that some natural languages would make use of exactly the opposite association, in which the agent is associated with the VP-internal object position, and the patient/theme is associated with the structural subject position, thereby having prominence over the agent. Marantz (1984) and Levin (1983) claim that this logical possibility is attested in so-called "deep ergative" languages, including Dyirbal (Dixon 1972) and a dialect of Inuktitut. Similarly, Dowty (1991: 581–582) suggests that the basic rules for associating semantic arguments with grammatical functions are reversed in some ergative languages,[6] pointing out that if so, "this provides an extremely strong reason why we should not try to collapse the notion of P[roto]-Agent with grammatical subject and P[roto]-Patient with grammatical object . . . , or adopt a theory which necessarily correlates them in this unique way." Thus, whether or not there are any truly deep ergative languages is a crucial issue for the UTAH.

It is helpful to begin by imagining what a deep ergative language would look like. If everything else were held constant, the allowable syntactic dependencies in such a language should be exactly the opposite of those in a language like English. For example, the agent and the verb should form a unit to the exclusion of the patient for purposes of word order, VP deletion, VP fronting, and the like. Furthermore, the agent in such a language should be able to be referentially dependent on the patient, but not vice versa – the reverse of the typical English pattern in (4). Finally, in nonfinite clauses headed by a morphologically simple transitive verb, it should be the patient of the verb that is phonologically null and understood as controlled by an argument of the matrix verb, not the agent as in English. The question is whether there are any such languages.

It is clear that some languages have an "ergative" Case system, where the patient of a transitive verb appears in the same Case and/or triggers the same kind of agreement as the sole argument of an intransitive verb (called absolutive Case), while agents of transitive verbs have a distinct Case and/or agreement (called ergative Case). Assuming that the sole argument of an intransitive verb is necessarily its surface subject, this Case/agreement pattern invites the hypothesis that the patient of the transitive verb is also a subject. This hypothesis is reinforced by the facts that "absolutive Case" is often morphologically unmarked and absolutive agreement is generally the farthest from the verb stem, as shown in (7) and (8); in these respects it is like nominative in most Indo-European languages (Campana 1992, Bittner and Hale 1996).

(7) a. Payi yara-Ø paninyu. DYIRBAL
there man(abs) come
"The man is coming."

b. Palan jukumpil-Ø pangkul yara-ngku palkan.
there woman(abs) there(erg) man-erg hit
"The man is hitting the woman."

(8) a. (Uanga) qungujup-p-u-nga. GREENLANDIC
me(abs) smile-ind-intrans-1s
"I smiled."

b. Anguti-p (uanga) urnip-p-a-a-nga.
man-erg me(abs) approach-ind-trans-3s-1s
"The man approached me."

However, it is well-known since Anderson (1976) that in the large majority of ergative languages, the evidence that the patient of a transitive verb might be its subject is restricted to these superficial morphological facts: control patterns and referential dependencies still pattern in very much the same way as they do in English.

Only in a small handful of languages such as Dyirbal and Greenlandic does the reversal seem to go deeper. For example, Levin (1983) points out that the unmarked word order in Dyirbal has the patient NP before the agent NP, which in turn is before the verb, as shown in (7b). If the patient NP is the syntactic subject, and the agent is the object, this is a straightforward instance of SOV word order – perhaps the most common kind across languages. If, on the other hand, the grammatical functions are interpreted the other way, (7b) would be an instance of basic OSV word order; this is a rare or unattested type. (Note, however, that the unmarked word order is the opposite in Greenlandic, as shown in (8b).) Second, Dyirbal has control(-like) purposive constructions in which there is a special subordinate verb form and a missing argument that is understood as co-referential with an argument of the first clause. Significantly, if the verb in the embedded clause is transitive, the missing NP must be the absolutive theme, not the ergative agent. Thus, Dyirbal can express the equivalent of (9b), but not (9a), whereas the facts in English are the opposite (see Dixon (1972) for the actual Dyirbal examples):

(9) a. The man$_i$ climbed up in order $-_i$ to see the bird.
OK English, *Dyirbal

b. The man$_i$ climbed up in order for the bird to see $-_i$.
OK Dyirbal, *English

Similar patterns pervade the grammar of Dyirbal: for example, only absolutive arguments can be "shared" in coordination-like clause chaining constructions, and only absolutive arguments can be understood as the head of a relative construction. This last constraint is found in other ergative languages as well, including Greenlandic (Bittner and Hale 1996). Finally, Bittner and Hale (1996: 565–568) show that in Greenlandic VP operators such as negation take scope over the ergative Case agent but not the absolutive Case patient; again, this is the exact reverse of the pattern found in English.

However, while some grammatical properties seem to reverse in these languages, others do not, as pointed out in Dixon (1979, 1994: sec 5.3). Perhaps the most significant is that the patient phrase can contain an anaphor that is referentially dependent on the agent phrase as in (10), but the agent phrase cannot contain an anaphor that is dependent on the patient (see Bittner (1994: ch. 4), Bittner and Hale (1996) for Greenlandic).

(10) Juuna-p qimmi-ni nirisip-p-a-i. GREENLANDIC
Juuna-erg dog-pl/3srefl feed-ind-trans-3s/3p

"Juuna$_i$ fed his$_i$ own dogs."

Dixon also mentions that in control phenomena involving complement-taking verbs with meanings like "can", "try", "want" and "begin", it is always the agent argument of the embedded verb that is controlled, not the theme argument. Again, this holds in Greenlandic, with the minor complication that the matrix verb generally shows up attached to the embedded verb at PF (Bittner 1994).

Moreover, Baker (1988a: 427–428) extends Dixon's list of invariant properties by pointing out that compounding and incorporation phenomena work the same way in both accusative languages and ergative ones (see also

Mithun (1984)). It is well-known that the theme argument of the verb root can appear in English deverbal compounds, but the agent argument cannot: one can have *dish-washing*, but not **husband-washing (of dishes)*. Presumably this is another reflex of the fact that themes are objects and appear structurally close to the verb in English, but agents are not (Roeper and Siegel 1978, Sproat 1985, Di Sciullo and Williams 1987, Grimshaw 1990). If so, one would expect this pattern to reverse in a deep ergative language. However, it does not; incorporation is common in Inuit, but the incorporated argument is always understood as the patient, never as the agent:

(11)	Juuna	alla-mik	ilinniartitsisu-siur-p-u-q.
	Juuna	other-instr	teacher-seek-ind-intrans-3sS

(Bittner 1994: 67)

"Juuna is looking for another teacher." NOT: "Another teacher is looking for Juuna."

See McKay (1975) for similar patterns in Rembarrnga, a morphologically ergative language related to Dyirbal.

On balance, then, we see that some syntactic phenomena reverse in ergative languages, but others do not. Dixon (1994: 233) criticizes Marantz (1984) and similar approaches to "deep ergativity" for their inability to capture this fact in a natural way. Instead, he claims that "the universal category of subject . . . plays a role in the grammar of every language." However, he distinguishes a second type of grammatical function, called a "pivot", which does differ significantly across languages: Dyirbal treats patients of transitive verbs together with the sole argument of intransitive verbs as pivots, whereas English treats intransitive subjects and the agents of transitive verbs as pivots. Pivots are distinct from subjects and belong to another layer of grammatical description, one concerned with the combining of clauses and coreference across clauses (see also Foley and Van Valin (1984)).

In fact, Dixon's insights translate rather directly into what has become the standard approach to ergativity in the P&P framework.[7] For reasons that are quite independent of ergativity, it has become standard to assume that the agent argument of a transitive verb in English is a subject in (at least) two ways: it is base-generated as the specifier of a VP projection where it is directly theta-marked; it then raises to the specifier of an Inflectional head to receive (or check) its nominative Case. Thus, the agent is both the subject of VP and the subject of IP. However, these two distinct senses of subject may diverge, resulting in a "deep ergative" language. Thus, suppose that the basic projection of arguments is the same in languages like Dyirbal or Inuit, but the verbs in these languages cannot license accusative Case on the underlying object. Then, it is the patient argument of the verb, not the agent, that must move to the specifier position of IP to receive/check nominative Case and trigger agreement on I (Bok-Bennema 1991, Campana 1992, Murasugi 1992, Bittner 1994, Bittner and Hale 1996).[8] The agent NP, on the other hand, remains in the specifier of VP and receives ergative Case by some other means (researchers vary on the exact mechanisms here). Simple versions of the two basic clause structures are compared in (12), where I leave open the possibility that there are additional functional categories and/or a more complex VP-internal structure.

(12) a. ENGLISH

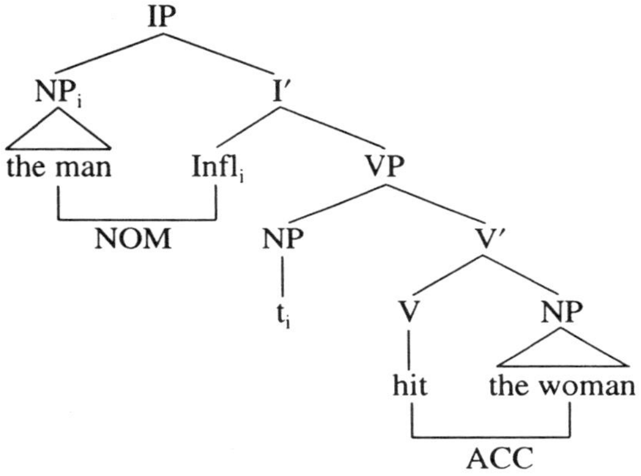

b. DYIRBAL/INUIT

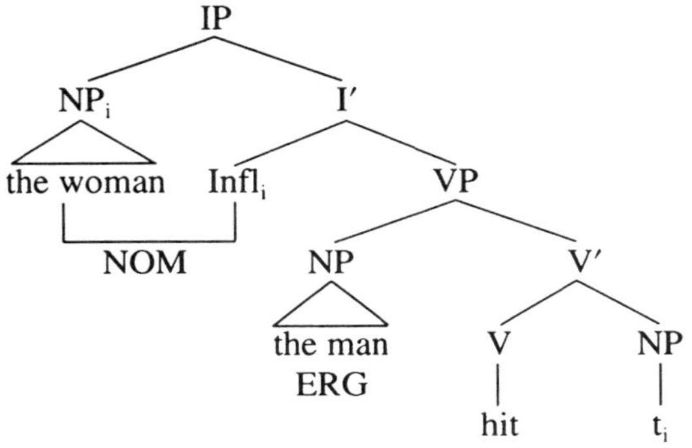

Several of the peculiar-looking facts of ergative languages now follow immediately. For example, the movement of the patient past the subject shows up overtly in Dyirbal, in the form of unmarked Patient-Agent-Verb order. Similarly, it follows from these representations that agents are outside the scope of VP operators in English, whereas patients are in Inuit. Finally, the purposive inflection in Dyirbal can be analyzed as a special form of

Infl that licenses "null Case", and hence its specifier must be a null element, perhaps PRO. This null element is then anaphorically dependent on the matrix clause. Plausibly relative clauses in Dyirbal and Inuit, and topic-chaining constructions in Dyirbal can be analyzed in a more or less similar way (see Bittner and Hale (1996) for discussion of participial relatives).[9]

However, the structural reversal is not total on this account. In particular, the inner structure of VP is the same in both ergative and accusative languages on this approach. Thus, for linguistic phenomena that have the basic VP as their domain, deep ergative languages and accusative languages are expected to work very much the same. For example, the agent c-commands the patient before movement; hence the patient can be anaphorically dependent on the agent but not vice versa (see (10)). (The movement of the patient past the agent does not change this relationship if that is an A-bar movement; see note 9.) Similarly, we explain why noun incorporation patterns are the same in ergative languages as in others: noun incorporation is an alternative to movement to receive Case (Baker 1988a), and it takes place entirely internal to the VP. Within this VP, the patient is in a close enough relationship to incorporate into the verb, but the agent is not. Finally, it makes sense that control of complement clauses also acts in the same way, since this kind of control is known to be sensitive to the thematic roles defined over VP-internal configurations (see Bittner (1994) for some discussion).

In conclusion, this P&P approach can be seen as a formal development of Dixon's intuition that "subjects" are the same in all languages, while "pivots" vary. The P&P equivalent of Dixon's "subject" is "subject of VP", whereas the equivalent of "pivot" is "subject of IP." Crucially, this theory not only accounts for the fact that "subject properties" seem mixed in ergative languages, but it gives insight into exactly what mixtures one finds. Roughly, ergative languages differ from accusative languages in their A-bar processes (quantifier scope, relative clauses, topics) and Case-related morphology, but are similar in terms of A-processes (anaphora, incorporation, complement control). If this approach is correct, it shows that ergative languages are not counter-examples to the UTAH after all. Rather, the basic projection of arguments is identical in the two kinds of languages, and it is subsequent movement processes that differ.

2.3. *A Note on Nonconfigurationality*

Similar issues for the UTAH are raised by the existence of so-called nonconfigurational languages, although for reasons of space I cannot do more than indicate where this large and fascinating topic fits into the issues at hand. Whereas some of the familiar subject-object asymmetries appear to be reversed in deep ergative languages, in nonconfigurational languages such as Warlpiri (Australian) and Mohawk (Amerindian) they appear to be neutralized. Thus, patterns like (3) in English cannot be replicated in these languages and it is difficult, perhaps impossible, to find direct evidence for a constituent that contains the verb and the object-theme but not the agent-subject. Rather, the NP arguments of a simple clause can generally appear in any order (subject to pragmatic constraints), and any NP can be omitted in discourse (see Hale (1983), Simpson (1991), Baker (1991, 1995b) and references cited there). Moreover, the nonconfigurationality of these languages is not a purely superficial (PF) phenomenon, because, in at least some languages, the asymmetries in referential dependency such as (4) are partially neutralized as well (see Simpson (1991: 177–182) for Warlpiri; Baker (1995b, ch. 2) for Mohawk). Thus, such languages again call into question the idea that subjects have consistent phrase structure positions distinct from objects.

However, just as the syntactic reversal of agent and theme is not complete in ergative languages, so the neutralization of differences between agent and theme is not complete in nonconfigurational languages. Typically, some subject-agent/object-theme asymmetries can still be found. Strikingly, the kinds of relationships that carry over unchanged to nonconfigurational languages are approximately the same as those that remain unchanged in ergative languages: agents bind anaphoric themes but not vice versa (Hale 1983), agents of nonfinite clauses are controlled (Hale 1983, Simpson and Bresnan 1983), themes and not agents are incorporated into the verb (Baker 1988a, Baker 1995b: ch.7), and so on.

These strong similarities suggest that nonconfigurationality should be approached in much the same way as ergativity. Thus, most P&P-based work on such languages assumes that the basic arguments of the verb project into the same initial positions within VP in nonconfigurational languages as in configurational (and ergative) ones. This allows the nontrivial similarities between the languages to be captured by the normal principles of Binding theory, control, and head movement.[10] Surface nonconfigurationality then arises because phonetically realized NPs in these languages do not necessarily – indeed in some cases *must* not – surface in their normal argument positions at S-structure/Spell-Out. This gives rise to the free word order of nonconfigurational languages, as well as some of their other seeming-peculiarities (Jelinek 1984). How this works out in detail probably varies a good deal from language to language. In mildly nonconfigurational head-final languages like Japanese, Hindi, and German, free word order seems to be the result of the leftward movement of NPs ("scrambling") (Saito 1985, 1992, Mahajan 1990, Webelhuth 1992). In Mohawk and other polysynthetic languages, free word order is the result of a kind of base-generated dislocation that is syntactically very similar to the Clitic Left Dislocation found in Romance languages (Baker 1995b: ch. 3). In Warlpiri and other Australian languages, free word order is probably a result of the fact that nominal secondary predication is very free (Speas 1990:

165–172). Thus, there is not and probably should not be a fully unified theory of nonconfigurationality.[11] However, if this general approach is on the right track, then the UTAH does apply to these languages, just as much as it does to ergative and accusative-configurational ones, with observable empirical consequences.

3. DIRECT VS. OBLIQUE INTERNAL ARGUMENTS

Having confirmed that the choice of the subject argument is determined by something like the UTAH, let us turn to direct objects. Here we will be particularly concerned with three-argument verbs, and assume that one argument (the causer of the event) has already been chosen as the subject. The crucial question, then, is which of the other two arguments is expressed as the direct object of the verb, and whether the facts in this domain are compatible with the UTAH. The remaining argument of the verb is then typically expressed as the object of a semantically appropriate adposition or semantic Case marker.

In the matter of subject selection, there is little controversy that the causer-to-subject rule applies to most verbs in many languages; the only questions are whether this rule should be extended to all predicates and all languages. However, in the domain of object selection there is much less agreement as to what the basic rule is. Part of the reason for this lack of consensus is the fact that a substantial percentage of the three-argument verbs in English alternate as to which argument shows up as the direct object. Two particularly important and well-studied alternations are the dative alternation in (13) and the locative alternation in (14).

(13) a. I gave the candy to the children.
b. I gave the children the candy.

(14) a. I loaded the hay onto the truck.
b. I loaded the truck with the hay.

Even those three argument verbs that do not alternate give little guidance as to which linking pattern should be taken as basic. Thus, *donate* appears only in the (13a) frame, *owe* appears only in the (13b) frame, *pour* only in the (14a) frame, and *fill* only in the (14b) frame. Moreover, superficial comparison with other languages simply adds to the confusion. For example, French has only the equivalent of (13a), while Sesotho has only the equivalent of (13b).[12] Given this situation, practically every imaginable view has adherents: some claim that (13b) is derived from (13a) (Larson (1988, 1990); also Baker (1988a), and much work in classical Relational Grammar); some believe that (13a) is derived from (13b) (Dryer 1987, Kiparsky 1987, Aoun and Li 1989); many believe that both (13a) and (13b) are base generated (Oerhle 1975, Jackendoff 1990a, Speas 1990, Dowty 1991, Collins and Thráinsson 1996). Moreover, Dryer (1987) argues that different languages make different choices in this respect: in some languages the equivalent of (13a) is basic, and in others the equivalent of (13b) is basic – a parameter of variation that he explicitly compares to the issue of ergativity. Indeed, the only thing that this entire range of researchers agrees on is that whatever account one has, it should be essentially the same for both the dative alternation and the locative alternation.[13]

Before considering the data, it is useful to survey once again the logical possibilities. Two approaches to these alternations are compatible with the UTAH. The first is to say that one or the other of the linking patterns in (13) and (14) is basic, and the other is derived from it by some kind of movement. The second is to claim that the thematic roles in the (b) sentences are subtly different from those in the (a) sentences, and this justifies constructing two different syntactic structures (see Speas (1990), among others). The solution that would refute the UTAH is one which said that the (a) and (b) sentences do not differ in thematic roles but are both base-generated as a result of different subcategorization frames associated with the verbs in a partially idiosyncratic manner; this was the standard view in the late 1970s and early 1980s (see also Jackendoff (1990a)). In fact, I will argue that the dative alternation and the locative alternation are quite different in these respects, thereby disagreeing with the standard view. The dative alternation is a result of movement, with sentences like (13b) being derived from underlying structures like (13a) by a combination of P-incorporation and NP-movement. In contrast, the locative alternation results from two different conceptions of the event in question: one in which the hay is seen as primarily affected, and one in which the truck is seen as primarily affected (Rappaport and Levin 1985, Pinker 1989, Dowty 1991). Once the viewpoint is picked, the affected argument (i.e., the theme) is consistently generated as the direct object. If this is correct, then the minimal contrast between the two alternations illustrates elegantly the two options allowed by the UTAH, while giving reason to think that it is correct to rule out the intermediate option. Moreover, I will survey some evidence that suggests that the same is true in other, superficially different languages, thereby supporting the idea that the basic object linking rule is universal, contra Dryer (1987).

3.1. *Objects in English*

Let us begin with English, considering first the semantic side of the issue. The crucial question is whether (13a) and (13b) mean the same thing or not, and similarly for (14a) and (14b). The answer to this question depends in part on how fussy one wants to be. On a crude level, the (a) and (b) sentences can often be used to describe the same events; in this sense they are synonymous. On a very detailed level, the (a) and (b) sentences differ at least with respect to matters of topic and focus, so that they do not always sound equally good in every discourse environment. However, the crucial matter with respect to the UTAH is whether the two sentences differ specifically in terms of their thematic roles, where this is a proper subpart of a complete semantic and pragmatic characterization. In fact, I believe that at this medium-grain level of description (14a) and (14b) differ, but (13a) and (13b) do not.

Take first the locative alternation. There is a clear intuition that the object argument in both versions of (14) is "totally affected": in (14a), all the hay is loaded into the truck, but the truck need not be completely loaded, whereas in (14b) the truck is completely loaded, but there may be unloaded hay left over. In both cases, then, the NP expressed as the direct object is seen as undergoing a change of state (Pinker 1989) and thus "measures" the progress of the event named by the verb (Tenny 1994). Dowty (1991: 591–592) brings out this intuition by invoking the fact that verbs which are normally accomplishments aspectually often become activities when their theme argument is a bare plural or mass noun. Now, in locative alternation constructions, the argument that is expressed as the direct object determines the aspectual quality of the whole clause; whether the oblique argument is determined or not has no effect, as shown by the *in an hour/for an hour test* in (15) (see Dowty 1979).

(15) a. John sprayed this wall with paint in an hour / (#)for an hour. (OK, but atelic)
b. John sprayed paint onto this wall #in an hour / for an hour.
c. John sprayed subway cars with this can of paint #in an hour / for an hour.
d. John sprayed this (whole) can of paint onto subway cars in an hour / #for an hour

Dowty concludes from this that *paint* is the "incremental theme" in (15b,d), while *this wall* and *subway cars* are incremental themes in (15a,c). In other words, the thematic roles associated with the participants in the event differ in the two versions of the locative alternation.

If one tries to replicate these judgments for the dative alternation, however, results are not nearly so clear. If one asks whether the candy or the children are totally affected in (13), it seems that (for this particular example anyway) both must be. Moreover, when one constructs examples parallel to those in (15) by putting bare plural NPs in the various argument slots, one gets the following pattern, according to my judgments:

(16) a. I have read stories to the children for an hour / #in an hour
b. I have read the children stories for an hour / #in an hour
c. I have read the story to children ?for an hour / in an hour
d. I have read children the story ?for an hour / in an hour

Here dative shift seems to have no effect on the judgments: whether *stories* is a bare plural or is determined decides whether the event is an activity or an accomplishment, and the status of *children* is irrelevant in both syntactic frames. Thus, by parity of reasoning, *stories* is the incremental theme in both versions of the dative alternation. Therefore we fail to find evidence that the two differ in their thematic roles.

In fact, the literature that argues for a base-generation account of the dative alternation does not claim that the two members of the alternation differ in delimitedness per se. Instead, researchers typically try to bring out the intuition that the "recipient" is affected by the action in (13b) in a somewhat different way. Essentially, the idea is that the transfer of possession involved in these kinds of verbs must succeed in the double object frame, whereas it need not in the NP-PP frame. Thus, (17b) suggests that the children actually learned some amount of French more strongly than (17a). Similarly (18b) suggests that the ball actually reached Bill, whereas (18a) does not, and (19b) is weird because the dead lover cannot perceive the song.[14]

(17) a. I taught French to the children.
b. I taught the children French.

(18) a. I threw the ball to Bill.
b. I threw Bill the ball.

(19) a. She sang a song for her dead lover.
b.#She sang her dead lover a song.

Thus, the (b) sentences suggest that the recipients undergo a kind of change of state in that they come to possess something (knowledge of French, the ball, an experience of a song). While I agree that there is something to this judgment, I think it must be stated at the level of "suggests," rather than "asserts" or "implies". Thus, the sentences in (20) may be stylistically awkward, but they do not feel to me like contradictions and I can imagine finding them in texts.[15]

(20) a. I taught the children French, but they didn't learn it at all.
b. I threw John the ball, but it didn't reach him because of the strong wind.
c. Mary sang her lover a song, but he didn't hear it because he had just died.

It is a priori very attractive to have a unified analysis of dative shift and the locative alternation, so it is tempting press the subtle differences in (17)–(19) into service as evidence for such an analysis. However, the evidence is weak at best, and the contrast between (15) and (16) clearly points the other way.

In addition, there are many syntactic tests that confirm that the dative alternation has a different status than the locative alternation. I will briefly survey a variety of these. Their common property is that they distinguish the shifted benefactive/goal argument of a dative verb from the theme argument of a dative verb and the direct object of either version of the locative alternation. My claim then is that these tests show that the theme of a dative verb, and the objects of both versions of the locative alternation are underlying direct objects, but benefactive/goal arguments are not.[16] However, space limitations permit me to give only very brief discussions of the theoretical underpinnings of the tests.

The first test involves adjectival secondary predication. Secondary predicates obey a c-command condition, such that they must both c-command and be c-commanded by their subjects (Williams 1980: n. 1). As a result, depictive and resultative APs can be predicated of the direct object, but not the object of a PP, even when this would be pragmatically plausible:

(21) a. I put *the food* on the table *hot*.
b.*I put the ice-cream into *the oven hot*.

Now locative alternation verbs work just as one would expect on the basis of their superficial syntax: an AP can be predicated of the direct object but not of the object of the PP, regardless of which expresses the location and which the material (Williams 1980: 204).[17]

(22) a. John loaded *the hay* onto the wagon *green*.
b.*John loaded the hay onto *the wagon full*.
c.*John loaded the wagon with *hay green*.
d. John loaded *the wagon full* with hay.

With dative verbs, however, Williams observes a further restriction: an AP cannot be predicated of the goal even when it is not expressed as the object of *to*.

(23) a. I gave *the meat* to Mary *raw*.
b.*I gave the meat to *Mary hungry*.
c. I gave Mary *the meat raw*.
d.*I gave *Mary* the meat *hungry*.

Indeed, (23d) is the only situation in which an AP cannot be predicated of a bare NP that is inside VP. Williams introduces a special stipulation to cover this case, saying that "If X is in the VP, then X is predicated of the theme of V." However, this is ad hoc; moreover, it violates the conjecture of Rappaport and Levin (1988), Belletti and Rizzi (1988), and Grimshaw (1990) that thematic roles are relevant only to the construction of initial syntactic structure and cannot be referred to directly by syntactic principles.

A more interesting generalization that can be gleaned from (23) is that the predication possibilities in the dative-shifted sentence are identical to those in the NP-PP sentence. This makes sense if the dative shifted construction is derived from the NP-PP construction. Specifically, suppose that a secondary predicate must be a dependent of (the inner) VP, as seems to be true observationally. As such, it will be in a mutual c-command relationship with a normal direct object. Next, suppose that we derive the dative shift as in Larson (1988), with the minor difference that what Larson calls "dative-case absorption" is treated as an instance of Preposition Incorporation in the sense of Baker (1988a). When the preposition is incorporated, it no longer can license Case on its object; therefore the goal must move to a position outside the inner VP to receive/check structural accusative Case. (For concreteness, I assume this position is the specifier of Aspect Phrase, following Travis (1991).) As a result of this movement, the goal comes to be before the theme and asymmetrically c-commands it, as shown in (24).

(24)

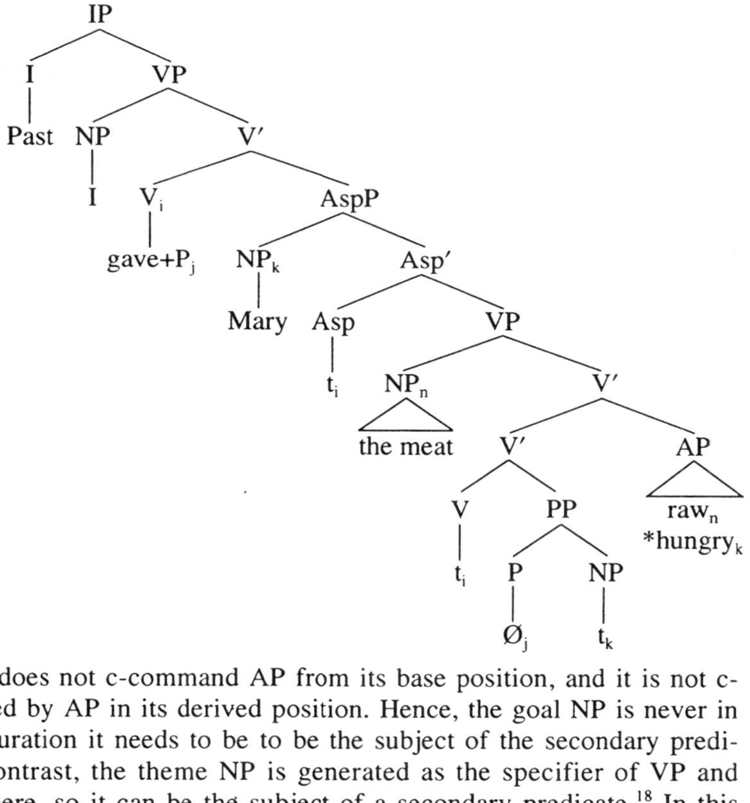

Now NP_k does not c-command AP from its base position, and it is not c-commanded by AP in its derived position. Hence, the goal NP is never in the configuration it needs to be to be the subject of the secondary predicate. In contrast, the theme NP is generated as the specifier of VP and remains there, so it can be the subject of a secondary predicate.[18] In this way, we eliminate Williams' stipulation, and motivate a derivational approach to the dative shift. Moreover, the fact that *the wagon* in (22d)

can be the subject of an AP predicate shows that it is in fact an underlying object, base-generated in Spec, VP (contra Larson (1990) and Aoun and Li (1993)).

Other differences between the dative alternation and the locative alternation appear in the domain of *wh*-movement. It is a well-known but somewhat mysterious fact that it is rather bad to extract the first object of a double object construction in English and some other languages (see Stowell (1981), Baker (1988a) and references cited there).

(25) Which woman do you think I should ?give/*buy t perfume?

Naturally the theme-direct object in the NP-PP structure can be easily extracted:

(26) Which perfume do you think I should give t to/buy t for Mary?

More interestingly, it is also perfectly grammatical to extract the direct object from either version of a locative alternation:

(27) a. Which boxes do you think I should load t onto the truck?
b. Which truck do you think I should load t with hay?

The same asymmetry shows up in rightward movements, such as heavy NP shift. As is well-known, most direct objects can extrapose to the right over some other constituent when they are long and/or focused. However, this movement is sharply impossible for the goal object of a double object construction (Stowell 1981, Kayne 1984: ch. 9, Larson 1988).

(28) a.*I gave t candy every child that came to the door.
b. I gave t to Johnny every piece of candy I could find.
c. I loaded t with hay three carts and one wheelbarrow.
d. I loaded t onto the cart a stack of books that had been sent to the library.

Again, the goal NP of the double object construction has unique syntactic behavior.

It is not clear what accounts for the deviance of (25) and (28a). One possibility that is compatible with the current framework is mentioned in Kayne (1984: 202, n. 19). Suppose that when the goal NP moves to the derived object position in a structure like (24), it pied pipes the null preposition along with it, for some reason. Then extracting the NP from this moved PP violates the Subject Condition (also known as the Left Branch Condition, or the Condition on Extraction Domains): one is moving a proper subpart of the structural subject of a functional category. In contrast, simple object extraction takes the whole subject (which is allowed); perhaps it even originates in the VP-internal theta-position where it is lexically governed. Alternatively, Baker (1988a) simply stipulates that it is impossible to extract the complement of a null preposition.[19] Whatever the correct analysis, these facts clearly show that there is something syntactically special about the goal in a double object construction.

Further evidence comes from derived nominals. Kayne (1984: ch. 7) discusses at length the fact that while the NP-PP frame can easily appear in a nominalization, the NP-NP frame cannot. Kayne was primarily concerned with Romance-based derived nominals formed by affixes such as *-ment*, *-ion*, and *-age*, but he mentions in a footnote (pp. 161–162, n. 31) that the same facts hold for native Germanic nominals derived by *-ing*, at least for some speakers. Thus, Fraser (1970: 92, 98) gives as bad the following, and I agree.[20]

(29) a.* Jim's giving of Mary (of) the book
b.* the renting of the men (of) the house
c.* his teaching of John (of) mathematics

Similar nominalizations based on the NP-PP frame of the verb are grammatical:

(30) a. Jim's giving of a book to Mary
b. the renting of the house to the men
c. his teaching of mathematics to John

Kayne does not discuss the locative alternation directly, perhaps because the locative alternation verbs, being mostly monosyllabic verbs of Germanic origin, do not have derived nominalizations (see Pesetsky (1995: 147)). However, *-ing* nominals are possible with these verbs, and I find nominalizations corresponding to either argument frame quite acceptable:[21]

(31) a. the loading of the truck with hay
b. Mary's spraying of the wall with paint

(32) a. the loading of the hay onto the truck
b. Mary's spraying of paint onto the wall

In particular, the contrast between (31) and (29) is quite clear.

Several accounts of these nominalization facts are possible. For example, one could follow Chomsky (1986) and relate them to more general facts about Case assignment in nominalizations. Chomsky points out that *of*-insertion cannot apply to Case-mark the embedded subject in the nominalization of an Exceptional Case Marking verb:

(33) a. I believe [John to be the winner] (Chomsky 1986: 189)
b.* the belief of John to be the winner (Chomsky 1986: 191)

Chomsky concludes from this that the preposition *of* is really a realization of genitive Case assigned by the noun. Moreover, genitive Case is a type of inherent Case, which (unlike accusative Case) can only be assigned by a head to an NP if the head θ-marks the NP. Since *belief* does not assign a θ-role to *John* in (33b), the genitive Case expressed by *of* is impossible in this situation. This theory can be extended to explain why the examples in (29) are bad. As before, we assume that the goal is θ-marked by a (null) preposition even in the dative shifted construction. As such, it is not θ-marked by the derived noun; therefore, it cannot receive genitive Case from that noun. Neither can it get Case from the null preposition, so the structure is ungrammatical. In the locative alternation, however, each bare NP is a theme argument, directly θ-marked by the head; therefore either one can appear as an *of*-phrase in a nominal.

A fourth difference between the dative alternation and the locative alternation is found in synthetic compounds. In compounds headed by a locative alternation verb, either the material or the location can appear as the nonhead, as long as other factors are controlled for:[22]

(34) a. hay-loading, glassware-packing
b. truck-loading, box-packing

However, the goal argument of a dative shift verb can never be in a synthetic compound:

(35) a. secret-telling, book-reading
b. *spy-telling, *child-reading

This asymmetry can be explained in terms of the observation that there is no room for a preposition in a simple synthetic compound. Thus, it follows that if a given nominal is θ-marked by a preposition, it will not be able to appear in a compound either. This can be seen apart from dative shift in the ungrammaticality of examples like **Relative-depending is unwise* (compare *Depending on relatives is unwise*). The (35b) examples are ruled out for the same reason, given that goals always receive their θ-role from a (possibly null) preposition. In contrast, (34) shows once again that either argument of a locative verb can be directly θ-marked by the verb.[23]

Further evidence that locative alternations are syntactically different from dative alternations comes from quantifier scope interactions. In an NP-PP frame either the theme or the goal can take wide scope if both are quantified expressions. However, in the double object frame, the first NP must have wide scope with respect to the second. Thus, (36a) is ambiguous but (36b) is not; it can only mean that there is a single student who must do all the work (Aoun and Li 1989, 1993, Larson 1990, Hornstein 1995).

(36) a. The teacher assigned one problem to every student. (Larson 1990: 604)
b. The teacher assigned one student every problem.

However, no such scope-freezing effect is found in the locative alternation. Both versions of the locative alternation are scopally ambiguous; in particular, a wide scope reading of the oblique argument in (37b) is possible, at least for some English speakers.[24]

(37) a. I loaded one crate of books onto every library cart.
b. I loaded one library cart with every crate of books.

Again, the dative double object construction stands out as being syntactically unique.

Unfortunately, there is no satisfactory analysis available for the scope-freezing effect in double object constructions.[25] One possibility worth exploring would be to relate it to the fact that the first object in a double object construction cannot be *wh*-moved or heavy NP-shifted. Perhaps this object also cannot undergo the LF movement rule of Quantifier Raising, for the same reason. This would partly explain why the scope possibilities are more limited. However, there are many problems to be overcome, and at best this will reduce the scope-freezing effect to another ill-understood phenomenon. Nevertheless, we can be optimistic that, whatever the final analysis is, it will support the idea that only the dative double object construction has an underlying structure that does not match its surface configuration.

A final difference between the dative alternation and the locative alternation involves how they interact with the phenomenon of unaccusativity. Many verbs in English can be used either transitively or intransitively according to the pattern in (38).

(38) a. They dropped a rope (down).
b. The rope dropped (down).

A few of these verbs also take part in the dative shift alternation when they are transitive:

(39) a. They dropped the rope (down) to John.
b. They dropped John (down) the rope.

When the agent argument is omitted from the NP-PP argument structure, the theme-object can assume the subject position to derive an acceptable sentence:

(40) The rope dropped (down) to John.

However, Baker (1992c, 1995a) points out that when the agent is omitted from the NP-NP frame, no grammatical sentence can result. In particular, the goal-object cannot move to the subject position to license its Case and satisfy the Extended Projection Principle (this particular example is from Wasow (1977: 332); see also Evereart (1990)):

(41) *John dropped t (down) the rope.

This sentences is only acceptable on the irrelevant reading in which the subject is understood as the agent of the verb; it cannot be understood as a moved goal or benefactive. More generally, there seem to be no non-agentive change-of-possession verbs that undergo the alternation in (42); thus, Levin (1993: 47) observes that "The dative alternation does not have an intransitive counterpart."[26]

(42) a. THING GO to PERSON.
b. PERSON GO THING.

However, there are many unaccusative locative alternation verbs, such as *swarm*:

(43) a. The bees swarmed in the garden
b. The garden swarmed with bees

(See Levin (1993: 53–55) for an extensive list and brief discussion.) These examples are parallel to those with *load*, except there is no agent, and as a result the totally affected theme shows up in the subject position. Thus, the theme of a dative verb and either argument of a locative verb can become the subject of an unaccusative structure, but the goal of a dative verb cannot.

Baker (1992c, 1995a) claims that this pattern of facts can be explained if one assumes with Larson (1988) that the goal always starts lower than the theme in verbs of change of location or possession. When an agent is present and dative shift occurs, the goal becomes higher than the theme by moving out of the lower VP into the derived object position (Spec, AspP), as shown in (24). However, when there is no agent, the inner VP contains all the arguments of the verb, and hence counts as a Complete Functional Complex in the sense of Chomsky (1986). Movement of the goal over the theme and out of such a VP thus violates condition A of Chomsky's Binding theory: the trace of the movement fails to be bound within the smallest Complete Functional Complex that contains a subject distinct from that trace. However, no such problem arises in locative alternation examples, because the location is higher than the material not as a result of movement, but rather as a result of being viewed as the theme of the event. When this happens, the location argument projects directly into the specifier of VP position, and there is no intervening NP to prevent it from moving to the subject position.

Let us summarize what we have learned about complement alternations in English. Lexical semantic judgments indicate that the two members of a locative alternation differ more than the two members of a dative alternation. In particular, which participant counts as totally affected and delimits the action changes in locative alternations, but not in dative alternations. Given this, it is reasonable to say that the locative alternation results from different choices as to what is considered the theme of the event, but this is less plausible for the dative alternation. Next, when we turn to syntactic behavior, it turns out that the goal object of a double object construction has many peculiar properties that distinguish it from other superficial objects, including location objects. Most of these are restrictions: the goal object cannot be the subject of a secondary predicate, cannot undergo *wh*-movement or heavy NP shift, cannot be assigned genitive in a derived nominal, cannot be the nonhead of a synthetic compound, must take wide-scope with respect to the second NP, and cannot become the subject of an unaccusative verb. These restrictions can, to a substantial extent, be understood if one says that the goal NP originates within a PP even in double object constructions; it then moves past the direct object to a distinct "derived object" position. If all this is correct, then there is an important correlation between lexical semantics and syntax: where there are few semantic differences, there are syntactic oddities pointing to a nontrivial derivation (the dative alternation); where there are significant semantic differences, there is no sign of such a derivation (the locative alternation). This pattern of facts supports the UTAH. Furthermore, we make the strong prediction that all other complement alternations in English should fall into one of these two classes. This remains to be tested in full, but seems consistent with what is known so far.[27]

This section has also given evidence that helps us to refine the statement of the UTAH. In particular, there is good evidence that the double object construction is derived from an underlying structure that is isomorphic to that of the NP-to-NP frame, rather than vice versa. If this is correct, then we can conclude that for English three-place verbs with a theme and a goal, the theme is consistently expressed as an NP in the Specifier of VP, while the goal is inside a PP that is the complement of V.

3.2. *Do Languages Vary in the Projection of Objects?*

The next question, then, is whether this projection rule is universal, or whether it varies parametrically. Prima face evidence that it might vary comes from the fact that many languages have only the double object construction. Mohawk (Iroquoian) and Sesotho (Bantu) are two languages of this kind:

(44) a. O'neróhkwa' y-a-hiy-atʌnyéht-ʌ-' ne
box trans-fact-1sS/MsO-send-ben-punc NE

Shawátis.
John

"I sent John a box."

b.*O'nerohkwa' y-a-k-atʌ'yeht-e'
box trans-fact-1sS/NsO-send-punc

Shawatís-hne.
Shawatis-loc

"I sent a box to John."

(45) a. Ntate o-f-a bana lijo. (Machobane 1989:113)
father SP-give-fv children food
"My father gives the children some food."

b.*Ntate o-f-a lijo ho bana.
father SP-give-fv food to children
"My father gives some food to the children."

In such languages, one could still say that the (a) examples are derived from a source similar to the (b) examples, but only at the cost of saying that "dative shift" (however expressed) is obligatory. This looks like an unwarranted degree of abstractness, making it desirable to consider alternatives in which the (a) examples are generated directly. In fact, Dryer (1987) develops a set of arguments along these lines within a modified Relational Grammar framework. He draws an explicit parallel between the apparent crosslinguistic variability of object choice in sentences like these and the variability in subject choice that results in ergative languages. Languages in which the goal of a ditransitive verb and the theme of a monotransitive verb seem to map into a single grammatical function Dryer calls "primary object languages"; they contrast with "direct object languages" in which themes are consistently the underlying object whether or not a goal is present.

The natural translation of Dryer's ideas into the current P&P framework is to assume that in primary object languages the goal projects directly into the specifier of VP and the theme projects as the complement of V if and only if there is a goal.[28] Indeed, Larson (1988: 351, n. 18) seems open to the possibility that there may be such languages, citing Johns' (1984) work on Inuktitut as a possible case in point. However, I will argue that there are in fact no "deep primary object languages" in this sense. Rather, a close look shows that the same projection rule that works in English is at work in both primary object languages and direct object languages. My strategy for building this argument is simply to show that the "goal objects" of triadic verbs in Mohawk and Sesotho show the same peculiarities of behavior that goal objects do in English. Such facts then provide evidence that the basic principles of constructing the underlying syntactic representation are also the same across the three languages.

3.2.1. *Primary Object Languages*

Consider first the semantic issue of delimitedness. Which NP of a triadic verb counts as the measurer of the event referred to by the verb in Mohawk and Sesotho: the theme as in English, or the goal? If it were the latter, this would be evidence that what corresponds to the goal in English actually has theme/direct object properties of a certain kind. However, in Mohawk there is clear evidence that points the other way. The standard *in an hour/for an hour* test does not work well in this language (cf. Baker (1995b: 290)), but Mohawk has an adverbial particle *eso* "many" that may modify the event argument of the VP it attaches to. If the modified verb has an "incremental theme" that measures out the event, many events will correspond to many tokens of the kind referred to by that theme argument. Thus, one can recognize the theme of the verb in Mohawk by attaching *eso* to the VP and seeing which NP (if any) is understood as there being many of. These dynamics can be seen with the simple transitive verb in (46).

(46) Eso wa-ha-tshʌri-' ne onhúhsa'.
a.lot fact-MsS-find-punc NE egg
"He found a lot of eggs."

Literally, this means that there were many events of him finding an egg; thus the Mohawk user easily infers that there were many eggs found, since egg-finding events are naturally individuated by the eggs found. However, even if the subject agreement prefix were changed to plural, this sentence would not be interpreted as "a lot of people found the egg," since VPs are delimited by their themes, not their agents (Tenny 1994). Now consider the use of *eso* with a dative verb:

(47) Eso wa'-khe-tsikét-a-nut-e' ne rati-ksa'-okú'a.
a.lot fact-1sS/3pO-candy-feed-punc NE MpS-child-pl
"I gave a lot of candy to the children."
NOT: "I gave candy to a lot of children."

Here *eso* clearly implies that much candy was given, not that many children were given candy. Thus, "candy" is the incremental theme, even when a goal NP is present, and in spite of the fact that the goal is the "primary object" for purposes of things like agreement. See Aissen (1987) for similar facts in Tzotzil (Mayan), another language with "obligatory dative shift".

I do not have direct evidence of themehood and delimitedness in Sesotho. However, Machobane (personal communication) reports that the semantic restrictions alleged to hold of the English double object construction (see examples (17)–(19)) are undetectable in their Sesotho translations. Thus, there is no evidence of this kind for a difference in θ-roles.

Next, let us turn to the morphosyntactic properties of goal-objects in Mohawk and Sesotho. The first type of evidence comes from compounding and noun incorporation. In Mohawk, the sole object of many monotransitive verbs can incorporate into the verb to form a kind of compound verb (Postal 1979, Baker 1988a, Baker 1995b). One can then ask which object of a dative ditransitive verb is incorporable. The answer is clearly that the theme-object can be incorporated, but the goal object cannot, as illustrated in (48).

(48) a. Se-'wáhr-a-nut ne érhar.
2sS/MsO-meat-Ø-feed NE dog
"Feed the (male) dog some meat!"

b.*O-'wáhr-u se-náhskw-a-nut.
NsO-meat-nsf 2sS/(ZsO)-pet-Ø-feed
"Feed the pet some meat!"

Note that even in (48a) the goal object triggers object agreement, showing it to be the "primary object" in Dryer's sense. Thus, noun incorporation is sensitive to the direct-indirect object distinction, even though Mohawk seems to be a primary object language in several other respects. Exactly the same pattern of facts is found in Southern Tiwa, Nahuatl, Mayali, Chukchee, and indeed all languages that are known to have syntactic noun incorporation. Baker (1988a, 1995b) analyzes these facts as showing that the goal NP is the complement of a null P, as in English. This P prevents the goal from incorporating into the verb by the Head Movement Constraint. However, these patterns also show a clear similarity to those involving synthetic compounds in English (see (35)).[29]

Bantu languages do not have true noun incorporation, but some have a kind of synthetic compounding. I have no information about this in Sesotho, but Sproat (1985) discusses compounds in the related language Chichewa. A simple example is (49), where the theme of a monotransitive verb is the nonhead in the compound.

(49) m-pala-matabwa (Sproat 1985: 225)
Cl-scrape-wood
"wood-scraper" (i.e. "carpenter")

However, goal objects cannot exist in such a compound:

(50) *m-patsa-ana ma-siwiti (Sproat 1985: 228)
Cl-hand-child cl-sweets
"a child-hander of sweets"

This can be interpreted as evidence that the goal is not a direct object argument of the verb in Chichewa any more than it is in English or Mohawk.[30]

Another peculiarity that goal objects in Chichewa share with their English counterparts is the deviance of extracting goal objects by *wh*-movement (Baker 1988a). In a simple transitive clause, the sole object of the verb can be fronted by clefting. When a recipient-benefactive is added to the structure (along with an applied affix), it becomes the primary object of the verb in the sense that it is adjacent to the verb, it may be replaced by a clitic pronoun, and it becomes the subject if the verb is passivized. However, the goal object cannot naturally be clefted:

(51) a. Uwu ndi-wo mtsuko u-mene ndi-ku-ganiza kuti
this be-agr waterpot cl-which 1sS-pres-think that

Mavuto a-na-umb-ir-a mfumu.
Mavuto SP-past-mold-appl-fv chief

"This is the waterpot which I think that Mavuto molded the chief."

b.*Iyi ndi-yo mfumu i-mene ndi-ku-ganiza kuti Mavuto
this be-agr chief cl-which 1sS-pres-think that Mavuto

a-na-umb-ir-a mtsuko.
SP-past-mold-appl-fv waterpot

"This is the chief who I think that Mavuto molded a waterpot."

This pattern of facts in Chichewa is virtually identical to the pattern in English, even though "dative shift" is optional only in the latter. Again, this suggests that *mfumu* "chief" in (51) is a derived object, but not a base-generated one. The only way one can extract the goal in Chichewa is by including an object clitic that acts as a kind of resumptive pronoun for the benefactive argument. (Similar object clitics always appear in Sesotho and Mohawk, so the restriction on extracting the goal object is not detectable in those languages.)

The last and perhaps the most illuminating comparison between the primary object languages and English is in the domain of unaccusative verbs. Recall that a goal phrase cannot become the surface subject of an unaccusative verb in English, as shown in (41). This was accounted for by assuming that the goal is always generated lower than the theme in English. In transitives, the goal can move past the theme into a VP-external position, but this is impossible with unaccusatives because when there is no agent role to assign the VP becomes a Complete Functional Complex that contains a subject (the theme) distinct from the benefactive/goal. Baker (1992c, 1995a) also points out that passive clauses pattern more or less like transitive clauses, rather than like unaccusatives, as shown by the relative acceptability of (52).

(52) (?)John was dropped t a rope.

This is expected if the passive clause actually contains a syntactically represented but covert agent argument (Baker, Johnson and Roberts 1989). Now if goal NPs were generated higher than themes in primary object languages, the minimal contrast between (41) and (52) should disappear. This prediction is not borne out. Thus, in Sesotho the benefactive/goal can perfectly well become the subject of a passive:

(53) 'Me o-pheh-ets-o-e (t) nama
mother 3sS-cook-appl-pass meat

"My mother has been cooked the meat."

However, the benefactive cannot become the subject of an unaccusative verb.

(54) *Nkhono li-hol-el-a (t) lintja.
grandma agr-grow-appl dogs
"The dogs are growing for my grandma."

Benefactives can appear with unaccusative verbs in Sesotho, but only if the theme argument of the verb is its surface subject and, in addition, the benefactive is expressed by a pronominal clitic. (This is to avoid the problem that unaccusative verbs cannot assign structural Case.) Similarly, a benefactive argument can be added rather freely to most transitive verbs in Mohawk, as in (55) (the benefactive is pro-dropped thanks to the presence of object agreement).

(55) Wa'-ha-ake-nohare-'s-e' ne atya'tawi.
fact-MsS-1sO-wash-ben-punc NE shirt
"He washed the shirt for me; he washed me the shirt."

Benefactive arguments can also be added to unaccusative verbs, but with some restrictions. In particular, the benefactive must trigger object agreement, rather than subject agreement, showing that it has remained inside VP and is still c-commanded by the theme argument. (56) illustrates this for the verb *ate-nohare* "come clean", an unaccusative verb derived from *nohare* "wash".

(56) Wa'-wak(*k)-ate-nohare-'s-e' ne atya'tawi.
fact-1sO(*1sS)-srfl-wash-ben-punc NE shirt
"The shirt came clean for/on me."

Mohawk does not have a passive construction to compare this with, but it does have a reflexive "voice" that has the same general structure (see Baker (1995b: sec. 5.1)). Significantly, in the reflexive form of *nohare*, the benefactive argument may (and must) trigger subject agreement, not object agreement.

(57) Wa'-k(*wak)-atate-nohare-'s-e' ne atya'tawi.
fact-1sS(1sO)-refl-wash-ben-punc NE shirt
"I washed the shirt for myself."
(lit. "I was self-washed t the shirt.")

Thus, benefactive arguments can escape the VP only if an agent is present in Mohawk, although this is seen by agreement patterns rather than by visible NP movement given the nonconfigurational nature of the language. These Sesotho and Mohawk facts are readily explicable if the theme is projected higher than the goal, but not if it is the other way around.

Moreover, the same pattern seems to hold in other Bantu languages, as well as in polysynthetic languages, such as Mayali and Nahuatl.

In conclusion, we have found no evidence to suggest that the projection rules for themes and goals are any different in Mohawk, Sesotho, or similar "primary object languages" than they are in English. On the contrary, the syntactic patterns are remarkably consistent across this range of languages. Therefore, the analyses of the peculiarities of dative objects in terms of a process of dative shift should generalize to these languages as well.

3.3.2. *A Note on Direct Object Languages*

There is, however, another way to interpret the similarities between English, Mohawk, and the Bantu languages: one could say that English too is a primary object language. In fact, Dryer (1987) himself argues for this view, claiming that sentences like (13b) are basic, sentences like (13a) being derived from them by an "antidative" rule. If this is correct, then there might still be important differences in how languages project their arguments, but those differences will not show up by comparing English with Mohawk or Sesotho. Instead, we need to compare these languages to true "direct object languages", which have no dative shift at all.

In fact, it is not so clear that there are any such languages. Many languages do not show any Case-frame alternation with triadic verbs, the goal argument invariably showing up in dative Case or its equivalent. Japanese is a well-studied language of this type. However, even though there is no Case marking alternation, there is a word order alternation in Japanese: the theme object can appear before or after the goal argument, as shown in (58).

(58) a. John-ga Mary-ni/*o hon-o age-ta.
John-nom Mary-dat/acc book-acc give-past
"John gave a book to Mary."

b. John-ga hon-o Mary-ni age-ta.
John-nom book-acc Mary-dat give-past
"John gave Mary a book."

This word order variation is normally attributed to an optional process of scrambling, which is pervasive in Japanese. However, recent literature has shown that this particular instance of scrambling has peculiar properties that make it more like A-movement than other kinds of scrambling. In particular, the goal asymmetrically c-commands the theme in (58a), while the theme asymmetrically c-commands the goal in (58b) for purposes of anaphora and bound pronouns (Saito (1992); see also Mahajan (1990) for

Hindi). This reversal of prominence is exactly comparable to what one finds in the English dative alternation (Barss and Lasnik 1986, Larson 1988); thus, it is reasonable to think of the alternation in (58) as a kind of dative shift.

In fact, there is a good deal of evidence that these Japanese sentences have very much the same properties as their English counterparts. For example, Japanese allows a certain kind of floated quantifier that must be in a mutual c-command relationship with its subject (Miyagawa 1989), like secondary predicates in English. It turns out that (for most speakers) such quantifiers can be predicated of the theme-object but not of the goal in both sentences in (58) (compare English (23) and Mohawk (47)). Second, Japanese allows certain kinds of synthetic compounds, particularly if the head is a Sino-Japanese morpheme. Theme arguments can appear in such compounds, but goal arguments cannot ((?)*shoohin-jyuyo* "prize-giving" vs. **seeto-jyuyo* "student-giving"; *shorui-soofu* "document-sending" vs. **yakunin-soofu* "official-sending"; compare (35) in English, (50) in Chichewa, (48) in Mohawk). Third, if the theme and goal arguments are both quantified expressions, their relative scope is ambiguous when the word order is as in (58b), but the goal necessarily takes wide scope over the theme when the word order is as in (58a) (Hoji 1985). Hoji interprets this as evidence that (58b) is derived from (58a) by scrambling (see also Aoun and Li (1993: ch. 7) and others); however, it is striking that the pattern of facts exactly replicates the scope freezing effect found in double object constructions in English (see (36)). Finally, Baker (1992c, 1995a) shows that the goal argument of a dative verb can become the subject when the verb is passivized in Japanese, but not when an unaccusative version of the verb is used; this is parallel to (41) in English, (54) in Sesotho, and (56) in Mohawk. In all these ways, then, the Japanese alternation in (58) behaves just like a dative alternation, with (58a) comparable to the double object construction. These facts raise many intriguing questions about the nature of dative Case and about what triggers dative shift.[31] However, they give no evidence against the UTAH's claim that the rules associating thematic roles to syntactic positions are invariant across languages. There is much to be done to show that other languages that appear to lack dative shift are actually like Japanese in these respects, but the evidence available so far from languages like Hindi and German appears to confirm this (see also Collins and Thrainson (1993) on Icelandic).

4. ON THE FORMULATION OF THE UTAH

So far we have surveyed reasons for believing that arguments bearing similar thematic roles are expressed in similar initial structural positions both within and across languages. Although there are significant differences between accusative, ergative, and non-configurational languages, and between primary-object and direct-object languages, these differences do not involve the basic projection of NPs but rather their surface licensing. The alternations in the realization of arguments of a predicate that one does find are either the result of different conceptualizations of the event, or the result of syntactic movement processes.

Agreeing then that some version of the UTAH should be accepted, the next question is which one? How can one refine this vague hypothesis into a specific principle and defend its details? In this section, I discuss three areas of controversy that have arisen with respect to these questions: (i) What thematic roles is the UTAH sensitive to and how are they ordered? (ii) Does the UTAH stipulate the exact positions of each argument, or does it only put conditions on their position relative to one other? (iii) Are thematic roles or aspectual notions the primary determinants of basic syntactic structure? Once these questions are answered, we will have a rather precise picture of what the operative principle(s) actually are.

4.1. *Details of the Thematic Hierarchy*

Recent work on the UTAH and related topics often states the relevant principle in terms of a thematic hierarchy. For example, Larson (1988: 382) proposes the following:

(59) Thematic Hierarchy
Agent > Theme > Goal > Obliques (manner, location, time, . . .)
If a verb a determines θ-roles $\theta_1, \theta_2, \ldots, \theta_n$, then the lowest role on the Thematic Hierarchy is assigned to the lowest argument in constituent structure, the next lowest role to the next lowest argument, and so on.

Speas (1990) adopts this principle directly, and Grimshaw's (1990) view is similar. Other theoretical frameworks that do not subscribe to the UTAH often capture the same effects by stating grammatical conditions not over phrase structure configurations (like c-command) determined by the Thematic Hierarchy, but directly in terms of the Thematic Hierarchy itself. Either way, it is clearly an important matter to establish what the exact hierarchy is. However, this has proved to be difficult – a problem that has created some skepticism about whether the approach as a whole is on the right track.

Consider first the question of exactly how the thematic roles are ranked. We have implicitly said much about this already. Once the issue of deep ergative languages has been dealt with, it is uncontroversial that the agent is ranked higher than all other roles. More controversial is the relative ranking of theme and goal. I have assumed and in some cases argued that the theme is higher than the goal, but many researchers in this area assume the opposite (Jackendoff 1972, Grimshaw 1990, Li 1990, Bresnan and Moshi

1990, Foley and Van Valin 1984). One source of the controversy comes from the existence of the dative alternation, and the difficulty of determining which version is basic and which (if either) is derived. This has already been dealt with at length. In particular, I consider the fact that goals cannot be subjects of unaccusative verbs to be strong evidence that they are lower than themes, given the long historical relationship between thematic hierarchies and subject choice, traceable back to Fillmore (1968).

What then are the arguments that goals should be ranked higher than themes? Some of them are embedded in frameworks of assumptions that are too different from the current one to permit easy comparison here. However, Grimshaw (1990), working in roughly the same framework, discusses two: light verb constructions in Japanese, and compounding in English.[32] The English data has already been touched on. Grimshaw points out the contrast in (60).

(60) a.(?) gift-giving to children
b. *child-giving of gifts

She says that (60b) is bad because the goal is assigned in a smaller domain (the compound word) than the theme, which is assigned in N′. This order of assignment contradicts her version of the thematic hierarchy. In contrast, I attributed the ungrammaticality of examples like (60b) to the fact that the goal role is necessarily assigned by a preposition, and Ps cannot appear in compounds. Evidence that this second interpretation is the correct one comes from compounds formed from verbs that have an optional theme argument. According to Grimshaw's account, it should be possible for the goal to appear as the nonhead in these circumstances, as long as the theme role is not assigned. In fact, goal-verb compounds are still completely impossible, as shown by examples like **child-reading* or **spy-telling*. Thus, English compounds do not support a hierarchy with goals higher than themes.

The facts from Japanese Light Verb Constructions are not as well understood. The basic form of Grimshaw's argument is this: Japanese has constructions that consist of an argument-taking noun and a dummy verb. The arguments of the noun can in general be expressed in two ways: either as genitive phrases inside the NP, or as constituents governed by the dummy verb. However, there is a constraint: the theme can only appear outside the NP if the goal does as well. Grimshaw again interprets this as evidence that theme is lower than goal on a thematic hierarchy, together with a principle like (59). However, other constructions work in exactly the opposite way. For example, Baker (1989) uses similar reasoning in his study of the Serial Verb Constructions found in West African languages. In these languages, a phrase headed by a triadic verb such as "give" can appear embedded within a projection of some other verb. When this happens, the theme argument of the three-place verb may appear as the object of the higher verb, but the goal object must always appear in the first projection of the dative verb. (61) is a minimal contrast from the Nigerian language Edo that shows this.

(61) a. òzó [$_{Vx}$ rhié íghó [$_{Vx}$ hàé úyì]].
Ozo take money pay Uyi
(Stewart, personal communication)

"Ozo took money and paid it to Uyi."

b.*òzó [$_{Vx}$ guàlo̱ úyì [$_{Vx}$ hàé (íghó)]].
Ozo find Uyi pay money

"Ozo found Uyi and paid him the money."

Thus, Grimshaw's reasoning does not extend smoothly to all comparable cases. I claim that (61) shows the true hierarchical relationship between the goal and the theme, and that a different kind of account is needed for the light verb facts (see Baker (1995b: 353–356) for a preliminary sketch of an alternative account).

One attractive dividend of the view that goals are ranked lower than themes is that they can then be collapsed with other locative expressions, such as the PP arguments of verbs of putting. The theme clearly c-commands the locative argument of such verbs, and there is no dative shift to cloud the matter. Now if goals ranked higher than themes, and themes ranked higher than locations, as proposed by Kiparsky (1987), Bresnan and Kanerva (1989), and other LFG work, then the two roles clearly cannot be collapsed into a single macrorole. However, there is often a rather smooth continuum between locative phrases and goal phrases. Given that the PPs in (62b,c,d) are locational paths on anyone's theory, it seems artificial to say that the PP in (62a) is not a locational path as well.

(62) a. John threw the ball to Bill.
b. John threw the ball (all the way) to the fence.
c. John threw the ball toward the fence.
d. John threw the ball into the dugout.

Of course, (62a) differs from (62b,c) in that it may (or even must) undergo dative shift in some languages; this is part of the motivation for distinguishing them. My claim, however, is that this is not a *thematic* distinction; rather it is due to other factors, such as the semantic redundancy of the preposition in (62) (Larson 1988, Baker 1992a), and perhaps the fact that animate nouns must bear structural Case in many languages. In this way, one can avoid proliferating thematic roles that are difficult to distinguish from one another in practice.

This leads naturally into the other controversial question of how many thematic roles there are. Current theories range from a high of something like 10–15 down to a low of two (Dowty's Proto-agent vs. Proto-theme distinction; Talmy's (1985) Figure vs. Ground distinction). So far, we have found more reason to collapse roles than to distinguish them. I have implicitly treated goals and recipient-benefactives as the same through out; now we have seen that these can be collapsed with location arguments as well. Presumably most source arguments such as *from John* in *I stole a book from John* also fit into this class; together they constitute a broad category of path/location (Jackendoff 1983).[33] Similarly, in section 2.1 I briefly argued that the role experiencer, often used in the analysis of psych verbs, only confuses the theory of linking. Rather the "experiencers" of verbs like *fear* are (relatively) ordinary agent/causers, who create mental representations of a certain kind, while the "experiencers" of verbs like *frighten* are patient/themes that undergo a change of (mental) state. Perhaps some "experiencers" are goals as well (see below). However, these do not seem to form a coherent class. Thus, the core cases of thematic roles reduce down to only three: agent/causer, patient/theme, and path/location.

Of course, other thematic roles have been proposed, such as instrument and comitative. However, these are virtually never subcategorized arguments of a verb, and their linguistic expression is highly variable across languages. Indeed, some languages have no direct expressions of them at all (Mohawk, for example). This suggests that they are not primitive thematic roles, but rather constructs defined in terms of the more basic roles. Thus, a comitative is usually either a second agent or a second theme (cf. Baker (1992b)). Similarly, Jackendoff (1987) shows that instruments are intermediate agent-themes: they are things which the agent acts upon, which then in turn act upon the ultimate theme. Clearly, there is more to say about how these and other secondary roles are worked into the syntax of different languages, but they should not be part of the basic statement of the UTAH. If this is correct, then Theta theory is rather coarse grained. It reduces to two key oppositions: agent vs. patient/theme, with the agent external, and patient/theme vs. path/location, with the theme external.

4.2. *Relative UTAHs and Absolute UTAHs*

The second area of debate related to the UTAH concerns how rigid the requirements it puts on a syntactic structure are. Baker's (1988a) original statement implied that particular thematic roles were associated with particular syntactic positions in an absolute sense. However, many other researchers assume that only the relative positions of the arguments are important. On this view, it does not matter exactly what syntactic position (say) a theme phrase is generated in, as long as it is higher than any goal phrase and lower than any agent phrase in the same clause. We may call a condition of this kind the Relativized UTAH, or RUTAH. Larson's (59) is a form of RUTAH, as he makes explicit in Larson (1990). Similarly,

Grimshaw's (1990) arguments concerning the thematic hierarchy reviewed above assume something like a RUTAH; see also Belletti and Rizzi (1988), Speas (1990), Li (1990), and most other work that uses a thematic hierarchy. In investigating this issue, I look first at the evidence that seems to require a RUTAH, and then at some evidence that points in the opposite direction.

4.2.1. *Evidence for a Relativized UTAH*

Many different reasons have been proposed for adopting the RUTAH rather than the UTAH. For example, Larson (1990) does so for certain theoretical reasons that do not necessarily arise in my approach.[34] However, Speas (1990: 73) expresses perhaps the clearest reason that needs to be considered – the fact that in some cases the expression of arguments seems to be context-dependent. The example she cites involves the recipient role, which may be a subject (as in (63a)), but only if there is no agent present in the clause (as in (63b)).

(63) a. John received a package from Baraboo.
b. Mary sent a package to John from Baraboo.

This seems to be a counterexample to the UTAH, but is consistent with a RUTAH that says that agents rank higher than recipients. Similarly, it is well-known that instruments can appear in the subject position in English, but again only if there is no agent.

(64) a. John loaded the truck with a crane/pitchfork.
b. The crane/*pitchfork loaded the truck. (Levin 1993: 80)

Grimshaw (1990) has a similar conception in mind when she points out that there are no syntactic differences between transitive psych verbs like *hate* and ordinary agent-patient verbs like *kill*, even though the particular thematic roles seem to be different. This follows if syntax is sensitive to the relative rankings of the thematic roles, but not their exact value.

(65) a. Mary hates John.
b. Mary killed John.

However, an absolute version of the UTAH can still be maintained in the face of such examples if one adopts Dowty's (1991) idea that the basic thematic roles are prototype concepts rather than categorically defined ones. On this view, it is possible to say that *John* in (63a), *the crane* in (64b), and *Mary* in (65a) are all (proto-)agents, and as such belong in the subject position. This is justified by the fact that each of these NPs shares certain semantic entailments with the prototypical agent *Mary* in (65b), although they do not all share the same ones. For (64b), in particular, there is good reason to think that the subject is a slightly peculiar agent/causer rather than an instrument; this makes it possible to explain why some artifacts can appear as subjects, but others cannot. Both a pitchfork and a crane are equally good instruments in (64a), but only the crane can be seen as having the kind of quasi-independent causing role necessary to be considered an agent. The situation is less clear with *hate* and especially *receive*, but both typically have animate subjects whose internal properties partly determine whether the eventuality occurs or not (Mary's personality in the case of *hate*; John's decision to accept the item in at least some uses of *receive*). In contrast, *John* is a goal, not an agent in (63b) and *the knife* is an instrument, not an agent in (64b); hence they show up in PPs.

Of course we must still explain why *John* can be an agent in (63a) but not in (63b). Dowty's answer is that the event expressed by (63b) contains a better candidate for proto-agenthood, namely Mary; she has more agent-like semantic entailments. Thus, adopting this line does not eliminate all relativity from the analysis. Rather, it moves the relativity from the statement of the UTAH into the cognitive realm of what is perceived as an agent. RUTAH theories say that recipients can be subjects only in the absence of agents because agents outrank recipients; the prototype theory says that certain participants in an event are less prone to being seen as agents than others are, but the one seen as an agent is always the subject. The question is not whether a degree of relativity is necessary or not, but rather at what stage the relativity comes into the picture.

Perhaps the most sophisticated, closely argued, and impressive use of the RUTAH is Belletti and Rizzi's (1988) analysis of psych verbs in Italian. The basic challenge posed by this class of verbs has already been discussed in section 2.1: in short, it stems from the fact that nearly-synonymous verbs seem to have different linking patterns only in this narrow semantic domain. The RUTAH gives Belletti and Rizzi the flexibility that they need to develop an elegant syntactic solution to this problem. Their idea is that the experiencer argument of every psych verb must be generated in a higher syntactic position than the "theme" argument (or, better, the stimulus). For *fear*-class psych verbs, the experiencer is inserted into the normal subject position, and little else happens. However, the experiencer of *frighten*-class psych verbs is generated further down, leaving the subject position open for the stimulus argument to move into. Belletti and Rizzi support their analysis with a series of empirical arguments that show that the structure of clauses with *frighten*-class verbs is not as simple as it seems, but involves a nontrivial syntactic derivation.

For the simplest facts of *frighten*-class verbs, the appeal to the RUTAH can be replaced by Dowty's prototype conception of agenthood, as before. We can say that the stimulus is seen as the cause of a certain (change of) state in the experiencer with *frighten*, though not with *fear*; it therefore qualifies as an agent/causer, and is inserted into the subject position by the normal projection rule, as argued by Pesetsky (1987, 1995) and Dowty

(1991). However, the task is not complete, because we still owe Belletti and Rizzi an account of why *frighten*-verbs have so many syntactic peculiarities (see also Grimshaw (1990: 19–25)). Dowty (1991) ignores these peculiarities, and Pesetsky (1987) puts them aside as semantic.

Here is a tentative proposal that has the right general character. Part of the difficulty with psych verbs is that it is not clear what kind of lexical/thematic analysis to assign them. So far, I have assumed that *frighten* means basically "x cause [y to be in FEAR (with respect to z)]". Such a conceptual representation should give rise to an ordinary transitive clause. Suppose instead that its lexical semantic representation is more like "x cause [[FEAR (of z)] to go to y]". Here "fear" is conceived of as an abstract thing that goes into the experiencer, rather than an abstract state that the experiencer enters. The stimulus is the causer, as before, but now the experiencer is a type of goal, rather than a type of theme, that role being taken by the emotion itself. Each element of this account can be motivated by superficial morphology in some languages: *frighten*-class verbs are often causatives morphologically (e.g., in Japanese (Pesetsky 1995: 7, 46–47)); experiencers often bear dative Case identical to that of goals (e.g., many South Asian languages); psych predicates are often nominal rather than verbal (e.g., Palauan (Georgopoulos 1987), Warlpiri (Simpson 1991)). Then, by normal rules of projection, one gets (66).

(66)

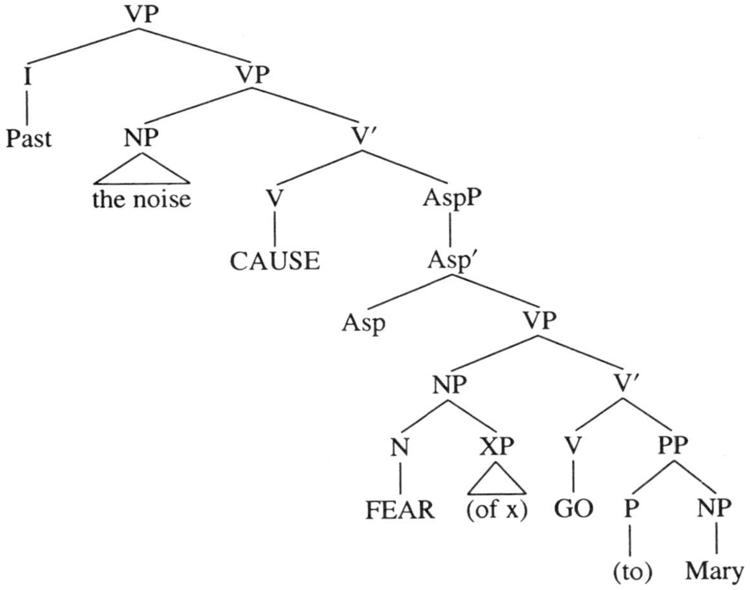

Several things then happen to this basic structure. First, the abstract elements FEAR, GO, and CAUSE somehow combine to give *frighten*. I leave open whether this is done by incorporation in the sense of Baker (1988a) applying in the syntax, followed by late lexical insertion along the lines of Halle and Marantz (1993), or whether the combination happens by a kind of pre-syntactic incorporation as in Hale and Keyser (1993) (but see section 5). Second, dative shift takes place just as in (24), incorporating the preposition into the predicate and moving its object into Spec, AspP.

This proposal goes a long way toward explaining the peculiarities of the experiencer-object that have been noted in the literature; it has very much the same properties as the goal object of a double object construction. For example, Belletti and Rizzi (1988) show that the object of a *frighten*-type verb is a mild island for movement processes in Italian, an effect that is also detectable in English:

(67) a.? Which company does international unrest frighten [the president of t].
b. Which company does the international community fear [the president of t]?

The awkwardness of (67a) can be attributed to a Left Branch Violation (compare *??Which company did John give the president of a bribe?*). Similarly, the literature shows that *frighten*-class verbs in English cannot be nominalized (**the movie's amusement of the children*, Grimshaw (1990: 118–123), also Rappaport (1983), Pesetsky (1995)), they cannot form synthetic compounds (**a child-frightening storm*, Grimshaw (1990: 15–16, 25), and they do not have unaccusative variants (**Mary frightened*, Grimshaw (1990: 36), attributed to M.-L. Zubizarreta). In all of these ways, *frighten*-class verbs are like dative shift verbs.[35]

Finally, there are certain questions about the stimulus subjects of these verbs. Belletti and Rizzi (1988) show that they have several properties normally associated with derived subjects, the most striking of which is that something in the subject can be anaphorically dependent on the direct object:

(68) a. *Each other's friends like John and Mary
b.(?) Each other's friends worry John and Mary

On the other hand, Pesetsky (1995) and Grimshaw (1990) show that the stimulus subject also has certain properties of a base-generated subject. Borrowing liberally from Pesetsky (1995), we could potentially resolve this contradiction by saying that the stimulus subject is indeed base-generated in the agent-subject position, but it shares some properties with derived subjects by virtue of binding an empty category that is the argument of the abstract noun that characterizes the emotion. Semantically, this is rather natural; the most obvious reading of *The noise frightened Mary* is that the noise caused Mary to have fear of the noise itself (but see Pesetsky (1987, 1995) for other, putatively different readings). Thus, the derived structure of (66) is (69).

(69)

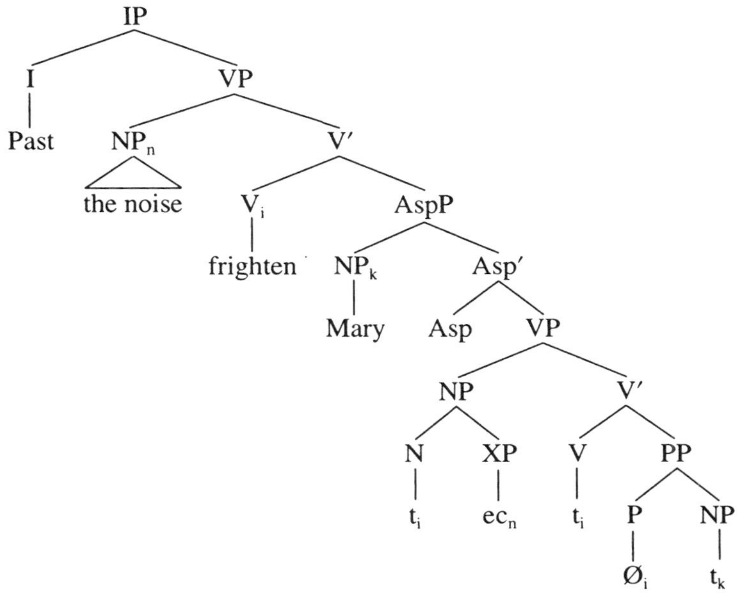

Here, the stimulus subject can be anaphorically dependent on the experiencer object because even though it is not c-commanded by the object, it is linked to a position that is (see Barss (1986)). There would be many important theoretical problems to face in fleshing out this analysis[36]; however, it seems to have approximately the right cluster of properties to explain the behavior of *frighten*-class psych verbs, as well as being consistent with an absolute UTAH.

4.2.2. *Reasons for an Absolute UTAH*

So far, we have surveyed some of the reasons for holding a relativized version of the UTAH, and have seen that they are not necessarily conclusive. Now let us see if there are reasons to prefer an absolute version of the UTAH.

One obvious place to look for evidence distinguishing the two is the syntax of verbs that take a single nominal argument. For such verbs, the RUTAH strictly speaking puts no restrictions on how the single argument is expressed in the syntax. For example, if a verb has only an agent argument, the RUTAH in (59) requires only that the agent c-command all of its co-arguments. This condition is satisfied trivially, even if the agent is generated as an immediate complement of the verb, because it has no co-argument by hypothesis. Conversely, a verb that has only a theme argument could project that argument into a high structural position; it would still be the lowest argument in the clause. In contrast, the absolute UTAH says that these variations are not possible. As such, it automatically induces the so-called Unaccusative Hypothesis: the idea that the sole argument of an agentive intransitive verb is a subject at all levels, but the sole argument of a nonagentive intransitive verb is generated as an initial object (Perlmutter 1978, Burzio 1986). Therefore, if the Unaccusative Hypothesis is true universally, this supports the UTAH over the RUTAH.

In fact, Perlmutter's Unaccusative Hypothesis is now widely accepted in P&P-style theories, and has proved to be a very productive idea in the analysis of many different kinds of languages. There has been some debate about whether it is true universally, and about whether the unaccusative predicates of a given language can be predicted on universal lexical semantic grounds (see Rosen (1984)). The UTAH is committed to a positive answer to both of these questions, and the bulk of current work tends to support this, once one is adequately sophisticated in one's treatment of lexical semantics and the syntax of particular languages. For example, Levin and Rappaport-Hovav (1995) show that, once the details of lexical semantics are attended to, which predicates are unaccusative and which are unergative is quite consistent across a range of well-studied languages, including English, Dutch, Italian, Hebrew, and Russian. At the same time, more and more work is accumulating that shows how insightful analyses of phenomena in less-studied languages can be given if the Unaccusative Hypothesis is accepted, supporting the idea that it holds universally. I mention only a few instances from languages already mentioned in this article: Baker (1995b) finds five differences between unergative and unaccusative verbs in Mohawk: (i) the argument of an unaccusative verb but not an unergative verb can be incorporated; (ii) the quantifier *eso* "many" can be floated off of the argument of an unaccusative verb only; (iii) benefactive applicatives made from unergative verbs can have a transitive agreement prefix, but those made from unaccusatives cannot; (iv) morphological causatives can be formed from unaccusatives only; (v) morphological purposive constructions can be formed from unergatives only.[37] In Chichewa and other Bantu languages, unaccusative verbs allow a locative inversion construction in which a locative expression becomes the surface subject (Bresnan and Kanerva 1989); however, benefactive applicative constructions cannot be formed from unaccusative verbs except under special circumstances (Alsina and Mchombo 1988, Machobane 1989). In West African languages, unaccusative verbs but not unergative verbs can appear as the second verb in certain kinds of Serial Verb Constructions (Baker 1989). And so on. Thus, while there are still languages in which there is little or no known evidence for the Unaccusative Hypothesis, they are becoming fewer and fewer. Moreover, I am not aware of any empirical arguments *against* the Unaccusative Hypothesis in a particular language.

The major remaining controversy concerning the Unaccusative Hypothesis is whether the phenomena attributed to it should be explained in terms of syntactic structure or in terms of semantic conditions. In most cases, a P&P account of such phenomena comes in two phases: first the meaning of the clause determines whether the argument of the verb is inserted in a direct object position or in a subject position, and then syntactic conditions defined over the resulting structural configuration determine whether a given operation is possible or not – for example, whether one can add a resultative predicate in English, or whether a partitive *ne* clitic can be extracted in Italian, or whether an impersonal passive is possible in Dutch. Given the logic of this situation, it is natural to ask whether one can cut out the middleman by stating the relevant conditions directly in terms of the meaning of the clause. This line of argument is developed by Zaenen (1993) for Dutch, and Van Valin (1987, 1990) for Italian. If it is successful, then the unergative-unaccusative distinction might not support the UTAH after all.

Levin and Rappaport-Hovav (1995) examine this issue at some length, and formulate a reasonable reply to it. Given that unaccusativity is determined by lexical semantics, it will nearly always be possible to state *descriptively adequate* rules that have purely semantic conditions. The question, however, is whether such a theory will be able to *explain* why those conditions hold. In several interesting cases, the semantic-based conditions look ad hoc, whereas syntactic-based conditions seem to uncover interesting connections with other phenomena, and thus achieve a greater level of generality. The particular case Levin and Rappaport-Hovav examine in some detail is resultative secondary predication in English, which is possible with unaccusative verbs (*The river froze solid*) but not unergatives (**John laughed sick*). Grimshaw (1990: 42) makes the same point with respect to *ne*-cliticization in Italian: she claims that Van Valin's analysis is essentially stipulative, whereas the kind of analysis offered in Belletti and Rizzi (1981) unifies this phenomenon with other instances of syntactic movement – including noun incorporation, morphological causatives, subject-auxiliary inversion in English, and ultimately perhaps even the subject-object asymmetries found with *wh*-movement (Baker 1988a). It is very unlikely that a substantive semantic condition could give a unified account of this range of phenomena, whereas a syntactic condition involving locality relationships between a trace and its antecedent can. Thus, Levin and Rappaport-Hovav conclude that unaccusativity is semantically determined and syntactically represented. If so, then the absolute UTAH is supported.

Given then that the Unaccusative Hypothesis is true, we should reconsider whether it is really impossible to capture it in a RUTAH-based framework. Of course it is not. For one thing, one could stipulate the Unaccusative Hypothesis as an extra condition in addition to the RUTAH; this is approximately the view of Grimshaw (1990). A more attractive way to proceed is to try to reduce one or the other class of intransitive verbs to a transitive construction. One possibility is that unergative clauses are really transitive clauses with some kind of covert theme-object; the presence of this object then forces the agent to be external. Chomsky (1995: 247–248) adopts this as a way to capture the difference between unergatives and unaccusatives in his highly impoverished "bare phrase structure" theory, building on Hale and Keyser (1993). Alternatively, one could say that unaccusative clauses are really transitives with a suppressed agent; the presence of this agent forces the theme to be relatively internal, as in transitive clauses (see Levin and Rappaport-Hovav (1995), building on unpublished work by Gennaro Chierchia). However, neither of these proposals is very well motivated empirically: one simply does not see cognate objects with all unergatives in most languages, nor are unaccusatives consistently derived from transitives morphologically. Furthermore, both of these methods of reducing intransitive clauses to transitive ones would need to be supplemented with an explanation of *why* an agent cannot be projected into syntax without a theme or vice versa. Thus, I conclude that the absolute UTAH is a preferable approach to unaccusative phenomena, assuming that it is otherwise tenable.

The Unaccusative Hypothesis concerns the representation of agents and themes. In principle, one should be able to raise the same kinds of questions concerning themes and goals: Must a goal be the innermost complement of V even when there is no theme? Must a theme be the specifier of the inner VP even if there is no goal? This is harder to evaluate, both because there are not many syntactic differences between the two VP internal positions, and because the presence of the preposition with the goal complicates the issues. However, there is some evidence that points to an absolute version of the UTAH in this domain as well. In (61), I showed that the Edo verb *hae* "pay" can share its theme argument with a higher verb in a Serial Verb Construction, but it cannot share its goal argument in the same way; this was interpreted as evidence that themes are structurally higher than goals. Now it so happens that *hae* can also appear without the theme argument in a sentence like "Kate paid Julia." Nevertheless, its goal argument still cannot be shared with the higher verb; (61b) is ungrammatical even when the theme NP is omitted. This suggests that the goal must be strictly in the smallest projection of V, regardless of whether there is a theme present as well. A similar case is (48) in Mohawk, which shows that themes but not goals can incorporate into the verb. Now, the theme argument of *nut* "feed" in Mohawk is optional. Thus, if the RUTAH underlay these facts, one might expect that when the theme is omitted, the goal phrase could be projected in the position normally reserved for the theme, and then could incorporate from there. This is false: (48b) is ungrammatical even if *o'wahru* "meat" is omitted. Facts like these suggest that it is not competition with the theme that forces the goal into its peculiar syntactic position, but rather some absolute requirement on goalhood.

Possibly relevant data from English comes from the so-called conative alternation, in which the verb has two arguments, one of which is an agent-subject and the other of which can be realized as either an NP or a PP (Levin 1993: 41–42).

(70) a. I stabbed the loaf of bread (with a knife).
b. I stabbed at the loaf of bread (with a knife).

If the RUTAH were true, one could imagine this alternation being semantically vacuous: since there is only one non-agent argument, it can assume either the direct object position or the indirect argument position freely. (Note that the preposition in the conative alternation is fixed as *at* for most verbs, and therefore can be considered semantically redundant.) However, the alternation is clearly not semantically vacuous: rather, (70a) entails that my knife actually made contact with the bread and probably penetrated its surface, whereas (70b) only entails that the bread was the target of my stab. Since the direct object in (70a) is affected by the event, it is reasonable to consider it a theme, while the PP in (70b) is more like a goal. Therefore, (70) actually shows that themes systematically show up as direct objects and goals as PP complements, even in the absence of another internal argument. This again supports the absolute version of the UTAH.[38]

4.3. *Thematic Roles and Aspectual Roles*

The last issue concerning the formulation of the UTAH I will consider is whether it is thematic roles that determine the syntactic position of arguments, or whether it is aspectual notions that do so (Tenny 1994, McClure 1994, Borer 1995). Roughly speaking, aspectual notions are those that are involved in expressing the state of completion of the event referred to by the verb: whether it is completed, in progress, continuing, repeated, and the like. The idea that aspectual roles might play a key role in linking theory grows out of the convergence of several lines of research. The first is investigations of the locative alternation, where the argument that "measures out" the event is the direct object in both versions, in spite of the fact that in other respects the same kind of situation is described (see section 3.1). The conative alternation just discussed is similar in this respect: the internal argument measures the progress of the event when it is a direct object but not when it is oblique. Facts like these lead Tenny (1987, 1994) to the conclusion that there is a close relationship between being a syntactic direct object and performing this kind of aspectual role. A second thread comes from the Van Valin-Zaenen observation that some of the putative differences between unaccusative verbs and unergative verbs actually boil down to differences in the aspectual notion of telicity (roughly, whether the event reaches a natural conclusion or not): telic verbs are unaccusative, and atelic ones are unergative (see also Tenny (1994), Grimshaw (1990), Borer (1995)). The third thread comes from the domain of psych verbs, where some researchers who have not recognized a *thematic* distinction between the *fear*-class and the *frighten*-class have recognized an aspectual difference: *frighten* may refer to an inchoative, caused change of state (an accomplishment or achievement), whereas *fear* is stative. These lines of research converge into Tenny's (1987, 1994: 115–116) Aspectual Interface Hypothesis (AIH):

(71) *Aspectual Interface Hypothesis*
The universal principles of mapping between thematic structure and syntactic argument structure are governed by aspectual properties related to measuring-out. . . . Only the aspectual part of thematic structure is visible to the universal linking principles.

More specifically, Tenny (1994: ch. 1) argues that the argument that measures the progress of an event must be a direct object, the argument that defines when the event is over must be an oblique internal argument, and an external (subject) argument cannot play any role in measuring out or delimiting the event described by the verb. The question then is whether it is aspectual roles or thematic roles that determine underlying syntactic structure.

In fact, this may be more a terminological question than an empirical one, depending on one's theory of aspect and thematic roles. Thus, Tenny presents the AIH not so much as an alternative to the UTAH, but as a refinement of it; it defines which facets of a rather rich thematic/conceptual representation can be relevant to syntax. She points out that there is a close and nonaccidental correlation between the Gruber/Jackendoff notion of a theme, and her notion of a Measure argument. The theme of an event is the participant that undergoes a change of location or state in the event; as such, the position of that participant in space or its physical properties provide a suitable measure of the progress of the event toward completion. Similarly, there is a close connection between the goal thematic role and Tenny's "terminus" aspectual role. If these close correlations were to become true equivalencies by a refinement of either theory, then there would be no difference between the UTAH and the AIH. Indeed, some of the differences that Tenny points out crucially assume that thematic theory is relatively fine-grained, and makes a variety of distinctions that are not relevant to linking (e.g. agent vs. instrument, benefactive vs. malefactive). However, I have argued for a rather coarse-grained thematic theory – one that distinguishes about the same number of thematic roles as Tenny has aspectual roles. This decision contributes further to the convergence of the two ideas. Therefore, one can expect the differences between an aspect-based theory and a thematic-based theory to be few.

A close look, however, may reveal that there are some. Levin and Rappaport-Hovav (1995) explicitly consider this issue as it applies to intransitive verbs. They discover that the connection between aspect and unaccusativity is not as tight as has been claimed. (72) shows that clauses with unaccusative verbs can be either telic or atelic, as shown by the standard test of whether the clause is compatible with the adverb *for X time* (atelic) or *in X time* (telic).

(72) a. The ball bounced/rolled/spun for five minutes/#in five minutes. (atelic)
b. The soup cooled/the train descended for five minutes/in five minutes. (telic/atelic)
c. The vase broke/shattered/arrived #for five minutes/in five minutes. (telic)

Conversely, unergative verbs are often atelic activities, but examples like (73b) are telic (McClure 1994).

(73) a. Mary snored for an hour/#in an hour. (atelic)
b. Mary won #for an hour/in an hour. (telic)

Levin and Rappaport-Hovav also show that the state/event distinction is not relevant to determining which verbs are unergative and which are unaccusative. For example, they show that posture verbs like *sit*, *stand*, and *lean* are unergative when they take animate subjects and have a "maintain position" meaning (*Mary stood in line for an hour*) but they are unaccusative when they take inanimate subjects (*The statue stood in the park for 50 years*). Here there is a clear difference in agency (i.e. whether the event is internally caused), but no difference in aspect: both uses of *stand* are stative. Similar remarks hold for verbs of light and smell emission, they claim. This broader range of examples thus suggests that aspectual distinctions do not determine the underlying structure of a clause, but something more like thematic roles does.[39]

This issue can also be investigated in the area of transitives. Here too there is reason to doubt that reference to thematic roles can be replaced by reference to aspectual notions. Tenny (1994) discusses the fact that while all "measure" arguments are direct objects, not all direct objects are "measures". Thus, (74a) is a telic event, with *the cart* providing the measure, but (74b) is an atelic event with no measure argument.

(74) a. John washed the cart in half an hour.
b. John pushed the cart for half an hour.

Thus, Tenny's aspect-based linking rules determine which argument of the verb is its direct object in (74a), but they do not extend readily to determine which is the object in (74b). This seems like a failure to capture an important generalization, since the linking in (74b) is clearly not accidental.

In contrast, it is easy to state generalizations that cover both (74a) and (74b) in thematic terms: John is clearly the agent/causer of the event in both cases, while a change is asserted of the cart in both cases (a change of state in one case, a change of position in the other). Many other instances of this kind arise, where the same clause is ambiguous between an activity and an accomplishment reading, but the grammatical functions remain constant.

A third potential difficulty for aspect-oriented approaches to linking is that it is not clear whether they can be extended to account for stative transitive verbs. Tenny (1994) explicitly puts stative predicates aside in most of her discussion, conjecturing that there are in fact no universal linking principles that apply in such cases (see especially pp. 129–130, n. 35). Similarly, Grimshaw (1990: 29–30) points out that her aspect-based theory of psych verbs faces a problem that stems from the fact that *frighten*-class verbs may (and sometimes must) have stative readings; these clauses cannot be distinguished aspectually from *fear*-class verbs, which are also stative, even though the linking pattern seems different.

(75) a. This dog frightens/pleases John.
b. John fears/likes this dog.

In contrast, it is at least conceivable that a thematic account of the linking patterns in (74) could be extended to explain the patterns in (75) in a unified fashion, presumably by making use of Dowty's (1991) idea that agent and theme are prototype categories. Such an account would capitalize on the subtle but real intuition that (75b) comments more on John's character and tastes, while (75a) comments on a particular quality of the dog, in the way sketched in section 2.1. If this line is successful, it confirms the intuition that linking in stative predicates is not accidental, even though it cannot be determined in purely aspectual terms.

4.4. *Summary: The UTAH*

This section has explored three prominent controversies concerning linking theory and the exact formulation of UTAH-like principles. My conclusions have been that the UTAH is sensitive to a medium-coarse grained version of Theta theory, one that distinguishes three primary (proto)-roles: agent/causer, theme/patient, and goal/path/location. The conditions that it puts on the structural realization of these roles seem to be absolute, rather than relative, and they map the theme to a higher position than the goal. Finally, aspectual notions converge with thematic ones in an important range of cases, but seem not to be adequately general. With these insights in hand, we can finally state the linking principles that give content to the UTAH:

(76) (i) An agent is the specifier of the higher VP of a Larsonian structure.

(ii) A theme is the specifier of the lower VP.
(iii) A goal, path or location is the complement of the lower VP.

These rules are extremely simple; the substantial complexities of the data stem from the possibility of NP-movement in unaccusative clauses and dative shift configurations, and from choices that arise when categorizing the participants of a particular event into thematic roles.

5. THE MEANING OF THE UTAH AND ITS PLACE IN GRAMMAR

Now that we have an established version of linking theory to consider, this final section presents some tentative reflections on what it might mean for linguistic theory and for the relationship between language and other aspects of the mind. At stake is the question of whether the UTAH should be stated as an explicit principle of human language, as has been done so far, or whether it is rather an indirect reflection of the basic architecture of this aspect of human cognition. For concreteness, the discussion will be couched in terms of the Minimalist Program, Chomsky's (1995) recent house-cleaning and re-evaluation of the Principles and Parameters theory, in which every aspect of the theory of grammar is held up to the test of whether it can be justified in terms of "virtual conceptual necessity." However, the specific points that arise from this kind of inquiry should be of more general interest.

Before raising technical matters, one should ask whether something like the UTAH is "in the spirit of" the Minimalist Program. While Chomsky himself has been relatively silent on this question, I believe that the answer is clearly yes. A leading idea of the Minimalist Program is that there should be a natural interface between the representations computed by the language faculty and the performance systems that use those representations. Indeed, Chomsky conjectures that much of the observed structure of language is motivated by the goal of meeting this kind of "bare output condition" in an optimal way. In particular, there should be a natural interface between the level of LF and what Chomsky calls the "Conceptual-Intentional system" (C-I). The UTAH can be seen as part of the theory of this interface. If one follows the common practice of assuming that thematic roles are part of the conceptual system, then the UTAH asserts in essence that there must be a homomorphic, perhaps even an isomorphic relationship between this aspect of the conceptual system and the corresponding linguistic representation.

One can make a useful comparison between the UTAH and the Theta Criterion of Chomsky (1981) in this regard. Chomsky (1993) points out that the Theta Criterion is trivially true at the level of LF as it is understood in the Minimalist Program: if functors (such as verbs) do not take the right number of arguments (such as NPs), the system "crashes", failing to produce something with a usable interpretation. However, it is also true that if a functor takes more than one argument, it must have some way to tell which argument is which; this is necessary in order to distinguish restaurant reviews ("Man eats shark") from suspense movies ("Shark eats man"). The UTAH performs this function of distinguishing the different arguments of the verb by way of virtually the only method available in Chomsky's very spare system: it "merges" the arguments into the representation at systematically different points.[40] Therefore, there does seem to be a place for the UTAH within the limits of "virtual conceptual necessity."

Keeping the role of the UTAH in mind allows us to resolve certain conflicts between the Minimalist Program and the original versions of the UTAH. The most obvious conflict stems from the fact that Baker (1988a) stated the UTAH as a condition that held at the level of D-structure, prior to any movements. Chomsky (1993), however, argues that there should be no such level: it is not required by "virtual conceptual necessity," there were few substantive principles that held uniquely at D-structure, and certain paradoxes disappear once one is allowed to do movements and merges in any order. If this is correct, then the UTAH is either false or it is enforced at some other point. In fact, realizing that conceptually the UTAH is part of the theory of the relationship between language and the C-I system tells us where it should fit in the grammar: like the Theta Criterion, it should be understood as an output condition on LF, the interface level related to C-I.[41] There is one slight complication: to apply the UTAH at LF one must say that it looks not at simple NPs, but rather at the tails of chains, in order to factor out the effects of movement. However, this is no real difficulty, since chains are taken to be the fundamental LF objects in this system in any case (Chomsky and Lasnik 1993).

The second way in which specific Minimalist proposals seem to impact negatively on the UTAH concerns Chomsky's (1995) adoption of a "bare phrase structure" system. In short, Chomsky proposes to eliminate all reference to different bar levels, thereby removing any theoretical significance from one-bar level categories, and moving to a purely relative definition of X° and X^{max} level categories. Depending on the details, this proposal could undercut the ability to define the kinds of positions needed to state the UTAH correctly. In particular, since "specifier" and "complement" become relative notions, the bare phrase structure system seems more compatible with the RUTAH than with the UTAH (see, for example, section 4.2.2 for Chomsky's approach to the unergative-unaccusative distinction). Furthermore, Baker (1995a) conjectures that the reason linguistic theory seems to make use of exactly three proto-thematic roles is because X-bar theory defines exactly three kinds of positions – sister of X°, sister of X', and outside XP – so thematic distinctions are neutralized to the point that they fit into this template provided by the language faculty. However, if X-bar theory is in fact derivative (see also Speas (1990)), then this claim cannot be maintained.

This technical question about position types turns out to be related to a deeper conceptual one. Above, I claimed that the function of the UTAH was to show which NP fills which argument slot in the theta-grid of the verb. The question is whether it does so according to an arbitrary system or a principled one. To take a special case, is the fact that agents are found in positions external to themes and not vice versa an arbitrary choice made by particular languages, an arbitrary choice made by Universal Grammar, or a natural and principled choice? We have already ruled out the view that it is an arbitrary choice of particular languages by arguing that there are no "deep ergative" languages in the sense of Marantz (1984). It would be desirable to rule out the view that it is an arbitrary choice of Universal Grammar as well.

Ironically, Marantz (1984) also contains the seeds of how to do this, when he proposes that there is a semantic basis for the fact that agents are projected external to themes (at least in English), using data from idioms and other semi-idiosyncratic constructions. Formally speaking, within the (neo-)Larsonian view of phrase structure we have adopted, the agent NP is an argument of a higher verb and the theme NP is an argument of an embedded verb. This Larsonian structure dovetails nicely with work on lexical semantics, which generally decomposes standard transitive verbs into (at least) two predicates along the lines of (77) (Dowty 1979, Jackendoff 1983, Foley and Van Valin 1984, Hale and Keyser 1993).

(77) [x cause [y be/become PREDICATE]]

Here x is defined to be the agent argument and y is defined to be the theme. Given that these predicate decompositions are independently motivated on semantic grounds, it is very attractive to identify the causative part of the lexical semantic representation with the higher verb of the Larsonian shell,[42] and the be/become+PREDICATE part with the lower verb position. This is proposed by Hale and Keyser (1993) and has been adopted by Chomsky (1995: 315–316) and many others.[43] If this is correct, then the agent has prominence over the theme not by the extrinsic stipulation of some kind of thematic hierarchy, but by semantic compositionality: the agent is the argument of one predicate, the theme is the argument of another predicate, and the second predicate is an argument of the first. If syntactic structure is a projection of gross lexical semantic structure in this way (and if the lexical semantics of verbs is not grossly different across languages), it follows that there are no deep ergative languages or completely nonconfigurational languages.

In addition to taking away the apparent arbitrariness of the statements concerning where the theme and the agent appear, this approach makes it possible to distinguish unergative verbs from unaccusative verbs within a bare phrase structure system without claiming that either is a disguised transitive. On the semantic version of Larsonian structure, the agent NP is not generated in the higher VP shell because there is no room for it in the lower VP; rather, it is generated there because it is the argument of a CAUSE verb (or configuration), and hence is an agent by definition (Hale and Keyser 1993, Chomsky 1995). This carries over immediately to the case where the agent is the argument of a monadic verb; it will appear in the same position as the agent of a transitive verb, even if there is no theme argument in the lower VP. The three-way contrast between transitives, unergatives, and unaccusatives is therefore represented as in (78).[44]

(78) a. Transitive:

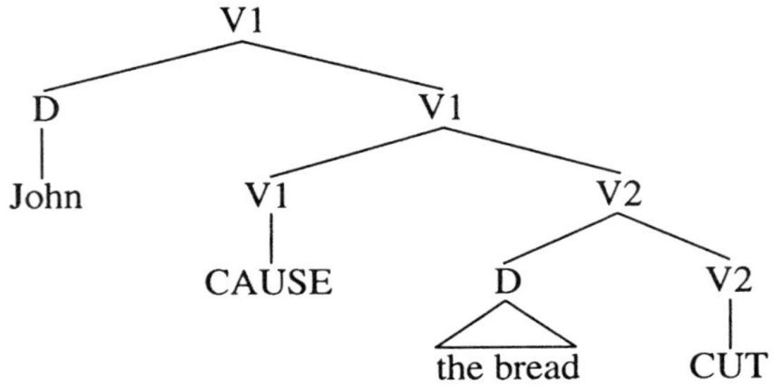

John cut the bread.
[x cause [y be linearly-separated]]

b. Unergative:

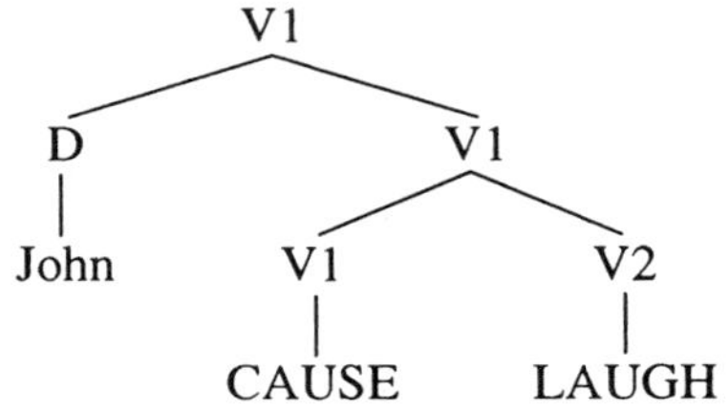

John laughed.
[x cause [LAUGH]]

b. Unaccusative:

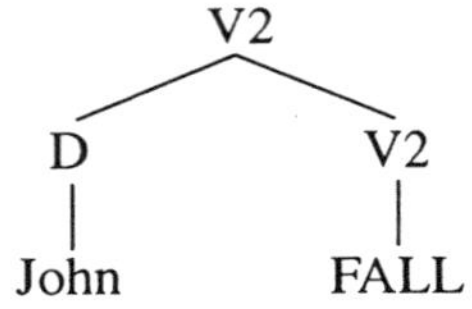

John fell.
[x become DOWN]

These representations follow Chomsky (1995), except for (78b). The idea is that the abstract element LAUGH is a one-place predicate of events; it means that laughter happened. *John laughed* then means that John was the immediate cause of an instance of this kind of event. Thus, (78b) and (78c) are structurally different without positing an otherwise unmotivated nominal cognate object within the V2 of (78b).

If this is the right account of why agents and themes end up where they do, the next question is whether similar considerations can explain why themes have prominence over goals and other path arguments. This question has not often been considered as such, to my knowledge. However, there is reason to think it should be possible. The trick is to propose a suitable semantic decomposition for the state or event that is expressed by the $V2^{max}$. Suppose for concreteness that $V2^{max}$ expresses a state.[45] States can be viewed as a pair consisting of an individual and a predicate, such that the predicate holds of the individual (cf. Kamp and Reyle (1993: 673)). The individual in this pair is the theme, by definition. What then is the goal? It must be an argument that helps define the predicate that holds of the individual. For example, *John put the book on the shelf* refers to an event which consisted of John causing a state, where the state consisted of a certain predicate holding of the book, and the predicate was being in a particular position with respect to the shelf. Translating these relationships into a syntactic structure gives (79).

(79)

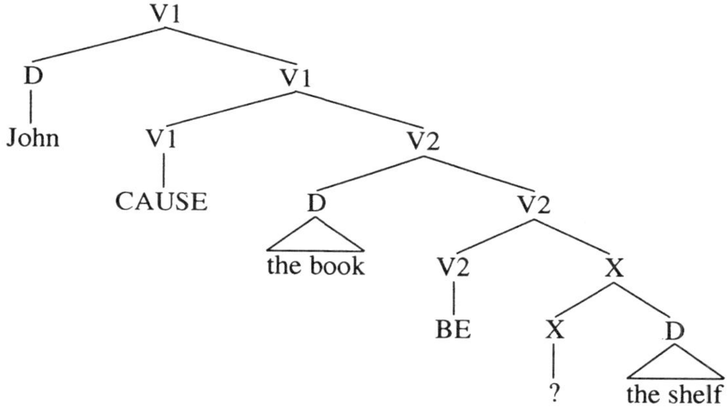

Here I assume that BE is a two-place relation that takes a thing and a predicate and creates the corresponding state. I leave open the exact nature of the element X, which takes a thing and creates a predicate; the easiest assumption would be that X is simply the preposition *on*, but one may want to leave room for other kinds of cases.[46] In any case, the theme in (79) has prominence over the goal, because it is semantically a direct argument of BE and the goal NP is only part of an argument of BE. Crucially, I suppose that it would be hard to give a semantic decomposition for a state in such a way that the goal is an immediate constituent and the theme is more deeply embedded. If this is so, then we have a second important convergence between lexical-semantic predicate decomposition and the results of syntactic tests (see section 3).

If this kind of lexical decomposition approach begun by Hale and Keyser and brought into the syntax by Chomsky and others is correct, then the UTAH essentially disappears as a separate condition of grammar. The basic function of the original UTAH was to regulate where the various arguments of a predicate are expressed. This is a nontrivial task if predicates have multiple arguments of the same type, because one must keep track of which NP is associated with which argument position. If, however, syntactic structure is built from the lexical decomposition of a verb, such that each predicate in the decomposition takes a single NP argument, the UTAH becomes trivial. All that remains is a simple convention that an argument must be in a local configuration with its argument-taker; the rest follows from compositional semantics. We have then reduced the UTAH to a matter of "virtual conceptual necessity".

As a final remark, it is worth pointing out that there is a slightly different way of interpreting this material that would have substantial ramifications for comparing P&P theory with other approaches to syntax and for assessing the role of language in cognition. Throughout this paper, I have assumed that linguistic representations and conceptual representations are two different things, following a broadly Jackendovian line (Jackendoff 1983, Jackendoff 1990b). Subject and object are syntactic notions, defined by the language faculty, while agent and theme are conceptual notions, defined over conceptual representations. The UTAH says that there must be a natural, homomorphic relationship between the two representations. This is in accordance with Chomsky's Minimalist conjecture that language is in some sense an optimal way of satisfying "bare output conditions" defined by the language-external systems (Chomsky 1995: 219–222). However, it is worth observing that this minimalist conception significantly blurs the distinction between P&P theory and functionalist approaches to language, which characteristically de-emphasize syntax as a separate study and focus on its connections with cognition, lexical semantics, and discourse pragmatics. Moreover, if the relationship between LF and Conceptual structure becomes *too* natural, approaching the status of an isomorphism, it becomes appropriate to question whether there are two representations at all; instead, there could be only one representation that is seen from two different perspectives. Thus, a more radical interpretation of the UTAH could be that it shows that there is no difference between the linguistic level of LF and "Conceptual structure". Researchers like Jackendoff (1983, 1987, 1990b) and Pinker (1989) have assumed that this could not be, because conceptual representations need to be much richer and more complex than syntactic representations are in order to support other aspects of cognition. However, current work in syntax suggests that syntactic structure – particularly LF – is somewhat more complicated than Jackendoff and Pinker have assumed (see, for example, section 3, especially (24), and (66)). If at the same time it could be shown that a somewhat more restrictive conceptual representation than Jackendoff assumes could adequately support other aspects of cognition, identifying the two would become a real possibility. Clearly, linguists alone will not be able to answer this question fully. However, it is interesting that Chomsky himself seems to vacillate between these two positions. Thus, in Chomsky (1994: 4), C-I is clearly presented as a performance *system*, distinct from the language faculty, that interprets LFs; on the other hand, Chomsky (1993: 2–3) uses C-I as a synonym for LF, referring to a *representation* built by the language faculty.[47] Which of these two positions is the true one could be the deepest question raised by the study of UTAH-like phenomena, with implications for the relationship of language to thought and beyond.

McGill University

NOTES

* Research for this article was supported by the Social Sciences and Humanities Research Council of Canada, grant 410-95-0979, and by FCAR of Quebec, grant 94ER0578. I have had the opportunity to discuss various issues in this article in a syntax seminar at McGill University and in colloquium talks at the University of Pennsylvania, USC, and the University of California-Irvine. In addition, I have benefited from discussing these issues with Lisa Travis, Nigel Duffield, O. T. Stewart, Miwako Uesako, Hironobu Hosoi, Mika Kizu, and Jim McGilvary. I thank all these people and groups for their valuable input.

[1] Here in order to be explicit I am taking a "language production" viewpoint, in which the conception is given and the problem is to find a suitable linguistic expression of it. The same stages would be run through in reverse if one took a "language perception" viewpoint, where the linguistic expression (i.e., the PF) is given and the problem is to find the matching conceptual representation (LF). Thus, no inherent directionality should be assumed in these associations.

[2] For example, Larson correctly points out that Baker (1988a) does not hold to the strictest imaginable sense of the UTAH in his analysis of the passive. Baker claimed that the agent role was assigned to the specifier of IP in normal active sentences, but to the head of I containing the morpheme -EN in corresponding passive sentences. These are not *identical* structural relationships, but they were held to be *equivalent* positions inasmuch as both are "minimally external" to the VP (outside VP but inside the next highest maximal projection).

[3] Suppressed here is the possibility that the various PPs might also differ in their syntactic positions. I suspect that this is the case, but in this article I concentrate on goals and other paths, except for a brief remark about instruments and comitatives in section 4.

[4] There may also be an instructive comparison between *fear/like* verbs and "representation-source" clauses such as *John memorized the poem*, discussed by Dowty (1991: 569–570). Dowty argues that the subject and object of *memorize* are relatively ordinary agents and patients. *John liked the poem* is similar in that it means that John created (or at least acquired) a particular kind of mental representation of the poem – a positively valued one.

[5] Perhaps other transitive verbs with noncanonical subjects such as the goal-subject verbs *receive, inherit, own* can be handled in a similar way (see Dowty (1991: 581) and section 4.2.1 below).

[6] In addition to Dyirbal, Dowty mentions certain Mayan languages. However, see Aissen (1995) for evidence that Tzotzil at least is not a deep ergative language.

[7] One exception to this near-consensus is Johns (1992), who argues for a position that is close to Marantz's "deep ergative" view of Inuktitut. However, the evidence for her account is primarily morphological, not syntactic.

[8] Essentially the same derivation has been proposed for "patient topic" constructions in

Tagalog and other Austronesian languages by Guilfoyle, Hung, and Travis (1992). This captures the intuition that these languages are partially ergative in some sense.

[9] Another common property of ergative languages is that the absolutive NP can be extracted by various kinds of *wh*-movement whereas the ergative NP often cannot. This can be understood if one assumes that the movement of the patient NP to Spec, IP, although Case-driven, is actually a kind of A-bar movement (Campana 1992, Bittner and Hale 1996). Since the patient NP is the highest position in the clause, it can readily be moved further, but it blocks A-bar movement of the ergative subject past it, by some kind of Relativized Minimality (Campana 1992, Nakamura 1993).

[10] However, the reader should be aware that many researchers draw a very different moral from these facts about nonconfigurational languages: they conclude that anaphor-binding, control, and incorporation must not determined by c-command and other structural properties, but rather by something else – either a functional representation (Bresnan (1982), Simpson (1991) and other work in Lexical Functional Grammar), or cognitive and pragmatic considerations. Much can be said to compare these approaches, but this is not the place to say it.

[11] See Chamorro (1992) and Baker (1995b) for some comparison of the Mohawk-type of nonconfigurationality with the Hindi/Japanese-type, and Baker (in progress) for some comparison of the Mohawk and Warlpiri types.

[12] Less is known about the locative alternation crosslinguistically. It seems that some languages have only the (14a) pattern (Mohawk is one such language); it is not clear that any languages have only the (14b) version.

[13] See also Pesetsky (1995). To be strictly accurate, Dowty (1991) anticipates a unified treatment for dative and locative alternations, but doesn't completely commit himself to one. Similarly, Tenny (1994: 81–83) expresses a preference for a base-generation approach to the dative alternation, similar to the one she has for the locative alternation, but leaves it out of the formulation of her principles. Dryer (1987) and Collins and Thrainsson (1996) say nothing about the locative alternation.

[14] These data and most like them can be traced back to Green (1974). However, Green herself questions the existence of dative movement only for *teach* (and *show*), saying that as far as she can tell nonidiomatic examples with *give* are essentially synonymous. See notes 23, 32, and 38 for other peculiarities of *teach* that are probably related.

[15] Compare Gropen et al. (1989: 242), who say that a sentence like (20b) "sounds somewhat self-contradictory" and say of a sentence like (20c) that the nondative-shifted alternate "may sound a bit less anomalous." Thus, while they draw the opposite conclusion from mine, they admit that the key judgments are far from categorical. I tentatively assume that these differences, to the extent that they are real, are due to the topic-focus differences between the two versions of the dative shift, and not to differences in the semantic/thematic roles.

[16] The reader should not be confused by the fact that there are also syntactic tests that treat all four classes of direct object as the same. For example, all four must be adjacent to the verb, must become the subject of a passive clause, and may cliticize to the verb (e.g. in Bantu languages). I assume that these properties are sensitive not to the base object position (the Spec of the inner VP), but rather to the derived object position (the Spec of Aspect Phrase).

[17] Williams' examples are not a perfect minimal pair in that *green* is a depictive predicate of *hay*, that describes its state throughout the event, whereas *full* is a resultative predicate that characterizes the wagon's state at the end of the event. The difference is presumably not crucial however. Thus, in *?I loaded the refrigerator with sodas warm*, *warm* is a depictive predicate of *refrigerator* and not of *sodas* (although the example is not as felicitous as one would like, and some speakers reject it).

[18] Thus, the fact that the theme NP can be a subject of predication even in a dative shift construction argues against Larson's original claim that the theme becomes an adjunct, as pointed out by Paul Kiparsky (personal communication). It also argues against the claim

that the theme NP in a double object construction is the object of a null preposition, as proposed by Emonds (1985) and Pesetsky (1995).

[19] Another possibility compatible with my framework is Larson's (1988) analysis of the paradigm in (28) in terms of "light predicate raising." Larson's account does not generalize to *wh*-extraction, but this may be appropriate since the heavy-NP shift contrast is much sharper. Baker (1988a, 1988b) argues that the deviance of (25) and (28a) is not simply a parsing effect created by the juxtaposition of two unmarked NPs: he shows that the same effect is found in dative constructions in Chichewa even when no theme NP is present, but it is not found in superficially similar instrumental constructions that have sequences of two bare NPs.

[20] However, Kayne cites Jespersen as having examples like *the giving of words figurative meanings*. The generative tradition of concentrating on Romance-based derived nominals rather than *-ing* nominals can be traced back to Chomsky (1970), who is rather tentative about extending the lexicalist analysis to *-ing* nominals. However, this biases the matter – needlessly, I believe – against both the locative alternation and the dative alternation, which are largely properties of the Germanic vocabulary of English, as is well-known.

[21] In this I disagree with Pesetsky (1995), who finds the (32) pattern unacceptable on the basis of a handful of noncanonical locative alternation verbs that (atypically) allow Romance-style derived nominals. I believe that the verbs Pesetsky uses actually participate in a somewhat different alternation.

[22] In particular, one must take verbs where both the material and location arguments are optional; otherwise the examples are ruled out by Selkirk's (1982) First Order Projection Condition.

[23] A similar effect can be seen in adjectival passives: either the material argument or the location argument may be the subject of the adjectival passive of a verb like *load* (*the recently loaded truck, the recently loaded hay*; Levin and Rappaport (1986: 634)); however, the goal cannot be the subject of the adjectival passive of a dative verb (*the untold story*, **the untold person*; Wasow (1977: 344)). Levin and Rappaport (1986) suggest that the ungrammaticality of examples like this last one is due to the fact that there is no place for the preposition needed to assign the goal role. On the exceptional behavior of verbs like *teach*, see Wasow (1977) and note 38 below.

[24] Note that because of the "total affectedness" effect, the object of *with* in (37b) must refer to enough stuff to completely load a cart. I believe that failure to attend to this factor has caused some confusion in the literature; thus, Larson (1990) and Aoun and Li (1993) (citing unpublished work by Schneider-Zioga) give flawed examples and wrongly conclude that the scope-freezing effect is found in locative alternations also. Nevertheless, a few speakers have reported to me that they still find the wide-scope interpretation of *every crate* difficult in (37b).

[25] See Aoun and Li (1989, 1993) and Hornstein (1995) for interesting proposals. However, these proposals have conceptual flaws, do not generalize to the full range of cases, and crucially assume syntactic structures for the double object construction that are different from the Larsonian one that I am arguing for.

[26] Pesetsky (1995: 124–125) claims that the verb *get* shows this alternation, since one can say both *The book got to Sue* and *Sue got the book*. See Baker (1995a: 30 n. 3) for a reply, claiming that these two sentences are actually derived from two different senses of the highly polysemous verb *get*.

[27] See section 4.2.2 for a brief discussion of the so-called conative alternation. Verbs of fulfilling such as *present* undergo the alternation in (i), which has superficial similarities to both dative shift and the locative alternation.

(i) a. Napoleon presented the medal to the soldier.
b. Napoleon presented the soldier with the medal.

Preliminary evidence suggests that this is essentially a variant of the double object construction in which inherent Case on the object is spelled out as *with* rather than as a null Case. Thus, clauses like (ib) cannot be nominalized (Kayne 1984: 153, 156), show the scope freezing effect (Larson 1990: 605), and do not have unaccusative versions (Levin 1993: 66) – all properties that are reminiscent of the double object construction. Other than this, it seems like a good bet that all other diatheses in English are the result of differing thematic analyses of the event, like the locative alternation. See Pinker (1989), Dowty (1991), Levin (1993), and Tenny (1994) for discussion of some relevant cases.

[28] Dryer himself would probably not approve of this implementation of his idea. Toward the end of his article he points out that many languages are not uniform in how they distribute "object properties" over the two objects of a ditransitive verb: some processes pick out "primary objects" and some "direct objects", even in the same language. In this he draws a parallel to the phenomenon of split ergativity, which is also more common than "pure" or "deep" ergativity. Therefore, he claims that the grammatical functions Primary Object and Secondary Object do not replace Indirect Object and Direct Object, but rather coexist with them and supplement them. (The simpler idea that the Primary Object is the "real" Direct Object in some languages he attributes to Comrie (1982), among others.)

[29] Further, we would expect that if these languages have locative alternations, the material argument could incorporate when the location argument is expressed as a locative oblique, and the location argument could incorporate when the material argument is expressed as an instrumental oblique. Mohawk apparently does not have locative alternation verbs, but the prediction seems to be correct for Chukchee (Nedjalkov 1976: 206–209).

[30] (50) may also be ruled out by Selkirk's (1982) First Order Projection Condition. This problem would be solved if an N representing the theme were also included in the compound, but Sproat shows that this too is impossible, perhaps because of Case theory. The ideal example to make my point would be a verb like *patsa*, where the theme argument is optional; however, it is likely that there is no such verb in Chichewa.

[31] For example, they suggest that dative Case has at least two syntactic sources: it is assigned by a null preposition *to* to its complement (Emonds 1985), or it is a variant of accusative, checked in the specifier of Aspect Phrase. They may also point to instances of NP-movement that are not Case-driven.

[32] In a footnote, she also mentions Li's (1990) important study of V-V compounding in Chinese. In fact, I believe that Li's paper contains only one example that might show the goal to be higher than the theme: the compound *jiao-dong* "teach-understand", which means "x taught z to y so that y understood z." Since the y argument of "understand" is higher than the z argument, the same must be true of the y and z arguments of "teach", according to Li's principles. However, it is not clear that *teach* is really (always) an agent-theme-goal verb (see notes 14, 38). Li gives no similar examples with more canonical dative verbs like *give*, *send*, *ask*, or *bring*.

[33] However, Zushi (1992) gives interesting evidence that some source phrases – roughly those that imply the consent of the source – rank higher than themes in Japanese. Presumably this follows from the fact that such sources are exercising volition, and hence count as a kind of (secondary) agent.

[34] Specifically, Larson needs the RUTAH in order to maintain his view that adjuncts are innermost arguments, and because he projects theme NPs in adjoined positions in dative shift structures. I do not adopt either of these positions. On my view, the landing site of dative movement is Spec, AspP, not Spec, VP, so there is no competition with the theme for the Spec, VP position (see (24) and note 18).

[35] My judgments of *frighten*-class verbs with resultative AP predicates are mixed. Most freely formed expressions sound rather bad, as the theory predicts: **She was depressed, but the clown amused her happy*, **The loud noise frightened John dead*. However, certain semi-idiomatic expressions are perfect, as are some non-AP predicates: *The economic situation worried Mary sick*, *The loud noise frightened John to death*.

[36] Among them are: What kind of empty category is the ec in (69)? Does the stimulus subject form a chain with this empty category? (If so, then the chain has two thematic roles; if not, then the dependency should not count for binding purposes, given standard assumptions.) Why is dative shift obligatory with these verbs – even in Romance, where dative shift does not otherwise happen? A hint concerning this last question may come from Green's (1974) observation that dative shift is obligatory even with *give* when there is a stimulus subject and/or an abstract theme. Thus, one can say: *The loud noise gave Mary a scare*, but not *??The loud noise gave a scare to Mary.*

[37] Significantly, the feature of Mohawk that looks at first like it will give the easiest evidence for the Unaccusative Hypothesis – the split agreement pattern on intransitive verbs – turns out *not* to be an unaccusative diagnostic (Baker 1995b: ch. 5). I believe that the unreliability of this kind of superficial morphological evidence has contributed greatly to the impression of Rosen (1984) and others that unaccusativity involves a substantial degree of idiosyncrasy.

[38] The one semantically vacuous NP-PP alternation in English is dative shift. However, this is usually blocked when no theme is expressed: one has *I read to the children* but not *#I read the children*, *I baked for Mary* but not *#I baked Mary*. These facts are more consistent with the UTAH than the RUTAH, but missing is an account of why dative shift is barred here. One possibility is that the theme is present as some kind of empty category, and this must reach the specifier of Aspect Phrase position to be properly licensed. If so, then the goal cannot move to that position.

There are a few exceptions to this generalization, including *teach, pay, feed, serve, write*; thus, one can say *I taught the children* and *I fed the children*. In fact, when these verbs have no theme, the "goal" NP loses most of the syntactic properties associated with goal objects: for example, it can be in a derived nominal, an adjectival passive, or a synthetic compound (Wasow 1977). See also notes 14, 23, and 32. Note furthermore that some of these verbs in Romance languages alternate between having a dative argument and an accusative argument (Borer 1984, citing Eric Werli), even though the these languages do not have dative shift. Finally, it is probably significant that these verbs are morphologically causatives in many languages: "teach" is literally "cause-to-know", and "feed" is "cause-to-eat" (cf. Green (1974)). Put all together, these facts suggest that the animate argument of these verbs may be a theme when there is no other internal argument.

[39] In fact, Levin and Rappaport-Hovav's (1995) linking rules do not use thematic roles, either; their view is that thematic roles should be eliminated (or defined) in terms of Lexical Semantic Structures. However, their substantive linking rules can be interpreted thematically without too much difficulty. They are stated as follows:

(i) *Directed Change Linking Rule (DCLR):*
The argument of a verb that corresponds to the entity undergoing the directed change described by that verb is its direct internal argument.

(ii) *Existence Linking Rule (ELR):*
The argument of a verb whose existence is asserted or denied is its direct internal argument.

(iii) *Immediate Cause Linking Rule (ICLR):*
The argument of a verb that denotes the immediate cause of the eventuality described by that verb is its external argument.

(They also propose a default linking rule, omitted here.) The DCLR is very similar to the statement that themes are direct objects; it almost repeats the original Gruber-Jackendoff definition of what a theme is (with a slight refinement). Similarly, the ICLR generalizes the statement that agents are subjects to a somewhat broader range of causes. Finally, there seems to be no inherent barrier to collapsing the DCLR and the ELR into a single rule, given that they are unorderable, and the arguments of some verbs are redundantly classified as internal arguments by both.

[40] Other, more obvious ways of marking which argument is which are not available at LF in the Minimalist Program. For example, linear order is defined only at PF in Chomsky's system, while Case features are uninterpretable and must be eliminated before LF. The idea is that where these exist they are PF reflexes of a more fundamental phrase structure asymmetry. The kind of data reviewed in sections 2 and 3 seems to support this.

[41] An alternative, worth considering, is that the UTAH is built into the inner workings of Merge, the operation that builds phrase markers. Thus, Merge could stipulate that an argument combines with a phrase X only if it discharges the kind of theta role associated with X by the UTAH. As a theory of sentence production, this seems natural, but as a theory of basic linguistic competence it seems clumsy and stipulative compared to the view in which UTAH is a matter of how fully constructed LFs are interpreted by C-I.

[42] Larson himself considers the higher V to be a semantically null position, motivated by purely formal requirements of X-bar theory. However, these requirements become unstateable within the bare phrase structure theory. (See also Chomsky (1995) for other Minimalist problems with Larson's original proposal.)

[43] The idea works nicely for accomplishments in particular. It can be extended to activities, including unergatives, as explained below. The hard case is stative transitives, such as *see* or *like*. These are considered to have simple lexical-conceptual structures by many authors. I have been assuming that they can be included in the same theory if one uses a prototype approach and thematic rather than aspectual representations. Perhaps a lexical decomposition such as [x cause [y be represented visually/favorably (in x's mind)]] would be appropriate.

[44] Here I use "bare phrase structure" labels, with no bar levels. Also, functional categories are omitted here for simplicity, including the Aspect which would come between the two verbal projections in the case of a transitive or an unergative. A variant of this proposal would be to say that V2 can only be a state, not an event. Then (78c) would be the representation for (say) *John stinks*, and to get *John fell* one would embed V2 under a monadic V1 that meant BECOME, not CAUSE (Travis, in preparation). Related to this is the question of whether V1 and V2 are members of exactly the same syntactic category, which I leave open.

[45] This is adequate for true goals, which define the endpoint of an event, and hence its resulting state. Whether other kinds of paths can also be expressed purely in terms of resulting states is unclear. For example, is it adequate to express *John threw the ball towards the tree* as [John CAUSE [ball BE [closer to tree]]], or does one need [John CAUSE [ball GO [toward tree]]]? If the latter is required, then the text proposal must be generalized to include V2 operators such as the Jackendovian GO function in addition to simple BE.

[46] In work in progress, I explore the idea that the category adjective can be characterized crosslinguistically as an element that fills the X position in a representation like (79).

[47] I recognized the difference between these two slightly different usages because of discussion of the matter with Jim McGilvary, who I thank.

REFERENCES

Aissen, Judith (1987) *Tzotzil Clause Structure*. Reidel, Dordrecht.

Alsina, Alex and Sam Mchombo (1988) 'Lexical mapping in the Chichewa applicative construction', in *19th Annual African Linguistics Conference*. Boston University, 1988.

Anderson, Stephen (1976) 'On the notion of subject in ergative languages', in: Charles Li (ed.), *Subject and Topic*. Academic Press, New York, pp. 1–23.

Aoun, Joseph and Audrey Li (1989) 'Scope and constituency', *Linguistic Inquiry* **20**, 141–172.

Aoun, Joseph and Yen-hui Audrey Li (1993) *Syntax of Scope*. MIT Press, Cambridge, Mass.
Baker, Mark (1985) *Incorporation: A Theory of Grammatical Function Changing*. Ph.D. dissertation, MIT.
Baker, Mark (1988a) *Incorporation: A Theory of Grammatical Function Changing*. University of Chicago Press, Chicago.
Baker, Mark (1988b) 'Theta theory and the syntax of applicatives in Chichewa', *Natural Language and Linguistic Theory* **6**, 353–389.
Baker, Mark (1989) 'Object sharing and projection in serial verb constructions', *Linguistic Inquiry* **20**, 513–553.
Baker, Mark (1991) 'On some subject/object non-asymmetries in Mohawk', *Natural Language and Linguistic Theory* **9**, 537–576.
Baker, Mark (1992a) 'Thematic conditions on syntactic structures: Evidence from locative applicatives', in: I. M. Rocca (ed.), *Thematic Structure: Its Role in Grammar*. Foris, Berlin, pp. 23–46.
Baker, Mark (1992b) 'Unmatched chains and the representation of plural pronouns', *Natural Language Semantics* **1**, 33–72.
Baker, Mark (1992c) 'Why unaccusative verbs cannot dative-shift', in *NELS*. University of Massachusetts-Amherst, University of Ottawa.
Baker, Mark (1995a) 'On the structural positions of themes and goals', in: Johan Rooryck and Laurie Zauring (eds.), *Phrase Structure and the Lexicon*. Kluwer, Dordrecht, pp. 7–34.
Baker, Mark (1995b) *The Polysynthesis Parameter*. Oxford University Press, New York.
Baker, Mark, Kyle Johnson and Ian Roberts (1989) 'Passive arguments raised', *Linguistic Inquiry* **20**, 219–251.
Barss, Andrew (1986) *Chains and Anaphoric Dependence: On Reconstruction and Its Implications*. Ph.D. dissertation, MIT.
Barss, Andrew and Howard Lasnik (1986) 'A note on anaphora and double objects', *Linguistic Inquiry* **17**, 347–354.
Belletti, Adriana and Luigi Rizzi (1981) 'The syntax of ne: some theoretical implications', *The Linguistic Review* **1**, 117–154.
Belletti, Adriana and Luigi Rizzi (1988) 'Psych-verbs and θ-theory', *Natural Language and Linguistic Theory* **6**, 291–352.
Bittner, Maria (1994) *Case, Scope, and Binding*. Kluwer, Dordrecht.
Bittner, Maria and Kenneth Hale (1996) 'Ergativity: towards a theory of a heterogeneous class', *Linguistic Inquiry* **27**, 531–604.
Bok-Bennema, Reineke (1991) *Case and Agreement in Inuit*. Foris, Berlin.
Borer, Hagit (1984) *Parametric Syntax: Case Studies in Semitic and Romance Languages*. Foris, Dordrecht.
Borer, Hagit (1995) 'Passive without theta grids', ms., University of Massachusetts-Amherst.
Bresnan, Joan (1982) 'Control and complementation', in: Joan Bresnan (ed.), *The Mental Representation of Grammatical Relations*. MIT Press, Cambridge, Mass., pp. 282–390.
Bresnan, Joan and Joni Kanerva (1989) 'Locative inversion in Chichewa: A case study of factorization in grammar', *Linguistic Inquiry* **20**, 1–50.
Bresnan, Joan and Lioba Moshi (1990) 'Object asymmetries in comparative Bantu syntax', *Linguistic Inquiry* **21**, 147–185.
Burzio, Luigi (1986) *Italian syntax: A Government-Binding Approach*. Reidel, Dordrecht.
Campana, Mark (1992) *A Movement Theory of Ergativity*. Ph.D. dissertation, McGill University.
Chamorro, Adriana (1992) *On Free Word Order in Mohawk*. M.A. thesis, McGill University.
Chomsky, Noam (1970) 'Remarks on nominalization', in: R. Jacobs and P. Rosenbaum (eds.), *Readings in English Transformational Grammar*. Ginn, Waltham, Mass., pp. 184–221.

Chomsky, Noam (1981) *Lectures on Government and Binding*. Foris, Dordrecht.
Chomsky, Noam (1986) *Knowledge of Language: Its Nature, Origin, and Use*. Praeger, New York.
Chomsky, Noam (1993) 'A minimalist program for linguistic theory', in: Kenneth Hale and Samuel Jay Keyser (eds.), *The View from Building 20*. MIT Press, Cambridge, Mass., pp. 1–52.
Chomsky, Noam (1994) *Bare Phrase Structure*, ms., MIT.
Chomsky, Noam (1995) *The Minimalist Program*. MIT Press, Cambridge, Mass.
Chomsky, Noam and Howard Lasnik (1993) 'The theory of principles and parameters', in: Joachim Jacobs,Arnim von Stechow,Wolfgang Sternefeld, and Theo Vennemann (eds.), *Syntax: An International Handbook of Contemporary Research*. Walter de Gruyter, Berlin, 506–569.
Collins, Chris and Höskuldur Thráinsson (1996) 'Object shift in double object constructions and the theory of case', *Linguistic Inquiry* **27**, 391–444.
Comrie, Bernard (1982) 'Grammatical relations in Huichol', in: Paul Hopper and Sandra Thompson (eds.), *Syntax and Semantics 15: Studies in Transitivity*. Academic Press, New York, pp. 95–115.
Di Sciullo, Anna Maria and Edwin Williams (1987) *On the Definition of Word*. MIT Press, Cambridge, Mass.
Dixon, R. M. W. (1972) *The Dyirbal Language of North Queensland*. Cambridge University Press, Cambridge.
Dixon, R. M. W. (1979) 'Ergativity', *Language* **55**, 59–138.
Dixon, R. M. W. (1994) *Ergativity*. Cambridge University Press, Cambridge.
Dowty, David (1979) *Word Meaning and Montague Grammar*. Reidel, Dordrecht.
Dowty, David (1991) 'Thematic proto-roles and argument selection', *Language* **67**, 547–619.
Dryer, Matthew (1987) 'On primary objects, secondary objects, and antidative', *Language* **62**, 808–845.
Emonds, Joseph (1985) *A Unified Theory of Syntactic Categories*. Foris, Dordrecht.
Everaert, Martin (1990) 'NP-movement "across" secondary objects', in: Joan Mascaro and Marina Nespor (eds.), *Grammar in Progress*. Foris, Dordrecht, pp. 125–136.
Fillmore, Charles (1968) 'The case for Case', in: Emond Bach and R. T. Harms (eds.), *Universals in Linguistic Theory*. Holt, Rinehart, and Winston, New York, pp. 1–88.
Foley, William and Robert Van Valin (1984) *Functional Syntax and Universal Grammar*. Cambridge University Press, Cambridge.
Fraser, B. (1970) 'Some remarks on the action nominalization in English', in: R. Jacobs and P. Rosenbaum (eds.), *Readings in English Transformational Grammar*. Ginn, Waltham, Mass., pp. 83–98.
Georgopoulos, Carol (1987) 'Psych nouns', in: Joyce McDonough and Bernadette Plunkett (eds.), *Proceedings of NELS 17*. Graduate Linguistics Student Association, Amherst, Mass., pp. 211–231.
Green, Georgia (1974) *Semantics and Syntactic Regularity*. Indiana University Press, Bloomington, Ind.
Grimshaw, Jane (1990) *Argument Structure*. MIT Press, Cambridge, Mass.
Gropen, Jess, Steven Pinker, M. Hollander, R. Goldberg and R. Wilson (1989) 'The learnability and acquisition of the dative alternation', *Language* **65**, 203–257.
Guilfoyle, Eithne, Henrietta Hung and Lisa Travis (1992) 'Spec of IP and Spec of VP: Two subjects in Austronesian languages', *Natural Language and Linguistic Theory* **10**, 375–414.
Hale, Kenneth (1983) 'Warlpiri and the grammar of nonconfigurational languages', *Natural Language and Linguistic Theory* **1**, 5–49.
Hale, Kenneth and Samuel Jay Keyser (1993) 'On argument structure and the lexical expression of syntactic relations', in: Kenneth Hale and Samuel Jay Keyser (eds.), *The View from Building 20*. MIT Press, Cambridge, Mass., pp. 53–110.

Halle, Morris and Alec Marantz (1993) 'Distributed morphology and the pieces of inflection', in: Kenneth Hale and S. J. Keyser (eds.), *The View From Building 20*. MIT Press, Cambridge, Mass., pp. 111–176.

Hoji, H. (1985) *Logical Form Constraints and Configurational Structures in Japanese*. Ph.D. dissertation, University of Washington.

Hornstein, Norbert (1995) *Logical Form: From GB to Minimalism*. Blackwell, Oxford.

Jackendoff, Ray (1972) *Semantic Interpretation in Generative Grammar*. MIT Press, Cambridge, Mass.

Jackendoff, Ray (1983) *Semantics and Cognition*. MIT Press, Cambridge, Mass.

Jackendoff, Ray (1987) 'The status of thematic relations in linguistic theory', *Linguistic Inquiry* **18**, 369–412.

Jackendoff, Ray (1990a) 'On Larson's treatment of the double object construction', *Linguistic Inquiry* **21**, 427–455.

Jackendoff, Ray (1990b) *Semantic Structures*. MIT Press, Cambridge, Mass.

Jelinek, Eloise (1984) 'Empty categories, case, and configurationality', *Natural Language and Linguistic Theory* **2**, 39–76.

Johns, Alana (1984) 'Dative "movement" in Eskimo', in: D. Testen, V. Mishra and J. Drogo (eds.), *Papers from the Parasession on Lexical Semantics*. Chicago Linguistic Society, Chicago.

Johns, Alana (1992) 'Deriving ergativity', *Linguistic Inquiry* **23**, 57–88.

Kamp, Hans and Uwe Reyle (1993) *From Discourse to Logic*. Kluwer, Dordrecht.

Kayne, Richard (1984) *Connectedness and Binary Branching*. Foris, Dordrecht.

Kiparsky, Paul (1987) *Morphology and Grammatical Relations*, ms., Stanford University.

Larson, Richard (1988) 'On the double object construction', *Linguistic Inquiry* **19**, 335–392.

Larson, Richard (1990) 'Double objects revisited: A reply to Jackendoff', *Linguistic Inquiry* **21**, 589–632.

Levin, Beth (1983) *On the Nature of Ergativity*. Ph.D. dissertation, MIT.

Levin, Beth (1993) *English Verb Classes and Alternations*. University of Chicago Press, Chicago.

Levin, Beth and Malka Rappaport (1986) 'The formation of adjectival passives', *Linguistic Inquiry* **17**, 623–661.

Levin, Beth and Malka Rappaport-Hovav (1995) *Unaccusativity: At the Syntax-Lexical Semantics Interface*. MIT Press, Cambridge, Mass.

Li, Yafei (1990) 'On V-V compounds in Chinese', *Natural Language and Linguistic Theory* **8**, 177–208.

Machobane, Malillo (1989) *Some Restrictions on the Sesotho Transitivizing Morphemes*. Ph.D. dissertation, McGill University.

Mahajan, Anoop (1990) *The A/A' Distinction and Movement Theory*. Ph.D. dissertation, MIT, Cambridge, Mass.

Marantz, Alec (1984) *On the Nature of Grammatical Relations*. MIT Press, Cambridge, Mass.

McClure, William (1994) *Syntactic Projections of the Semantics of Aspect*. Ph.D. dissertation, Cornell University.

McKay, G. R (1975) *Rembarnga: A Language of Central Arnhem Land*. Ph.D. dissertation, Australian National University.

Mithun, Marianne (1984) 'How to avoid subordination', in *Berkeley Linguistics Society*, pp. 493–509. Berkeley Linguistics Society, Berkeley, 1984.

Miyagawa, S. (1989) *Syntax and Semantics 22: Structure and Case Marking in Japanese*. Academic Press, San Diego.

Murasugi, Kumiko (1992) *NP-movement and the Ergative Parameter*. Ph.D. dissertation, MIT.

Nakamura, Masanori (1993) 'An economy account of wh-extraction in Tagalog', in:

Proceedings of the West Coast Conference on Formal Linguistics, CSLI, Stanford, Calif., 1993.

Nedjalkov, V. P. (1976) 'Diathesen und satzstruktur im Tschuktschischen', in: Ronald Lötsch and Rudolf Ruzicka (eds.), *Satzstruktur und genus verbi*. Akademie Verlag, Berlin, pp. 181–211.

Oerhle, Richard (1975) *The Grammatical Status of the English Dative Alternation*. Ph.D. dissertation, MIT.

Perlmutter, David (1978) 'Impersonal passives and the Unaccusative Hypothesis', in *Papers from the Fifth Annual Meeting of The Berkeley Linguistics Society*. Berkeley Linguistics Society, Berkeley, Calif.

Pesetsky, David (1987) 'Binding problems with experiencer verbs', *Linguistic Inquiry* **18**, 126–140.

Pesetsky, David (1995) *Zero Syntax*. MIT Press, Cambridge, Mass.

Pinker, Stephen (1989) *Learnability and Cognition: The Acquisition of Argument Structure*. MIT Press, Cambridge, Mass.

Postal, Paul (1979) *Some Syntactic Rules of Mohawk*. Garland, New York.

Rappaport, Malka (1983) 'On the nature of derived nominals', in: Lori Levin, Malka Rappaport and Anne Zaenen (eds.), *Papers in Lexical Functional Grammar*. Indiana University Linguistics Club, Bloomington, Ind.

Rappaport, Malka and Beth Levin (1985) 'A case study in lexical analysis: The locative alternation', ms., MIT.

Rappaport, Malka and Beth Levin (1988) 'What to do with θ-roles', in: Wendy Wilkins (ed.), *Syntax and Semantics 21: Thematic Relations*. Academic Press, San Diego, Calif., pp. 7–36.

Roeper, Tom and M. E. A. Siegel (1978) 'A lexical transformation for verbal compounds', *Linguistic Inquiry* **9**, 199–260.

Rosen, Carol (1984) 'The interface between semantic roles and initial grammatical relations', in: David Perlmutter and Carol Rosen (eds.), *Studies in Relational Grammar 2*. University of Chicago Press, Chicago, pp. 38–80.

Saito, Mamoru (1985) *Some Asymmetries in Japanese and Their Theoretical Implications*. Ph.D. dissertation, MIT, Cambridge, Mass.

Saito, Mamoru (1992) 'Long distance scrambling in Japanese', *Journal of East Asian Linguistics* **1**, 69–118.

Selkirk, Elisabeth (1982) *The Syntax of Words*. MIT Press, Cambridge, Mass.

Simpson, Jane (1991) *Warlpiri Morpho-Syntax: A Lexicalist Approach*. Kluwer, Dordrecht.

Simpson, Jane and Joan Bresnan (1983) 'Control and obviation in Warlpiri', *Natural Language and Linguistic Theory* **1**, 49–64.

Speas, Margaret (1990) *Phrase Structure in Natural Language*. Kluwer, Dordrecht.

Sproat, Richard (1985) *On Deriving the Lexicon*. Ph.D dissertation, MIT.

Stowell, Timothy (1981) *Origins of Phrase Structure*. Ph.D. dissertation, MIT.

Talmy, Leonard (1985) 'Lexicalization patterns', in: Timothy Shopen (ed.), *Language Typology and Syntactic Description*. Cambridge University Press, Cambridge, pp. 57–149.

Tenny, Carol (1987) *Grammaticalizing Aspect and Affectedness*. Ph.D. dissertation, MIT, Cambridge, Mass.

Tenny, Carol (1994) *Aspectual Roles and the Syntax-Semantics Interface*. Kluwer, Dordrecht.

Travis, Lisa (1991) 'Inner aspect and the structure of VP', in *NELS 22*. Newark, Delaware, 1991.

Van Valin, Robert (1987) 'The Unaccusative Hypothesis versus lexical semantics: syntactic vs semantic approaches to verb classification', in: Joyce McDonough and Bernadette Plunkett (eds.), *Proceedings of NELS*. University of Massachusetts, Amherst, GSLA, pp. 641–662.

Van Valin, Robert (1990) 'Semantic parameters of split intransitivity', *Language* **66**, 221–260.

Wasow, Thomas (1977) 'Transformations and the Lexicon', in: Peter Culicover, Thomas Wasow and Adrian Akmajian (eds.), *Formal Syntax*. Academic Press, New York, pp. 327–360.

Webelhuth, Gert (1992) *Principles and Parameters of Syntactic Saturation*. Oxford University Press, New York.

Williams, Edwin (1980) 'Predication', *Linguistic Inquiry* **11**, 203–238.

Zaenen, Anne (1993) 'Unaccusativity in Dutch: integrating syntax and lexical semantics', in: James Pustejovsky (ed.), *Semantics and the Lexicon*. Kluwer, Dordrecht, pp. 129–161.

Zushi, Mihoko (1992) 'The syntax of dative constructions in Japanese', ms., McGill University.

MICHAEL BRODY

PERFECT CHAINS

1. TOWARDS PERFECT SYNTAX

1.1. *Duplications, Conditions on Chains, Economy*

In the Principles and Parameters theory representational conditions on various levels carried most of the burden of restricting syntax. In the minimalist framework representational conditions will only hold at interface levels, the only levels that exist. Let us assume the strong version of the minimalist hypothesis according to which syntactic interface conditions are "bare output conditions", that is conditions forced on syntax by the interpretive systems that are fed by the syntactic computations. Suppose furthermore that most of the effects of representational conditions of the Principles and Parameters theory turn out to be the effects of either bare output conditions or of conditions holding within the syntax-external systems. If so, then we may expect the syntactic computation, whose task is to assemble interface representations from a set of lexical items, to be near-trivial.

In any case the syntactic system may turn out to be significantly more trivial than in standard minimalist theories. One area where simplification is achievable is the derivational duplication of representational concepts. A central case is the independently motivated interface notion of Chain which captures the same relations as the derivational rule of Move, making the latter redundant and in fact untenable in a restrictive system. Notice that eliminating Move in favor of Chain does not necessarily make the theory strictly non-derivational: see the one step derivational theory of Brody (1995a,b). (This is not to say, however, that it would not be possible to construe this theory in a strictly representational fashion.) Eliminating Move will however necessarily make the architecture of the mapping system between lexical items and the two interfaces radically simpler: since there are no intermediate structures between the lexical input and the semantic interface, this level has to serve as the input to the SPELLOUT component. There is therefore only a single syntactic interface level, say the level of Lexico-logical Form (LLF) of Brody (1993a, 1995a), which is the input to both semantic interpretation and the SPELLOUT component.

There are various other related distinctions and duplications that seem equally dubious. For example, Chomsky (1995) proposes a representational definition in addition to the derivational system of interface assembly (in effect an additional definition) of what counts as a well-formed syntactic

Liliane Haegeman (ed.), Elements of Grammar, 139–167.

object (cf. Brody 1995b for some discussion). Or take the additional distinction he makes between deletion (interface invisibility only) and erasure (essentially invisibility also for Move), where erasure occurs only if this would not violate the representational duplicate definition of well-formed syntactic object. Such duplications, and distinctions that build on these duplications, should have no place in a restrictive system of syntax.

Another area where we might expect the system of interface assembly to be radically simplified has to do with economy conditions. Strong empirical argument is necessary to motivate the undesirable complication of the system of assembly which would make it powerful enough to compare derivations – especially in view of the attendant computational complexity. It does not seem unreasonable to think that economy conditions will be eliminable without the introduction of any additional apparatus. More recent versions of economy conditions that "compare locally" seem to represent no major improvement in computational complexity. Suppose that at any stage in the derivation only the possible continuations of the derivation already constructed are compared. But clearly, for any comparison of full derivations we can construct an equally complex comparison of "continuations", simply by embedding the appropriate structure. Notice that in order for the comparison to be meaningful, it cannot be restricted to look only at a single step in the relevant derivations. The derivations in which a step or a series of steps will be compared must all be carried out fully, if only to check that they converge, given the assumption – an inevitable one as Chomsky (1995) explains – that economy conditions select only among converging derivations.

A third set of concepts and conditions that should have no place syntax-internally in a restrictive system of interface assembly pertain to the Chain/Move relation. Assuming that the relation is part of syntax proper, various conditions specific to this relation, like Uniformity, c-command, Last Resort, Minimal Chain Link and Procrastinate, should still be attributable to the syntax external systems (either as matters internal to the interpretive components or as properties imposed by these on syntax, i.e. bare output conditions) or should be eliminable in some other way. Uniformity was discussed in this light in Brody (1995b), treatment of the other minimalist conditions on Chain/Move is the main subject of the present paper.

1.2. *Interactions with The Interpretive Components*

In Brody (1995a,b) I proposed an interface assembly system based on the notions of copy and immediate domination that complies with these restrictions. I used the term perfect syntax to refer to the theory that postulated such a near-trivial assembly system. There are two additional general constraints related to the interaction of the assembly system with the interpretive components that the standard minimalist framework does not incorporate, but we might expect perfect syntax to meet. One of these has to do with the nature of the interaction between syntax and the interpretive systems. In the standard minimalist framework it is suggested that imperfections in syntax may be due to the effect of the interpretive components. Bare output conditions will be satisfied optimally, but this may necessitate departures from perfection. In particular it is often suggested that the fact that syntax has the Chain/Move relation is an imperfection due to output conditions. Chomsky (1995) contains also the further suggestion that the optimal operation of Move is covert (feature-movement only) and overt movement of categories is again due to interpretive (PF) pressures. These pressures could have to do for example with strong checking features holding at PF (although this assumption is rejected in Chomsky 1995) or with the necessity of moved features pied piping full constituents to avoid PF crash.

The idea that the components interacting with syntax force additional imperfect operations on this system seems to raise problems. Without further assumptions, whose nature seems unclear, for the external systems to cause the addition of imperfect operations to syntax it is necessary that perfection in syntax and the demands of the external system be in conflict. But it seems difficult to think of a case where the external demands could not be met in some alternative way without sacrificing perfection. If so, then given usual methodology, we would expect the system to choose the more perfect option. To look at the actual proposals concerning Move, consider the hypothesis that the existence of this operation is forced by the bare output condition of full interpretation. This requires certain features to be checked at LF by features of lexical items generated elsewhere. But if Move is an imperfection, there are in principle many ways in which it could be avoided without violating full interpretation. For example, the checking features could freely delete or they could be generated in a position that is accessible to the lexical item without movement etc. It is not easy to see why all the alternative options should be in principle unavailable.

(Notice incidentally that the proposal that Move is forced by bare output conditions interacts only with some redundancy with Chomsky's (1995) assumption that strong features are intolerable in the derivation. Given the additional distinction between +/– Interpretable checking features, Move will sometimes be forced by full interpretation (to eliminate weak non-interpretable features of hosts) and sometimes by both derivation-technological reasons and full interpretation (to eliminate strong non-interpretable features and (non-interpretable) "strength" of interpretable features). See below in sections 2 and 4 for related discussion.)

Similar comments apply to the question of overt Move. If overtness of Move is an imperfection and the optimal way of satisfying the constraints requiring movement is covert feature-movement, then overt movement of categories within the mapping between lexical items and (L)LF could be avoided for example by eliminating strong features, or by restricting overt movement to the SPELLOUT component. (See Brody 1995b for evidence that this latter possibility is not what actually happens.) Many other options are imaginable, which seem extremely difficult to rule out on principled grounds.

Let us avoid such problems and assume that the syntax-external components cannot force imperfect additions to syntax. This is then the first general condition promised above, related to the interaction of syntax with the interpretive systems. Returning to the concrete case of Chain/Move, this is simply an instance of the copy relation. It is not necessary to take this relation to be an imperfection, indeed within the assembly system of Brody (1995b) this would not even be possible. In this theory the copy relation is involved also in categorial projection and is the only basic concept apart from the hierarchical notion of immediate domination. As for chains corresponding to "overt movement" of a full category, again this is simply the copy relation, where only the highest copy is visible for the SPELLOUT component. In the case of "expletive-associate" (Brody 1993a, 1995a) or "feature-movement" (Chomsky 1995) chains, the copy relation is not between full lexical items, but between features. See Brody (1995a,b) for some discussion of why it may not be correct to eliminate syntax internally the distinction between chains where the copy relation is between full lexical items and chains where it is between features, by treating "covert movement" relations as full copies with a lower SPELLOUT position.

Given the distinction between feature copy chains and full category copy chains, it is possible to view one of the two instances of the relation as an imperfect version of the other. For example, in the spirit of Earliness (Pesetsky 1989) or Transparency (Brody 1995a), we might take the full categorial copy to be the default operation, and consider copying a proper subset of features as a degenerate case, that occurs only where full category copy chains are not licensed by the relevant checking features. Such an assumption would still disallow the addition of imperfect syntactic properties or relations but it would countenance a special type of syntactic imperfection: the imperfect instantiation of a perfect syntactic relation, namely the copy relation.

It would clearly be better, however, to avoid even this limited kind of imperfection. Instead of viewing one of the two chain-types as an imperfect version of the other, we could assume, in the spirit of the elsewhere principle (cf. especially Williams 1995), that category copy chains, which involve more fully specified copies, take precedence over feature copy chains. Category copy chains will then block feature copy chains whenever the (strong) checking heads license the category copies.

Suppose further that the option of copying a full category is conditioned by the morphological properties of the head with which the copy will establish a checking relation. A head may or may not license a full category in its checking domain. In fact it seems necessary to distinguish heads that license a full category word (X^0)-internally, hence in principle license an "overt" X^0-chain and heads that license a full category in their word-external checking domain, hence in principle allow "overt" XP-chains. (Further, unless multiple checking of the same feature, as for example in multiple overt *wh*-movement languages, is only apparent and can be treated in some alternative way, we may in fact have to have three choices both word internally and word-externally: a head licensing zero, one or multiple full categories.)

Licensing a full category in the checking domain is, I assume, a matter of morphology, internal to the SPELLOUT component. When the relevant head is "weak" with respect to a position in the checking domain and does not license a full category there, then only a "feature movement" chain can surface. In such a case a full categorial copy chain could not be expressed by the morphology. Notice that this view not only displaces the strong/weak distinction from the syntactic component, it also eliminates the distinction, in the sense of collapsing it with an independently necessary parameter which determines the number of categorial specifiers (more precisely categories in the checking domain) of a given functional head.

I argued so far for the assumption that the interpretive components cannot directly influence the nature of the syntactic computation, although they can filter its output. In this respect the semantic/conceptual and the SPELLOUT component behave similarly. There is however also a conspicuous difference between them: syntactic elements are generally identical to elements to which the semantic/conceptual system needs to refer. Suppose that the discussion of the strong/weak distinction above is on the right track and "strength", ie. the licensing of the "categoriality" of checking relations does not take place syntax internally. Then little reason remains to assume that syntax ever needs to make use of elements or features that have only morpho-phonological but no semantic/conceptual interpretation. This leads directly to the second general constraint pertaining to the interaction of syntax with the interpretive components. The perfect (L)LF assembly system should be constructed using only elements that the semantic/conceptual interpretive system provides. This condition, which I shall refer to as radical interpretability, is natural, and I will give some indication below that it may be tenable empirically.

Radical interpretability is related to the condition that requires syntactic representations not to contain non-interpretable features (or features without "effect" on the interpretive components) – call this interpretability. But the requirement that all features in a given structure must have either semantic or morpho-phonological content is not only weaker but may also be stronger in one respect than radical interpretability. In contrast to interpretability, radical interpretability requires all syntactic elements to be semantically interpretable, but not necessarily actually interpreted in a given structure. The latter requirement may be too strong. As just noted, in perfect syntax there can be no distinction between interface invisibility and invisibility for the computational system. But the stronger construal of radical interpretability would rule out even the concept of interface invisibility which may be necessary for checking theory. It will be crucial for the theory of checking to be presented in section 4 below, that in a checking configuration merger of checker and checked feature result in a single feature for interpretive purposes. Checking will thus presumably have to make either the checker or the checkee, or both (creating a new composite feature), invisible.

Although there seems to be no difficulty in taking the existence of the copy relation as such not to be a departure from perfection, as noted earlier the minimalist framework assumes several a priori unexpected conditions on this relation, which clearly could not be part of the perfect assembly system. In what follows I will argue that those conditons on Chain/Move that do not dissolve on closer examination should be thought of as either constraints on the interpretive components or as bare output conditions. In the next section I shall start with the c-command and the cyclic properties of Move. After critically examining two approaches in the standard minimalist framework to eliminating these stipulations (sections 2.1 and 2.2), I shall turn to an improved analysis that is made possible by the assumptions of perfect syntax (section 2.3). Section 3 will discuss the MLC and section 4 looks at checking theory.

2. STRONG FEATURES, C-COMMAND AND THE CYCLE

2.1. *Weak vs Strong Checking Features*

In earlier versions of the minimalist framework it was assumed that weak checking features have to be checked by a moved element by LF and strong features by PF. This ensured that both weak and strong checking features forced movement to occur and strong features furthermore forced movement to occur overtly. Chomsky (1995) makes somewhat different assumptions about strong features. He argues that strong features not only force overt movement, they also ensure the cyclicity of this operation. He suggests that strong features once Merged must be checked/eliminated "quickly" by Move or Merge. "Quickly" is defined essentially as in (1):

(1) The derivation terminates if an element H with a strong feature is in a category not headed by H

(1) entails the cycle for overt movement. Movement targeting a position in a given phrase P (and checking a strong feature of its head H there) must now precede movement targeting a higher position outside P. This is because a P-external position will necessarily be in a phrase not headed

by H. Hence the strong feature of H will have survived in a phrase not headed by H, contrary to (1). (1) also ensures a form of c-command (m-command) for overt movement between the moved category and its trace. In order to overtly move α to a position that is not in the minimal domain of the head of a phrase that dominates α, to let α check a strong feature there, a structure must have been built which violates (1).

These appear to be welcome consequences: if possible we clearly do not wish to stipulate either c-command (which is only one of infinitely many possible structural relations) or the cyclic property for Move. This approach to the cycle and to c-command however does not seem promising for three reasons. First (1) appears to lack genuine independent motivation. Secondly its explanation, to be discussed below, is untenable and therefore (1) remains stipulative. Thirdly (1) would not be general enough. I shall take these points one by one, starting with the question of independent motivation. This involves mainly the question of strong features forcing overt movement.

Given the assumption that strong features cannot be inserted covertly, which Chomsky takes to be the consequence of wider considerations, (1) is taken to entail that strong features force overt movement, since the strong feature on a head H must be eliminated before the phrase H projected is merged with some other element. But covert movement will occur only after the whole structure has been assembled (after the SPELLOUT point). One problem here is that if H is the highest head in the tree then the theory predicts that its strong feature, introduced overtly, can be checked covertly. This is incorrect: a strong +wh feature on the root C for example cannot be satisfied by covert Move.

Notice that given Chomsky's (1995) assumption that strong features can only be satisfied by categories (section 2.1, p. 11), the strong +wh feature on the root C would force movement of a category rather than a feature, whether it is satisfied overtly or covertly. (The PF pied-piping theory of overt movement includes a least effort type assumption that entails that covert movement does not involve categories (section 4.4). But the least effort assumption is not strong enough to rule out category movement in this case since it requires nothing more than features to move, only when movement of nothing more is forced. Here movement of a category is forced by the strong feature under the assumption that strong features can only be satisfied by categories.)

Note also that in any case the conjunction of the assumption that strong features can only be satisfied by categories with the PF pied-piping theory creates a redundancy. The fact that overt movement must involve categories is now entailed by both, suggesting that at least one of the two ideas should be modified. Suppose we reject the PF pied-piping theory (see Brody 1995b for arguments) and assume for the sake of argument that strong features must be satisfied by categories, whereas weak ones can also be satisfied by features. This should suffice then as a strong/weak distinction, there should be no need to duplicate this in terms of a derivational property of quick elimination of the feature. The distinction does suffice in a theory where (L)LF is the input to SPELLOUT, and therefore the question of invisible (covert) movement of categories does not arise. (Recall that for reasons not strictly relevant to the discussion of (1), I suggested a somewhat different theory of the strong/weak distinction in section 1 above: strong but not weak features license categories in the checking domain, and strong features cannot be satisfied by features due to blocking.)

The direct empirical evidence for (1) is that it might allow adjuncts to intervene between the two elements of the checking relation as e.g. in (2). If adjunction does not close off a projection, then the strong feature of the inflectional head can be checked by the subject, still within the projection of this head. The dubious status of adjunction configurations in general (e.g. Chomsky 1995, Brody 1994, 1995b), and in the particular case of adverbials (Cinque 1995), weakens this point considerably. If such adjuncts are heads or specifiers, then the argument will not go through.

(2) John probably has left already

The result is quite questionable also on directly empirical grounds: many clear cases of checking configurations require adjacency that does not tolerate intervening adverbials, for example wh-checking in English or in Hungarian:

(3) a. Who (*suddenly) did Bill discover

b. Kit (*tegnap) latott Mari
Who+acc yesterday saw Mary

Let us next look at the question of whether (1) can be attributed to some more general consideration. In Chomsky (1995) it is claimed that (1) follows from (4), where (4) itself is claimed to be a consequence of other considerations.

(4) Nothing can join to a non-projecting category

"Non-projecting" here cannot mean a category C that is embedded in some phrase not headed by C. This is because in the standard minimalist framework under this interpretation (4) would exclude covert movement. Could "non-projecting" in (4) mean a category that does not project as a result of the joining operation, i.e. could (4) express an extension of the generalization that it is always the target of Move that projects (cf. Chomsky 1994, 1995, Brody 1995a,b for different approaches to this principle)? But this reading is irrelevant since the requirement that the target projects does not entail (1). If Move lands in an embedded position, its target could still in principle project.

It appears that we must choose the first reading of (4) and in order to distinguish weak and strong features we need to restrict it to overt movement:

(5) Nothing can overtly join to a non-projecting category

But although (5) does not refer to feature strength, it is just as much a stipulation as (1). It is simply a statement of the overt cycle which (1) therefore failed to explain.

Let us turn to the third set of problems with the explanation of the cycle and the c-command property of Move in (1): even if the principle was otherwise tenable, it would not be general enough. (1) stipulates that overt movement is cyclic. How about Merge? As Chomsky notes, "it applies at the root only". Embedded Merge would be more complex than at the root. "Any such complication (which could be quite serious) would require strong empirical motivation" (Ch. 4.3, p. 11). Of course this does not entail the extension requirement for Merge, the remark just explains why a theory that entails it would be desirable. (A problem for the standard minimalist theory is that the same consideration applies to any embedded operation, overt or covert. Thus it applies also to covert object shift which is allowed in the standard minimalist framework.)

Thus in the theory based on (1), the c-command property of Move and the cycle are ensured only partially, and by a conspiracy of stipulations. (1) entails the cyclicity of overt Move, the stipulation in (5) would entail the extension requirement for overt Merge – further conditions will be necessary to rule out covert countercyclic Move and covert Move to non c-commanding positions. If overt embedded Merge is taken to be ruled out for the same reason as overt embedded Move (as in (5)), then still further stipulations are necessary to rule out covert embedded Merge. (Recall that Uniformity entails that covert Merge is available in principle.)

Chomsky also appears to note that the explanation of cyclicity and c-command based on (1) is not a full solution. He observes that "it would be interesting to strengthen [the] conclusion: to show . . . that overt targeting of an embedded category (hence lowering and non-cyclic raising) is not possible, hence *a fortiori* not necessary" (section 4.1, p. 16). But the remark seems to me to somewhat misstate the issue which does not have to do with the modality of the restriction but with its generality.

2.2. *C-command by Merge*

Crediting Kawashima and Kitahara (1994) and Eric Groat (p.c.), Chomsky briefly sketches a more general solution to the problems of cyclicity and c-command. This is based on the theory of Epstein (1994) where

(6) "C-command is just the relation that holds between α and elements of β when α is attached to β by Merge or Move" (section 4.1, p. 16)

Hence an embedded operation that attaches α to β will establish no c-command relation between elements in the tree higher than β and α. Given the further assumptions that all terminals must be ordered at PF and that terminals are ordered at PF only by c-command relations holding between them (or between categories dominating them) at LF (Kayne 1995), such embedded operations will be prohibited in the overt syntax. They would result in terminals preceding β and those dominated by α being unordered. Thus overt Merge and Move must be cyclic. Similarly overt Move to a non c-commanding position, whether lowering or "sideways" (i.e. where no c-command relation is established between α and its trace), is prohibited.

Again, there are a number of problems with this solution. First, the assumption that LF c-command determines PF precedence establishes an LF–PF link that might cause a PF crash. But this conflicts with what seems to be the optimal assumption, that within core grammar there are no such LF–PF interactions. (Cf: "We thus adopt the (non-obvious) hypothesis that there are no PF–LF interactions relevant to convergence . . ." (section 1, p. 1).)

Secondly, since traces need not be ordered at PF (cf. Chomsky 1995, section 8), all improper overt operations will still be allowed as long as they are followed by cyclic raising. For example, lowering (from P) followed by raising (to P′, not lower than P) is still allowed:

(7) * $[_{IP}$ John $[_{VP}$ t believed $[_{IP}$ t to have arrived a man yesterday]]]
P′ P

(8) * $[_{IP}$ Who $[_{VP}$ t wondered [t +WH [Mary left]]]]
P′ P

In (7) *John* lowered from its thematic VP-spec position into the non-thematic spec-IP position of the embedded clause. It cannot remain here since no c-command relation would hold between itself and, say, the matrix verb *believe*. If it subsequently cyclically moves to the matrix spec-IP, then no PF violation remains: *John* c-commands the rest of the sentence and its traces, invisible at PF need not be ordered. The same problem is raised by the "round trip" A′-movement derivation in (8). While one might think of various ways of ruling out such derivations, it is clear that the c-command and the cyclicity properties of overt Move do not follow fully from the approach under consideration.

There are further problems of coverage, echoing the shortcomings of the strong feature theory of cyclicity and c-command considered above. This theory allows countercyclic covert Move (like object shift) since covert operations do not feed PF, hence they need not establish a c-command based full ordering. But this means that the theory does not extend to any covert operation: countercyclic covert Merge, covert lowering and covert "sideways" Move will also be incorrectly allowed.

2.3. *The Cycle and C-command in Perfect Syntax*

As a first step, observe that the problems with the solution based on c-command ordering can be largely remedied on the assumption that elements of LF rather than of PF representations are ordered by this relation. This assumption immediately eliminates the problem of linking LF and PF representations: no such link is necessary. Since traces are represented as visible copies at LF, the possibility of saving an illegitimate operation of Move which lands in a non c-commanding position or applies countercyclically by a later legitimate application disappears. The traces/copies also must be ordered at LF, hence the possibility of making an illegitimate operation avoid exclusion by turning the element in the landing position into an invisible trace ceases to exist. Furthermore, if all elements must be ordered by LF c-command then all Move and Merge operations (overt or covert) will now have to be cyclic and all applications of Move (overt or covert) will have to target a c-commanding position. Thus the problems relating to the covert applications of these rules disappear also.

A salient consequence of assuming Epstein's definition of c-command and stating the ordering requirement of Kayne's Linear Correspondence Axiom at LF is that there will be only a single cycle in the derivation of LF. This should not be problematic if covert Move does not affect PF material. That "covert Move" relations do not affect the placement of the category and its phonology anywhere in syntax was argued in Brody (1993a, 1995a), see also Chomsky (1995), Brody (1995b). Of course the assumption makes it also unnecessary to consider the SPELLOUT point in the syntactic derivation to be different from LF.

The assembly system of Brody (1995a,b) which satisfies the strictures of perfect syntax is not cyclic: the elements of the input list (a concept related to the notion of numeration) are joined simultaneously in one step. The cycle is incompatible with the requirement that the syntactic derivation create no intermediate structures between the input list and the interface level LF (Brody 1995a). But the question of how to ensure the cycle may be a pseudo-issue if the cycle in fact is unnecessary. Cyclic effects can be noticed only where the application of some constraint can be illegitimately avoided by a noncyclic derivation. But if the constraints in question in fact apply to or beyond the syntactic output representation (the expected case in perfect syntax, where they will be constraints on the interpretive components or bare output conditions) then it will generally be impossible to avoid them through changing the derivational history.

A typical case is the late insertion of intervener type cycle violations for the minimal link condition (MLC). But if the MLC (or any other condition with the relevant effect) applies to the fully formed LF representation (cf. section 3 below), then the derivational history of the structure will be irrelevant: the effect of the MLC cannot be avoided at LF where the intervening elements are necessarily present. In (9) for example the intervening subject *it* will necessarily occur between *John* and its trace at LF.

(9) *John seems it is certain t to go

(10) *Who were [pictures of t] bought [pictures of t]

Similarly, the subject island violation of (10) cannot be voided by first applying *wh*-movement and then passive if the presence of a subject-internal trace is determined on the basis of the output representation.

Thus no cycle should be necessary in perfect syntax given the general architecture of the theory, where constraints apply to the output of the assembly system. There will be then nothing to explain: the optimal case. The question of excluding lowering operations may similarly turn out to be a pseudo-issue due to the minimalist duplication of the concept of Chain by Move. In perfect syntax lowering and raising cannot be distinguished: chains are neutral with respect to this dimension. Again the situation is optimal: the theory is designed in such a way that there is nothing to explain. (The question of hierarchical directionality does arise in the treatment of the Generalized Projection Principle, but this is demonstrably a matter for the interpretive component since this principle constrains also nonsyntactic features. Cf. Brody 1995a,b.)

All that remains then is the question of chains connecting positions that are not related by c-command. One possibility would be to exclude such chains by adopting a version of the Epsteinian solution to the assembly system of perfect syntax. We could require that there must be a syntactic relation at LF between the members of a given chain and assume that the only syntactic relation that exists is the one created by the operation of Insert (cf. Brody 1995a,b). Thus c-command is just the relation that holds between α and elements of β on one hand and (irrelevantly for the present problem) the head of β and elements of α (including α) on the other, when the operation Insert joins α and β by making β immediately dominate α. Alternatively, if ellipsis involves chains, as suggested by Chomsky (1995), then chains whose members are not in a c-command relation in fact exist. The question then shifts to differentiating ellipsis chains from others in terms of c-command – presumably a problem in the interpretive component and not in the assembly system.

This raises a different though related issue of whether all relations involving c-command reduce to the chain relation or whether the interpretive component will need to refer additionally to c-command. I will not attempt here to go beyond noting the issue. Thus one possibility is to resurrect the early Principles and Parameters theory view that the c-command requirement on chains is due to the anaphoric nature of traces/non-head elements (copies) of chains. Then chain-members are not forced to be in a c-command relation by syntax, and the interpretive system has access to this relation. On the other hand the obvious counter-example of anaphora to the alternative hypothesis, according to which all c-command relations reduce to chain-relations can be fairly straightforwardly accommodated. Thus ordinary anaphors have been treated as involving a chain/move relation, while bound (variable) anaphora, a less plausible candidate for a chain analysis, has been argued to require precedence rather than c-command (Williams 1994, Brody 1994, see also Hornstein 1994 for a contrary view and some discussion in section 3 below).

3. THE MINIMAL LINK CONDITION (MLC) AND COVERT A′-CHAINS

The MLC in Chomsky (1995) restricts elements moving to a given target K to the closest one among those that have the property that they can enter into a checking relation with K. This version of the MLC covers cases like superraising (11b), superiority (12b) and *wh*-island violations (13b).

(11) a.**It seems t(it) is certain John to meet Mary
b.**John seems it is certain t(John) to meet Mary

(12) a. Who t(who) saw what
b.?*What who saw t(what)

(13) a. * Who did you wonder [$_{CP}$ t(who) [$_{IP}$ t(who) gave this book to whom]]
b. ? To whom did you wonder who gave this book t(to whom)

The MLC does not allow these derivations since in each case there is a nearer element to the target of movement that has appropriate checking features. In (11b) this is the expletive subject *it*, in (12b) and (13b) the *wh*-phrase *who* in subject and spec-CP position respectively. The MLC would therefore allow the derivations in the a. examples in (11) through (13). Such a derivation happens to give a grammatical result in (12), but crashes in (11) and (13). Chomsky points out that under such a formulation the MLC could not be an economy condition: if crashing derivations could block a converging one then presumably no operation would ever take place. So he takes the MLC to be part of the definition of Move.

The restrictive assembly system of perfect syntax aims to avoid both economy conditions and stipulated conditions on chains/movement like the MLC. There are also empirical reasons for questioning the generalization the MLC expresses. Superraising, Superiority, *Wh*-island violations appear to have very different (un)grammaticality status, raising initial doubts about a principle that treats them uniformly. Judgements range from the completely hopeless superraising case through the intermediate superiority effects to the only mildly deviant and sometimes fully grammatical *wh*-island violations. As is well known, the *wh*-island cases improve probably to full grammaticality with infinitival complements, as for example in (14). Since the MLC cannot be made sensitive to the presence or absence of tense in any obvious way, it will rule out also such cases.

(14) Which crimes does the FBI know how to solve

Another problem with the MLC is that it is not compatible with covert A′-movement: covert A′-movement of *wh-in-situ* and similar elements would regularly violate the MLC, as exemplified in (15) where the *wh-in-situ* should be understood with matrix scope.

(15) Who wondered who t bought what

Chomsky (1994, 1995) assumes that A′-movement can take place only in the overt derivation, but it is not clear why A- and A′-movement/chains should differ in this way. Furthermore the assumption makes some of the standard evidence for covert A′-movement/chains puzzling. *In-situ* neg-phrases are sensitive to complement non-complement divide as was first observed by Kayne (1981) (see also Jaeggli 1981, Rizzi 1982, Longobardi 1991 for the same effects in other Romance languages). This is parallel to overt A′- chains as exemplified in (16) and (17)

(16) a. Who did you say that Mary saw
b. *Who did you say that saw Mary

(17) a. Jean n'exige que Pierre voit personne
J not requires that P has seen no one

b. *Jean n'exige que Pierre soit arrêté
J not requires that P be arrested

Or as argued first by Longobardi, the relation between the *in-situ* neg-phrase and its scope (marked by *non*) shows subjacency effects:

(18) Complex NP Constraint
* Non approverei la tua proposta di vedere nessuno
"I would not approve of your proposal of seeing anybody"

(19) Sentential Subject Condition:
?* Chiamare nessuno sarà possible
"To call no one will be possible"

(20) Adjunct Condition:
a. *Non fa il suo dovere per aiutare nessuno
"He does not do his duty in order to help anyone"

b. *Per ottenere nulla ha fatto il suo dovere
"In order to obtain nothing has he done his duty"

As observed by Watanabe (1991), *wh-in-situ* in Japanese type languages also has properties that parallel those of overt movement/chains. (21) is an example, where the *wh-in-situ* within the *wh*-island creates a degraded grammaticality status:

(21) ??John-wa [Mary-ga nani-o katta [ka dooka]] Tom-ni
top nom what-acc bought whether dat

tazuneta no
asked Q

"What did John ask Tom whether Mary bought t?"

Hornstein (1994), who assumes the MLC and rejects covert A′-movement, attempts to neutralize Longobardi's examples by assuming that they involve A-movement. This does not appear to lead to an easily tenable position however for two reasons. First, as Longobardi made clear, the relation has typical A′-chain locality properties, in particular it can escape from embedded tensed clauses:

(22) Non approverei che tu gli consentissi di vedere nessuno
"I would not approve that you allow him to see anybody"

Secondly, as (21) shows, covert *wh*-relations show similar effects. But *wh*-chains are prototypical A′-relations.

A different theory that would neutralize the evidence of the examples in (18) through (21) might claim that all syntactic A′-movement is subject to the MLC and that syntactic A′-movement occurs only to satisfy some checking feature of a +wh/+Neg head. This point is neutral with respect to whether the movement of the *in-situ* neg-phrase in (18)–(20) and the *wh*-phrase in (21) involves overt movement (of, say, an empty operator as in Watanabe 1991) or covertly (say, as movement of formal features, as in Chomsky 1995). The crucial distinction would be between *in-situ* elements that need to move to satisfy some checking feature and *in-situ* elements that do not have similar motivation to move. The two groups correspond to the primary and the secondary or parasitic wh/neg-chains respectively of Brody (1995a). The *wh-in-situ* not constrained by the MLC in (15) would belong to the group of secondary relations, while the *in-situ* elements exhibiting movement characteristics in (18) through (21) would be primary ones. Could it be claimed then that only primary relations involve syntactic movement/chains, and hence only these show movement/ chain characteristics including the MLC?

Such a claim would be incompatible with the checking theory to be discussed in section 4 below, in which no distinction can be made between primary and secondary chains with respect to their behavior in checking relations. There is also direct empirical evidence that appears to show that the claim that only primary relations involve syntactic movement/chains would not be correct: secondary relations also show island effects. Neg-phrases participating in secondary relations show parallel locality behavior to parasitic gaps. As Kayne (1983) showed, although parasitic gaps can be separated from the primary gap by an island, within this island they show movement diagnostics with respect to further islands. As pointed out by Longobardi (1991), secondary neg-phrases appear to do likewise. Some of his examples are reproduced in (23)–(24).

(23) Parasitic neg-phrases:
 a. (In a Sentential Subject)
 (?) Chiamare nessuno [secondary neg-phrase] servirà a niente, ormai
 "To call nobody will do any good now"

 b. (In an Adjunct)
 Non fa niente per aiutare nessuno [secondary neg-phrase]
 "He does not do anything in order to help anyone"

(24) a. Adjunct island inside Subject island:
 * Partire per incontrare nessuno [secondary neg-phrase] servirà a niente
 "To leave in order to meet no one will do any good"

 b. Adjunct island inside another:
 * Non fa niente per scoprire la verita indagando su nessuno [secondary neg-phrase]
 "He doesn't do anything in order to discover the truth by investigating anyone"

In Brody (1995a) I argued for extending the analysis in terms of parasitic chains to *wh*-relations. Chomsky (1986) drew the conclusion about parasitic gaps on the basis of such locality evidence that they must involve movement. If we draw the same conclusion here about secondary neg-and *wh*-relations, then the relation of the *in-situ wh*-phrase in (15) to its scope position must involve a chain/Move relation. The analysis creates difficulties then for the MLC, since in examples like (15) with matrix scope for the *wh-in-situ*, this condition will be violated.

Various further problems for the MLC arise from properties of superiority effects. These can be alleviated in several types of constructions including (25), where the *wh-in-situ* is associated with the matrix *wh*-phrase (cf. Lasnik and Saito 1992) and (26) where the *wh-in-situ* is d-linked (cf. Pesetsky 1987)

(25) Who wondered what who bought

(26) Which book did which girl buy

From the perspective of the MLC, such cases are difficult to understand and therefore they raise doubts about this condition. The alternative quasi-semantic treatment of superiority based on work by Chierchia (1991), put forward independently by Williams (1994) and Hornstein (1994), on the other hand is able to make sense of such apparent counterexamples.

The analysis, which relates the phenomenon to weak crossover, claims that a *wh-in-situ* is or contains an element whose interpretation is dependent on the A-position copy of the *wh*-phrase in spec-CP. Superiority violations arise when this dependency is illegitimate. For present purposes it does not matter if this is because the antecedent of the dependent element D must precede D (Williams 1994, Brody 1994) or because it must "almost c-command" (Hornstein 1994) D. Such an analysis captures the three way parallel between the crossover and the superiority violations in (28) and (29) and the lack of pair-list interpretation in (30) (cf. especially Hornstein 1994 for details and much additional argument):

(28) What did who buy (what)

(29) Who did his father meet (who)

(30) What did everyone say (what)

In none of the three cases does the trace of the *wh*-phrase in spec-CP c-command or precede the dependent element (*who, his* and *everyone* respectively). Furthermore in (25) the trace of the matrix *wh*-phrase does c-command and precede the *wh-in-situ*, thus the latter element can be associated with the matrix *wh*-phrase without incurring a superiority violation. (26) also becomes understandable on the assumption that a d-linked *wh*-phrase need not be a dependent element. (Notice that we cannot meaningfully make a similar exemption from the MLC for d-linked *wh*-phrases by allowing these to be crossed. The MLC is a formal no-crossing requirement not directly sensitive to the interpretive status of the elements involved.)

To summarize so far, the island behavior of neither overt nor covert A′-movement conforms to that predicted by the MLC. Furthermore the condition incorrectly predicts superiority violations in various cases and is incapable of capturing the similar behavior of weak crossover, pair-list reading and superiority constructions. Discounting superiority and *wh*-islands, the major remaining effect of the MLC is the exclusion of superraising. Here again there are alternatives. One possibility might be to restrict theta role percolation in the spirit of Williams (1994). Brody (1995a,b) argues for an interpretive mechanism of feature percolation in chains, that involves thematic roles alongside non-syntactic selectional features. Suppose that NP-traces can receive but cannot directly percolate (transmit) theta roles to higher chain members: they can do this only via the subject–predicate relation under a stricter locality condition. Let us assume for concreteness that the theta role can be inherited from the NP-trace vertically by the smallest predicate VP that includes the trace, and which can in turn assign it to its subject via the predication relation. Vertical transmission is possible only from from (Caseless) NP-traces. This may be a subject trace as in raising or an object trace, as in passives and ergatives. This will allow successive cyclic chains but no superraising in English.

In (11b) for example the theta role of the most deeply embedded verb, *meet*, will be assigned to the VP-internal NP-trace from which it will percolate to the predicate VP *t meet Mary*. This assigns the theta role to the subject, again a Caseless trace that allows further percolation to the next predicate. The subject of this predicate is the expletive *it*, however, so this receives the theta role. No further percolation can take place and the matrix subject *John* will remain without a theta role. The account predicts also that superraising will be possible in multiple subject languages (Ura 1994) on the assumption that in these a predicate can sometimes enter multiple predication relations. (Under the theory of theta role and selectional feature percolation of Brody (1995a,b), a theta role assigned to a chain C must percolate to all members of C, regardless of their status as arguments or expletives. Given this background, a structure like "*There seems it to be certain t to be a man in the garden," in which the relation of the expletive *there* to its trace violates the superraising condition, will be ruled out by the assumptions concerning percolation just made, without the need to invoke an expletive replacement mechanism or some equivalent.)

The MLC thus largely dissolves, as perfect syntax leads us to expect it would: most of the phenomena in its scope turns out to involve interpretive relations that should be constrained within the interpretive component. Dependency, in the sense used here in the account of superiority and related phenomena, is clearly a semantic relation, and so is the mechanism of theta role percolation. This is just a particular case of percolation of selectional features, only a subset of which are syntactic – cf. Brody (1995a,b).

Numerous questions remain in the area of locality phenomena, which a fuller treatment would need to address. Let us look here at one case that might appear related to the MLC: the well-known *wh*-island effect that shows up even in constructions like (14). This is the so called scope reconstruction – in fact a dependent reading of the *wh*-phrase on a quantifier c-commanding its trace. This reading does not obtain even in otherwise grammatical *wh*-islands (on "scope reconstruction" cf. e.g. Longobardi 1984,

Rizzi 1990, Williams 1994, Hornstein 1994). Thus (31a) can be construed as a question asking about each individual which book that individual read, where they all potentially read different books. Such a construal is possible also where the quantifier is in an embedded clause as in (31b). (31c) on the other hand only has a reading "which book is such that you wondered whether everyone read that book", i.e. on which everyone read the same book. Similar judgement obtains with the infinitival embedded clause in (31d).

(31) a. Which book did everyone read
b. Which book did you believe everyone to have read
c. Which book did you wonder whether everyone read
d. Which book did you wonder whether to believe everyone to have read

Hornstein proposes that the MLC is responsible for this difference: it always prevents extraction from the *wh*-island. (14) and (31c,d) will then involve an island internal empty operator movement (cf. Cinque 1990) construed with the matrix wh-phrase. The dependent reading of the *wh*-phrase in (31c,d) will be impossible since the MLC effectively prevents "reconstruction" of the *wh*-phrase into the island: the trace in the island will be the trace/copy of the empty operator and not that of the *wh*-phrase. This account raises numerous questions. First of all, if our discussion so far is correct, the standard minimalist version of the MLC has little independent motivation, hence invoking it here would be quite stipulative. Other problems have to do with the empty operator: what is its landing site, what checking relation triggers its movement (there are no plausible candidates)? Yet others have to do with the scope of the phenomena. Since the effect shows up in other types of islands, Hornstein (1994) suggests assimilating all relevant island violations to *wh*-islands. If all islands have a filled A′-spec then crossing these will be ruled out by the MLC (note 26, p. 181). This would make it necessary to postulate a filled A′-spec (in addition to postulating a head that is necessary to check the empty operator) also in complex NP constructions and adjuncts where the same effect obtains. The marginal structures in (32) cannot have the "scope reconstruction" reading either.

(32) a.??Which book did you deny the fact that everyone read
b.??Which book did you meet Mary before everyone read

But there is no evidence for any of the three empty elements that this account needs to postulate (empty blocking A′-spec, empty Operator, empty head to check the empty Operator). Thus it is unlikely that that the MLC is responsible for "scope reconstructions" effects. (This is not to say that it is inconceivable that some notion of crossing is at issue in the examples in (31), although (32) raises some doubts even about this much weaker claim. In the context of Rizzi's (1990) relativized minimality it was reasonable to put examples like (32) aside as due to some other notion of barrier, since relativized minimality captured a rich generalization in that it constrained also the behavior of adjuncts. But this is not true of the MLC. One important respect in which the MLC differs from relativized minimality is that it refers to argument-type elements. Thus if it was taken to constrain also adjuncts, it would predict the same type of violation: correctly or not, it would not capture the adjunct argument asymmetry with respect to extraction from islands.)

4. CHECKING THEORY

4.1. *Bare Checking Theory*

Let us start with subject verb agreement. The checking theory of Chomsky (1993) assumes that in addition to agreement features appearing on the verb and the subject, mediating features occur on the agreement node. In "'John hits Bill' . . . The ϕ-features appear in three positions in the course of the derivation: internal to *John*, internal to *hits*, and in AGR_S". In effect the mediating features are present in duplicate: "AGR must in fact have two kinds of features: V-features that check V adjoined to AGR and NP-features that check NP in SPEC-AGR." The mediating features delete when checked, so "at PF and LF the ϕ-features appear only twice, not three times: in the Noun Phrase and verb that agree." (p. 42)

In Brody (1995c) I argued against such mediating features. The major objection against NP- and V-features was that at LF the ϕ-features of subject/object-verb agreement should only occur on the subject, they do not appear to have a consistent additional interpretive function on the verb. Additional copies of checking features would presumably be excluded by the principle of full interpretation. But under a checking theory where Agr has separate V- and NP-features, there will still be two copies of the relevant features at LF after the mediating features have deleted. One of these will be on the subject and the other on the verbal head.

Such considerations led to a theory without splitting of Agr features: The approach, which I called "bare checking theory", takes seriously one of the original intuitions behind checking theory, that "movement" or rather non-trivial chain formation is forced by bare output conditions at the LF interface. According to bare checking theory, chains are formed because of the way information is stored in the lexicon. The lexical items in a sentence duplicate certain features – the checking features – these duplications must disappear by LF through checking. Checking of a given feature F is forced by the fact that the multiple copies of F are interpretively redundant and would violate the principle of full interpretation. (We may assume that checking involves marking the redundant copies of some feature invisible, perhaps as a result of merger of features in some sense. Merger might make both checking features invisible creating a single visible LF unit.)

Given bare checking theory, checking takes place because multiple instances of what is in fact one feature are not tolerated at the interface. It is not necessary then to invoke non-interpretability of features to force a checking configuration. Bare checking theory is thus consistent with radical interpretability according to which all features have semantic content.

Dispensing with NP- and V-features leaves the further question of whether mediating features (now without the split into NP- and V- features) exist. The basic assumption of bare checking theory does not require the elimination of the mediating features in Agr, although it would not disallow this move either. This theory is not compatible with the splitting of the features of Agr into NP- and V-features since this would result in two copies of ϕ-features at LF. But if ϕ-features are present in three position, then bare checking theory will simply require all three positions to merge by LF through checking.

Nevertheless I will assume that mediating features do not exist. Apart from simplicity considerations, an argument against these in Brody (1995c) was that the evidence for the third copy of ϕ-features is missing even where it could be expected to occur. When the feature on Agr is weak we would expect it to show up at PF. It is only by stipulation (namely that unchecked weak features are invisible or delete in the PF component) that this incorrect prediction is neutralized. I assumed therefore that within bare checking theory subject verb agreement involves only a single checking relation: the ϕ-features of the verb and the subject are checked directly against each other. (On the assumption that checking must involve spec-head configurations in functional phrases, this will entail the formation of NP- and V-chains.)

Chomsky (1995) also develops a theory that is not compatible with the existence of mediating ϕ-features. He proposes to eliminate the Agr node altogether. Although he does not discuss the matter, eliminating Agr could give the result we seek: after subject verb checking there will be only a single set of ϕ-features present at LF. Chomsky rejects the Agr node for reasons that are not dissimilar to those given in Brody (1995c) for rejecting mediating features. Apart from simplicity (section 4.1, pp. 16–17), Chomsky notes that unlike other functional categories like C, T or D for example, Agr does not contain interpretable (either LF or PF) features (section 10). "We therefore have fairly direct evidence from interface relations about T, C and D but not AGR" (p. 8).

Notice, though, two differences. First the argument from PF invisibility does not distinguish between (semantically/conceptually) interpretable and non-interpretable features: it argues against triplications irrespective of this dimension. Chomsky's argument on the other hand is relevant only for features that have no interpretation at either interface.

Secondly, the argument in Brody (1995c) questioned only the existence of mediating features while Chomsky argues against the Agr node itself. But the question of whether the Agr node exists is in fact composed of two issues: only one of which is the question of the mediating features. Even if these do not exist, it might be that some node α above T projects a phrase which hosts both a member of the subject chain (in its spec) and a member of the verbal X^0 chain that enter into a checking relation here. One possibility is that T or perhaps all categories have the option of projecting recursively: α would then correspond to the higher T node. Thus we could retain the spec and the head positions as appears to be empirically desirable, without assuming the existence of mediating ϕ-features. The condition of interpretability (cf. section 1.2 above) could be satisfied jointly by the the two T nodes. (Similarly, recursively projecting Vs may be a way of creating multi-layered VPs.)

Consider next English interrogatives.

(33) I wonder (what) who +WH [(who) saw what]

(34) a. I wonder who +WH Bill saw (who)
b. Bill saw who

(35) Who did +WH Mary (did) see (who)

(36) Did +WH John see Mary

In (33) there are three instances of the *wh*-feature (two on the *wh*-phrases and one on the embedded C node). But there is only one question. So by full interpretation the *wh*-features must all merge. This is possible if both *wh*-phrases form a chain that has a member that forms a checking relation with the +wh head. Thus bare checking theory entails the existence of A′-chains that express "covert A′-movement" relations, in accordance with our earlier conclusions. As noted in section 1, a chain corresponding to an "overt movement" relation is the default case, it will occur if the relevant head (here the +wh C) is "strong" enough to license a categorial element in the checking domain in the morphological component; in the case of an XP-chain word-externally as a specifier. (On the reasons for "extended structure preservation" that prevents word-internal phrases see Brody 1995b.) Given the generalization that SPELLOUT operates only on the highest copy in a chain, the lexical item will show up in spec-CP. In English this head licenses a single spec, hence additional *wh*-phrases checked by it must remain *in-situ* forming feature-chains only.

(34b) will be possible only with a -wh C and an echo interpretation. If it had a +wh C then the two *wh*-features in the structure should merge through checking by full interpretation. This makes a chain necessary, linking the *wh*-phrase to the checking domain of the +wh C. Since this head licenses an overt specifier in morphology, the chain must be a full copy chain as in (34a).

In (35) the auxiliary *did* must have a *wh*-feature. We can analyze (35) in two ways. The choice between these depends on whether features on heads mediating spec-head relations between other elements can exist. If they do, then both C and T can have a *wh*-feature and T (together with the auxiliary) forms a chain because these must merge through checking. Additionally the *wh*-feature on *who* must also merge with this complex, hence an XP-chain is also formed. These will be chains involving copies of full categories since the relevant C licenses both a word-internal and a word-external categorial element in its checking domain. Alternatively if mediating features are dispensed with, then the T with the *wh*-feature and the *wh*-phrase both form a chain linking them to CP because this is the only way that they can establish a checking relation. (This latter alternative corresponds essentially to the account in Rizzi 1991, see also Brody 1990, 1995c.)

If yes-no questions contain an empty (*wh*-)operator in spec-CP then the analysis of (36) will not significantly differ from that of (35). If not, then (36) will be parallel to (34), modulo the difference between an X^0-chain and an XP-chain.

Notice that we must apparently allow merger of a set of checking features without all of these occupying positions in the same checking domain. In a language that exhibits the pattern in (37), this structure will contain three instances of the +plural feature, but only one plurality: that of the DP. The +plural feature of the XP-chain of *they* apparently merges with the other two in two distinct spec's. Given the independently necessary assumption that checking features are properties of the chains and not of the members of the chain (cf. Brody 1995b), this should create no problems. At LF there is only a single +plural feature in (37), that of the XP-chain.

(37) They(pl) seem(pl) (they(pl)) clever(pl)

4.2. *The Minimalist Checking Theory and the +/–Interpretable Distinction*

Let us next consider briefly the current version of checking theory in the minimalist framework of Chomsky (1995). He suggests that interpretable features like categorial features and ϕ-features on nouns do not need to be checked, whereas noninterpretable features like for example Case or ϕ-features on verbal heads or "strength" (presumably a feature) of an interpretable feature must be checked because this makes it possible to eliminate these, as required by full interpretation. (In fact he assumes further that once checked, these features are not visible for the remaining syntactic computation either.) Thus checking relations and indirectly movement and chain relations are forced by noninterpretable features. These must be eliminated, and they can be eliminated only when already checked.

The principle of radical interpretability is incompatible however with existence of noninterpretable features: according to this principle all syntactic features must be potentially interpretable. As we have seen, under bare checking theory it is not necessary to make use of noninterpretable features: checking relations are forced by the duplication of interpretable features. Furthermore the checking theory based on this distinction seems to lead to less optimal analyses. Consider for example the analysis of interrogatives within this theory.

The *wh*-feature is clearly interpretable hence not in need of being checked. A +wh feature will be checked only if it is "strong" and then overtly (some of the problems with the notion of strength used here were discussed in section 2 above). Thus in English the *wh*-feature on C is strong and hence it can be checked either by (T+)*did* as in (36) or by a *wh*-phrase as in (34). Since a strong feature can be satisfied by a single element, the analysis raises the question of why (38a) is unacceptable. Here the strong *wh*-feature of C is satisfied by the hosted verbal element.

(38) a. did John give which book to Mary
b. +WH John gave which book to Mary

Chomsky suggests that (38a) "converges as gibberish". (Notice that (38a) would then contrast with (38b), which crashes since the strong *wh*-feature on C has not been checked.) But since Chomsky rejects covert A′-movement type syntactic relations, he needs to assume the existence of some interpretive mechanism to link *in-situ wh*-phrases to their scope. It is then unclear why (38a) is gibberish, why it cannot be interpreted with the interpretive strategy generally used for *in-situ wh*-phrases. As we have seen, under bare checking theory, where all *wh*-features must merge, the problem does not arise: *which book* in (38a) must form a chain linking it to the *wh*-feature of the auxiliary (and perhaps also of C). Further, the chain must be a full category copy chain, that is one that corresponds to overt movement of the minimalist framework, since English C is strong, i.e. it licenses a specifier in addition to an element in the word (X^0)-internal checking domain.

(Further elaboration, like for example multiple strong features are necessary to generate (35) within Chomsky's system of assumptions. Note that (35) like many other examples will also violate the MLC of the minimalist system: the *wh*-phrase moves to CP even though another element that could (and does) legitimately move there, namely the verbal complex, is nearer.)

A major prediction in the theory where noninterpretable features are crucially involved is the exclusion of movement from Case positions. On the assumption that Case is noninterpretable and that such features once checked are invisible for further computation, the derivation of (39) will crash. The Case feature of the DP *John* are checked and deleted in the embedded clause (together with the Case feature of the embedded T). Hence the noninterpretable Case feature on the matrix T cannot be checked and deleted when DP raises, and therefore the derivation will crash at LF.

(39) a. *John seems [t saw Mary]
b. *There seems [a man was clever]

If this is the only case where noninterpretable features are needed then the explanation is less appealing. Additionally *easy-to-please* and grammatical superraising suggest that the generalization in terms of Case is too strong:

(40) John is easy [Op to please t]

(41) John seems [t′ Mary liked t]

If the analysis in Brody (1993b) is correct then in (40) we have a chain [John, Op, t] that involves two Case positions. Similarly in the grammatical superraising cases, which pattern like (41) (Ura 1994), the superraising chain [John, t′, t] appears to involve two Case positions. Notice that if *John* in (41) is taken not to check (accusative) Case in the position of t, then *John* in (39a) (and *a man* in (39b)) should similarly be able to avoid Case-checking in the lower clause. This would however eliminate the explanation of the ungrammaticality of (39): these DPs could check the Case feature of the matrix T and the derivation would converge. (Ura suggests that in the grammatical superraising constructions lack of Case assignment to the trace correlates with the possibility of filling the position with a *pro* element. This generalization would still incorrectly allow (39) in subject *pro* drop languages like Italian or Hungarian.)

The contrast between (39) and (40)/(41) suggests that the subject non-subject difference may be relevant. Nominative subjects correlate with and presumably check Tense. We could thus attribute the ungrammaticality of (39) to Tense conflict instead of Case-conflict: subject raising in these examples illegitimately establishes an (indirect) chain-relation between two independent tenses. If null Case of PRO is assigned by an inflection with "unrealized" Tense (Stowell 1982, Martin 1992, Boskovic 1994), then the account will generalize to chains involving infinitival subject positions:

(42) a. *John is illegal t to go there
b. *John tried PRO to be illegal t to go there

5. CONCLUSION, UNIFORMITY, LAST RESORT, PROCRASTINATE

Although various issues remain, the results so far seem encouraging. Stipulative conditions of the minimalist framework on the Move/chain relation, like the cycle/c-command, and the MLC appear unnecessary or attributable to the interpretive components as perfect syntax leads us to expect. Checking relations and indirectly (non-trivial) chain formation is forced by bare output conditions. Given bare checking theory this need not involve noninterpretable features that would violate radical interpretability. I have discussed in detail and rejected the remaining major stipulative condition on Move/chain, namely Uniformity, in Brody (1995b). I argued there that a well-designed theory should not make available devices that would make it possible to violate the condition, which requires that all chain members be of the same projection level. If projectional levels are not defined relationally, then the question of uniformity cannot even arise. Since chains are sets of copies the chain members necessarily share also the projection level property.

Finally let me comment briefly and incompletely on two more conditions: Last resort and Procrastinate. Last resort can be thought of as an interface condition on the assumption that all categories must be licensed by full interpretation. This licensing involves participation in either (a) a projectional relation (selectional/ modificational relation or categorial projection) or (b) in a checking relation. Since by the generalized projection principle projectional relations are relevant only for chain roots (cf. Brody 1995b), non-roots of non-trivial chains (i.e. "Move" of the minimalist framework) can be licensed only by a checking relation.

I assumed that in the default case chains are formed on full categorial copies, feature chains occur only when full copies are not licensed in the checking domain of some head. This preference for "overt movement" type relations is consistent with the Transparency principle and incompatible with Procrastinate which would require feature chains as the default case. (For Transparency and arguments against Procrastinate cf. Brody 1995a.)

There is a particular prediction of Procrastinate that our account so far has nothing to say about. The ungrammaticality of the examples in (43) has been attributed to this principle. Procrastinate will predict this, if at the embedded subject position it prefers insertion (of the expletive *it, there*), over the raising of the associate (*a man*). Instead of the ungrammatical (43), we will then derive the grammatical (44).

(43) a. *There seems a man to have arrived
b. *It was believed a man to have been here

(44) a. There seems (there) to have arrived a man
b. It was believed (it) to have been a man here

Let us consider the alternative of claiming either that the embedded subject position simply does not exist, or that its inflection is weak, and licenses only a featural subject. On either of these assumptions, the embedded subject position cannot be occupied by the associate and (43) cannot arise. This entails immediately that English object shift must be overt: *him* in (45) cannot be in the embedded subject position. (For independent arguments for the overtness of English object shift see e.g. Johnson 1991, Koizumi 1993, Lasnik 1994.)

(45) John believed him to be clever.

The stronger claim that the governed and Caseless subject positions of the Principles and Parameters theory do not exist entails also giving up the successive cyclicity of A-chains since intermediate A-chain links occupy such subject positions. If A-chains are not successive cyclic, then the intermediate traces will not be present in (46a) and (47a) to act as interveners for the binding relations indicated. (The principle C violation in the b. examples shows that c-command holds between the relevant elements.)

(46) a. John seems to $Mary_x$ [(t) to appear to her_x//*$herself_x$ [(t) to have met me]]
b. *John seems to her_x [(t) to appear to $Mary_x$ [(t) to have met me]]

(47) a. John seems to $Mary_x$ [(t) to be considered [(t)clever] by her_x//$herself_x$]
b. *John seems to her_x [(t) to be considered [(t) clever] by $Mary_x$]

Hence we will presumably have to account for the binding relations in examples like (46a), (47a) along the lines of Williams' (1980) Predicate Opacity Condition (see also Reinhart and Reuland 1993 for relevant discussion): anaphors need to be bound and pronominals free within their predicate – in (46a), (47a) this is within the intermediate level of the structure.

Consider the alternative assumption: the subject positions are only weakly licensed, and intermediate traces in A-chains involve only feature copies. This will make it possible to retain the theory of feature percolation sketched in section 3 above. The feature copies can then act as interveners for the binding theory. If this analysis is correct, it would represent a case where a full copy is higher in a chain than a feature copy. The scenario would be unexpected in the minimalist theory: a "covert movement" type relation cannot be followed by an "overt movement" relation. (This is not to say of course that the configuration is not achievable through stipulation, say by deleting the intermediate copy up to its formal features.)

On the other hand given the assembly system of Brody (1995a,b), such a configuration would be expected to occur. Here copies of features or of full categories and their content can be freely made (subject to the blocking effect by full category copies, as discussed above). Unless further constraints prevent this, feature copies and full copies can be inserted in the structure in any c-command order. In particular a full categorial copy may be higher than several feature copies (which in turn may be higher than another full copy), as appears to be necessary to retain successive cyclic A-movement in the context of the above assumptions.

REFERENCES

Boskovic, Zeljko (1994) 'Selection and the categorial status of infinitival complements', *NLLT*.

Brody, Michael (1990) 'Some remarks on the focus field in Hungarian', *UCLWP* **2**, University College, London.

Brody, Michael (1993a) *Lexico-Logical Form*. Ms., University College, London.

Brody, Michael (1993b) 'Theta theory and arguments', *Linguistic Inquiry* **24**, 1–23.

Brody, Michael (1994) 'Dependence and phrase structure', *UCLWP* **6**, University College, London.

Brody, Michael (1995a) *Lexico-Logical Form. A Radically Minimalist Theory*. MIT Press, Cambridge, Mass.

Brody, Michael (1995b) *Phrase Structure and Projection*. Ms., University College, London, to appear in *Linguistic Inquiry*.

Brody, Michael (1995c) 'Hungarian focus and bare checking theory', in *Arbeitspapiere des Sonderforschungsbereichs 340*, University of Tubingen.

Chierchia, G. (1991) 'Functional wh and weak crossover', *The Proceedings of the WCCFL 10*. Stanford Linguistics Association, Stanford, pp. 75–90.

Chomsky, Noam (1986) *Barriers*. MIT Press, Cambridge, Mass.

Chomsky, Noam (1993) 'A minimalist program for linguistic theory', *MIT Occasional Papers in Linguistics*, MIT, Cambridge, Mass.

Chomsky, Noam (1994) *Bare Phrase Structure*, ms., MIT, Cambridge, Mass.

Chomsky, Noam (1995) 'Chapter 4'. ms., MIT.

Cinque, Guglielmo (1991) *Types of A'-dependencies*. MIT Press, Cambridge, Mass.

Cinque, Guglielmo (1995) 'Adverbs and the universal hierarchy of functional projections', Tromso GLOW abstract.

Hornstein, Norbert (1994) *LF: The Grammar of Logical Form. From GB to Minimalism*. Ms., University of Maryland.

Jaeggli, Osvaldo (1981) *Topics in Romance Syntax*. Foris, Dordrecht.

Johnson, Kyle (1991) 'Object positions', *Natural Language and Linguistic Theory* **9**, 577–636.

Kawashima, R and Hisatsugu Kitahara (1995) 'Strict cyclicity, linear ordering and derivational c-command', to appear in *WCCFL 14*.

Kayne, Richard (1981) 'ECP extensions', *Linguistic Inquiry* **12**, 93–133.

Kayne, Richard (1983) 'Connectedness', *Linguistic Inquiry* **14**, 223–249.

Kayne, Richard (1995) *The Antisymmetry of Syntax*. MIT Press, Cambridge, Mass.

Koizumi, Masatoshi (1993) 'Object Agreement Phrases and the Split VP Hypothesis', *MITWPL* **18**. MIT, Cambridge, Mass. .

Lasnik, Howard (1994) Antecedent contained deletion and/or pseudo-gapping. Talk, presented at MIT.

Lasnik, Howard and Mamoru Saito (1992) *Move* α. MIT Press, Cambridge, Mass.

Longobardi, Giuseppe (1991) 'In defense of the correspondence hypothesis: island effects and parasitic constructions in logical form', in: C.-T. James Huang and Robert May (eds.), *Logical Structure and Linguistic Structure*. Kluwer, Dordrecht.

Martin, Roger (1992) *On the Distribution and Case Features of PRO*. Ms., University of Connecticut.

Pesetsky, David (1987) 'WH-in-situ: movement and unselective binding', in: Eric Reuland and A. ter Meulen (eds.), *The Representation of (In)definiteness*. MIT Press, Cambridge, Mass, pp. 98–129.
Pesetsky, David (1989) *Language Particular Processes and the Earliness Principle*. Ms., MIT.
Reinhart, Tanya and Eric Reuland (1993) 'Reflexivity', *Linguistic Inquiry* **24**, 657–720.
Rizzi, Luigi (1982) *Issues in Italian Syntax*. Foris, Dordrecht.
Rizzi, Luigi (1990) *Relativized Minimality*. MIT Press, Cambridge, Mass.
Rizzi, Luigi (1991) *Residual Verb Second and the Wh-Criterion*. Ms., Universite de Geneve.
Stowell, Timothy (1982) 'The tense of infinitives', *Linguistic Inquiry* **13**, 561–570.
Ura, Hiroyuki (1994) *Varieties of Raising and the Feature-based Phrase Structure Theory* (chapter 1). Ms., MIT.
Watanabe, Akira (1991) *Wh-in-situ, Subjacency and Chain Formation*. Ms., MIT.
Williams, Edwin (1980) 'Predication', *Linguistic Inquiry* **11**, 208–238.
Williams, Edwin (1994) *Thematic Structure in Syntax*. MIT Press, Cambridge, Mass.
Williams, Edwin (1995) *Blocking and Anaphora*. Ms., University of Princeton.

JANE GRIMSHAW

THE BEST CLITIC: CONSTRAINT CONFLICT IN MORPHOSYNTAX[1]

1. INTRODUCTION

This paper illustrates the application of Optimality Theory (Prince and Smolensky 1993) to the domain of morphosyntax. It deals with a strictly delineated set of data, concerning the behavior of clitic combinations in the Romance languages, and draws very heavily on research presented in Bonet (1991, 1995).

The phenomenon of interest is the occurrence of what Bonet calls "opaque clitics": clitics whose form in certain combinations is unexpected given the choice of clitics in isolation. I will argue that these effects can be insightfully characterized under a theory of optimization: the unexpected clitic forms are the best available, given the need to avoid duplicative sequences of clitics.

The situation is one in which there is a conflict between two goals. One goal is to utilize the very best clitic, the one which occurs in isolation. Another goal is to avoid duplication. I will show that variation among languages and dialects can be explained as a choice between different ways of resolving the conflict. One clitic can delete (avoiding duplication), one clitic can change form, or the language can insist on the very best clitic and live with the duplication. These choices are the inevitable result of alternative rankings of the constraints in the system, as expected under optimality theoretic assumptions.

The chief points of Optimality Theory as presented in Prince and Smolensky (1993) are these. First, all constraints are universal. Second, constraints can be violated in well-formed sentences. A grammar is a ranking of the universal constraints which determines which constraint is satisfied in case of a conflict. The optimal form (that which best satisfies the constraints under the ranking in the grammar) is grammatical, all non-optimal candidates are ungrammatical. An optimal output form for a given input is selected from among the class of competitors in the following way: a form which, for every pairwise competition involving it, best satisfies the highest-ranking constraint on which the competitors conflict, is *optimal*. (Grimshaw, to appear). The input in the cases at hand is a set of specifications for morphosyntactic properties: reflexivity, person, number, gender and case. The constraints and their rankings determine what clitic form is the best realization of the input.

One set of constraints, entirely familiar from the phonological litera-

Liliane Haegeman (ed.), Elements of Grammar, 169–196.

ture, functions to regulate the relationship of the input to the output, imposing a "faithful relationship" between the two. In particular, there are constraints requiring that the input and the output have identical specifications for the morphosyntactic features mentioned above:

FILL FEATURE	Only features in the input can appear in the output
PARSE FEATURE	All features in the input must appear in the output

These constraints are violated whenever an opaque clitic occurs (and elsewhere as we will see).

A further set of constraints targets specific values of these features. *1, *2 and *3 are violated by any form with a first, second or third person specification respectively. I suggest that they form a universal markedness hierarchy, such that *2 dominates *1, and *1 in turn dominates *3 in the grammar of every language, although there is no attempt made here to explore this fully. Similarly there are constraints which penalize case specifications, specifically *DAT for dative and *ACC for accusative, and I suggest that these also form a universal markedness hierarchy in which *DAT dominates *ACC.

The final constraint is the constraint against duplication, which is clearly related to the Obligatory Contour Principle (Leben 1973, McCarthy 1986), which I call "*XX", and which is violated by combinations of identical elements. This is clearly part of a much more general group of constraints, including the OCP, the double-*ing* constraint (Ross 1972) constraints on case such as the "double *o*" constraint of Japanese, and the Case OCP discussed in Mohanan (1994). Assuming that all of these involve heads, the constraint can be stated as ruling out sequences of identical functional heads.

*XX Sequences of identical functional heads are ill-formed

It is the ranking of the faithfulness constraints relative to *XX which supports the system of clitic combinations. When the faithfulness constraints dominate *XX then a faithful parse of the input is the result and the output clitic is the one that maximally would be found in isolation, even though it violates *XX. When *XX dominates a faithfulness constraint, then the clitic will change or disappear in order to satisfy *XX.

The constraint rankings are of two types; the universal markedness hierarchies which were mentioned above, and the language particular rankings.

Universal Markedness Hierarchies
*2 > *1 > *3
*DAT > *ACC

Some language particular rankings are common to the clitic systems of

Italian and Spanish. These, together with the common lexicons discussed shortly, determine a shared core in the clitic systems.

FILL PERS > PARSE NUM
FILL R > PARSE PERS, PARSE NUM, and PARSE CASE

The remaining language particular rankings are the locus of cross-linguistic variation, as mentioned above. I will discuss the alternative rankings and their consequences as they become relevant.

2. THE STRUCTURE OF THE CLITIC SYSTEM: ITALIAN

While teaching grammars of Italian often describe the clitic system in terms such as "the accusative pronoun clitics, the dative pronoun clitics, the accusative reflexives and the dative reflexives", this characterization misses some of the fundamental properties of the clitic system. For example, *vi* is the only 2nd person plural form: it is used for reflexive and non-reflexive situations and it is used as a dative and an accusative. *Si* is used for 3rd person reflexives, regardless of their person, number, gender and case. What this suggests is that it is unilluminating at best to characterize each clitic as a fully specified set of morphosyntactic features: we then have to posit multiple *vi*'s (one for each page of the grammar book), multiple *si*'s and so forth. Alternatively, we can treat clitics as potentially underspecified bundles of morphosyntactic features. In a situation where a clitic with a given specification is called for, an output clitic with exactly that specification will be the best realization, but if there is no such clitic available, an underspecified clitic which best matches the input may suffice. This is where optimality comes into play.

For example, it could be that *si* occurs as the reflexive, third person, plural, feminine, accusative because it is specified for all these features. Or it could be that it is not specified for all of these features but no alternative clitic with a better specification is available. This is the line that will be pursued here.

Once we think about clitics in these terms, it is clear that the different clitics vary in how much morphosyntactic information they encode. *si*, the extreme, encodes none: it is not marked for reflexivity "R", person, "P", number, "N", gender "G", and case "C". When a clitic is not marked for a feature, this is indicated by enclosing the abbreviation for the feature in parentheses, hence "(R)" indicates that that the clitic is unmarked for reflexivity, i.e. has no reflexivity specification.

Specifically, I will assume the clitic lexicon given in (1).[2]

(1)	si	(R)(P)(N)(G)(C)	self
	mi	(R) 1 sg (G)(C)	me, to me
	ti	(R) 2 sg (G)(C)	you, to you
	ci	(R) 1 pl (G)(C)	us, to us
	vi	(R) 2 pl (G)(C)	you, to you
	lo/la	-R (P) sg m/f acc	him, her, it
	li/le	-R (P) pl m/f acc	them
	gli/le	-R (P) sg m/f dat	to him, her, it

The fault lines in the system involve the R specifications and the P specifications. There is a group of clitics which ranges across reflexive and non-reflexive uses, marked as (R) in (1). A second group is non-reflexive only, -R in (1). With respect to the person dimension, there is a group of clitics which mark person (1st or 2nd) and a group which do not. This latter group will in fact only occur as the output for a 3rd person input, because, as we will see, the clitics which mark person are better outputs for 1st and 2nd person inputs. Finally, there is *si*, which marks nothing. The two fault lines, the R and P specifications, are connected. Apart from *si* all and only (R) clitics mark person. Apart from *si*, all and only -R clitics are (P). Other generalizations hold but will not be analyzed here: for example, all and only (R) clitics are (G) and (C), so the (R) clitics don't vary for gender and case and the -R clitics do.

The most interesting clitic in this analysis is *si*, the clitic which is usually described as a reflexive clitic. In this view it is really no such thing. It is a clitic which has no properties. This is in essence the proposal of Bonet (1995), slightly rephrased.

3. CLITICS IN ISOLATION

The first step is to illustrate the operation of the system in the simple cases. How does it settle on the right lexical choice when a clitic occurs in isolation? We begin with an input for which there is a nearly perfect solution, given the above analysis of the clitic system (I ignore gender here in the interests of simplicity). Assume an input which specifies a non-reflexive 3rd person plural accusative clitic. The actual correct output is *li* or *le* depending on the choice of gender.

(2) Input is -R
input: ⟨[-R 3 pl acc]⟩

candidates		PARSE R	FILL R	PARSE PERS	FILL PERS	PARSE NUM	FILL NUM	PARSE CASE	FILL CASE
a. si	(R)(P)(N)(C)	*		*		*		*	
b. mi	(R) 1 sg (C)	*		*	*	*	*	*	
c. ti	(R) 2 sg (C)	*		*	*	*	*	*	
d. ci	(R) 1 pl (C)	*		*	*			*	
e. vi	(R) 2 pl (C)	*		*	*			*	
f. lo/la	-R (P) sg acc			*		*	*		
☞ g. li/le	-R (P) pl acc			*					
h. gli/le	-R (P) sg dat			*		*	*	*	*

Since the winning candidate violates only PARSE PERS, and every other candidate violates this constraint and others, there is no evidence for constraint ranking in this tableau, g. being the winner under every ranking. It is thus impossible to tell from this case which violations are "fatal" and which are incidental. Under these assumptions, all the -R clitics work in the same way: they are all faithful realizations of an input, apart from their failure to parse the person specification. (Later in the paper I will argue that singular and masculine are in fact not marked, hence ultimately the optimal clitic here will violate PARSE GEND as well, if the input is masculine. The constraint system still picks the same candidate as optimal, however, and this should be clear in what follows.)

The (R) clitics do not have a specification for reflexivity. Since every input is specified as either reflexive or nonreflexive, an (R) clitic cannot be an entirely faithful realization of any input. Why, then, are they selected as output forms? Suppose the input is 2nd person reflexive. This is illustrated in (3).

(3) Input is R, non-third person
input: ⟨[R 2 pl acc]⟩

candidates		Parse R	Fill R	Parse Pers	Fill Pers	Parse Num	Fill Num	Parse Case	Fill Case
a. si	(R)(P)(N)(C)	*		*		*		*	
b. mi	(R) 1 sg (C)	*		*	*	*	*	*	
c. ti	(R) 2 sg (C)	*				*	*	*	
d. ci	(R) 1 pl (C)	*		*	*			*	
e. ☞ vi	(R) 2 pl (C)	*						*	
f. lo/la	-R (P) sg acc	*	*	*		*	*		
g. li/le	-R (P) pl acc	*	*	*					
h. gli /le	-R (P) sg dat	*	*	*		*	*	*	*

All candidates fail Parse R. The -R clitics will do worse on an R input than the (R) clitics, since the -R specification guarantees failure on Fill R in addition to Parse R. However, the -R clitics can do better on the case constraints (and the gender constraints, not shown) than the (R) clitics, since the (R) clitics do not parse case. So we must rank Fill R above Parse Case (and Parse Gend) to eliminate the -R group. (In this case, the person specification in the input is such that the -R clitics must fail the person constraints in addition, so it might appear that the ranking of the person constraints might do the job here, but this is not true as we will see shortly.) To put the situation in intuitive terms, the system prefers a clitic which does not contradict the R specification of the input over one which faithfully parses the case specification.

For these constraints, this ranking is sufficient to guarantee the choice of *vi* as optimal. It violates only Parse R, which all the other candidates also violate, and Parse Case, which is satisfied only by candidates which violate Fill R. Every other candidate violates at least two additional constraints. However, the constraint *2, to be encountered crucially in the next section, will prefer first and third person clitics to *vi*. In fact, then, it is necessary to rank Parse Pers over *2, to ensure faithful parsing of the 2 in the input.

Finally, consider *si* in its various incarnations in Italian. As a first example, we can take the form realizing a 3rd person plural reflexive input, as in (4).

(4) input: ⟨[R 3 pl acc]⟩

candidates		Parse R	Fill R	Parse Pers	Fill Pers	Parse Num	Fill Num	Parse Case	Fill Case
a. si	(R)(P)(N)(C)	*		*		*		*	
b. mi	(R) 1 sg (C)	*		*	*!	*	*	*	
c. ti	(R) 2 sg (C)	*		*	*!	*	*	*	
d. ci	(R) 1 pl (C)	*		*	*!			*	
e. vi	(R) 2 pl (C)	*		*	*!			*	
f. lo/la	-R (P) sg acc	*	*	*		*!	*!		
g. li/le	-R (P) pl acc	*	*	*					
h. gli/le	-R (P) sg dat	*	*	*		*!	*!	*!	*!

In analyzing this tableau, it is helpful to divide it into two parts: the (R) clitics and the -R clitics. Among the (R) clitics, *si* satisfies Fill Pers, which is violated by all the other candidates. *si* violates Parse Num, which *ci* and *vi*, the plurals, satisfy. Hence *si* will be victorious if Fill Pers >> Parse Num. Among the non-reflexive clitics, *li* or *le* is the winner. All other candidates share the R and Pers faithfulness violations and violate other constraints in addition.

Now we can do a reduced comparison, looking at the optimal candidate from each of the two parts of the previous tableau:

(5) Reduced comparison: the best (R) clitic versus the best -R clitic
input: ⟨[R 3 pl acc]⟩

candidates		Parse R	Fill R	Parse Pers	Fill Pers	Parse Num	Fill Num	Parse Case	Fill Case
a. ☞ si	(R)(P)(N)(C)	*		*		*		*	
g. li/le	-R (P) pl acc	*	*!	*					

This comparison reveals a crucial ranking: Fill R >> Parse Num, and Parse Case. (Evidence for Fill R >> Parse Case has already been given.) For a reflexive input, the grammar of Italian chooses a clitic that is not irreflexive in form, even though it does not encode the input properties of number and case. Faithfulness to the reflexivity of the input, in so far as this is possible in the system, is given priority over faithfulness to its number, case (and also gender, not discussed here).

Note that both constraint rankings are crucial. The ranking of Fill R >> Parse Num, Parse Case successfully chooses the (R) clitic over all -Rs, but it will not choose *si* from among the (R) clitics. Fill Pers >> Parse Num is needed for that.

The appearance of *si* as the impersonal subject is illustrated in (6):

(6) Lo **si** sveglia
3rd-acc impers. wakes-up
"one wakes him up"

Must we stipulate that *si* is chosen as the impersonal subject? Given the analysis proposed here, which follows Bonet's insight, *si* is the least marked clitic, having no specifications. Thus if the grammar of Italian stipulates that the impersonal is a clitic, the choice of *si* is predictable. Suppose, for example, that the input for an impersonal is just [3 pl]. (Impersonal subjects trigger plural participial agreement, Cinque (1988).)

(7) The impersonal is the least marked clitic
input: ⟨[3 pl]⟩

candidates		PARSE R	FILL R	PARSE PERS	FILL PERS	PARSE NUM	FILL NUM
a.☞ si	(R)(P)(N)(C)			*		*	
b. mi	(R) 1 sg (C)			*	*!	*	*!
c. ti	(R) 2 sg (C)			*	*!	*	*!
d. ci	(R) 1 pl (C)			*	*!		
e. vi	(R) 2 pl (C)			*	*!		
f. lo/la	-R (P) sg acc		*!	*		*	*
g. li/le	-R (P) pl acc		*!	*			
h. gli/le	-R (P) sg dat		*!	*		*	*

si violates PARSE NUM, but FILL R dominates this constraint, so all -R candidates are eliminated. (*si* violates only PARSE PERS in addition, and every other candidate violates this constraint too.) The singular (R) clitics *ti*, *mi* violate everything that *si* does plus additional constraints, so they are eliminated. The plural (R) clitics satisfy PARSE NUM, but violate FILL PERS. Since FILL PERS ≫ PARSE NUM, *si* beats *ci* and *vi*. So the constraints and rankings which chose *si* in the previous case, choose *si* now, and it is not an accident at all that same clitic is used for both.

The observation that the impersonal subject clitic is the same as the reflexive clitic has been a puzzling one: what do they have in common? (See Cinque 1988 for a detailed discussion of the uses of *si* in Italian.) This line of reasoning suggests that what they have in common is not some elusive reflexivity or other syntactic/semantic property, but the simple absence of morphosyntactic detail. (A reasonable further target, then, would be the extension of this solution to the so-called "inherent reflexives", where the clitic (*si* with a third person subject, *mi* with a first person subject etc.) does not, at least not obviously, correspond to an argument at all. If the grammar of Italian specifies that the verb form involves a clitic, it should be possible to predict the choice of clitic from the constraints given here.)

So far *si* has the property that it violates every PARSE constraint, since it parses nothing in the input. It also satisfies every FILL constraint: since it has no specification for any of the morpho-syntactic features, it cannot have a specification which contradicts that of the input. However, it cannot be the case that *si* parses nothing at all. If *si* parses nothing at all then it is necessarily equivalent to the null candidate. Why, then, is it preferred to realize the clitic at all, rather than omitting it? The null candidate, like the *si* candidate, would violate the PARSE constraints and not the FILL constraints. The problem is illustrated in (8), for the input analyzed above in (4)–(5).

(8) *si* versus null candidate, without constraint PARSE CL
input: ⟨[R 3 pl acc]⟩

candidates		PARSE R	FILL R	PARSE PERS	FILL PERS	PARSE NUM	FILL NUM
a. si	(R)(P)(N)(C)	*		*		*	
b.	(R)(P)(N)(C)	*		*		*	

The answer must be that there is a further constraint which prefers parsing of any kind over no parsing at all. For present purposes let us call this constraint PARSE CLITIC, though it is perhaps more general in form. Furthermore, the proper analysis of *si* must be that it does parse the feature Cl, even though it parses nothing else. Now the constraint will eliminate the null candidate, as illustrated in the table in (9), which compares the null candidate with *si* for the same [R 3 pl acc] input.

(9) *si*/*se* versus null candidate, with constraint PARSE CL
Input: ⟨[Cl R 3 pl acc]⟩

Candidates		PARSE CL	PARSE R	FILL R	PARS PERS	FILL PERS	PARSE NUM	FILL NUM
a. si	(R)(P)(N)(C)		*		*		**	
b.	(R)(P)(N)(C)	*!	*		*		**	

On any ranking among these constraints, PARSE CL will select *si* over the null candidate. Subsequently we will see that alternative rankings of PARSE CL control the choice between deletion of a clitic and its realization. Until they become important again, however, I will omit Cl from inputs, and the PARSE CL constraint from tableaux.

In the analysis developed here, a crucial role is played by the ranking of FILL PERS ≫ PARSE NUM. There is another possibility here and throughout, in which *si* is selected by a markedness constraint *PERS, a constraint which dislikes person specifications. When PARSE PERS is violated, *PERS will choose a form which has no person specification over one which has the wrong one. In a system where *PERS ≫ PARSE PERS, there would be no clitics marked for person, and the same point holds for all features. I will not pursue this possibility here, postponing it for a further study which addresses the issue of how the lexicon of clitics is to be properly understood.

In this paper, I take the clitic lexicon as given, and show how the constraint system derives constancy of forms in isolation and variation in combination. However, one of the interesting points of Optimality Theory is that it makes it possible to derive grammatical inventories themselves from rankings of constraints (Prince and Smolensky (1993), Grimshaw (to appear), Grimshaw and Samek-Lodovici (to appear). A constraint such as *PERS finds its natural place in such an analysis. Although I do not develop this point here, it should be noted that even in the present paper, the constraint ranking is playing a critical role in determining the lexicon of clitics that is actually realized in these languages.

Tableau (10) illustrates this point for a relatively straightforward example. Recall that the choice of *vi* as the optimal candidate for [R 2 pl acc] input requires the ranking FILL R ≫ PARSE CASE. This was shown in (3) above. This is because the *vi* clitic fails to parse the case in the input, and the -R clitics can successfully do this. Hence we must count the FILL R violation as dominating the effects of PARSE CASE. What happens under other rankings? The answer is that we can derive a system with no second person pronouns. (10) shows the fatal violation of PARSE CASE that *vi* suffers.

(10) PARSE CASE ≫ FILL R, PARSE PERS, FILL PERS
input: ⟨[R 2 pl acc]⟩

candidates		PARSE NUM	FILL NUM	PARSE CASE	FILL CASE	PARSE R	FILL R	PARSE PERS	FILL PERS
a. si	(R)(P)(N)(C)	*		*		*		*	
b. mi	(R) 1 sg (C)	*	*	*		*		*	*
c. ti	(R) 2 sg (C)	*	*	*		*			
d. ci	(R) 1 pl (C)			*		*		*	*
e. vi	(R) 2 pl (C)			*!		*			
f. lo/la	-R (P) sg acc	*	*			*	*	*	
g. ☞ li/le	-R (P) pl acc					*	*	*	
h. gli/le	-R (P) sg dat	*	*	*	*	*	*	*	

If PARSE CASE dominates FILL R and the person constraints, then the optimal candidate will be the -R variant which successfully parses the case, even though it counterspecifies reflexivity and fails both person constraints. Such a grammar will have no second person pronoun. (The same choice is optimal for an input with a -R specification, where the g. candidates satisfy FILL R in addition to the constraints they satisfy in (10).) This is an illustration of the interplay between constraint rankings and lexical inventories, documented in Prince and Smolensky (1993).

Returning to the main theme, the rankings established so far are these:

FILL PERS ≫ PARSE NUM
FILL R ≫ PARSE NUM, AND PARSE CASE

These are constant across all the Romance dialects and languages discussed here. We will see shortly that other rankings, those involving *XX in particular, show significant variation.

4. CLITIC COMBINATIONS: *XX

The central hypothesis of this paper is that clitic combinations are regulated by a violable constraint like the Obligatory Contour Principle, which prohibits clitic duplication. The ranking of this constraint relative to the faithfulness constraints determines what happens in clitic combinations. When *XX dominates a faithfulness constraint, the faithfulness constraint will be violated and the form which occurs will be the one that best fits the input given the constraint rankings. It may even be the case that only one of the input clitic specifications is realized in the output, the other deleting. When *XX is dominated by the relevant faithfulness constraint(s), the *XX violation will be ignored and the clitics which occur will be exactly those that occur in isolation.

The data in (11) (from Bonet 1995) illustrates the alternation found in Italian between *si* and *ci*. The clitic *si* is the best output for the impersonal input, as we saw above in (7), and it is also the best output for a 3rd person reflexive input (as shown above in (4–5)). Both of these clitics occur in combination with other clitics, as (11a,b) show (although *si* is replaced with *se* in clitic combinations, a substitution which I will not analyze here.) When we would expect to find two occurrences of *si*, however, or perhaps *si* plus *se*, this is not possible. Instead, we find the combination *ci* plus *si*. This use of *ci* is an example of what Bonet (1995) calls an "opaque clitic": *ci* is generally the first person plural clitic but in this situation it is not encoding first person.

(11) a. Lo **si** sveglia — impersonal *si*
3rd-acc impers. wakes-up
"one wakes him up"

b. Se **lo** compra — reflexive *si/se*
refl. 3rd-acc buys
"s/he buys it for herself/himself"

c. **Ci si** lava — impersonal plus reflexive (**si si*)
ci si washes
"one washes oneself"

Let us assume for simplicity that *ci* in the output corresponds to the impersonal subject input (which is plural in Italian as noted above), although the same prediction is made with respect to choice of forms if *ci* corresponds to the reflexive. To realize the impersonal input with *si* violates *XX. To realize it with *ci* results in an incorrect person specification, hence the ranking of FILL PERS below *XX is crucial.

(12) *si si* > *ci si* (Tableau ignores case and gender, also candidates with dative -R clitics)
Input: ⟨[3 pl] [R 3 pl]⟩

Candidates		*XX	PARSE R	FILL R	PARS PERS	FILL PERS	PARSE NUM	FILL NUM
a. si+si	(R)(P)(N)+(R)(P)(N)	*	*		**		**	
b. li/le +si	-R (P) pl + (R)(P)(N)		*	*!	**		*	
c. lo/la+si	-R (P) sg + (R)(P)(N)		*	*!	**		**	*
d. ☞ci+si	(R) 1 pl +(R)(P)(N)		*		**	*	*	
e. mi+si	(R) 1 sg + (R)(P)(N)		*		**	*	**!	*!
f. vi+si	(R) 2 pl + (R)(P)(N)		*		**	*	*	
g. ti+si	(R) 2 sg + (R)(P)(N)		*		**	*	**!	*!

The singular clitics in c. e. and g. are the same as the corresponding plurals, except that they have a violation of FILL NUM plus an extra violation of PARSE NUM, so the singular candidates can be eliminated. Since all candidates fail PARSE R once and PARSE PERS twice, we can eliminate these constraints from consideration. The resulting greatly reduced tableau is in (13).

(13) *si si* > *ci si* (Tableau ignores case and gender, also candidates with dative -R clitics)
Input: ⟨[3 pl] [R 3 pl]⟩

Candidates	*XX	FILL R	FILL PERS	PARSE NUM	FILL NUM
a. si+si (R)(P)(N)+(R)(P)(N)	*			**	
b. li/le +si -R (P) pl + (R)(P)(N)		*!		*	
d. ☞ci+si (R) 1 pl +(R)(P)(N)			*	*	
f. vi+si (R) 2 pl + (R)(P)(N)			*	*	

Recall that *ci* is not the best clitic for the impersonal input when it is in isolation. This is because it counter-specifies the person of the input, and since FILL PERS ≫ PARSE NUM, the fact that it successfully parses the number in the input, which *si* does not, is irrelevant. In order for *ci* to be selected here, then, there is a crucial ranking between *XX and FILL PERS. The ranking selects *ci* with its FILL PERS violation over *si*. We also see in (13) evidence for a further ranking. The non-reflexive plural clitics can realize the input with no FILL PERS violation, because they have no person specification, while *ci* is specified as 1. The non-reflexive clitics do, however, have a -R specification and thus induce a violation of FILL R, hence provided that FILL R ≫ FILL PERS the non-reflexive candidates will be eliminated. This assumes that the input is not -R, of course, as does the original analysis of impersonal *si* in (7).

Finally, the markedness constraint *2, which universally dominates *1, selects *ci* over *vi*. (Note that the existence of *1 is inferred only, there is no direct evidence for such a constraint. If it does exist, then it must be ranked below *XX, in order that the violation of *1 which *ci* incurs not result in incorrect choice of *si* as optimal.) The crucial language particular rankings involved in the *si*/*ci* alternation are thus those in (14).

(14) Crucial Rankings: *XX ≫ FILL PERS, FILL R ≫ FILL PERS,
*XX ≫ *1

5. RE-RANKING TO GET *SI SI* DIALECT

Bonet (1995) notes that there is a dialect of Italian (Conegliano), illustrated in (16), which does not show the *si*/*ci* alternation. Here instead, *si* appears twice.

(15) Standard Italian
Ci si lava
ci si washes
"one washes oneself"

(16) Conegliano
Si si lava
si si washes
"one washes oneself"

Bonet observes that this is quite puzzling because it undermines any attempt to derive the *si/ci* alternation from a universal constraint against like occurring with like. If such a constraint existed, it would rule out the existence of Conegliano. If such a constraint does not exist, how do we explain the *si/ci* alternation? Under an optimality theoretic account, this dilemma is resolved. It is both the case that the general constraint exists and the case that grammatical sentences can violate it. This is what will arise if the *XX constraint is dominated by a crucial faithfulness constraint. In particular, if FILL PERS ≫ *XX, as in (17), the grammar will select the *si si* output, since it satisfies FILL PERS.[3]

(17) Re-ranking of *XX and FILL PERS
Input: ⟨[3 pl] [R 3 pl]⟩

Candidates	PARSE R	FILL R	PARS PERS	FILL PERS	*XX	PARSE NUM	FILL NUM	*2	*1
a. ☞si+si (R)(P)(N)+(R)(P)(N)	*		**		*	**			
d.ci+si (R) 1 pl +(R)(P)(N)	*		**	*!		*			*

Thus the existence of the Conegliano dialect is predicted: it is simply the result of re-ranking a faithfulness constraint with *XX.

6. SPANISH *SE* ELLIPSIS

As noted earlier, there is more than one way to resolve the problem posed by clitic duplication. One is to change one of the clitics into another form as in Italian, another is to delete one. Bakovic (p.c.) points out that Spanish opts for the latter in at least some dialects: the generality of this phenomenon remains to be determined.

(18) a.* Se se lava
"one washes oneself"

b. Se lava

In the earlier discussion of the success of *si* and the success of the null candidate at parsing input specifications, we saw that since *si* parses none of the person, number, gender and reflexivity of the input, it is preferred over the null candidate only by virtue of its success in satisfying the constraint PARSE CL which is satisfied if the output is any clitic, regardless of how unsatisfactory a parse the clitic may offer. The "reduction" of *se se* to just *se* results if the *XX constraint dominates PARSE CL, provided that FILL PERS ≫ PARSE CL also. This is illustrated in the tableaux below, in which *XX and FILL PERS both dominate PARSE CL.[4]

(19) *se se* > *se* (Tableau radically simplified)
Input: ⟨[Cl 3sg] [Cl R 3 sg]⟩

Candidates		*XX	PARSE R	FILL R	PARS PERS	FILL PERS	PARSE CL	PARSE NUM	FILL NUM
a. se+se	Cl (R)(P)(N)+Cl (R)(P)(N)	*!	*		**			**	
b. me+se	Cl (R) 1 sg+.Cl (R)(P)(N)		*		**	*!		*	
c. ☞ se	Cl (R)(P)(N)		*		**		*	**	

Since PARSE R, FILL R, PARSE PERS and FILL NUM do not distinguish among the key candidates, we can eliminate them all and simplify the tableau as follows.

(20) *se se* > *se*
Input: ⟨[Cl 3sg] [Cl R 3 sg]⟩

Candidates		*XX	FILL PERS	PARSE CL	PARSE NUM
a. se+se	Cl (R)(P)(N)+Cl (R)(P)(N)	*!			**
b. me+se	Cl (R) 1 sg+.Cl (R)(P)(N)		*!		*
c. ☞ se	Cl (R)(P)(N)			*	**

Candidate a. is eliminated in favor of c. if *XX ≫ PARSE CL: the two candidates are identical on all other constraints. This leaves candidates b. and c. The reduced candidate c. does worse than b. on two constraints: PARSE CL and PARSE NUM, and better only on FILL PERS, so the following rankings are required in addition:

FILL PERS ≫ PARSE CL, PARSE NUM

We now need to briefly reconsider what was said above concerning Italian and the Conegliano dialect, taking the effects of PARSE CL into account. Clearly, since all the key candidates perform the same with respect to PARSE R, FILL R, PARSE PERS and FILL NUM, we can continue to eliminate them from the tableaux. We need only consider possible alternative rankings among the remaining constraints.

The next tableau shows the ranking which yields the Conegliano facts: here PARSE CL and FILL PERS both dominate *XX.

(21) *si si > si si*
Input: ⟨[Cl 3 pl] [Cl R 3 sg]⟩

Candidates	PARSE CL	FILL PERS	*XX	PARSE NUM
a. ☞ si+si Cl (R)(P)(N)+Cl (R)(P)(N)			*	**
b ci+si Cl (R) 1 sg+.Cl (R)(P)(N)		*!		*
c. si Cl (R)(P)(N)	*!			**

Note the crucial role played in (21) by the ranking of FILL PERS over *XX. If PARSE CL ≫ *XX then a form with two clitics will always result when the input has two units, but whether the two clitics are identical as in (21) or distinct as in (22) depends on the ranking of *XX and FILL PERS. The choice of *si si* over *ci si* depends also on the previously discussed ranking of FILL PERS over PARSE NUM, which is violated one more time in the optimal candidate than in the *ci si* candidate.

(22) shows that the *ci si* pattern results when *XX dominates FILL PERS as well as PARSE CL.

(22) *si si > ci si*
Input: ⟨[Cl 3 pl] [Cl R 3 sg]⟩

Candidates	*XX	PARSE CL	FILL PERS	PARSE NUM
a. si+si Cl (R)(P)(N)+Cl (R)(P)(N)	*!			**
b. si Cl (R)(P)(N)		*!		**
c. ☞ ci+si Cl (R) 1 pl +Cl (R)(P)(N)			*	*

When *XX dominates PARSE CL and PARSE CL dominates FILL PERS, the *ci si* pattern is the outcome, since the counterspecification of person is less serious in its consequences than the duplication of clitics or failure to parse a clitic. The same output is selected if PARSE CL dominates *XX and PARSE CL ≫ FILL PERS. In other words, it results from every system where PARSE CL ≫ FILL PERS, and **XX ≫ FILL PERS, regardless of the ranking of *XX and PARSE CL.

The general result is as follows. The duplication of *si* is a point of conflict in the constraint system. On the one hand, faithfulness requires realization as *si* for both inputs, but on the other hand *XX prohibits this outcome.

What we have seen is that a variety of resolutions are possible, depending on the ranking of a few key constraints: *XX, PARSE CL, FILL PERS and PARSE NUM. Depending on how they are ranked, the solution will be to live with the duplication, to delete a clitic, or to replace one of the offending clitics with a less faithful alternative.

7. SPANISH "SPURIOUS *SE*"

The data in (23), again taken from Bonet (1995), illustrate the phenomenon known as "spurious *se*" in Spanish (Perlmutter 1971). When a third person accusative and a third person dative combine, the dative is replaced by *se*.

(23) a. El premio, **lo** dieron a Pedro ayer.
the prize 3rd-acc gave(3rd-pl) to Pedro yesterday

b. A Pedro, **le** dieron el premio ayer.
to Pedro 3rd-dat gave(3rd-pl) the prize yesterday

c. A Pedro, el premio, **se lo** dieron ayer. (***le lo** ***lo le**)
to Pedro the prize se 3rd-acc gave(3rd-pl) yesterday
"they gave the prize to Pedro yesterday"

An analysis of spurious *se* must explain why the expected output does not occur, why it is the dative that is replaced and not the accusative, and why *se* appears rather than some other clitic.

The general structure of the solution here is clear: the *le lo* combination violates some constraint which dominates the relevant faithfulness constraint and *se* appears in a not unexpected fashion. Assuming for now that it is *XX that *le lo* violates, we have the situation in (24).

(24) *XX includes *le* > *se*.
input: ⟨[-R 3 sg dat] [-R 3 sg acc]⟩ (case constraints omitted from consideration)

Candidates	*XX	PARSE R	FILL R	PARSE PERS	FILL PERS	PARSE NUM	FILL NUM
a. le + lo -R (P) sg dat + -R (P) sg acc	*!						
b. ☞ se + lo (R)(P)(N)(C) + -R (P) sg acc		*		*		*	
c. me + lo (R) 1 sg (C) + -R (P) sg acc		*		*	*!		
d. te + lo (R) 2 sg (C) + -R (P) sg acc		*		*	*!		
e. nos/os + lo (R) 1/2 pl (C) + -R (P) sg acc		*		*	*!	*	*

However, (24) also reveals that it is rather unclear why *le* + *lo* should violate *XX. They are not phonologically identical, unlike the cases we have seen so far. Moreover, although they are morphologically similar in that they are both descriptively third person, in the analysis given here they are unmarked for person, and represent the residual case. They are, of course, both -R clitics, and perhaps this suffices to trigger *XX. What makes this uncertain is the question of what other kinds of morphological identity might count for the constraint, and why. (Note that they are not morphologically identical, because one is dative and one accusative, moreover the spurious *se* effect is found when a singular combines with a plural, so identity of number is not relevant.)

These issues remain unresolved at this point. There are three ways to think about the nature of the constraint violation in the *le lo* combination. One is that it is really phonological, and the identity of onsets is sufficient to violate *XX. The second is that it is really morphological, and that the occurrence of two -R clitics violates *XX, or perhaps, if we revise the analysis of 3rd person, that the duplication of 3 is in violation of the constraint. The third possibility is that the source of the violation is a little different, and concerns the constraints on clitic order, which have sometimes been analyzed in terms of a "template" or output constraint, following the original proposal by Perlmutter (1971). Bonet proposes such a solution for certain opaque forms in Catalan. According to this view, the realization of clitics must conform to principles determining what count as good clitic sequences. For Spanish, Perlmutter (1971: 45) proposes the following condition: *se* II I III. According to this constraint, then, there is only one third person position ("III"), so one might hypothesize that the clitic combination *le lo* (and indeed some of the others discussed here) violates the templatic requirement and hence cannot be realized. Since there is only one position for a 3rd person in the template, a clitic which is not third person must "replace" a third person form in combinations.

While this idea has some initial appeal, its ultimate fate depends on the theory of these templatic restrictions. On further reflection it is hard to see how the templatic view really differs from saying that two (descriptively) 3rd person clitics cannot combine. In other words, it seems highly likely that the template requirements themselves are the result of the system of constraints at work in the selection of clitics. Recognizing that this issue needs to be resolved, I will continue to assume that *XX is at work here. Clearly, though, its status as the key constraint here is leading into questions beyond those we can address.

Returning to the tableau in (24), given the clitic inventory, all -R candidates violate *XX, for one of the reasons discussed above. The best of these candidates must be *le*, which best parses the input, hence of the -R clitics only *le* is shown in the tableau. The ranking *XX > PARSE R eliminates all the -R clitics.

For familiar reasons, *se* is the best choice of the remaining clitics. Of the candidates which satisfy *XX b. satisfies FILL PERS, which the others violate. But b. violates PARSE NUM, which c. and d. satisfy. Therefore FILL PERS ≫ PARSE NUM yields *se* as optimal.

Crucial rankings *XX > Parse R
FILL PERS ≫ PARSE NUM

Since PARSE CASE is violated in the optimal candidate, but satisfied in the candidate which violates *XX, we can also deduce that *XX ≫ PARSE CASE; however, the case constraints are not included in the tableau.

The next question is why *le*, rather than *lo*, is replaced by *se*. Tableau (25) shows the alternatives available if *le* is retained. The best candidate in this set is *le* plus *se*, candidate b, given the rankings just mentioned.

(25) Why keep *lo* and not *le*?
input: ⟨[-R 3 sg dat] [-R 3 sg acc]⟩

Candidates	*XX	PARSE R	FILL R	PARSE PERS	FILL PERS	PARSE NUM	FILL NUM
a. le + lo -R (P) sg dat + -R (P) sg acc	*!						
b. le + se -R (P) sg dat + (R)(P)(N)(C)		*		*		*	
c. le + me -R (P) sg dat + (R)1sg(C)		*		*	*!		
d. le + te -R (P) sg dat + (R) 2 sg (C)		*		*	*!		
e. le + nos/os -R (P) pl dat + (R) 1/2 pl (C)		*		*	*!	*	*

When we compare *le* plus *se* with *lo* plus *se*, it becomes clear that they are identical except with respect to the case on the retained item, accusative in one instance, dative in the other. Since each offers a faithful parse of the input case specification, no faithfulness constraint relating to case can distinguish them. Hence *le* + *se* and and *se* + *lo* are equally (un)successful parses for the input, and a markedness constraint must be at work. A constraint against dative (*DAT), universally ranked above a constraint against accusative if such exists (here *ACC), will have the right consequences.

(26) best of candidates which retain *lo*, and best of candidates which retain *le*:
input: ⟨[-R 3 sg dat] [-R 3 sg acc]⟩

Candidates	*XX	PARS E R	FILL R	PARSE PERS	FILL PERS	PARSE NUM	FILL NUM	*DAT	*ACC
a. ☞ se + lo (R)(P)(N)(C) + -R (P) sg acc			*	*		*			*
b. le + se -R (P) sg dat + (R)(P)(N)(C)			*	*		*		*!	

In this analysis, then, we can predict that *le lo* will be replaced by *se lo*. The only puzzle concerns the precise understanding of *XX in this context, raising the question of whether some other constraint will prove to lie behind the effect.

8. RERANKING TO DERIVE *LE LO*

Given the preceding discussion, it comes as no surprise that not every Romance language shows the spurious *se* effect. If PARSE R ≫ *XX, then the transparent clitics will surface, as they do in Italian (27), where *gli* plus *lo* surfaces as the complex *glielo*:

(27) Glielo venderà
"he will sell it to him/her"

This ranking picks the candidate which parses the -R specification of the input, and the best such candidate is the one which appears in isolation.

(28) *XX below PARSE R, no spurious *se*
input: ⟨[-R 3 sg dat] [-R 3 sg acc]⟩ (case constraints omitted from consideration)

Candidates		PARSE R	*XX	FILL R	PARSE PERS	FILL PERS	PARSE NUM	FILL NUM
a. ☞gli + lo	-R (P) sg dat + -R (P) sg acc		*		**			
b. si + lo	(R)(P)(N)(C) + -R (P) sg acc	*!			**		*	
c. mi + lo	(R) 1 sg (C) + -R (P) sg acc	*!			**	*		
d. ti + lo	(R) 2 sg (C) + -R (P) sg acc	*!			**	*		
e. ci/vi +lo	(R) 1/2 pl (C) + -R (P) sg acc	*!			**	*	*	*

9. FLOATING NUMBER

Bonet shows that in some dialects of American Spanish, the accusative clitic takes on the number associated with the dative argument, under spurious *se* conditions. (29a) is Iberian Spanish, (29b) the American Spanish dialect version.[5]

(29) a. El libro, a ellos, ¿quién **se lo** prestó?
the book to them who se 3rd-acc lent(3rd)
"'who lent the book to them?"

b. El libro, a ellos, ¿quién **se los** prestó?

The general idea here is a simple one. In a spurious *se* configuration, the input specification is not well parsed. In particular the number of the dative argument in the input is unparsed since *se* is unspecified for number. In (29b) the system selects the option of expressing the plurality of the argument "replaced" by *se*, by expressing it on the other argument. Thus (29b) involves suppressing the singular character of the direct object in order to express the plural character of the indirect object.

The conclusion we have to draw is that there is an asymmetry, not addressed here previously, between singular and plural. This motivates a further step in the analysis of the basic clitic systems, which is illustrated in (30)–(31). The input contains two number specifications, one for the accusative clitic and one for the dative. In the case where the number specifications of the two clitics differ, if the number of the dative clitic is realized on the accusative, it follows that the number of the accusative clitic is not realized. If, on the other hand, the number of the accusative is realized, the number of the dative will not be. Thus in either case, under assumptions made so far, there will be a violation of PARSE NUM. This is illustrated in (30). Since the realization of the number of the dative clitic on the accusative clitic will also violate FILL NUM, there is no way that the candidate with the number transferred can ever be optimal. (In the greatly reduced tableaux to be used here, only the constraints on which the candidates differ are included, and the constraint violations induced by *se*, those involved in the spurious *se* configuration, are not represented on the tableaux.)

(30) Why sg must be unmarked
input: ⟨[-R 3 pl masc dat] [-R 3 sg masc acc]⟩

Candidates which satisfy *XX		PARSE NUM	FILL NUM
☞ se + lo	(R)(P)(N)(G)(C) + -R (P) sg masc acc	*(pl)	
se + los	(R)(P)(N)(G)(C) + -R (P) pl masc acc	*(sg)	*!

The conclusion we must draw is that the singular must be unmarked, and the plural marked. More precisely, it must be the case that the representation of the singular clitics has no number specification, so that *lo* is properly represented as in (31a) instead of (31b), as we have assumed so far.

(31) a. [-R (P) (N) masc acc]
b. [-R (P) sg masc acc]

Under this representation, we still get the right result for candidates in isolation, as we can see in (32), which shows the outcome for a singular input.

(32) Selecting the right candidate in isolation: singular
input: ⟨[-R 3 sg masc acc]⟩

Candidates		PARSE NUM	FILL NUM
los	-R (P) pl masc acc	*	*!
☞ lo	-R (P) (N) masc acc	*	

When the input is plural, *los* will be selected:

(33) Selecting the right candidate in isolation: plural input: ⟨[-R 3 pl masc acc]⟩

Candidates		PARSE NUM	FILL NUM
☞ los	-R (P) pl masc acc		
lo	-R (P) (N) masc acc	*!	

Returning to the problem of floating number, and utilizing the asymmetry between singular and plural, the situation can now be summarized slightly differently. When the accusative clitic is singular, its number specification is never parsed, because the available clitics are unmarked for number. There is thus no additional cost with respect to parsing the number of this clitic if it is realized as a plural: the input singular is unparsed whether the clitic used is *los* or *lo*. In isolation, the option of realizing a singular input as *los* is prevented by FILL NUM, which penalizes the realization of the plural specification on the accusative clitic, as we saw in (32). In the floating number situation, therefore, there is a conflict between the goal of parsing the input number specification of the dative clitic, and improperly attaching plural specification on the singular input accusative argument. To put it in constraint terms, PARSE NUM and FILL NUM are in conflict in this case. If PARSE NUM ≫ FILL NUM, the number will float.

(34) Floating number if PARSE NUM > FILL NUM
input: ⟨[-R 3 pl masc dat] [-R 3 sg masc acc]⟩

Candidates	*XX	PARSE NUM	FILL NUM
se + lo (R)(P)(N)(G)(C) + -R(P) (N) masc acc		**!	
☞ se + los (R)(P)(N)(G)(C) + -R (P) pl masc acc		*	*

Realizing the accusative input with a plural clitic satisfies PARSE NUM for the plural specification, but violates FILL NUM on the accusative. There is a crucial assumption behind this proposal, which needs to be refined. The asssumption is that PARSE NUM is satisfied in the optimal candidate, despite the fact that the number specification is parsed in the wrong clitic. This is clearly the result that we want: it is better to parse the number in the wrong place than not to parse it at all. It is assumed here that a FILL NUM violation ensues when the accusative is realized as a plural, because the FILL constraint looks at the input for that clitic, rather than the input as a whole. In order to explicate this more precisely we need to draw upon the results of recent phonological research on correspondence, and I will turn to this shortly.

10. FLOATING GENDER

The more general prediction of this analysis is that for any input specification, its realization will float if PARSE F ≫ FILL F. Bonet (1995) discusses dialects of American Spanish, citing colloquial Mexican and Uruguayan, in which *se la* is the preferred output when the input dative is feminine, even when the input accusative is masculine. She cites the data in (35b), which contrasts with the Iberian Spanish (35a).

(35) a. Si ella me quiere comprar el caballo, yo **se lo** venderé.
if she 1st-dat wants buy the horse I se 3rd-acc will-sell (1st)
"If she wants to buy my horse, I will sell it to her"

b. Si ella me quiere comprar el caballo, yo **se la** venderé.
if she 1st-dat wants buy the horse I se 3rd-acc-fem will-sell(1st)
"if she wants to buy my horse, I will sell it to her"

For reasons entirely parallel to those discussed for singular number, this situation requires that masculine gender is unmarked and, more precisely, that there are no clitics marked as masculine. The correct representation of *lo* is as in (36a) rather than (36b).

(36) a. [-R (P) (N) (G) acc]
b. [-R (P) (N) masc acc]

I will not go through the details of how the correct candidate is selected in isolation, as the logic is exactly the same as for number. As was the case with number, in this analysis the "masculine" clitics do not parse the gender specification of the input, and hence always violate PARSE GEND even when the clitics occur in isolation. Hence *se* plus *lo* in (35a) violates PARSE GEND twice, while *se* plus *la* in (35b) violates the constraint only once. Provided, then, that PARSE GEND ≫ FILL GEND, gender will float as number does.[6]

(37) Floating gender if PARSE GEND ≫ FILL GEND
input: ⟨[-R 3 sg fem dat] [-R 3 sg masc acc]⟩

Candidates		PARSE GEND	FILL GEND
se + lo	(R)(P)(N)(G)(C) + -R (P) (N) (G) acc	**!	
☞se + la	(R)(P)(N)(G)(C) + -R (P) (N) fem acc	*	*

The same assumptions hold here concerning what count as violations of the PARSE and FILL constraints as above.

11. RERANKING FOR DIALECTS WITH NO FLOATING FEATURES:

Not surprisingly, in view of the previous discussion, the opposite ranking of the PARSE and FILL constraints yields dialects in which there is no floating. So where FILL F ≫ PARSE F, F will not float. Tableau (38) illustrates this for gender.

(38) No floating gender if FILL GEND ≫ PARSE GEND
input: ⟨[-R 3 sg fem dat] [-R 3 sg masc acc]⟩

Candidates	FILL GEND	PARSE GEND
☞se + lo (R)(P)(N)(G)(C) + -R (P) (N) (G) acc		**
se + la (R)(P)(N)(G)(C) + -R (P) (N) fem acc	*!	*

Finally, if the PARSE constraints for both gender and number dominate the FILL constraints, then both number and gender will float. The data in (39), again from Bonet (1995), illustrate this: (39a) is Iberian Spanish, (39b) illustrates the relevant American dialects.

(39) a. Si ellas me quieren comprar el caballo, yo **se lo** venderé.
if they(fem) lst-dat want(3rd-pl) buy the horse I se 3rd-acc will-sell(lst)

"if they want to buy my horse, I will sell it to them"

b. Si ellas me quieren comprar el caballo, yo **se las** venderé.
if they(fem) lst-dat want(3rd-pl) buy the horse I se 3rd-acc-fem-pl will-sell(lst)

"'if they want to buy my horse, I will sell it to them"

In this case the optimal candidate violates both FILL NUM and FILL GEND, but satisfies both PARSE NUM and PARSE GEND.

(40) Gender and Number float together
input: ⟨[-R 3μ pl fem dat] [-R 3 sg masc acc]⟩

Candidates which satisfy *XX	PARSE GEND	FILL GEND	PARSE NUM	FILL NUM
se + lo (R)(P)(N)(G)(C) + -R (P) (N) (G) acc	**!		**	
se + la (R)(P)(N)(G)(C) + -R (P) (N) fem acc	*	*	**!	
se+los (R)(P)(N)(G)(C) + -R (P) pl (G) acc	**!		*	
☞se+las (R)(P)(N)(G)(C) + -R (P) pl fem acc	*	*	*	*

I should point out that, in this analysis, the floating of gender and the floating of number are independent, so we expect to find dialects in which neither float, dialects in which both float, and dialects in which only one of the two floats.

As I mentioned above, there is a crucial assumption behind this proposal, which needs to be refined. The asssumption is that the PARSE constraints are satisfied when the features float, even though the features are parsed in the "wrong" clitic, but the FILL constraints are violated in this case; this requires assuming that the PARSE constraints look at the input as a whole while the FILL constraints look at the input for individual clitics. It is hard to see why such an asymmetry should be expected. We can explicate the situation rather differently, if we draw upon the results of recent phonological research on correspondence, presented in McCarthy and Prince (1995). In their discussion of reduplication and identity requirements they develop three constraint families. Considering only their role in constraining the relationships between inputs and outputs, the MAX family requires that every segment of the input has a correspondent in the output, the DEP family requires that every segment in the output has a correspondent in the input and the IDENT(F) family requires that correspondent segments are identical in feature F. The key point is that MAX and DEP only require that each piece of the input has a correspondent in the output, or vice versa, whereas the IDENT(F) constraints are sensitive to the location of the correspondent. Let us take the position that the number feature in the input is in correspondence with the number feature of the output and so forth, and that the set of feature specifications in the input is in correspondence with the set of feature specifications in the output. We can now apply this revised analysis to the case of floating number, for illustrative purposes, showing, as always, only the violations that result from the selection of the second clitic, and not those triggered by *se*.

(41) Floating number if MAX NUM >> IDENT NUM
input: ⟨[-R 3 pl masc dat] [-R 3 sg masc acc]⟩

Candidates		MAX NUM	DEP NUM	IDENT NUM
se + lo	(R)(P)(N)(G)(C) + -R (P) (N) (G) acc	**!		*
☞ se + los	(R)(P)(N)(G)(C) + -R (P) pl (G) acc	*		**

MAX holds for features and for the clitics as collections of features. In particular, it is violated for every feature in the input which does not have a correspondent in the output, so there are 5 violations overall for *se* in both candidates, three for *lo* in the first candidate and two for *los* in the second candidate. Crucially, MAX NUM is violated in *se lo* but not in *se los*. DEP NUM (and more generally DEP for all the output specifications) is satisfied in both candidates, since no feature in the output lacks a corresponding feature in the input, assuming crucially that the "pl" feature of the output is in correspondence with the "sg" specification in the input, i.e. that different values for the same feature, here number, are in correspondence with each other. Finally, IDENT NUM is violated by *se* in both candidates, since the correspondents are not identical with respect to number (taking the correspondents to be the collections of features between square brackets in the input and the collections of features between plus signs in the outputs). One correspondent, the input clitic specification, has number specified (among other features) while the other correspondent, the output clitic specification, has no number. IDENT NUM is also violated by the combination "sg in input plus pl in output" for the *los* candidate, hence this candidate has two violations of the constraint. What is going on, then, is that the fact that the plural feature is realized at all satisifes MAX, but IDENT NUM is violated in reflection of the fact that the plural specification is not in the correspondent clitic. IDENT NUM is playing the role here that FILL NUM played previously, penalizing the realization of the feature on the wrong clitic, while MAX NUM is playing the role in which PARSE NUM was previously cast, with the rather odd consequences noted earlier. The critical ranking, then, is MAX NUM >> IDENT NUM, and the other ranking will give dialects with no floating features.

That constraints developed in phonological research should provide an improved solution for the problems of clitic choice should hardly be surprising by now. In particular, both reduplication systems and the clitic systems under study here are domains in which notions of faithfulness and identity play a crucial role. In any event, it seems that separating the faithfulness constraints into these three types, as opposed to the previous two types, offers the conceptual clarification needed for a solution of floating number and gender.

13. CONCLUSIONS

There are a number of important issues which are not addressed at all in this paper, but require further investigation. One is the question already raised, of whether the optimality theoretic account can extend in an interesting way to the generalizations concerning clitic order, usually taken to reflect the operation of some kind of surface structure template as first discussed in Perlmutter (1971). The second issue, more directly challenging to the theory, is how to explain why certain clitic combinations are simply impossible. This is the case with, for example, Italian combinations like *mi mi*, where one is a dative and one an accusative, and for others discussed in Wanner (1977). Here there is no change in the clitic choice which results in grammaticality, and the only possible form is one in which one of the arguments is expressed as a phrase and not as a clitic. Optimality Theory offers two lines of attack on this problem. The ill-formed combination may be impossible because in fact there is a better output, one which better satisfies the constraints. It is possible, for example, that a phrasal expression competes with a clitic expression for status as the optimal output for a given input. Alternatively, the combination may be impossible because the null candidate is the optimal candidate in this case, hence no actual candidate survives. Both of these lines of analysis need to be pursued.

The choice of clitics in these Romance systems is highly systematic, as Bonet (1995) has already shown. The argument of this paper is that this systematicity can best be explicated in terms of the notion of optimization: the clitic used is the best one available in the circumstances. The "circumstances" are provided by the clitic inventory of the language and the rankings of the grammatical constraints, especially the ranking of faithfulness constraints relative to *XX. In this way, the constraints of Universal Grammar determine the actual set of words which appears in the sentence which realizes a given input.

Cross-linguistic variation here is limited to the effects of constraint rankings: the same basic clitic system exists in each case. The constraints themselves are stated over a set of independently needed morphosyntactic features, such as "person", "reflexive", and simply require faithful parsing of these features. The same constraints regulate the clitic alternations studied here as regulate the more mundane case of clitic choice where no alternations occur. Finally, we see the importance of the optimality theoretic notion of "minimal violation". While it is perfectly possible to select a clitic which violates a constraint, indeed many constraints, such violation must be compelled by a higher ranking constraint. Violation is not free. Hence we see clitic alternations under pressure from *XX, but clitics in isolation are not affected by this constraint, and hence appear in a standard form with no alternations.

Rutgers University

NOTES

[1] The research reported here was supported by grant SBR-9511891 from the National Science Foundation by Rutgers University. It has benefited from presentation at Keio University, Stanford University, the University of California at Santa Cruz, and the Third Australian Linguistic Institute at the Australian National University. Special thanks to the Rutgers Optimality Research Group, in particular Eric Bakovic, Ed Keer, Suzanne Preuss, Alan Prince, Melissa Trachtenburg and Vieri Samek-Lodovici for much helpful discussion, and to Eric Bakovic for important insights concerning Spanish.

[2] Italian has no clitic form for the plural counterpart of the datives *gli*/*le*.

[3] Alternatively, assuming the existence of *1 (see above), the ranking of *2, *1 ≫ *XX will give the *si si* dialect, regardless of the ranking of *XX and FILL PERS.

[4] A slight complication is that while Italian impersonal subjects seem to be plural (Cinque 1988: 536–537), their Spanish counterparts seem to be singular. I will show the Spanish input as [3 sg], and hence consider *me* in Spanish as the counterpart to *ci* in Italian, in assessing potential as the output for the impersonal.

[5] Kany (1951: 109–112) cites many examples of both floating number and floating gender (analyzed below), commenting that "grammarians and purists inveigh against this solecism".

[6] It is not clear why gender floats only with spurious *se*, and not also when the dative clitic is a first or second person, all of which are just like *se* in failing to encode gender.

REFERENCES

Bonet, i Alsina, M. Eulàlia (1991) *Morphology after Syntax: Pronominal Clitics in Romance*. Doctoral dissertation, Massachusetts Institute of Technology.

Bonet, Eulàlia (1995) 'Feature structure of Romance clitics', *Natural Language and Linguistic Theory* **13**, 607–647.

Cinque, Guglielmo (1988) 'On *si* constructions and the theory of *Arb*', *Linguistic Inquiry* **19**, 521–582.

Grimshaw, Jane (to appear) 'Projection, heads and optimality', *Linguistic Inquiry*.

Grimshaw, Jane and Vieri Samek-Lodovici (to appear) 'Optimal subjects and subject universals', in: Barbosa, Fox, Hagstrom, McGinnis and Pesetsky (eds.), *Is the Best Good Enough?* MITWPL/MIT Press.

Leben, Will (1973) *Suprasegmental Phonology*. Doctoral disseration, Massachusetts Institute of Technology.

McCarthy, John (1986) 'OCP effects: Gemination and antigemination', *Linguistic Inquiry* **17**, 207–263.

McCarthy, John and Alan Prince (1995) 'Faithfulness and reduplicative identity', ms. University of Massachusetts at Amherst and Rutgers University.

Mohanan, Tara (1994) 'Case OCP: A constraint on word order in Hindi', in: Miriam Butt, Tracy Holloway King and Gillian Ramchand (eds.), *Theoretical Perspectives on Word Order in South Asian Languages*. CSLI, pp. 185–216.

Perlmutter, David (1971) *Deep and Surface Structure Constraints in Syntax*. Holt, Rinehart and Winston.

Prince, Alan and Paul Smolensky (1993) *Optimality Theory: Constraint Interaction in Generative Grammar*. RuCCS Technical Report #2. Rutgers University Center for Cognitive Science, Piscataway NJ.

Ross, John Robert, (1972) 'Doubl-ing', *Linguistic Inquiry* **3**, 61–86.

Wanner, Dieter (1977) 'On the order of clitics in Italian', *Lingua* **43**, 101–128.

JIM McCLOSKEY

SUBJECTHOOD AND SUBJECT POSITIONS

1. INTRODUCTION

The notion of "subject" is fundamental in Aristotelian logic and in almost all Western traditions of thinking about philology and grammar.* It is also fundamental to certain strands of thought within the broad tradition of generative grammar – notably Relational Grammar and Lexical Functional Grammar. However, in the tradition which extends from the "Standard Theory" through the "Extended Standard Theory" to "Principles and Parameters Theory" and then to the "Minimalist Program", the notion of subject plays no formal role at all. Not only is "subject" not a primitive term in these theories, but in their most recent instantiations it is not even clear that there is any derived or defined notion which captures the traditional intuition of what a subject is (as there was, for instance, in the theory of Chomsky 1965). What we have seen, in a sense, is a progressive deconstruction of the traditional category "subject" so that the properties which are supposed to define it are distributed across a range of distinct (but derivationally linked) syntactic entities and positions. This theoretical eccentricity may turn out to have been foolish or wise, but it is certainly grounded in some of the deeper methodological instincts of generative grammar. My purpose in this contribution is to consider some recent proposals about the syntax of subjecthood, to try to place those proposals in a broader theoretical and historical perspective, and to evaluate their plausibility at least in a tentative way.

2. THE INTUITION

What might persuade someone that subjecthood is theoretically central? The answer, in part, must be that an impressively broad range of disparate phenomena seem to require reference to the notion.[1]

(i) The subject is the characteristic bearer of certain kinds of semantic roles (prototypically AGENT and perhaps also CAUSE and, more controversially EXPERIENCER).

(ii) The subject is more prominent than any other argument of the main verb. Its prominence is manifested in a variety of phenomena:
  a. the subject may bind reflexive and reciprocal pronouns appearing in other argument-positions but may not itself (if it is a reflexive or a reciprocal) be bound by elements in other argument-positions.
  b. the subject, at least in the typical case, takes wider scope than an element in any other argument-position.

Liliane Haegeman (ed.), Elements of Grammar, 197–235.

c. a subject, if it has the right semantic properties, licenses a Negative Polarity Item in some other argument-position. A Negative Polarity Item in subject-position cannot, however, be licensed by an appropriate element in another argument-position.

(iii) Subjects are typically formally marked – positionally and/or morphologically. Morphological marking may be on the subject itself (in the form of a case) or on the main inflectional element of the clause (in the form of agreement morphology).

(iv) It has sometimes been claimed that every clause must have a subject. This is not obviously correct, but it is clearly correct in some broad sense for some languages. There is no other argument-type or syntactic position for which this claim can be made with even remote plausibility. There are no languages, as far as I know, for which it has ever occurred to anyone to claim that every clause must have a direct object, or an indirect object or a prepositional complement or whatever.

(v) Subjects are almost always nominal. There is a well-known set of difficulties for this general claim (subject clauses if they exist, cases in English such as *Under the sink would be a good place to hide*, locative inversion constructions) but the general fact is so striking that it cannot be ignored. It is not remotely plausible to claim for any other syntactic position that it must be occupied exclusively by a phrase of a particular syntactic category.

(vi) Subjecthood is central in the system of promotion and advancement of nominals (to use the terminology of Relational Grammar). That is, there are many grammatical operations which create surface subjects by promoting nominals from other positions or ranks (passive, subject-to-subject raising, unaccusative advancement, *Tough* Movement and so on). These operations exhibit an impressive constancy across languages – in the way that they function and in the constraints that they are subject to.

3. A LITTLE HISTORY

In the *Aspects* framework which defined much work of the 1960's (Chomsky 1965), there is in fact a single position which is crucially implicated in all six of the identifying phenomena listed above. Given a phrase structural analysis of the sentence like that schematized below:

(1) a.

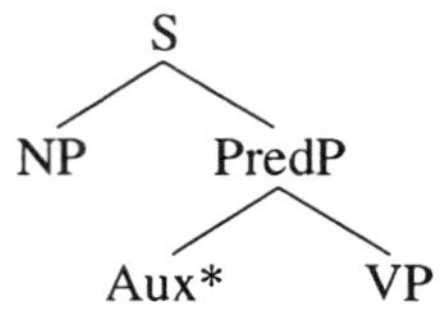

the NP–daughter–of–S position is the crucial position. Although it is anachronistic to speak of "semantic roles" in connection with this theory, it is true that the NP–daughter–of–S position is the position in which the AGENT argument of transitives and the EXPERIENCER argument of perception verbs and so on were assumed to appear at deep structure (and in which the "selectional restrictions" associated with assignment of such roles were enforced). This is also the position crucially implicated in the various operations which determine morphological properties of subjects – case and agreement especially (property (iii)). As for the question of prominence (property (ii)), following the work of Ross and of Langacker in the late 1960's (Ross 1969a, Langacker 1969), and that of Reinhart in the late 1970's (Reinhart 1976, 1979, 1983) the phrase-structural notion of command became, and has remained, the fundamental measure of relative prominence within the tradition we are discussing here (α is more prominent than β if α commands β and β does not command α). There is a variety of phrase structural relations in the "command" family (for general discussion see Barker and Pullum 1990), but all but one of them guarantee that the NP–daughter–of–S will be more prominent than any other argument-position. If the phenomena for which prominence is crucial are analyzed in terms of command relations, and if the "subject" relation is simply the phrase structural relation "NP–daughter–of–S", then the prominence of the subject is guaranteed.

The obligatory presence of a subject, and its obligatorily nominal character (properties (iv) and (v)) were simply stipulated in the initial phrase structure rule:

(1) b. S → NP PredP

As for the sixth property (the centrality of subject position in the operation of relation-changing rules of promotion), the relevant transformations (passive, subject raising and so on) were simply formulated so as to move nominal phrases into the NP–daughter–of–S position.

This conception of subjecthood is traditional and conservative in the sense that it associates subject properties with a unique syntactic position. It is radical in denying that the concept of subjecthood is a primitive of grammatical theory, but in maintaining rather that it is a derivative notion defined in terms of the primitives of phrase structure theory. It was this part of the *Aspects* conception of subjecthood that was to become controversial – in work of the 1970's and 1980's especially. One of the central issues that arises here is the issue of cross-linguistic generality. Assuming that one wants a way of referring to subjecthood that is invariant across languages, it is at least unclear that the phrase structural understanding provided by the *Aspects* theory is adequate. In the development of Relational Grammar and of Lexical Functional Grammar, it was argued that the syntactic and morphological encoding of subjecthood varies considerably across languages and language-types (pre-verbal position in English, immediate post-verbal position in Irish, final position in many Mayan languages, nominative marking in some languages, absolutive or ergative marking in others), but that the other properties are largely invariant across languages. One will want to say, for instance, that it is a general property of subjects, no matter how they are morphologically signaled, that they may bind reflexives or reciprocals in other argument positions, but that they may not themselves be bound from lower positions. One will also want to say with full cross-linguistic generality that passive creates derived subjects, that subjects of embedded clauses are raised to be subjects of matrix clauses under certain conditions and so on. From this perspective, it is natural to conclude that the *Aspects* understanding of subjecthood is irredeemably English-specific, confusing the grammatical encoding of the relation with the relation itself. From this position, it is in turn a short step to the assumption that "subjecthood" is properly construed as a primitive of the theory of grammar, and that the cross-linguistic generalizations governing passive, unaccusative advancement, raising and so on make direct reference to that notion.

This was not, of course, the conclusion drawn within the EST tradition. The strategy pursued there was to develop a theory of the subject-position and a theory of how that position determined subject properties, which was general enough to have some cross-linguistic credibility. There were a number of distinct analytical strands which made up this effort.

The development of the IP-model of sentence-structure in the early 1980's was one important element. It provided a model of clausal structure of sufficient abstraction and flexibility that it could lay some plausible claim to cross-linguistic generality. The analysis involved two crucial elements. The first is the idea that the sentence is universally a projection of inflectional information (tense, person, number and so on) and the second is that it is a regular X-Bar projection. This conception was flexible enough to handle clauses built around both verbal and nonverbal predicates (many languages have tensed non-verbal clauses; these could now be understood as cases in which Infl took a complement other than VP), and it brought with it the restricted flexibility of X-Bar theory to account for the known range of attested clause-types. The inflectional head could be initial or final in its projection; its specifier could be initial or final. The inflectional element (fused with the head of its complement in many cases) could move to the left across the subject to yield predicate-initial or verb-initial orders. What was constant across cases and types was the X-Bar notion of "specifier of the inflectional projection." This was the new unitary notion of subject-position.

(2)

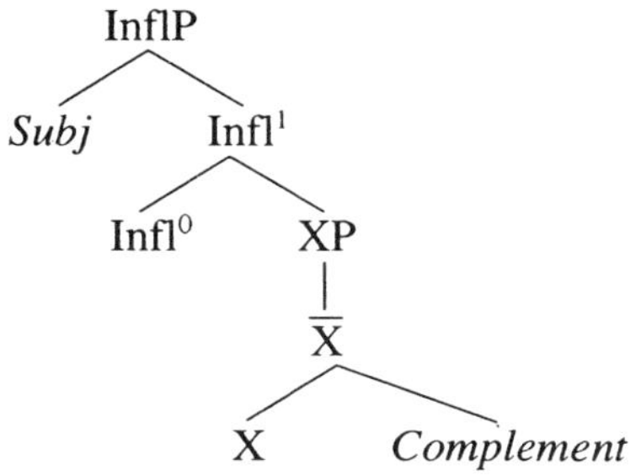

This conception represented a clear advance over earlier treatments. It simultaneously eliminated an anomaly in the theory of phrase structure (the status of the category S) and provided a framework in which variation in clause-type across languages could be reasonably accommodated. The view of clausal organization that it embodies (that it consists of a lexical layer embedded within an inflectional layer, both of them conforming to the architectural principles of X-Bar Theory) made available something like a theory of what a clause could be.[2]

Since the inflectional layer, furthermore, is held to properly contain the lexical layer, any nominal which occupies the specifier position of the inflectional projection will command all positions and material within the lexical layer. Since all non-subject arguments were assumed to appear within the lexical layer, the relative prominence of the subject with respect to other arguments is guaranteed.

Furthermore, the development of the theory of thematic relations and its interaction with the theory of movement provided a framework for understanding why promotion to subject has a central place in the grammars of natural languages.

At the core of this theory (developed primarily in Chomsky 1981) is the contention that movement into a position which is assigned a semantic role is impossible. Since complement positions in phrase structure are assumed to be projected from the argument-list associated with a lexical head, they can exist if and only if they are assigned a semantic role. Complement positions are necessarily thematic positions, then, and movement into such positions is impossible in principle. The inflectional projection, however, works differently. It bears inflectional features which must be licensed by being in an appropriately local relation with nominal phrases bearing matching features. The specifier position of IP is, as a consequence, always projected – whether or not a semantic role is assigned to it. This position, then, is uniquely privileged – it is the only potential argument position whose existence is licensed in the absence of semantic role assignment. It is, as a consequence, the only potential argument position which may function as a target for movement. Furthermore, the need to license features of the inflectional head with matching features on a nominal will typically force either the insertion of an expletive element or raising of a nominal from some lower position.

The existence of NP-movement is thus seen to be ultimately a product of the reification of clausal architecture into inflectional and lexical layers with their distinct properties. A connection is made between the requirement that there be a structural subject (the (second clause of the) EPP) and the existence of raising to subject-position. Both are rooted in the need to license morphosyntactic features by providing them with the nominal phrases that they need in a sufficiently local phrase structural relation. The charge of parochiality is voided in that in this conception no language-specific rules of passive or raising or the like are postulated. In fact, no element or construct in this account is language-specific.[3] The theory provides theoretical grounding for the observed prevalence of operations raising nominal phrases into "subject position" but it entails no reference, direct or indirect, to a theoretically primitive notion of subjecthood.

These were important and innovative developments. The understanding of subjecthood that emerges from them is conservative, however, in the sense that it retains the *Aspects* idea (which is in turn the traditional idea), that there is a unique position in which all the various subject properties are realized. The specifier position of IP, in this conception, is a position in which a range of very different functions is fulfilled. It is the position to which certain classes of semantic roles are assigned (notably the AGENT role), but it is also a position which is crucially implicated in the validation of the morphosyntactic features associated with subjecthood (nominative case on the subject, agreement morphology on the finite verb, and the specification of finiteness for the clause).

4. METHODOLOGY

As well as being in some fundamental sense conservative, the conception of subjecthood embodied in this theory is at odds with some of the central methodological instincts of generative syntax.

It is a truism that in even the simplest sentences of a natural language a single phrase may simultaneously enter into a complex array of overlapping grammatical relationships. To illustrate, consider the web of relations that the pronoun *what* enters into in a simple example such as (3):

(3) What did everyone eat?

What is an argument (a complement) of the verb *eat* and, as a consequence, is the bearer of a particular kind of semantic role. It is also a bearer of accusative case – in virtue of its relation with *eat* and in virtue of the fact that *eat* is transitive. It is an operator which can be assumed to bind a variable in object position and to enter into a certain scope relation with the element *everyone*.

Since its inception, generative grammar has been driven by the instinct that each such relationship is associated with a canonical position – complements to V occur in a distinctive position (sister of V); accusative nominal phrases occupy a distinctive position (sometimes identified with the complement position in VP, sometimes not); interrogative operators occupy a distinctive clause-peripheral position, and so on. It follows from this overall conception of how syntactic systems work that the pronoun *what* will naturally be assumed to occupy a range of distinct syntactic positions – one canonically associated with each of the grammatical functions and relations that it enters into. If one follows the instinct through consistently, this can only mean that the sentence (3) is associated with a series of representations in which each crucial relationship is encoded structurally in its canonical form. There will be one in which *what*, since it is an internal argument, is in complement position; there will be one, perhaps distinct, in which it is in the accusative position,[4] one in which it is in the operator position and so on. If one then adds to the mix the idea that all of these representations are constructed from the same vocabulary and by way of the same combinatorial processes (i.e. they are all (indexed) phrase structure trees), one arrives almost inevitably at the idea of the transformational derivation and the idea that an element like *what* in (3) occupies a series of distinct but derivationally linked positions.

Given this overall intuition about how grammatical systems work, the idea of a unitary subject position is an anomaly. Fundamental to the idea of a unitary subject-position is the claim that a single position is canonically implicated in a wide array of distinct functions and relationships. It is the nominative position; it is the position reserved for those elements which trigger agreement on the main inflectional element; it is the position in which a certain subset of semantic role-types are characteristically realized; it is a topic position; it is a target for movement; it is the position privileged by the EPP. Given the way in which generative syntax has developed over its now almost forty-year history, it is unsurprising that this clustering of functions should have been broken up and each one associated with a distinct canonical position. It is also unsurprising that the idea of subjecthood as a consequence should have been deconstructed and re-conceived – as inhering not in a single syntactic position, but rather in a sequence of distinct but derivationally linked positions. The development of the Internal Subject Hypothesis in work of the late 1980's can be seen as the working out of this always powerful analytical impulse.

5. DECONSTRUCTION

Viewed in this light, the development of the Internal Subject Hypothesis was in a certain sense inevitable (or at least predictable). This might be why the idea was formulated by many different researchers independently and simultaneously.[5] What drives most of these proposals is the impulse to separate out the functions of the lexical and inflectional layers. The lexical layer is the phrase structural domain in which argument realization (semantic role assignment) takes place; the inflectional layer is the phrase structural domain in which morphosyntactic features are given syntactic expression and licensed. It has no role in implementing semantic role assignment. All arguments, including the subject, are initially realized within a lexical projection. In many, or perhaps all, languages the nominal which initially occupies the highest argument-position within the lexical projection will bear a series of morphosyntactic features which will require that it raise into the inflectional layer where those features can be licensed.[6] The specifier position of the inflectional projection is thus a derived subject position only, and most clauses will contain not a unique subject position but rather at least a pair of derivationally linked positions, each associated with distinct subsets of the set of subject properties.

Two classes of arguments have been presented for the Internal Subject Hypothesis:

1. Arguments which seek to show that there is a derivational link between a subject in the specifier of IP and a lower VP-internal position. I will use the term "Lower Origin Arguments" for this group of arguments.
2. Arguments which seek to establish that the subject occupies a VP-internal position in audible syntax in certain languages or in certain constructions. I will call these "Lower Position Arguments."

In discussing some of the arguments that have been presented, I will proceed initially as if it were clear that there is just one inflectional projection (IP). This is false, of course. But the move will simplify the expositional task in various useful ways.

6. LOWER ORIGIN ARGUMENTS

6.1. *One*

It is a very old observation (see at least Schachter 1976, Williams 1977, Gazdar 1981, Goodall 1987, van Valin 1986) that examples such as (4) appear to be problematical for the view that the derived subjects of passives originate in complement positions within VP:

(4) a. The girls will write a book and be awarded a prize for it.
    b. Marta asked for red wine and was given white.

On the assumption that such examples involve coordination at the VP-level, they must involve a violation of the Coordinate Structure Constraint and its associated Across the Board convention for rule application (Ross 1967, Williams 1977, 1978). This is because the subjects (*The girls* in (4)a, and *Marta* in (4)b) must be taken to be base-generated in the specifier position of IP with respect to the left conjunct but to have been moved from complement position within VP with respect to the right conjunct. Since the movement analysis of Passive is otherwise well-supported, this is an uncomfortable paradox.

McNally (1992) and Burton and Grimshaw (1992) independently noticed, however, that the Internal Subject Hypothesis provides a straightforward resolution. If subjects originate in VP and undergo A-movement to the specifier of the inflectional projection, then examples such as those in (4) straightforwardly obey the ATB convention in that the subjects originate inside VP in both conjuncts:[7]

(5) The girls$_j$ will [$_{VP}$ t_j write a book] and [$_{VP}$ be awarded t_j a prize for it]

6.2. *Two*

One of the most celebrated arguments in favor of the Internal Subject Hypothesis was developed by Sportiche (1988) and involved the development of a new kind of understanding of the phenomenon of Quantifier Float:

(6) a. They all must have been drinking wine.
b. They must all have been drinking wine.
c.? They must have all been drinking wine.
d.? They must have been all drinking wine.
e.* They must have been drinking all wine.
f.?*They must have been drinking wine all.

The argument begins by maintaining that *they all* begins life as a syntactic unit in cases such as (6). Given this much, the distribution of the isolated quantifier *all* can be understood if, at a number of points in the raising of the subject from within VP to the specifier position of the highest inflection projection, the pronoun *they* can move on its own (failing to pied-pipe the quantifier, so to speak). The option is available at each step of the derivation, resulting in the multiple stranding possibilities seen in (6). Recent versions of the analysis (Shlonsky 1991, Koopman and Sportiche 1991: 222, Sportiche 1996, Merchant 1996, McCloskey 1995b) have typically assumed that the crucial movement proceeds from the specifier position associated with *all* or *both*, probably subsequent to an internal movement from the complement to the specifier position of the quantifier (Shlonsky 1991, Koopman 1993, McCloskey 1995b, Merchant 1996). If such approaches are on the right track, then subjects must originate in a lower position than that which they typically occupy – given (7), a position lower at least than that occupied by adverbs usually assumed to be left-adjoined to VP (Jackendoff 1972).

(7) a. They must simply all retake the exam.
b. They've just all taken leave of their senses.
c. They had barely all finished eating when the waiters began to clear the table.

The analysis is of course controversial. The principal alternative available at present is one according to which the quantifier and the raised DP never form a syntactic constituent, but in which the quantifier has an essentially adverbial function, left-adjoined to some part of the verbal or inflectional projection (Klein 1976, Dowty and Brodie 1984, Kayne 1984, Doetjes 1992, Baltin 1995, Bobaljik 1995 (Chapter Four)). Some versions of this approach (Doetjes 1992 for instance) also include the Internal Subject Hypothesis as a crucial element in the analysis.

But such treatments do not deal gracefully with the agreement shown between the floated quantifier and its associated DP – a regular feature of the construction across languages, and one which is captured straightforwardly on the stranding analysis (for further discussion, see Shlonsky 1991 and especially Merchant 1996). Furthermore, the adverbial analysis has difficulty accommodating the various cases that have been documented of what looks like stranding in complement-positions – cases where it is much more difficult to interpret the quantifier plausibly as being left-adjoined (Giusti 1990, McCloskey 1995b).

If this is so, and an approach like Sportiche's is on the right track, then *all* in the examples of (7) is a visible sign that the subject occupied a lower position at an earlier point in the derivation.

6.3. *Three*

Ladusaw (1988) points out that the relative scope of negation, modals and sentence-adverbs is straightforwardly determined by the surface position of those elements. The following examples (from Ladusaw 1977), for instance, are unambiguous:

(8) a. A Fiat isn't necessarily reliable.
b. A Fiat necessarily isn't reliable.

(9) a. Shelly usually doesn't do her homework.
b. Shelly doesn't usually do her homework.

These observations in turn suggest that the kind of scope determining mechanisms available for nominal phrases (Quantifier Raising in one widely accepted analysis), which can allow a DP to have wider scope than one would expect on the basis of its position in audible syntax, should not be available to modals, adverbials or to negation (Ladusaw 1988: 487).

This conclusion is natural within the terms of reference of Chomsky (1995: Chapter Four), in which the movement operations that might lead to a mismatch between surface position and relative scope are unavailable in principle to adverbs at least (given the assumption that movement is driven entirely by feature-checking mechanisms and the assumption that adverbs do not participate in such mechanisms).

The following observations also suggest that scope-enhancing covert movement should be unavailable in principle for negation. If there are no S-structure principles (Chomsky 1993, 1995), then the licensing mechanism for negative polarity items must be an LF condition. But notice now the following contrast:

(10) a. Which of the kids doesn't anyone like?
b.*Which of the kids does anyone not like?

In (10)a negation is carried along with the raised auxiliary by an overt movement into a position where it commands the subject position and may therefore license a subject Negative Polarity Item. In (10)b, no such overt raising takes place, and the Negative Polarity Item in subject-position is not licensed. To capture the contrast between (10)a and (10)b, it seems that we must assume that covert raising of the negation to a position where it would command the subject must be unavailable. Without this assumption there is no relevant LF difference between (10)a and (10)b. See McCloskey (to appear) for additional relevant discussion.

There are, however, well-known scopal interactions between these elements (modals, negation, sentence adverbs) and the subject. The following examples are thoroughly ambiguous:

(11) a. At least one player always loses.
b. Most guests might be late.
c. Every player didn't score.

These observations pose a dilemma. If there is no equivalent of QR for negation, modals or adverbs, it is not obvious how the subject DP in examples such as (11) can have narrower scope than the other logical operators in the clause. QR is by definition a scope-enhancing mechanism and should only cause the subject to have wider scope than its surface position might lead one to expect. But what is required to account for the ambiguities in (11) is a mechanism that would allow the subject to have narrower scope than one would expect on the basis of its overt position.

The internal subject idea provides a resolution of the dilemma. Its crucial contribution is the idea that the subject is linked in an A-Chain with a lower A-position inside VP. It is, in turn, a well-known property of the relation established by A-Movement that the moved nominal phrase may make its semantic contribution either at the head or at the tail of the A-Chain so formed, as seen most clearly in a case like (12):[8]

(12) $[_{IP}$ $[_{DP}$ At least one student$]_j$ tends $[_{IP}$ t_j to fall asleep in class]].

The ambiguity of (12) is straightforwardly accounted for if the DP *at least one student* may be interpreted either in the matrix subject position (in which it commands the inherently quantificational verb *tends*) or in the specifier of the lower IP (in which it is commanded by *tends*). If this is right, then the ambiguities in (11) are expected – on the assumption that the subject raises from a position in which it is commanded by negation or the modal or the sentential adverb to a position in which it commands them. See Koopman and Sportiche (1991: 222–223) and see especially Aoun and Li (1989, 1993) for a detailed proposal about the mechanism involved, and an extension to a comparative analysis of English and Chinese.[9]

6.4. *Four*

Another influential argument of the same type (in that it argues for the existence of a subject-trace inside VP and predicate categories more generally) has been advanced by Huang (1993), building on earlier work by Cinque (1984) and Barss (1986). The starting point for the argument is an apparent difference between fronted predicates and fronted arguments with respect to the way in which they interact with reconstruction effects for Binding Theory. The fronted DP argument in (13) contains an anaphor which allows two binding possibilities:

(13) a. $[_{DP}$ Which stories about themselves] did the teachers think that the kids preferred?
b. $[_{DP}$ Which portraits of each other] did the teachers think that the kids would like best.

In both examples of (13), the anaphor can be bound by either the higher subject (*the teachers*) or by the lower subject (*the kids*). The second possibility arises if Binding Theory possibilities are calculated as if the fronted argument occupied its base position; the first possibility arises if Binding Theory possibilities are calculated as if the fronted argument occupied the intermediate specifier of CP position, much as they are in a case like (14):

(14) The teachers weren't sure $[_{CP}$ which pictures of each other $[_{IP}$ would be published in the school paper]].

Predicates seem to work differently, however:

(15) . . . but $[_{VP}$ listen to each other] they say the children won't _.

(16) *They weren't sure how proud of each other she was.

In (15), the only available reading is the one associated with full reconstruction. That is, the antecedent for *each other* can only be $[_{DP}$ *the children*], not *they*. In (16), on the other hand, binding by the matrix subject is impossible. "Full reconstruction" into the base-position seems to be required and since there is no appropriate antecedent available in the lower clause, ungrammaticality results.

Huang's explanation for this pattern (an explanation also considered by Barss (1986)) is that the range of binding possibilities open to the fronted VP in (15) and the fronted AP in (16) is narrower than that available to fronted arguments. This is because the VP (and the AP) necessarily carries within itself the trace of the subject which has at an earlier point in the derivation been raised out of it – that is, a trace bound by the DP *the children* in (15) or the DP *she* in (16). The presence of this trace (since it is a subject in the relevant sense) closes off the possibility that the anaphor within VP might be bound by other elements.

This has been a celebrated and influential argument for the Internal Subject Hypothesis. Evaluating it, however, turns out to be a delicate matter. For one thing, the facts involving Condition C effects are considerably more complex than those involving Condition A effects (Huang 1993, Heycock 1995, Takano 1995). Heycock cites (17) for instance as showing that the fronted predicate may *not* contain a trace of the raised subject:

(17) How pleased with the pictures that Pollock$_j$ painted in his youth do you think he$_j$ really was _ ?

To the extent that (17) is judged grammatical it represents a severe difficulty for the hypothesis that the fronted adjective contains a trace necessarily bound by *he*$_j$. Such indexing should give rise to a Condition C violation of the same type and force as that seen in (18):

(18) *He$_j$ was very pleased with the pictures that Pollock$_j$ painted in his youth.

Heycock's counter-proposal is that the crucial contrasts reflect not the distinction between arguments and predicates, but rather the distinction between "referential" and "non-referential" expressions (more exactly between phrases whose interpretations involve quantification over individuals and those whose interpretation does not). She argues that the effects documented by Cinque, Barss and Huang derive from the fact that such non-referential interpretations can be arrived at only if the relevant expressions take narrowest possible scope with respect to all other operators. To provide for such an interpretation, then, the displaced phrases of (15)–(16) must appear in their base positions at LF (at which level the binding conditions are taken to apply).[10]

7. LOWER POSITION ARGUMENTS

It would be impossible to provide a survey here of all the analyses which have as one of their crucial components the idea that the subject remains inside VP in some language or in some construction. I will consider just four (hopefully typical) cases. The choice I have made among the various candidates reflects in part personal predilection, and in part an effort to present some of the cases that have seemed most persuasive and which have been most influential. In addition, I try to present some cases whose interest and importance seem to me to have been overlooked.[11]

7.1. *VSO Languages*

A substantial minority of the world's languages conform to the generalization that their basic word-order is of the type schematized in (19):

(19) [IP V [FIN] DP [NOM] *Complements Adjuncts*]

Irish is such a language:

(20) Cheannaigh siad teach ar an bhaile mhór
bought they [nom] house on the town big

anuraidh.
last-year

"They bought a house in town last year."

The Internal Subject Hypothesis provides a way of understanding at least some of these languages and clause-types. The hypothesis provides for the existence of schematic structures like those in (21) (in one of its versions at least):

(21)

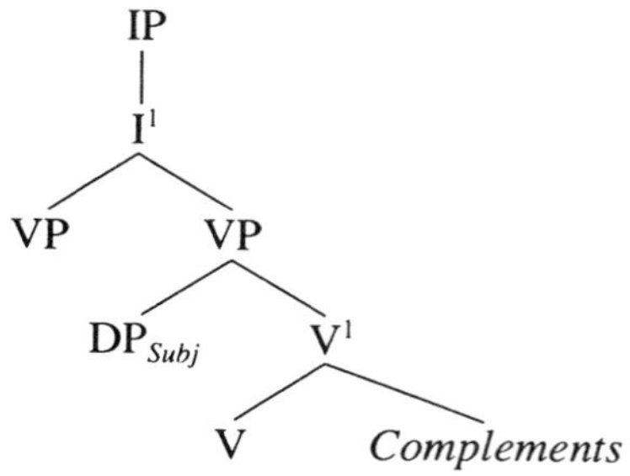

If we combine this fundamental idea with:

(i) the idea that in many (perhaps most) languages the finite verb raises to I.
(ii) the idea that the subject may in some languages and in some constructions remain inside VP,

then we derive the prediction that languages with the pattern of clausal organization illustrated in (20) and (19) should exist, with the structure seen in (22) (Koopman and Sportiche 1985, 1988, 1991; McCloskey 1991).

(22)

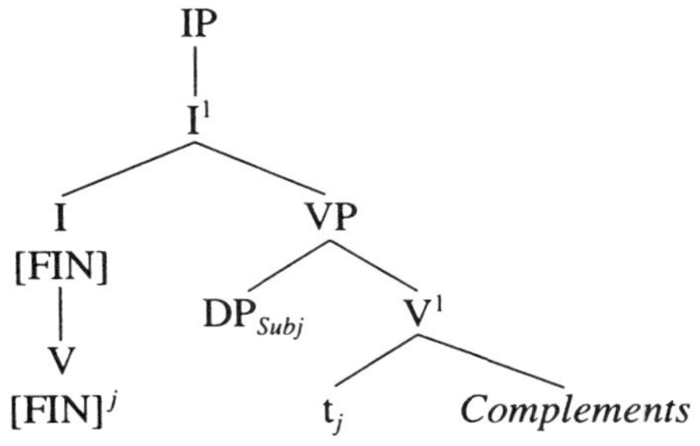

If this way of understanding (20) is right, then there is a major constituent break which separates the fronted finite verb (in I) from the rest of the clause.[12] In McCloskey (1991), I present detailed arguments (on the basis of ellipsis, coordination, right node raising phenomena) that this represents a correct understanding of clausal organization for Irish at least. Under the equivalent of VP-ellipsis, for instance, the subject must obligatorily elide, a contrast with English that follows right away given the structure in (22):

(23) Ní thánig muid 'na bhaile anuraidh
NEG came we home last-year

ach tiocfaidh – i mbliana.
but come [FUT] this-year

"We didn't come home last year but we will this year."

This analysis has a number of attractive properties. It predicts (correctly for all the cases I know of) that the prominence-relations (command relations) among the various argument-types will be the same in a VSO language as in SVO languages of the well-studied European type (the subject will be more prominent than any other argument because it commands every other argument). Nor does the theory of phrase structure need any special clause or provision to provide for the existence and properties of the VSO clause-type. All that is needed is the device of V to I raising – a device for which there exists considerable independent motivation (Emonds 1978, Pollock 1989, Belletti 1990, Shlonsky 1995 among many, many others), and in addition some provision for the possibility that the subject might not always raise out of VP. We will return at a later point to the question of what the property might be that lies behind that possibility (see Kuroda (1988) and Koopman and Sportiche (1991) for general discussion of the issue; see McCloskey (1996) for a proposal about what the specific property might be for Irish). For the present let us simply note that if movement is driven, in part or in whole, by the requirements of morphosyntax (feature-checking in the terms of Chomsky 1993, 1995) then morphosyntactic differences of one kind or another might well be reflected in differences in whether movement is triggered or not.[13]

7.2. *Negative Inversion in* AAVE

Many non-standard varieties of English (notably African-American Vernacular English – AAVE or "Black English") have emphatic negative constructions like those seen in (24):

(24) a. Ain't nothin' happenin'.
b. Can't nobody say nothin' to dem peoples!
c. Can't nobody tag you then.
d. Didn't nobody see it.

These constructions have recently been studied by Sells, Rickford and Wasow (to appear) (from which the examples in (24) are taken), building in part on earlier work by Labov et al. (1968). They argue that the construction results from leftward movement of the auxiliary (bearing with it the clitic negation) around the negative subject. Given just this much, it is hard to know whether the inversion here is I–to–C movement (which would reveal little about the position of the subject), or if the negative auxiliary remains in I.

For at least some varieties and idiolects, however, negative inversion applies in contexts which are known to be incompatible with I–to–C movement. Labov et al. (1968), for instance, report (25) as grammatical:

(25) I know a way that can't nobody start a fight.

The fact that inversion applies here in a relative clause and in the presence of an overt complementizer suggests strongly that it cannot reflect an application of I–to–C movement, which is quite generally impossible in these circumstances.

In the more recent data collected by Sells, Rickford and Wasow, inversion in the presence of an overt complementizer is usually at least degraded, but the negative auxiliary may still precede the subject in a variety of clause-types which generally forbid I–to–C fronting – in relative clauses ((26)a), and in selected clauses ((26)b).

(26) a. It's a reason didn't nobody help him.
b. I know ain't nobody leavin'.

If the auxiliary in (25) and (26) is not in C, then it must occupy some inflectional (head) position lower than C but higher than V. The subject must in turn occupy a position lower than the canonical subject position (specifier of IP). Given unitary Infl, that position must be the specifier of VP.[14]

7.3. *Imperatives in Ulster English*

Alison Henry (1995) describes another kind of nonstandard English ("Belfast English"), whose imperative constructions provide another kind of "Lower Position" argument. One of the distinguishing features of this dialect is that it has post-verbal subjects in imperatives (alongside the standard English pattern):[15]

(27) a. Go you away.
b. Open you that door.
c. Eat you your dinner.

Henry shows that the positioning of these subjects does not resemble the positioning of post-verbal subjects in Romance (their characteristic position is further to the left than in the Romance cases). She further argues that the imperative verb has raised out of VP (since it occurs to the left of VP-adverbs, as in (28)):

(28) Read you quickly that book.

Henry in fact argues that the verb raises to C in these constructions, but there exists crucial evidence that the subject remains in a low position. The evidence derives from a kind of Object Shift. In this variety of English, weak object pronouns in imperatives undergo obligatory leftward movement to a position to the left of sentential adverbs such as *always*. The crucial observation now is that in structures involving an imperative with a weak object pronoun, the imperative subject may appear on either side of the object:[16]

(29) a. Throw us you that rope.
b. Throw you us that rope.

(30) a. Bring them you over here to me.
b. Bring you them over here to me.

Henry argues that in (30)a, in which the subject appears to the right of the raised pronoun, it in fact remains within VP, a claim which is supported by the observation that in this rightward, or lower, position, it must follow adverbs often assumed to be VP-adjoined:

(31) a. Tell them always you the truth.
b.*Tell them you always the truth.

Furthermore, in compound tenses the subject appears after the nonfinite form of the verb, but before complements:

(32) a. Be picked yous for that team or I'll be furious.
b. Have gone you out before I get back.

Henry concludes that subject-raising is optional in these structures, and that the pattern in which the imperative subject appears to the right of a raised pronominal object is one in which it remains within VP (in the specifier of VP, specifically, according to her analysis).

Her conclusions are supported by certain observations concerning a closely related variety – that spoken in west Ulster, and in Derry City particularly. This variety also has post-verbal subjects in imperatives. But it has in addition an invariant imperative marker *gon* (from *go on*). There is some evidence that this element appears in the C-position; the fact that it interacts with VP-ellipsis in the way seen in (33) in particular is suggestive:

(33) **A**: Gon make us a cup of tea. **B**: Gon you.

If *gon* raises from an imperative head position to C, then examples such as (33) are entirely parallel to (34):

(34) **A**: He made us a cup of tea. **B**: Did he?

This suggests in turn that in a case such as (35):

(35) Gon make us a cup of tea.

the imperative verb does not occupy the C-position. Consider now (36):

(36) Gon open you that door.

The verb in (36) cannot have raised to C, if that position is occupied by the marker *gon*. Yet the subject remains to its right and therefore presumably below it, consistent with Henry's proposals. The position of the subject within VP in this west Ulster variety is confirmed by examples such as (37):

(37) Gon make us you a cup of tea.

Here, the weak pronoun *us* has undergone Object Shift as in Henry's analysis. The verb has raised out of VP, also as in her analysis, though not, probably, as high as the C-position, since that is occupied by *gon*. But the subject remains nevertheless below the target-position for Object Shift.

7.4. *Transitive Expletive Constructions*

One of the most powerful arguments for the internal subject idea has been its ability to make sense of a construction which was known to occur in a variety of languages but which had previously seemed utterly recalcitrant.

The core of the Internal Subject Hypothesis is the claim that there is an A-movement relation between the external subject-position and a lower position in which the subject is assigned its semantic role. Simplifying in a number of senses, let us assume for expository purposes that that internal position is the specifier position of VP. It is known, though, that the A-movement relation often co-exists with an expletive-argument relation, as in the English example in (38) and the French example in (39):

(38) a. [$_{DP}$ Three people]$_j$ were t_j arrested t_j at the airport.
b. [$_{DP}$ There]$_j$ were [$_{DP}$ three people]$_j$ arrested t_j at the airport.

(39) a. [$_{DP}$ Trois]$_j$ hommes ont été tués t_j hier.
b. [$_{DP}$ Il]$_j$ a été tué [$_{DP}$ trois hommes]$_j$ hier.

This being the case, if the Internal Subject Hypothesis is roughly right, then there should be languages and constructions in which the link between external and internal subject positions is mediated not by A-movement but by the presence of an expletive-argument chain with the usual properties. That is, we should find structures like (40) (in a head-initial language):

(40) [$_{DP}$ Exp]$_j$ . . . Infl [$_{VP}$ DP$_j$ V . . .]]

where DP is the external argument of an unergative or transitive verb. In a language with V–to–I movement, then, the result should be (41)a for a simple tense, (41)b for a compound tense:

(41) a. [$_{IP}$ Exp$_j$ $\underset{[FIN]}{V}$ [$_{VP}$ DP$_j$ Complements)]
b. [$_{IP}$ Exp$_j$ $\underset{[FIN]}{Aux}$ [$_{VP}$ DP$_j$ $\underset{[-FIN]}{V}$ Complements)]

It was realized in work of the late 1980's that this prediction is in fact borne out and that the Internal Subject Hypothesis provided an understanding of certain constructions which had proved resistant in the extreme to theoretical understanding.

A number of researchers (Falk 1989, Ottósson 1989, and especially Vikner 1991 and Sigurðsson 1991) pointed out that the Icelandic construction illustrated in (42) was of exactly the type whose existence was predicted by the Internal Subject Hypothesis:[17]

(42) a. það dansaði maður í garðinum
there danced a-man in the garden
"There danced a man in the garden."

b. það hefur maður dansað í garðinum
there has a-man danced in the-garden
"There has danced a man in the garden."

(43) a. það grefur kona gröf í garðinum.
there digs a-woman a-grave in garden-the
"There digs a woman a grave in the garden."

b. það hefur einhver borðað epli.
there has someone eaten an-apple
"There has someone eaten an apple."

Such structures (which have come to be known as Transitive Expletive Constructions following Jonas and Bobaljik (1993), Bobaljik and Jonas (1996)) are attested at least in Dutch,[18] in certain varieties of French (Legendre 1989), and in Finnish (Holmberg and Nikanne 1994). Expletive constructions based on unergative verbs are also found widely in the Scandinavian languages (for comparative discussion, see Falk 1989, Vikner 1991).

The fact that the Internal Subject Hypothesis made available a credible analysis for such constructions (which had previously yielded to no satisfactory theoretical understanding at all, despite a great deal of work) was a powerful argument in its favor.

8. A FURTHER DECONSTRUCTION

What do the arguments just surveyed actually establish? In combination, they make a powerful case that the canonical subject position (say the highest specifier position in the inflectional layer) has a derivational connection with a lower position. Given a theory of the clause in which the inflectional system is phrase structurally simple, there is just one A-position specifier in the space between the C-projection and the V-projection. It follows directly in such a system that if the subject does not originate in that position, then it must originate within VP. But of course this unitary view of the internal constitution of Infl has been widely abandoned, under the influence of work by Pollock (1989), Chomsky (1991), Belletti (1990) and many others. And there is at this point in the story a crucial interaction between the Internal Subject Hypothesis and these other developments. If Infl has a complex internal phrase structure, then establishing that the subject originates in a lower position than the canonical subject-position is not the same as establishing that it originates in VP.

What does seem to be true, however, is that one must accept one position or the other – either something like the Internal Subject Hypothesis is right, or else something like the "Split Infl Hypothesis" is right. It is not obvious how the range of observation and analysis surveyed here so far could be accommodated without one assumption or the other being adopted (or both of course). The minimal conclusion forced seems to be that there is no "subject position" – in the sense of a unitary position in which all subject properties are expressed and licensed. Rather, subject properties are distributed over a sequence of derivationally linked positions. In the larger context in which we have framed the present discussion, this is probably the most important conclusion to be reached.

In fact, further investigation has revealed that it is harder than originally thought to find cases in which the subject can be claimed with much confidence to occupy the VP-internal position. The Transitive Expletive

Constructions are emblematic in this regard. Consider again our earlier example:

(44) a. það grefur kona gröf í garðinum.
there digs a-woman a-grave in garden-the
"There digs a woman a grave in the garden."

b. það hefur einhver borðað epli.
there has someone eaten an-apple
"There has someone eaten an apple."

Subsequent detailed investigation (Holmberg 1993, Jonas 1992, and especially Jonas and Bobaljik 1993, Bobaljik and Jonas 1996) has established beyond any reasonable doubt that both visible "subject-positions" in (44) (the expletive and its associated indefinite) are in fact outside VP. A number of tests establish this conclusion, but most clearly and convincingly the interaction with Object Shift. One of the firm conclusions that emerges from work on Object Shift in the Scandinavian languages is that the target-position for Object Shift is external to VP (Holmberg 1986, Vikner 1991). It is observed by Jonas (1992), Jonas and Bobaljik (1993), and Bobaljik and Jonas (1996) that the indefinite subject of a Transitive Expletive Construction must appear to the left of this position:[19]

(45) a. það borðuðu margir strákar bjúgur ekki
there ate many boys the-sausages NEG
"Many boys did not eat the sausages."

b. það borðuðu bjúgur ekki margir strákar
there ate the-sausages NEG many boys
"Many boys did not eat the sausages."

It follows that the indefinite subject must be in a position external to VP but lower than the position occupied by the expletive. If the highest inflectional position is occupied by an expletive – either *það* itself or a null expletive whose presence is signaled by *það*[20] – then there must be two "subject positions" (a higher and a lower) in the syntactic space between C and V. Jonas and Bobaljik (1993), Bobaljik and Jonas (1996) identify that lower "subject-position" with the specifier of TP in the theory of clausal structure which derives from Chomsky (1991).

Similar observations are made and similar conclusions drawn with respect to colloquial Finnish by Holmberg and Nikanne (1994). In colloquial Finnish, one finds a range of Transitive Expletive Constructions similar to that found in Icelandic. Such constructions contain the expletive element *sitä* (which is the partitive form of the third person singular pronoun).

Sitä always immediately precedes the element (negation, auxiliary or main verb) which is inflected for subject agreement, suggesting strongly that it occupies the specifier of the subject agreement projection:

(46) Sitä leikkii lapsia kadulla.
EXP play children in-street

(47) Sitä eivät nämä lapset olisi ikinä oppineet
EXP NEG-P3 these children have [COND] ever learned

kävelemään
walk [-FIN]

"These children would never have learned to walk."

The expletive may be preceded by exactly one element, which must bear focus or contrastive stress; citing Vilkuna (1989), Holmberg and Nikanne analyze such elements as occupying the C-projection, the locus for contrastive stress and focus in Finnish.

(48) Onko sitä leikkinyt lapsia kadulla?.
have-Q EXP played children in-street

"Have there played children in the street?"

(49) Nämä lapset sitä eivät olisi ikinä oppineet
these children EXP NEG-P3 have [COND] ever learned

kävelemään.
walk [-fin]

"THESE CHILDREN would never have learned to walk."

The fact that the expletive must immediately precede the element that bears subject-verb agreement inflection, combined with the fact that it must follow elements analyzed as being in the C-projection, suggests strongly that it must occupy the highest inflectional projection (the subject-agreement projection, according to Chomsky (1991) and much subsequent work). The non-expletive subject may occupy a range of lower specifier positions (the specifier of TP, and the specifier of the Aux-projection in the analysis that Holmberg and Nikanne develop). It may not, however, remain within VP (Holmberg and Nikanne 1994: 182).

Zwart (1992) comes to the same conclusions concerning Transitive Expletive Constructions in Dutch.

A remarkably similar fate has overtaken the analysis of Irish clause-structure sketched in the previous section. It now seems clear that the subject in Irish finite clauses has in fact raised out of VP in the overt syntax. This position is argued for in some detail in McCloskey (1996) (see also Bobaljik and Carnie (1996)). The subject in Irish VSO structures must be taken, as in the case of the Icelandic expletive constructions, to occupy a lower "subject position" – one higher than VP, but lower than the position occupied, for instance, by *there* in English. This conclusion is suggested by concerns internal to the theory of movement and also by tests having to do with the distribution of sentential adverbs. The nominative subject of a finite clause appears routinely to the left of such adverbs:

(50) a. Deireann siad i gcónaí paidir roimh am luí.
say they always prayer before time lie[-FIN]
"They always say a prayer before bed-time."

b. Chuala Róise go minic roimhe an t-amhrán sin.
heard often before-it that-song
"Róise had often heard that song before."

c. Níor bhuail aon fhear amháin fós liom
NEG-[PAST] struck any man one yet with-me
a bhfuil a chuid éadaigh ghlain air.
comp is his share clothes [GEN] clean [GEN] on-him
"I haven't yet met one single man who has his clean clothes on."

If this interpretation is correct, then the subject must be external to VP in (50). But it has already been established that the subject in Irish occupies a position lower than the canonical subject position in an SVO language. Putting the conclusions together, it again emerges that there are two distinguishable subject-positions within the inflectional layer (see also Koopman and Sportiche (1991: 232–235) on Welsh).

According to the proposal made in McCloskey (1996), the properties of Irish VSO clauses are determined by a weak featural specification on the highest inflectional head but a strong featural specification on the lower inflectional head. The first specification means that there are no EPP effects in the language (expletives and their associated syntax are absent). The second means that there is obligatory ("Case-driven") movement of the highest DP-argument within VP to the second (lower) subject-position. Thus, promotion of a bare DP internal argument of a passive or unaccusative verb is obligatory in Irish as it is in English.[21]

These cases are emblematic. The proliferation of categories within the inflectional layer has made it difficult to point to cases where one can say with any confidence that the subject remains within VP. To really make the case, one would have to have a surer understanding of the phrase structure of the inflectional projections than anyone can reasonably claim to have at present.

This unclarity has combined with a revival of interest in some older concerns which were articulated clearly by Alec Marantz in the early 1980's.

One of the properties of the Internal Subject Hypothesis is that it blurs in a fundamental way the distinction between internal arguments and the external argument (a distinction introduced by Williams 1981). If all semantic role assignment is accomplished within lexical projections, then the structural difference between internal and external arguments is lessened.

The distinction remains important, though. Marantz (1984: 23–31), in particular, argues that there is a fundamental difference in the way that semantic roles are assigned to internal arguments and the way in which they are assigned to external arguments. According to Marantz, complements are arguments of the verb and are assigned their semantic role by the verb alone. Subjects, on the other hand, are arguments of VP, and are assigned their role by the VP – which is, in turn, a composition of the verb with its internal arguments. This asymmetry is reflected in an important difference in the way that internal and external arguments make their contribution to the process of semantic composition. Marantz points out that there are many cases in which the internal argument, when combined with the interpretation of the verb, can affect in a radical way the interpretation of the VP so formed and can, as a consequence, have radical effects on the kind of semantic role which is assigned to the subject. The examples in (51) and (52) are typical of this effect:

(51) a. She [took a book from the library].
b. She [took a nap].
c. She [took offence at his remarks].
d. She [took a well-earned rest].
e. She [took a bus to Waltham].
f. She [took her medicine].

(52) a. She [took to the water].
b. She [took to drink].
c. She [took to collecting stamps].
d. She [took to the place].

Angelika Kratzer (1994, 1996) has recently returned to these concerns and has shown that no currently known theory of argument structure can account for these observations, if it is assumed that the external argument (the pronoun *she* in the examples of (51) and (52)) is a direct argument of the verb. She proposes instead that there is a functional projection (which she calls *Voice*) which immediately dominates VP, and that it is this functional projection which is responsible for the assignment of roles associated with external arguments.[22]

The proposal found in Chomsky (1993, 1995) (which adapts earlier ideas of Hale and Keyser 1993) is close in spirit to Kratzer's, since it also assumes a distinguished element (in this case a phonologically null verbal element to which lower verbs adjoin) which is responsible for the assignment of the roles characteristic of external arguments. For both Kratzer and Chomsky, the crucial element has VP as its complement, and internal arguments originate within VP. For both also, unaccusative structures simply lack the higher projection and include only (the lower) VP. The differences between the Chomsky and Kratzer positions are real enough, but distinguishing them empirically is a very delicate matter. The fundamental issue at stake is the understanding of the real difference between functional projections (can they ever be implicated in semantic role assignment?) and lexical projections (do they correspond to the "open class" categories of traditional grammar?).

In any case, the two sets of proposals mark, in an important sense, a return to one of the earliest versions of the Internal Subject Hypothesis – that of Koopman and Sportiche (1985, 1988, 1991). Koopman and Sportiche held that the external argument is not actually internal to VP, but is rather adjoined to VP. The adjunction relation is the structural correlate of the predication relation which governs the realization of the external argument. The principal difference between this proposal and the more recent ones is the postulation of an empty head (*Voice* for Kratzer, *v* for Chomsky) to regularize the phrase structural expression of the crucial semantic relation.

These developments are important but they do not mark a radical departure from the essential insight of the Internal Subject Hypothesis – namely that semantic role assignment for subjects takes place at a position lower than the position(s) in which their morphosyntactic properties are licensed, and that the crucial position is in a very local syntactic relation with the projection (VP) in which internal arguments are realized.

But the postulation of a separate head responsible for the realization of external arguments has permitted the formulation of proposals which depart more radically from these assumptions. Since the head responsible for internal role assignment (V) is distinct from the head (*Voice* or *v*) responsible for external role assignment, it becomes possible to formulate theories in which the two heads are in a less local syntactic relation. Specifically, it becomes possible to propose that certain functional projections (Aspect, or the Object Agreement projection) intervene between the two. A variety of such theories has been proposed (see especially Travis 1992, Koizumi 1995, Harley 1995). They seem to draw their plausibility from two sources. The first is that, as we have seen, it has proved unexpectedly difficult to point with confidence to cases where the external argument appears unequivocally within VP (in a position, say, below the target-position for Object Shift). If the subject originates below all the inflectional projections, why should it prove so difficult to document cases in which it remains in such a position? The second is that certain difficulties for the theory of locality of movement (the difficulty, in particular, of how the subject can cross the position of a shifted object) disappear if one assumes that the subject always originates in a position higher than that of the shifted object. One version of this set of ideas is schematized in (53), in which V_e is the element responsible for introducing the external argument, and V_i is the element responsible for introducing the internal argument(s).

(53)

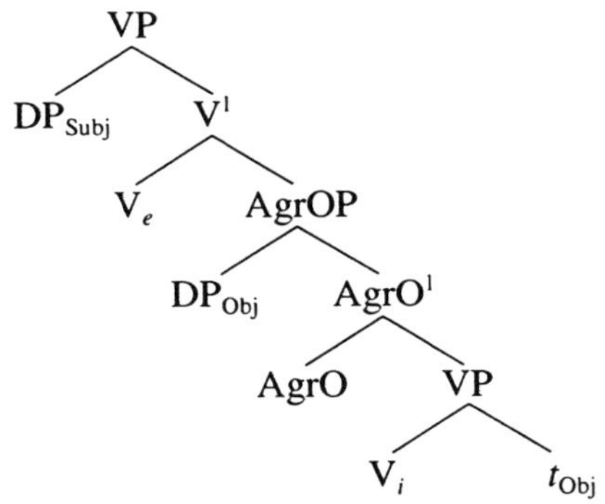

The hypothesis underlying theories of this general kind has come to be known as the Split VP Hypothesis.

These moves represent a more radical departure from the insight that the Internal Subject Hypothesis claims to capture. They also (in some of their articulations at least) relinquish a basic claim about clausal organization – namely that the projections responsible for semantic role assignment (whether lexical or functional) are contained within a layer of inflectional projections.

The empirical issues at stake are, in principle, clear – are there cases in which the external argument can be shown to originate below the target-position for Object Shift (the projection in which accusative case is assigned and object agreement checked)? The issue remains murky, but I'd like to end this survey by considering some cases in which the subject does seem to occupy a position below the target-position of Object Shift.

We should begin by noting that the Ulster English cases discussed earlier are of the crucial type. Recall that in these cases the imperative subject appeared below the Object Shift position for weak pronouns (see (29)a, (30)a and (37) above).

A similar situation obtains in the Celtic language Breton. Schafer (1994a, 1994b) considers a number of issues in the clausal structure of Breton. Breton is VSO in its finite clauses; but it is Verb Second in matrix (or more generally non-selected) clauses, as illustrated in (54):

(54) Lan a dreso buan ar c'hleud
Lan PTC fixes well the fence
"Lan fixes the fence well."

The underlying VSO character of the language emerges in those contexts where Verb Second is impossible – in relative clauses, for instance, or in complement clauses (see Schafer 1994b for details and analysis). What is interesting for our purposes here, though, is that Breton also has Object Shift of the kind familiar from the Mainland Scandinavian languages. Weak object pronouns must appear in a position to the left of the left edge of VP. In (55), for instance, the weak pronoun *anezhi* appears (and must appear) to the left of the manner adverbial *buan*. The evidence which suggests identifying this shifting of weak pronouns with Object Shift of the Scandinavian type is developed in detail in Schafer (1994a).

(55) a. Lan a dreso anezhi buan
Lan PRT fixes it well
"Lan fixes it well."

b.*Lan a dreso buan anezhi.

In (55), the subject has undergone fronting to initial position under Verb Second. But when we consider clauses in which this has not happened, it emerges that the subject must appear to the right of the shifted pronoun. This is shown for Verb Second (matrix clauses) in (56) and (57), in which a non-subject has been topicalized:[23]

(56) a. Breman e wel anezhan Maia
now PRT sees it Maia
"Maia sees it now."

b.*Breman e wel Maia anezhan.

(57) Dec'h neus roet anezhan Yann d'e verc'h
Yesterday has given it Yann to-his sister
"Yesterday Yann gave it to his sister."

In complement clauses, in which no constituent is topicalized, we see the same pattern:

(58) Sur on en'eus lakaet anezho Yann war an daol
sure I-am has put it Yann on the table
"I'm sure that Yann has put it on the table."

The position of the subject in (58) especially (below the Object Shift position and below the position of raised participles) suggests that the subject here may be within VP.

Finally, consider Irish. In nonfinite clauses in Irish, the object appears in a position to the left of the nonfinite verb, as seen in (59) (with an overt subject) and (60) (with a control subject):

(59) D'iarr sé orthu [gan [sin buaireamh ar bith
asked he on-them NEG that sadness any

a chur orthu]]
put [-FIN] on-them

"He asked them that that not cause them sadness."

(60) Níor mhaith liom [Ciarán a fheiceáil]
I-wouldn't-like Ciarán see [-FIN]

"I wouldn't like to see Ciaran."

There is a great deal of evidence that the object occupies a functional projection which deserves the name "object agreement projection." The head of this projection is the particle *a* which precedes the nonfinite verb in (59) and (60) (it can also be realized as an object agreement prefix under the usual conditions in which overt agreement is permitted in Irish). (McCloskey 1980, 1986, McCloskey and Sells 1988, McCloskey (in prep), Guilfoyle 1990, 1994, Duffield 1995, Bobaljik and Carnie (1996)).

Normally, an overt subject appears to the left of the preposed object (as in (59)), but under one circumstance it may appear in a different position. Under conditions that vary from dialect to dialect, the subject of a non-finite clause may be marked with the dative preposition *do*. When this is the case, the subject so marked has two positional options. It may appear in initial position as normal, as in (61):

(61) a. I ndiaidh dona Coláistí Ullmhúcháin druidim
after to-the Colleges Preparation close [-FIN]

"after the Training Colleges closed"

b. Tar éis do lucht na Parlaiminte an caisleán
after to people the Parliament [GEN] the castle

a thógáil
take [-FIN]

"after the Parliamentarians took the castle"

Alternatively, the dative-marked subject may, in formal registers, appear in post-verbal position:

(62) a. Le linn é a fhágaint dhom
when it leave [-FIN] to-me

"when I leave it"

b. Le linn an chaint sin a rá dó
while the talk DEMON say [-FIN] to-him

"while he was saying this"

c. Roimh an gcathair a shroicheadh dóibh
before the city reach [-FIN] to-them

"before they reached/reach the city"

If the dative subject remains inside VP, as an option, and if the verb in turn raises to adjoin to the object agreement projection, this is just the pattern that we would expect (assuming that VP is the complement of the object agreement projection). For more detailed discussion and analysis, see McCloskey (1995a, in prep).[24]

All of these cases[25] deserve much closer scrutiny than it is possible to give them here, but they are in combination at least suggestive. While unusual conditions have to be set up (morphosyntactic conditions that will call off the usual requirement of raising), it does seem to be possible on occasion to observe the subject occupying a position within VP. If the cases here are correctly interpreted, they pose difficulties for the Split VP Hypothesis, since within those conceptions the subject should never be able to appear below the target-position for Object Shift.[26] They provide support, rather, for the earlier view according to which inflectional projections may not be interspersed among the lexical projections (or the Θ-assigning projections).

9. UNDERSTANDING SUBJECTHOOD

If the general line of investigation considered here is roughly correct, then there are at least three subject-positions made available in principle by the theory of grammar. The lowest position (within VP or immediately above VP) is the position in which semantic role assignment takes place. There are, in addition, at least two higher positions within the inflectional projections which have a role in licensing various aspects of the morphosyntax of subjecthood.

What is the understanding of subjecthood that we are left with in the end? It is composite and derivational. There is no term in the theory of grammar which corresponds to "subject" and, in contrast with theorizing of the 1960's, 1970's and early 1980's, there is no "subject position." The properties that define subjecthood informally are distributed across at least three distinct syntactic positions. A subject is a nominal which has passed through all three positions in its derivational career and whose properties (referential and formal) must as a consequence be compatible with the various requirements imposed in those positions. There is no coherent distinction between "derived" and "underived" subjects. To the extent that the distinction is reconstructed, it is simply the difference between cases in which the DP originates in the most prominent argument position within VP (these are the "underived" subjects of earlier theorizing) and those in which the DP originates in one of the lower, or internal, argument-positions within VP.

In a sense, the theory denies the fact that subjects are typically animate agents (since it denies the distinction between derived and underived subjects). DP's will have the referential and semantic properties appropriate to the positions in which they originate and the roles which are assigned in those positions. A DP which originates in the most prominent argument-position will have the properties appropriate to the kind of role typically assigned in that position (AGENT, say). A DP which originates in one of the lower argument-positions will be required to have some different set of properties. If there is one argument, that will raise. If there are two or more arguments, that one will raise which is most accessible to the inflectional projections which license the morphosyntactic properties of subjects. There is no theory of what kind of nominal can be a subject, apart from the theory of argument-linking which says that certain role-types tend to be associated with the more prominent positions, and the theory of locality of movement which ensures that the relative prominence of nominals within VP will be preserved after they have raised into the inflectional layer (see Baker, this volume).

Why do subjects seem to be obligatory in many languages, and why is the subject necessarily nominal? A crucial part of the inflectional layer is the projection in which subject-verb agreement is checked (the highest projection according to Chomsky 1991, 1993, 1995). For some reason which remains unclear, the agreement relation requires a DP for satisfaction. Since this relation has to be satisfied at some point in the derivation, there will have to be in every sentence some DP which is in a position from which it can legally raise to the position where the crucial agreement relation can be established. This part of the theory is complete when there is an understanding of why the subject-agreement projection is an obligatory element within the inflectional layer (in general or in a given language).[27]

For the same reason, movement which is driven by the checking requirements of inflectional features will always be movement of a DP, and we have the beginnings of a theory of why the "cyclic NP-movements" of the *Aspects* theory are in fact NP(DP)-movements (rather than movements of some other category). Much of this understanding derives from the fundamental idea that clauses consist of a lexical projection or projections embedded within a set of nested inflectional projections. It is this principle of organization which leads to the necessary existence of DP-movement, and which gives rise to the complex web of derivational relationships which we name informally "subjecthood." The deeper question, of course, is why natural language should be organized in this bizarre way.

Linguistics
University of California, Santa Cruz
Santa Cruz, California 95064

NOTES

* I would like to thank Sandy Chung for the persistent scepticism which has forced me over the years to think about these issues more carefully than I otherwise would have. I would also like to thank the participants in a seminar on A-Movement that I taught at UCSC in the Fall quarter of 1994 in which many of the issues considered here figured prominently.

1 See Keenan (1976) for a useful and comprehensive survey of subject properties across languages. Space considerations prevent a full discussion of all the properties that have been attributed to subjects. We will have nothing to say, for instance, about the connection between subjecthood and topichood. Nor will we consider the many issues raised by the special properties of subjects in interaction with $\bar{A}$-Movement – ECP effects, and the "accessibility hierarchy" of Keenan and Comrie (1977). There is an intriguing tension between these two, in that the ECP has as a consequence that in a given language subject-extraction will in general be troublesome in a way that complement-extraction will not be. Yet the "accessibility hierarchy" makes the clearly correct claim that, in typological perspective, subjects are much more likely to be extractable than any other phrase-type.

2 An important antecedent being the conception of clausal organization found in Case Grammar (Fillmore 1968).

3 Except perhaps the EPP itself. More on this below.

4 The postulation of an inflectional projection implicated in the licensing of accusative case (Chomsky 1991), of course, drives a wedge between the "internal argument position" and the "accusative position" and can be seen as a further working out of the same methodological imperative. In a sense, that move deconstructs the notion "direct object" in the same way in which the notion "subject" has been deconstructed along the lines of the text discussion. To the extent that the analytical move deepens understanding of particular languages (in the understanding it provides of Object Shift phenomena in a variety of languages, for instance), one might conclude that the instinct has proved trustworthy. Likewise for subjects.

5 Kitagawa (1986), Koopman and Sportiche (1985, 1988, 1991), Kuroda (1988), Rosen (1989), Speas (1986), Wible (1990), Woolford (1991), Zagona (1982). Important antecedents include Fillmore (1968) and Ross (1969b).

6 The usual view is that this will happen in all languages either in the pre-audible part of the derivation – in which case its effects are directly observable, or else in the post-audible part of the derivation in which case its effects can be detected only indirectly if at all. Kuroda (1988), however, develops a theory by way of which a broad range of contrasts between Japanese and English can be understood on the assumption that the relative morphological impoverishment of Japanese (lack of agreement morphology in particular) reflects a substantial syntactic difference between the two languages as well. In such a language, raising of the subject will be unnecessary and impossible. This allows Kuroda to make a connection between the lack of agreement and the availability of scrambling. The specifier of IP is available as a target position for scrambling. Furthermore, since uniqueness of the specifier is not an intrinsic part of the theory of phrase structure but forced only by the bi-unique character of the agreement relation, the specifier of IP may be multiply filled, giving rise to multiple scrambling. These ideas are incompatible with the framework of Chomsky (1993), but perhaps compatible with the theory of Chomsky (1995: Chapter Four).

7 The logic of this argument implies that the subjects of small clauses (those seen in (i)–(iv) at least) must also originate in a lower position:

(i) With Gramm on the sidelines and believed to be running short of money, the race now looks a lot closer.
(ii) I watched Michelle open the door and be greeted by the assembled guests.
(iii) We had the prisoners line up and be photographed.
(iv) ? While PRO in custody and being interrogated, my courage failed me.

Such examples are in harmony with expectation if small clauses are functional projections (Kitagawa 1985, Hornstein and Lightfoot 1987, Bowers 1993, Chomsky 1993, Svenonius 1994, Sportiche 1995 (especially 291–302), Starke 1995, Contreras 1995, Guéron and Hoekstra 1995, Stowell 1995) and if their subjects originate within the lexical complement of the (lowest) functional head. If strict syntactic identity is really a condition on coordination, then examples such as (i)–(iv) must be taken to involve coordination at the intermediate bar-level of the functional projection if there is just one such projection.

[8] Perhaps also in such contrasts as that between (i) and (ii):

(i) The police arrested the demonstrators willingly.
(ii) The demonstrators were arrested by the police willingly.

See Jackendoff (1972), Lasnik and Fiengo (1974) for some discussion.

[9] Specifically, Aoun and Li argue that the absence of certain ambiguities in Chinese stems from the fact that subjects in that language have a different phrase structure status than in English. See also Wible (1990) for relevant discussion.

[10] Takano (1995) makes a proposal which is similar in spirit to Heycock's in that it also assumes that the fronted predicate must appear in its base position at LF, or act as if it appeared there. He derives this requirement, though, in a way that crucially depends on the Internal Subject Hypothesis, in that what forces full reconstruction, in his view, is the requirement that the subject trace within the predicate have a c-commanding antecedent at LF (i.e. that it meet the Proper Binding Condition on traces).

[11] Three of the most important and interesting cases will not be considered.

The first is Kuroda's (1988) extensive contrastive analysis of Japanese and English. This analysis is built on a version of the Internal Subject Hypothesis and anticipates much later work in interesting ways (see note 6 for some discussion).

The second is the work of Guilfoyle, Hung and Travis (1992) on a number of Austronesian languages.

The third is the rich and substantial body of work on post-verbal subjects in Romance languages (Kayne 1972, Kayne and Pollock 1978, Pollock 1983, 1986, Burzio 1986, Déprez 1988, Bonet 1989, Belletti 1990, Wible 1990, Rizzi 1991, Zubizaretta 1992, 1994, Belletti and Shlonsky 1995 (especially 500–506)), much of which now claims that the post-verbal subject occupies a VP-internal position, Evaluation of these claims is made difficult by two complicating factors. The first is that most of the languages impose an adjacency requirement of one kind or another on the relation between the main verb and the post-verbal subject. The force of this requirement varies considerably across the languages (being stronger, for instance, in French than in Italian), and it is in addition subject to a great deal of subtle idiolectal variation. There is no consensus about how to best understand this requirement (for Rizzi 1991 it reflects an adjacency requirement imposed on Case-assignment under government). A second complication is the fact that the postposed subject in all the languages seems to be inherently focused, suggesting to some (for instance Belletti and Shlonsky (1995: 500–506)) an analysis in which the subject moves to a distinguished focus position at the periphery of VP – in which case the implications for the Internal Subject Hypothesis are less than clear.

[12] One could achieve the same structural effect by analyzing the verb-fronting as moving an inflected verb from I to C around a subject in the specifier of IP; this is fairly clearly wrong for Irish (McCloskey, to appear), though perhaps right for other VSO languages (see Carnie, Pyatt and Harley (1994) on Old Irish).

[13] It is known that the analysis just sketched is not right for all VSO languages. Chung (1990), for instance, shows clearly that it is not right for Chamorro. It seems to be very unlikely that the category "VSO language" is other than epiphenomenal.

[14] This is not the conclusion drawn by Sells, Rickford and Wasow. Their discussion assumes that I–to–C fronting is free as long as the C-position is not lexically filled. The substantial

body of work on Verb Second phenomena, however (see Vikner 1991 for a survey), suggests that the possibilities are much more restricted than this.

15 Actually, Henry considers two distinct sub-dialects which differ in the range of verbs which tolerate a post-verbal subject. In the more restrictive dialect (which she terms Dialect A) only telic verbs of motion support the pattern in (27). In the more liberal dialect (Dialect B), a much broader range of verbs, including transitives, allow it. I will restrict my commentary here to the facts of the more liberal dialect. Henry's proposal about dialect A is that in these systems only (a subclass of) unaccusatives permit inversion, and that the post-verbal subject is an un-raised internal argument. Since we are dealing here with subjects and subjecthood, these patterns are of less concern to us.

16 Henry (1995: 71–72) shows clearly that the position of the weak pronoun is not a consequence of it having cliticized to the verb and raised with it. Rather the properties of the preposed pronoun closely mirror those documented for Object Shift in the Mainland Scandinavian languages and in earlier stages of English.

17 The exposition at this point ignores many important complexities – especially having to do with the analysis of the expletive element. We return to a more responsible and detailed treatment shortly.

Sigurðsson (1991) and Vikner (1991) both in fact hold that the indefinite subject in (42)b is in the specifier of a lexical projection. They assume, however, that it occupies the specifier of the verbal projection associated with the perfective auxiliary *hefur*, which has itself raised to I. More generally, the fundamental idea in both analyses is that the indefinite associate must occupy the highest specifier position within the lexical layer (in the specifier position of the highest auxiliary, for instance, in the case of multiple auxiliaries). The idea is in turn that the indefinite subject has raised to this position from its Θ-position – specifier of the VP projected by the main verb.

18 For an analysis of the Dutch construction along the same lines as that just sketched for Icelandic, see for instance Rullmann (1989).

The Dutch transitive expletive constructions have the additional curious property that both the subject and the direct object are subject to the (in)definiteness restriction (Bennis 1986), suggesting perhaps that objects are associated with a higher null object-expletive.

19 Joan Maling points out that (45)a with sentence-final negation is somewhat degraded for at least some speakers. The contrast between (45)a and (45)b seems to be strong and clear however.

20 This assumption is far from innocent, especially in the context of debates about the nature of the Verb Second phenomenon in Icelandic. The balance of evidence, however, suggests that it is correct, I believe. These difficulties do not arise for the Finnish cases discussed directly below.

21 If all this is correct, then the ellipsis process discussed earlier must now be taken to involve not ellipsis of VP, but rather ellipsis of a larger functional projection (complement to the head which hosts the raised finite verb). A possible interpretation is that the higher head is T (McCloskey 1996), and that T is the head which is crucially involved in the licensing of VP-Ellipsis.

22 Kratzer also assumes that the Voice projection is implicated in accusative case assignment, and thus arrives at a very direct structural interpretation of Burzio's Generalization.

See also Déchaine (1993 (especially Chapter 2), 1994) for distinct but related proposals.

23 On the positioning of the participle in (57), see Schafer (1994a).

24 Watanabe (1995: 249–281) discusses a range of cases in which subjects bearing a non-standard or oblique case-marking (genitive in Japanese for example) have the option of not raising, at least in the overt syntax. The present case perhaps deserved to be considered in the same context, although the interaction with $\bar{A}$-movement with which Watanabe is chiefly concerned is not an issue in the Irish data.

25 Jonas and Bobaljik (1993) claim that the subject may never appear below the Object Shift

position in Icelandic. However, subsequent research has revealed that the possibility does in fact exist under certain circumstances (Dianne Jonas, personal communication).

[26] They also pose difficulties for the position outlined in Kratzer (1994, 1996), since the accusative position in that conception is the specifier of VP, which is below the head responsible for external argument realization.

[27] See McCloskey (1996) for an argument that languages may lack this projection and that such languages will as a consequence lack the empirical effects associated with the Extended Projection Principle.

REFERENCES

Aoun, Joseph and Y.-H. Audrey Li (1989) 'Scope and constituency', *Linguistic Inquiry* **20**, 219–251.

Aoun, Joseph and Y.-H. Audrey Li (1993) *Syntax of Scope*. Linguistic Inquiry Monograph Twenty-One, MIT Press, Cambridge, MA.

Baltin, Mark (1995) 'Floating quantifiers, PRO and predication', *Linguistic Inquiry* **26**, 199–248.

Barker, Chris and Geoffrey Pullum (1990) 'A theory of command relations', *Linguistics and Philosophy* **13**, 1–34.

Barss, Andrew (1986) *Chains and Anaphoric Dependence: On Reconstruction and Its Implications*, unpublished Ph.D. dissertation, MIT.

Barwise, Jon and Robin Cooper (1981) 'Generalized quantifiers in natural language', *Linguistics and Philosophy* **4**, 159–219.

Belletti, Adriana (1990) *Generalized Verb Movement: Aspects of Verb Syntax*. Rosenberg and Sellier, Turin.

Belletti, Adriana and Ur Shlonsky (1995) 'The order of verbal complements: A comparative study', *Natural Language and Linguistic Theory* **13**, 489–526.

Bennis, Hans (1986) *Gaps and Dummies*. Foris Publications, Dordrecht.

Bobaljik, Jonathan (1995) *Morphosyntax: The Syntax of Verbal Inflection*, unpublished Ph.D. dissertation, MIT.

Bobaljik, Jonathan and Andrew Carnie (1996) 'A minimalist approach to some problems of Irish word order', in: Borsley and Roberts (1996), pp. 223–240.

Bobaljik, Jonathan and Dianne Jonas (1996) 'Subject positions and the roles of TP', *Linguistic Inquiry* **27**, 195–236.

Bonet, Eulalia (1989) 'Postverbal subjects in Catalan', *MIT Working Papers in Linguistics* **11**, Department of Linguistics and Philosophy, MIT, Cambridge, Massachusetts.

Borsley, Robert and Ian Roberts (eds.) (1996) *The Syntax of the Celtic Languages, a Comparative Perspective*, Cambridge University Press, Cambridge.

Bowers, John (1993) 'The syntax of predication', *Linguistic Inquiry* **24**, 591–656.

Burton, Strang and Jane Grimshaw (1992) 'Coordination and VP-internal subjects', *Linguistic Inquiry* **23**, 305–313.

Burzio, Luigi (1986) *Italian Syntax: A Government and Binding Approach*, Studies in Natural Language and Linguistic Theory, Kluwer Academic Publishers, Dordrecht, Boston and London.

Calabrese, Andrea (1992) 'Some remarks on focus and logical structures in Italian', *Harvard Working Papers in Linguistics* **1**, 91–127.

Cardinaletti, Anna and Maria Teresa Guasti (1995) *Small Clauses, Syntax and Semantics 28*. Academic Press, San Diego and New York.

Carnie, Andrew, Elizabeth Pyatt and Heidi Harley (1994) 'The resurrection: Raising to comp, evidence from old Irish', *Studies in the Linguistic Sciences* **24.2**.

Chomsky, Noam (1965) *Aspects of the Theory of Syntax*. MIT Press, Cambridge, MA.

Chomsky, Noam (1981) *Lectures on Government and Binding*. Foris Publications: Dordrecht.

Chomsky, Noam (1986a) *Knowledge of Language – Its Nature, Origin and Use*. Praeger, New York.

Chomsky, Noam (1986b) *Barriers*. Linguistic Inquiry Monograph 13, MIT Press, Cambridge, MA.

Chomsky, Noam (1991) 'Some notes on economy of derivation and representation', in: Robert Freidin (ed.), *Principles and Parameters in Comparative Grammar*. MIT Press, Cambridge, MA, pp. 417–454. Reprinted in Chomsky (1995: 129–166).

Chomsky, Noam (1993) 'A minimalist program for linguistic theory', in: Kenneth Hale and Samuel J. Keyser (eds.), *The View from Building Twenty*. MIT Press, Cambridge, MA, pp. 1–52.

Chomsky, Noam (1995) *The Minimalist Program*. MIT Press, Cambridge, MA.

Chung, Sandra (1990) 'VP's and verb movement in Chamorro', *Natural Language and Linguistic Theory* **5**, 225–244.

Cinque, Guglielmo (1984) 'Ā-bound *pro* vs. variable', ms, Universitá di Venezia.

Contreras, Heles (1987) 'Small clauses in Spanish and English', *Natural Language and Linguistic Theory* **8**, 559–619.

Contreras, Heles (1995) 'Small clauses and complex predicates', in: Cardinaletti and Guasti (1995), pp. 135–152.

Déchaine, Rose-Marie (1993) *Predicates Across Categories: Towards a Category-Neutral Syntax*, unpublished Ph.D. dissertation, Department of Linguistics, University of Massachusetts, Amherst.

Déchaine, Rose-Marie (1994) 'Ellipsis and the position of subjects', *NELS* 24, *Proceedings of the Twenty-Fourth Annual Meeting of the Northeastern Linguistics Society, GLSA*. Department of Linguistics, University of Massachusetts, Amherst, pp. 47–63.

Déprez, Vivienne (1988) 'Stylistic inversion and verb movement', Ms., MIT.

Doetjes, Jenny (1992) 'Rightward floating quantifiers float to the left', *The Linguistic Review* **9**, 313–332.

Dowty, David, and Belinda Brodie (1984) 'A semantic analysis of "floated" quantifiers in a transformationless grammar', in: M. Cobler, S. MacKaye and M. Westcoat (eds.), *WCCFL 3, Proceedings of the Third West Coast Conference on Formal Linguistics*. Stanford Linguistics Association, pp. 75–90.

Duffield, Nigel (1995) *Particles and Projections in Irish Syntax*. Studies in Natural Language and Linguistic Theory, Kluwer Academic Publishers, Dordrecht, Boston and London.

Emonds, Joseph (1978) 'The verbal complex V′-V in French', *Linguistic Inquiry* **9**, 151–175.

Falk, Cecilia (1989) 'On the existential construction in Germanic languages', *Working Papers in Scandinavian Syntax* **44**, 45–59.

Fillmore, Charles (1968) 'The case for case', in: E. Bach and R. T. Harms (eds.), *Universals of Linguistic Theory*. Holt, Rinehart and Winston, New York, pp. 1–88.

Gazdar, Gerald (1981) 'Unbounded dependencies and coordinate structure', *Linguistic Inquiry* **12**, 155–184.

Giusti, Giuliana (1990) 'Floating quantifiers, scrambling and configurationality', *Linguistic Inquiry* **21**, 633–641.

Goodall, Grant (1987) *Parallel Structures in Syntax: Coordination, Causatives, and Restructuring*. Cambridge University Press, Cambridge.

Guéron, Jacqueline and Teun Hoeskstra (1995) 'The temporal interpretation of predication', in: Cardinaletti and Guasti (1995), pp. 77–107.

Guilfoyle, Eithne (1990) *Functional Categories and Phrase Structure Parameters*, unpublished Ph.D. dissertation, McGill University.

Guilfoyle, Eithne (1994) 'VNPs, finiteness and external arguments', *NELS* 24, *Proceedings of the Twenty-Fourth Annual Meeting of the Northeastern Linguistics Society, GLSA*. Department of Linguistics, University of Massachusetts, Amherst, pp. 141–155.

Guilfoyle, Eithne, Henrietta Hung, and Lisa Travis (1992) 'Spec of IP and Spec of VP: Two subjects in Austronesian languages', *Natural Language and Linguistic Theory* **10**, 375–414.

Hale, Kenneth and Samuel J. Keyser (1993) 'On argument structure and the lexical expression of syntactic relations', in: Kenneth Hale and Samuel J. Keyser (eds.), (1993) The *View from Building 20*. MIT Press, Cambridge, MA, pp. 53–109.

Harley, Heidi (1995) *Subjects, Events and Licensing*, unpublished Ph.D. dissertation, MIT.

Henry, Alison (1995) *Belfast English and Standard English: Dialect Variation and Parameter Setting*. Oxford University Press, Oxford.

Heycock, Caroline (1995) 'Asymmetries in reconstruction', *Linguistic Inquiry* **26**, 547–570.

Holmberg, Anders (1986) *Word Order and Syntactic Features in the Scandinavian Languages and English*, unpublished Ph.D. dissertation, University of Stockholm.

Holmberg, Anders (1993) 'Two subject positions in IP in Mainland Scandinavian', *Working Papers in Scandinavian Syntax* **52**, 29–41.

Holmberg, Anders and Urpo Nikanne (1994) 'Expletives and subject positions in Finnish', *NELS* 24, *Proceedings of the Twenty-Fourth Annual Meeting of the Northeastern Linguistics Society, GLSA*. Department of Linguistics, University of Massachusetts, Amherst, pp. 173–187.

Hornstein, Norbert and David Lightfoot (1987) 'Predication and PRO', *Language* **63**, 23–52.

Huang, C.-T. James (1993) 'Reconstruction and the nature of VP: Some theoretical consequences', *Linguistic Inquiry* **24**, 103–138.

Jackendoff, Ray (1972) *Semantic Interpretation in Generative Grammar*. MIT Press, Cambridge, MA.

Jonas, Dianne (1992) 'Checking theory and nominative case in Icelandic', in: S. Kuno and H. Thráinsson (eds.), *Harvard Working Papers in Linguistics* Vol. 1, pp. 175–195.

Jonas, Dianne and Jonathan Bobaljik (1993) 'Specs for subjects: The role of TP in Icelandic', in: Jonathan Bobaljik and Colin Phillips (eds.), *Papers on Case and Agreement 1, MIT Working Papers in Linguistics 18*, pp. 59–98, revised version to appear in *Linguistic Inquiry*.

Kayne, Richard (1972) 'Subject inversion in French interreogatives', in: J. Casagrande and B. Saciuk (eds.), *Generative Studies in Romance Languages*, Newbury House, Rowley, MA, pp. 70–126.

Kayne, Richard (1984) *Connectedness and Binary Branching*, Foris Publication, Dordrecht.

Kayne, Richard and Jean-Yves Pollock (1978) 'Stylistic inversion, successive cyclicity, and move NP in French', *Linguistic Inquiry* **9**, 595–621.

Keenan, Edward (1976) 'Towards a universal definition of subject', in: Charles N. Li (ed.), *Subject and Topic*, Academic Press, San Diego and New York, pp. 303–334.

Keenan, Edward and Bernard Comrie (1977) 'Noun phrase accessibility and universal grammar', *Linguistic Inquiry* **8**, 63–101.

Kitagawa, Yoshihisa (1985) 'Small but clausal', *CLS* 21, *Proceedings of the Twenty First Regional Meeting of the Chicago Linguistics Society*. University of Chicago, Chicago Illinois, pp. 210–220.

Kitagawa, Yoshihisa (1986) *Subjects in Japanese and English*, unpublished Ph.D. dissertation, Department of Linguistics, University of Massachusetts, Amherst, published in the Distinguished Dissertations in Linguistics Series, Garland Press, 1994.

Klein, S. (1976) 'A base analysis of the floating quantifier in French', in: J. Kegl, D. Nash and A. Zaenen (eds.), *NELS VII, Proceedings of the Seventh Annual Meeting of the North Eastern Linguistics Society*, MIT.

Koopman, Hilda and Dominique Sportiche (1985) 'Theta theory and extraction', abstract in GLOW Newsletter.

Koopman, Hilda and Dominique Sportiche (1988) 'Subjects', Ms., UCLA.

Koopman, Hilda and Dominique Sportiche (1991) 'The position of subjects', *Lingua* **85**, 211–258.

Koopman, Hilda (1993) 'The internal and external distribution of pronominal DPs.'' Ms., UCLA.

Koizumi, Masatoshi (1995) *Phrase Structure in Minimalist Syntax*, unpublished Ph.D. dissertation, MIT.

Kratzer, Angelika (1994) 'The event argument and the semantics of voice', Ms., Department of Linguistics, University of Massachusetts, Amherst.

Kratzer, Angelika (1996) 'Severing the external argument from its verb', in: Rooryck and Zaring (1996), pp. 109–137.

Kuroda, Sige-Yuki (1988) 'Whether we agree or not: a comparative syntax of English and Japanese', *Linguisticæ Investigations* **XII**(1), 1–47.

Labov, William, P. Cohen, C. Robins and J. Lewis (1968) *A Study of the Nonstandard English of Negro and Puerto Rican Speakers in New York City*, Final Report, Cooperative Research Project No. 3288, United States Office of Education.

Ladusaw, William (1977) 'The scope of some sentence adverbs and surface structure', *NELS 8, Proceedings of the Eighth Annual Meeting of the Northeastern Linguistics Society, GLSA*. Department of Linguistics, University of Massachusetts, Amherst.

Ladusaw, William (1988) 'Adverbs, negation and QR', in *Linguistics in the Morning Calm 2, Selected Papers from SICOL-1986*. The Linguistic Society of Korea, Seoul, pp. 481–488.

Langacker, Ronald (1969) 'Pronominalization and the chain of command', in: D. Reibel and S. Schane (eds.), *Modern Studies in English*, Prentice Hall, Englewood, NJ, pp. 160–186.

Lasnik, Howard and Robert Fiengo (1974) 'Complement object deletion', *Linguistic Inquiry* **5**, 535–571.

Legendre, Géraldine (1989) 'French impersonal constructions', *Natural Language and Linguistic Theory* **8**, 81–128.

Marantz, Alec (1984) *On the Nature of Grammatical Relations*, MIT Press, Cambridge MA.

McCloskey, James (1980). 'Is there raising in Modern Irish?', *Ériu* **31**, 59–99.

McCloskey, James (1986) 'Case, movement and raising in Modern Irish', *WCCFL* Volume 4, *Proceedings of the West Coast Conference on Formal Linguistics*. The Stanford Linguistics Association, Department of Linguistics, Stanford University Fourth, Amherst, pp. 190–205.

McCloskey, James (1991) 'Clause structure, ellipsis and proper government in Irish', *Lingua* **85**, 259–302.

McCloskey, James (1995a) 'Case marking and clause-type in Irish', paper presented to the Celtic Linguistics Workshop, University College Dublin, June 1995.

McCloskey, James (1995b) 'Quantifier float and WH-Movement in an Irish English', presented to the Twenty-Sixth Annual Meeting of the Northeastern Linguistics Society, Harvard and MIT, November 1995.

McCloskey, James (to appear) 'On the scope of verb movement in Irish', to appear in *Natural Language and Linguistic Theory.*

McCloskey, James (1996) 'Subjects and subject-positions in Irish', in: Borsley and Roberts (1996), pp. 241–283.

McCloskey, James (in prep.) *Irish Syntax: Clauses and Clause-Types.*

McCloskey, James and Peter Sells (1988) 'Control and A-chains in modern Irish', *Natural Language and Linguistic Theory* **6**, 143–189.

McNally, Louise (1992) 'VP Coordination and the VP-internal subject hypothesis', *Linguistic Inquiry* **23**, 336–341.

Merchant, Jason (1996) 'Scrambling and quantifier float in German', *NELS* 26, *Proceedings of the Twenty-Sixth Annual Meeting of the Northeastern Linguistics Society, GLSA*. Department of Linguistics, University of Massachusetts, Amherst.

Ottósson, Kjartan (1989) 'VP-specifier subjects and the CP/IP distinction in Icelandic and Mainland Scandinavian', *Working Papers in Scandinavian Syntax* **44**, University of Lund: 89–100.

Platzack, Crister and Anders Holmberg (1989) 'The role of AGR and finiteness in Germanic VO-languages', *Working Papers in Scandinavian Syntax* **43**, University of Lund: 51–76.

Pollock, Jean-Yves (1983) 'Accord, chaînes impersonelles et variables', *Linguisticae Investigationes* **VII**(1), 131–181.
Pollock, Jean-Yves (1986) 'Sur la syntaxe de *en* et la paramètre du sujet nul', in: M. Ronat and D. Couquaux (eds.), *La Grammaire Modulaire*, Les Editions de Minuit: Paris, pp. 211–246.
Pollock, Jean-Yves (1989) 'Verb movement, universal grammar and the structure of IP', *Linguistic Inquiry* **20**, 365–424.
Reinhart, Tanya (1976) *The Syntactic Domain of Anaphora*, unpublished Ph.D. dissertation, MIT.
Reinhart, Tanya (1979) 'Syntactic domains for syntactic rules', in: F. Guenthner and S. J. Schmidt (eds.), *Formal Semantics and Pragmatics for Natural Language*, D. Reidel Publishing Company, Dordrecht.
Reinhart, Tanya (1983) *Anaphora and Semantic Interpretation*, The University of Chicago Press, Chicago and London.
Rizzi, Luigi (1991) 'Residual Verb Second and the WH-criterion', *Technical Report* **2**, Université de Genève.
Rooryck, Johan and Laurie Zaring (eds.) (1996) *Phrase Structure and the Lexicon*, Studies in Natural Language and Linguistic Theory, Kluwer Academic Publishers, Dordrecht, Boston and London.
Rosen, Sarah (1989) *Argument Structure and Complex Predicates*, unpublished Ph.D. dissertation, Brandeis University, published in the Distinguished Dissertations in Linguistics Series, Garland Press, 1990.
Ross, John R. (1967) *Constraints on Variables in Syntax*, unpublished Ph.D. dissertation, MIT. Published, 1986, as *Infinite Syntax!*, Ablex, Norwood, N.J.
Ross, John R. (1969a) 'On the cyclic nature of English pronominaliztion', in: D. Reibel and S. Schane (eds.), *Modern Studies in English*, Prentice Hall, Englewood, NJ, pp. 187–200.
Ross, John R. (1969b) 'Auxiliaries as main verbs', in: W. Todd (ed.), *Studies in Philosophical Linguistics* **1**. Great Expectations Press, Evanston, Illinois, pp. 77–102.
Rullman, Holtze (1989) 'Indefinite subjects in Dutch', in: Emmon Bach, Angelika Kratzer and Barbara Partee (eds.), *Papers on Quantification*, Report from NSF Grant BNS 8719999, Department of Linguistics, University of Massachusetts, Amherst.
Schachter, Paul (1976) 'A nontransformational account of gerundive nominals in English', *Linguistic Inquiry* **7**, 205–241.
Schafer, Robin (1994a) *Nonfinite Predicate Initial Constructions in Breton*, unpublished Ph.D. dissertation, University of California, Santa Cruz.
Schafer, Robin (1994b) 'Negation and Verb Second in Breton', *Natural Language and Linguistic Theory* **13**, 135–172.
Sells, Peter, John Rickford and Thomas Wasow (to appear) 'An optimality theoretic approach to variation in Negative Inversion in African-American Vernacular English', to appear in *Natural Language and Linguistic Theory.*
Shlonsky, Ur (1991) 'Quantifiers as functional heads: A study of quantifier float in hebrew', *Lingua* **84**(2/3), 159–180.
Shlonsky, Ur (1995) *Hebrew Syntax*, Ms., Université de Genève.
Sigurðsson, Halldor Ármann (1991) 'Icelandic Case-marked PRO and the licensing of Lexical Arguments', *Natural Language and Linguistic Theory* **9**, 327–363.
Speas, Margaret (1986) *Adjunctions and Projections in Syntax*, unpublished Ph.D. dissertation, MIT.
Speas, Margaret and Naoki Fukui (1986) 'Specifiers and Projections', in *MIT Working Papers in Linguistics* **8**, Department of Linguistics and Philosophy, MIT, Cambridge, Massachusetts.
Sportiche, Dominique (1988) 'A theory of floating quantifiers and its corollaries for constituent structure', *Linguistic Inquiry* **19**, 425–449.

Sportiche, Dominique (1995) 'French predicate clitics and clause structure', in: Cardinaletti and Guasti (1995), pp. 287–324.

Sportiche, Dominique (1996) 'Clitic constructions', in: Rooryck and Zaring (1996), pp. 213–276.

Starke, Michal (1995) 'On the format for small clauses', in: Cardinaletti and Guasti (1995), pp. 237–269.

Stowell, Tim (1995) 'Remarks on clause structure', in: Cardinaletti and Guasti (1995), pp. 271–286.

Svenonius, Peter (1994) *Dependent Nexus: Subordinate Predication Structures in English and the Scandinavian Languages*, unpublished Ph.D. dissertation, University of California, Santa Cruz.

Takano, Yugi (1995) 'Predicate fronting and internal subjects', *Linguistic Inquiry* **26**, 327–340.

Travis, Lisa (1992) 'Derived objects, inner aspect and the structure of VP', Ms., McGill University.

van Valin, Robert (1986) 'An empty category as the subject of a tensed S in English', *Linguistic Inquiry* **17**, 581–586.

Vikner, Sten (1991) *Verb Movement and the Licensing of NP-Positions in the Germanic Languages*, Thèse de Doctorat, Université de Genève, revised version, Universität Stuttgart.

Vilkuna, M. (1989) *Free Word Order in Finnish: Its Syntax and Discourse Functions*, Finnish Literature Society, Helsinki.

Watanabe, Akira (1995) *Case Absorption and Wh-Agreement*, Ms., Kanda University of International Studies.

Wible, David (1990) *Subjects and the Clausal Structure of Chinese and English*, unpublished Ph.D. dissertation, University of Illinois, Urbana-Champaign.

Williams, Edwin (1977) 'Across the board application of rules', *Linguistic Inquiry* **8**, 419–423.

Williams, Edwin (1978) 'Across the board rule application', *Linguistic Inquiry* **9**, 31–43.

Williams, Edwin (1981) 'Argument structure and morphology', *The Linguistic Review* **1**, 81–114.

Woolford, Ellen (1991) 'VP-internal subjects in VSO and nonconfigurational languages', *Linguistic Inquiry* **22**, 503–540.

Zagona, Karen (1982) *Government and Proper Government of Verbal Projections*, unpublished Ph.D. dissertation, University of Washington, Seattle.

Zubizaretta, Maria Luisa (1992) 'Word order in Spanish and the nature of nominative case', Ms., USC.

Zubizaretta, Maria Luisa (1994) 'Word order, prosody and focus', Ms., USC.

Zwart, C. Jan-Wouter (1992) 'Dutch expletives and small clause predicate raising', *NELS 23, Proceedings of the Twenty-Third Annual Meeting of the Northeastern Linguistics Society, GLSA*. Department of Linguistics, University of Massachusetts, Amherst, pp. 477–491.

JEAN-YVES POLLOCK

NOTES ON CLAUSE STRUCTURE[1]

1. INTRODUCTION

The present article will review, and elaborate upon, some of the many recent proposals concerning sentential functional projections, verb incorporation and "checking theory" (see Chomsky 1992) that have been published or circulated in recent years. In particular an effort will be made to identify the various functional projections distinguished under the so-called "Split Inflection Hypothesis" (henceforth SIH) in English and French and develop a theory of what it is that makes them [±strong] or [±opaque], in the terminology of Pollock (1989), Chomsky (1989) and Chomsky (1992).

Section 2 will summarize the data and arguments that led Pollock (1989) and Chomsky (1989) to posit the SIH in the first place. Section 3 will answer the fundamental objections to the SIH put forth in C. L. Baker (1991) and Iatridou (1990). Section 4 will attempt to remedy the real empirical and conceptual problems of Pollock (1989) by drawing upon and/or modifying various conceptions of verb to Inflection incorporation and checking theory that have been proposed in, e.g., Belletti (1990), Kayne (1989), Laka (1990), Johnson (1991), Speas (1991) Chomsky (1989), (1992) and others.

My main contribution to this fast-growing literature will be developed in section 5 and will consist in showing that the seldom recognized functional category of mood – but see Rivero (1994), Fassi-Fehri (forthcoming) – should be the head of a MoodP, which I will claim is the highest functional projection in French and Romance as well as Old, Middle and Modern English clauses. I will show that there are very good empirical reasons to suppose that the syntax of Modern English adverbs and the loss of main verb movement in interrogative and negative sentences like (1), and the well-formedness of their French counterparts in (2) should be seen as a consequence of a universal morphological constraint on overt checking and the presence or absence of mood in the inventory of morphologically manifested verbal suffixes in the two languages, and/or the respective "strength" of agreement morphology in the two languages. In order to make the required distinction between the two languages on a non ad-hoc basis, I shall attempt to develop the first elements of a theory of what it is that makes a functional head [±strong].

(1) a.*I kissed hardly Mary
b.*I kissed not Mary
c.*Kissed you Mary?
d.*I suggest that he lose not any time

Liliane Haegeman (ed.), Elements of Grammar, 237–279.

(2) a. J'embrassai à peine Marie
b. Je n'embrassai pas Marie
c. Embrassas-tu Marie?
d. Je suggère qu'il ne perde pas de temps

2. MOTIVATING THE "SPLIT INFLECTION HYPOTHESIS".

Pollock (1989) was led to suggest the SIH because of a number of empirical claims and descriptive generalizations concerning the comparative (ad)verb syntax of English and French. The basic generalization is formulated in A:

A. There exists a systematic correlation in English and French between the syntax of (main) verbs in interrogative and negative sentences and the properties of adverb and floating quantifier placement in main clauses.

A was first made in Emonds (1978) and given further support by Kayne's (1984: 228, fn. 18) insightful remark about the properties of British English *have* with respect to negation, questions and adverbs. Although it has since come under explicit or implicit criticism (see e.g. C. L. Baker (1991), Iatridou (1990), Ouhalla (1990), Johnson (1992)) I think it is fair to say that the great majority of researchers have held it to be valid. The diachronic work in Battistella and Lobeck (1991), Kroch (1990), Roberts (1993) has given it further support. Kroch (1990), Roberts (1993, section 3.3.3) show for instance that there is indeed a statistically significant correlation between the disappearence of sentence type (3) and the simultaneous demise of negative and interrogative sentence types (4) and (5):

(3) S + Main V + Adv + O
(4) S + Main V + not + O
(5) Main V + S + O ?

If A was not a valid correlation that statistical regularity would remain unexplained. I will therefore continue to consider A correct here.[2] As Emonds (1978) had done, Pollock (1989, section 1.2) expressed that correlation in terms of the contrast between two *a priori* possible ways of deriving morphologically inflected verb forms, inflection lowering, held to yield the inflected forms of main verbs in English, and main verb incorporation to inflection, held to characterize the inflected forms of main verbs in French.[3] This can be summarized as in B:

B. The correlation in A is to be expressed in terms of the respective properties of Verb movement in the different clause types of English and French.

In Pollock (1989), B was further articulated as B1, B2, and B3:

B1. The lexical restrictions on Verb movement in English tensed clauses are not idiosyncratic properties of English since the very same are also at work in Verb movement to inflection in French infinitives (and in Verb to Comp in Italian, Spanish and Portuguese).

B1 relied on the obvious similarity between paradigms like (6) and (7):

(6) a.* John ownsn't a car
 b. John doesn't own a car
 c.* John likesn't Mary
 d. John doesn't like Mary
 e. John hasn't a car
 f. John isn't happy
 g.* John seemsn't happy

(7) a.* Ne posséder pas voiture en banlieue rend la vie difficile
 b. Ne pas posséder de voiture en banlieue rend la vie difficile
 c.* N'aimer pas Marie
 d. Ne pas aimer Marie
 e. N'avoir pas de voiture en banlieue rend la vie dificile
 f. N'être pas heureux, . . .
 g.* Ne sembler pas heureux

If B1 is correct, any analysis of the restrictions on English (main) verb movement in (6a,c,g) relying on language particular properties should be considered inadequate, since it would of necessity fail to carry over to (7a,c,g) in French.[4]

B2. Verb movement affects a head and is therefore subject to the constraints that all heads abide by, in particular the Head Movement Constraint (HMC) of Travis (1984), Chomsky (1986), Baker (1988).

Since the HMC (or the deeper principles that the HMC can be deduced from) is blind to the individual lexical properties of the moved heads, the contrast between the behaviour of main verbs and auxilary verbs in (6) and (7) led Pollock (1989) to posit it was the syntactic reflex of a non language particular lexical distinction between the two types of verbs. That distinction was formulated there as in B3:

B3. The auxiliary vs main verb asymmetry at work in (6) and (7) follows from:
 (α) the respective thematic properties of the two classes of verbs: auxiliary verbs have no thematic grid to asssign, while main verbs do.

(β) some (partly) langage specific property of the (head) position verbs move to.

B3 (α) chooses to view the auxiliary vs main verb distinction in universal semantic terms rather than in language-particular morphological terms. The reason for this is that a morphological approach to the exceptional behavior of *be* and *have* in English tensed clauses could not naturally carry over to the equally exceptional behavour of *être* and *avoir* (and *be* and *have*) in French (and English)[5] infinitives where the relative "richness" of the morphological paradigms of *être/avoir* (and *be/have*) in tensed sentences is entirely missing.

Concerning B3(β), the article made the claim in C:

C. There are opaque vs transparent functional positions from which it is (im)possible for a verb to assign its thematic grid.

Seen in that light, (6) and (7) follow from the Θ-criterion – analyzed as a principle holding at every level of representation – if the positions the verbs move to are [+opaque]. On that view [-finite] tense in French and [-finite] C in Italian in Aux-to-Comp constructions are also [+opaque] functional positions. Furthermore, since the restrictions on Modern English Verb movement in tensed clauses are to be seen in the same light as Verb movement in French and Italian infinitives – see B1 above – they too follow from the transparent vs opaque opposition. There is therefore a language specific distinction between *transparent* finite inflection in French and *opaque* finite inflection in Modern English. Modern English finite inflection also differs minimally from Elizabethan, Middle and Old English finite inflection since at those earlier stages English, like German and Dutch, had French-like main verb movement in finite sentences. Comparing the various stages in the history of English can therefore give us a clue as to what triggered the [–opaque] → [+opaque] change. As first suggested in the generative literature, to the best of my knowledge, in Roberts (1985), Pollock (1989: 6.4) linked it to a change in the morphology, more precisely, to the loss of the singular vs plural person distinctions of "strong" inflection (see also Roberts (1993: chapter 3)). To capture that generalization about strong vs weak (person) inflection it was suggested that the strong vs weak opposition in tensed clauses was be identified with the [±opaque] parameter concerning Θ-assignment.

Granting A, B and C, the English and French contrasts and similarities shown in (8) were dealt with in a uniform fashion, the contrasts simply following from the overt, therefore learnable, morphological differences between English and French finite inflection.

(8) a. John has not disappeared
a′. Jean n'a pas disparu

b. John is not happy
b′. Jean n'est pas heureux
c.* John seems not happy
c′. Jean ne semble pas heureux
d. Is he happy?
d′. Est-il heureux?
e.* Seems he happy?
e′. Semble-t-il heureux?

Granted A, it follows further that the respective properties of adverb syntax in French and English are also a reflex of the properties of Verb movement in the two languages, i.e. are a consequence of the [+/–opaque] [+/–strong] distinction, with (9a) vs (9b) to be seen in the same light as (8b) vs (8c).

(9) a. John is never happy
a′. Jean n'est jamais heureux
b.* John seems never happy
b′. Jean ne semble jamais heureux

Thus my (explicit) claim was that any treatment of adverbial syntax failing to relate (9) and (8) should be considered inadequate since it would be insufficiently general.

Pollock (1989) also made the claim in D :

D. The D-structures of finite clauses and infinitives and gerunds are identical and only differ with respect to the feature composition of inflectional projections and/or Comp.

D has two possible interpretations that must be kept apart. It might mean that some features associated with a functional category vary in different clause types. So, for instance, it has often been claimed that Tense is present in both infinitival and tensed clauses but that these differ in some feature associated with it. More radically, however, D might be taken to mean that certain functional projections are altogether absent in certain clause types. So for example Tense has convincingly been argued to be missing entirely in past participial clauses in French, thus accounting for the absence of negative/pronominal clitics in sentences like **j'ai ne pas compris*, **j'ai le vu* in French (cf. Pollock (1989: 413)). Pollock (1989) rested however on the idea that French and English infinitives, gerunds and tensed clauses had exactly the same functional projection(s). I come back to this in section 5.4 below.

Accepting the conclusion that negative placement and adverb placement in infinitives, gerunds and tensed clauses are to be viewed as a reflex of the respective properties of Verb movement in the three sentence types, Pollock (1989) observed that Chomsky's widely accepted claim that there are no clause specific syntactic computations, the fact that, *à peine* and *mal* are only VP initial adverbs and the acceptability of (10a) and (10b) lead one to posit the existence of a [–opaque] functional position in French occupying a position immediately below *pas* to which all verbs may optionally move in French

(10) a. A peine/mal comprendre l'italien . . .
b. Comprendre à peine/mal l'italien . . .
c. Ne pas comprendre l'italien . . .
d. Ne pas être/avoir . . .
e. N'être/avoir pas . . .
f.* Ne {comprendre, sembler, parler, . . .} pas . . .

For the same reason, the contrast between (10c) and (10f) and the acceptability of (10e) require there to be a [+opaque] functional position in French infinitives above *pas* to which only *être* and *avoir* (and more exceptionally the three modals *vouloir*, *devoir* and *falloir* in a very literary style) may (optionally) move. (11a) shows the resulting "split" functional structure thus arrived at for French infinitives; (11b) is the corresponding functional structure which D leads us to adopt for all French clauses.

(11) a. $[_S$ NP $F_{1[+opaque]}$ pas $F_{2[-opaque]}$ $[_{VP}$ (adv) $_{VP}]]$
b. $[_S$ NP $F_{1[\pm opaque]}$ pas $F_{2[\pm opaque]}$ $[_{VP}$ (adv) $_{VP}]]$

As the preceding summary shows unambiguously, the crucial motivation for the SIH in Pollock (1989) rested almost exclusively on syntactic considerations with morphology playing at best a rather indirect part,[6] although naturally the article did give F_1 and F_2 morphological characterization and further fleshed out the split inflection idea by suggesting, as Kayne (1987) had done for different empirical reasons, that (some) languages have a functional NegP as well, thereby adding one item on the list of verbal functional projections.

The article suggested that F_1 was to be identified morphologically with tense and that F_2 was subject agreement. Under that translation and taking functional negation into acccount, (11b) comes out as (12):

(12) $[_{TP}$ NP T $[_{NegP}$ Neg $[_{AgrP}$ AGR $[_{VP}$ (adv) $_{VP}]]]$I

On the assumption that (12) also adequately characterizes the D-structure of English tensed clauses, infinitives (with *to* either in T or in AGR) and gerunds, all the facts reviewed so far, repeated for convenience in (13), follow straightforwardly.

(13) a. Jean embrasse souvent Marie/*kisses often Mary
b. Jean n'embrasse pas Marie/*kisses not Mary
c.* Jean ne pas embrasse Marie
d.* Jean souvent embrasse Marie

f. Ne pas embrasser Marie serait dommage
g.*N'embrasser pas Marie serait dommage
h. Souvent/à peine embrasser Marie est agréable/triste
i. (Ne pas) embrasser (souvent) Marie est agréable/triste
j. {Not to, To not} often kiss/*To not kiss often Mary/*To kiss not Mary

Given (12), it is also possible to fairly directly relate the [±opaque] nature of F_2 in the two languages to the morphological properties of AGR in Modern English (but see section 4.1 below). Thus (12) and the [±opaque] parameter also offer an account of the various stages in the history of (ad)verb placement in English in affirmative, interrogative and negative sentences and virtually[7] reduce them to a change in the "strength" of (subject) singular vs plural person agreement morphology.

In addition to A, B, C and D and their technical execution there were at least two other leading ideas in Pollock (1989).

First, since the presence of a [–transparent] F_2 made it impossible for main verbs to ever reach the highest functional position in a clause it was claimed that English had developed a specific substitute for main verbs, *do* and its non lexical counterpart ϕ. These were assumed to be generated in F_2 and moved to F_1 (or to C in questions). Choice of *do* vs ϕ was claimed to be regulated by the ECP on the one hand and an "avoid lexical *do*" principle on the other, which I informally claimed to be related to Chomsky's (1981) "avoid pronoun principle" on the grounds that *do*'s role as main verb substitute made it comparable to pronominals, therefore amenable to that principle of economy.

Second, to account for the obligatory character of verb movement in French and English tensed clauses it was claimed that (finite) Tense – though not Tense in infinitives – was an operator that had to bind a verb trace at D-structure.

3. OBJECTING TO THE SIH AND TO THE CORE GRAMMAR ANALYSIS OF ENGLISH AND FRENCH (AD)VERB SYNTAX

As just emphasized, Pollock's (1989) arguments in favor of the SIH are almost entirely based on syntactic considerations in which generalizations A, B, C and D play a crucial part. Naturally, if one wishes to argue against the SIH, these generalizations should be denied and/or the particular executions chosen to express them shown to be inadequate. Iatridou (1990) and C. L. Baker (1991) attempt to do precisely that.

3.1. *Iatridou (1990)*

Iatridou's (1990) chief goal is to show that Pollock's (1989) empirical arguments in favor of the two distinct functional positions F_1 and F_2 of (11) above, essentially based on so-called "short Verb movement" in infinitives, are without force. Her arguments rest on two claims. She observes first that it is possible to derive strings like (14),

(14) Aux + Adv + Present/Past Particple

(with Aux = *have/be*, *avoir/être*) without having to assume any kind of Aux movement on the plausible assumption that adverbs can be generated within the Aux's complement clause, IP_2 in (15):

(15) $[_{IP_1}$ . . . $[_{VP}$ Aux $[_{IP_2}$ . . . ADV V]]]

Thus, contrary to what Pollock (1989) claims, sentences like, say, *ne pas être bien/souvent/toujours récompensé pour son travail, c'est dur à supporter* (Not to be well/often/always rewarded for one's work is hard to put up with) do not establish the need for the movement to F_2 shown in (16):

(16) $[_{IP_1}$ PRO ne F_1 pas $[_{F_2}$ être$_i$] $[_{VP}$ Adv e_i $[_{IP}$ récompensé]]]

Secondly, she claims that both members of *Adv V O* vs *V Adv O* pairs like (17),

(17) a. A peine comprendre l'italien après dix ans d'étude dénote un manque de don pour les langues
b. Comprendre à peine l'italien après dix ans d'étude dénote un manque de don pour les langues

can be base-generated as such and therefore do not require postulating any intermediate functional head position.

Iatridou's criticism based on (15) vs (16) is correct. In fact Pollock (1989) was only assuming that *some* Aux Adv V sequences *could* be generated via movement as sketched in (16). It certainly assumed, like Iatridou, that some adverbs can – indeed must – be generated inside the various participial clauses subcategorized for by *have/be* and *avoir/être*, a conclusion forced on us by pairs like (18) in English for example.

(18) a. I believe $[_{IP}$ John not to be $[_{IP}$ $[_{VP}$ completely revising his thesis]]]
b.*I believe $[_{IP}$ John not to completely be $[_{IP}$ $[_{VP}$revising his thesis]]]

As a consequence derivations like (15) cannot be excluded; therefore examples like (19a) fail to show that there *must* be an F_2 position below *not* in English *be/have* + participle clauses since they can be analyzed as in (19b) where no movement has taken place.

(19) a. I believe John not to be frequently rudely criticizing Bill
b. I believe [$_{IP_1}$ John not to [$_{VP_1}$ be [$_{IP_2}$ frequently [$_{VP_2}$ rudely [$_{VP_2}$ criticizing Bill]]]]]

If we are to establish the existence of F_2 on the basis of adverb syntax in cases like these, we must choose adverbs which for one reason or another cannot be generated inside IP_2. It is not easy to construct unambiguous examples of this type, especially in English, though it may not be totally impossible.

As Jackendoff (1972: 51) has shown, there is a subset of adverbs that can only occur in pre-Aux or post-Aux position in English. These include *merely*, *truly*, *simply*, *utterly*, *virtually*, *scarcely* and a few others. It appears further that in a substantial number of cases two adverbs belonging to this particular class cannot felicitously occur in a simple clause, as shown, for example, by the rather poor acceptability of (20) for quite a few speakers:

(20) a.??John merely virtually lost his mind over Mary
b.??I believe John to merely virtually lose his mind over Mary

In complex sentences and in sentences containing *be*, *have* + participial clauses the acceptability of these adverb sequences improves noticeably for a number of speakers:

(21) a. John has merely virtually lost his mind over Mary
b. I believe John to have merely virtually lost his mind over Mary

I shall interpret this contrast by claiming that in (21) *merely* belongs to the main clause and *virtually* to the participial clause, as sketched in (22) where each of the two adverbs modifies an IP of its own, as it should:

(22) a. John has$_i$ merely e$_i$ [$_{IP}$ virtually lost his mind . . .]
b. I believe [$_{IP}$ John to have$_i$ merely e$_i$ [$_{IP}$ virtually lost his mind . . .]]

Given these premisses notice that (23a), whose acceptability is comparable to that of (22), establishes that *have* has moved from its VP internal position to a functional position below *not*, as indicated in (23b).

(23) a. Not to have merely virtually lost one's mind under such circumstances is a miracle
b. [$_{IP}$ Not to have$_i$ merely e$_i$ [$_{IP}$ virtually lost one's mind . . .]]

In short, although Iatridou's observations concerning the derivation of sequences like (14) are correct, it still seems possible to contruct arguments in favour of F_2 in English infinitives based on adverb syntax, although, admittedly, the empirical data for this position based on adverb syntax are not as sharp as one would wish in English.[8]

Fortunately the correctness of the SIH in general and the distinction between F1 and F2 in particular can be argued for on a much broader empirical basis in French, where the data are unmarred by the additional complexity due to auxiliaries and participial clauses. The arguments are based on paradigms like (24):

(24) a. Ne pas bien/mal comprendre l'italien . . .
b. Ne pas comprendre mal/bien l'italien . . .
c. A peine comprendre l'italien . . .
d. Comprendre à peine l'italien . . .
e.* Ne comprendre pas l'italien . . .

Iatridou's (1990) solution to the simultaneous existence of (24a,b), (24c,d) and the like (and the ungrammaticality of (24e)) is a reformulation of an informal suggestion in Di Sciullo and Williams (1987: 101) that French, but not English, allows for complex predicates like (25):

(25) $[_V$ V Adv]

This solution amounts to denying generalizations A and B, repeated below, since the (non) existence of complex predicates like (25) obviously does not have anything to do with negative or interrogative syntax.

A. There exists a systematic correlation in English and French between the syntax of (main) verbs in interrogative and negative sentences and the properties of adverb and floating quantifier placement in main clauses.

B. The correlation in A is to be expressed in terms of the respective properties of Verb movement in the different clause types of English and French.

One clearly would like to see some argument in favor of the rejection of those generalizations. Iatridou (1990) offers none and does not mention the extremely damaging fact that adverbs in *V* + *Adv* + *O* sequences can be freely modified by *très/trop/assez* etc. as in (26):

(26) a. J'ai entendu Pierre répondre très bien à cette critique
(I have heard Pierre answer very well to that criticism)

b. Manger trop souvent de la viande, c'est mauvais pour la santé
(To eat too often meat is bad for one's health)

This shows unambiguously that the intruding constituent between the verb and its direct object is phrasal, hence that it cannot have been incorporated into the inifinitival verb.

It must be emphasized that I am not trying to deny that there are Adv to V incorporation processes in a great variety of languages. There are in fact well-documented cases. So for example Lonzi (1991) has argued convincingly that Italian *ben* – the reduced form of *bene* – (obligatorily) left-adjoins to participles in examples like (27c), analyzed by her as $[_V [_{Adv}$ben] [capito]].

(27) a.* Ha bene capito la questione
b.* Ha capito la questione ben
c. Ha ben capito la questione

Similarly, Rivero (1990) has shown adverb to verb incorporation to be a very productive process in Modern Greek where one gets alternations like those illustrated in (28a)–(28b):

(28) a. *dískola* (hard), *kaká* (bad), *sigá* (soft(ly)), *gorgá* (fast))
b. *diskologenó* (give birth with difficulty), *kakologó* (talk bad(ly)), *sigotragudó* (sing soft(ly)), *gorgopetó* (fly fast)

Incorporated adverbs in Greek show vowel/stress modifications. Compare for example *dískola* and *diskolo+genó*, *gorgá* and *gorgo+petó* etc. We know that the forms in (28) are $[_V$ Adv + V] structures because they can be preceded by clitics like *to* (= it) or the future tense morphemes *tha* that can only precede verbs (Rivero (1990: 13–14 and *passim*):

(29) a. To fagitó tha vrási
(the food FUT boil)
b. To fagitó tha vràsi sigà
(the food FUT boil softly)
c. To fagitó tha sigovrási
(the food FUT soft-boil)

What is important for our present purposes is that Rivero (1990) also shows that adverbs external to VP, like the Greek counterparts of *perhaps*, *possibly*, *hardly*, never incorporate and that stative verbs like *know*, *possess*, *own* can never host incorporated adverbs. As she demonstrates, the very same pattern of facts is found in Nahuatl, which suggests that the incorporation process that yields complex predicates like (25) obeys very general constraints,[9] hence also applicable to French on the null hypothesis. It is very implausible, therefore, to suggest an incorporation analysis for French *V + Adv + O* sequences like (30) where the verbs are stative and the adverbs VP external:

(30) a. Savoir à peine l'italien après cinq ans d'étude . . .
(To know hardly Italian after five years of study . . .)
b. Ce bandit, que l'on dit posséder probablement un compte en Suisse, . . .
(That crook, who is said to possess probably a bank account in Switzerland, . . .)

Independently of the *très/trop/assez* facts mentioned above, this would suffice to show that, unlike Pollock's (1989), Iatridou's (1990) account of *V + Adv + O* sequences in French is insufficently general. Notice also that although the complex verb idea may have some plausibility for that subset of adverbs which can in some intuitive semantic sense be said to make up a "complex predicate" with the head verb semantically, it entirely lacks that sort of support where *V + Floating Q + O* sequences are concerned, as in (31a):

(31) a. J'ai entendu [mes amis chanter tous cette chanson]
     b. J'ai entendu [mes amis tous chanter cette chanson]

For all such examples an incorporation analysis would have to make the extremely unnatural claim that a quantifier can be part of a complex predicate semantically. If that unpalatable conclusion is to be avoided Iatridou's (1990) analysis cannot capture the obvious parallelism between (32) and (33) in English and (31) and (34) in French:

(32) a.* I heard my friends sing all this song
     b. I heard my friends all sing this song

(33) a.* I heard my friends sing often this song
     b. I heard my friends often sing this song

(34) a. J'ai entendu mes amis chanter souvent cette chanson
     b. J'ai entendu mes amis souvent chanter cette chanson

On the contrary, the (optional) V to F_2 analysis of Pollock (1989) can; I conclude that the SIH crucially contributes to the analysis that gives generalizations A and B formal content, is an indispensable element in our understanding of the syntax of adverbs and floating quantifiers in French and lends itself to a comparative and diachronic analysis of English and French which appears to be beyond the scope of the (informal) suggestions offered in Iatridou (1990).

3.2. *C. L. Baker (1991)*

C. L. Baker's (1991) main goal is to redefine the "core" vs "periphery" distinction as introduced in current linguistic theorizing in Chomsky (1981) and impute the great bulk of the syntax of negation in English tensed sentences to a language specific periphery consisting of the rule in (36) and the auxiliary assumptions in (37):

(36) . . . not . . . V_{finite} . . . → V_{finite} . . . not (obligatory)
[+special] [+special]

(37) (a) Preverbal adverbs are recursively generated in V′ adjunction positions subject to the usual scope differences: $[_{V'}$ Adv $[_{V'}$ . . .]]

(b) *Not* is a preverbal adverb of the *seldom, hardly, never* etc. type.

(c) There is a "special purpose VP" and "limited use phrase" of the shape [$_{V'}$ do [$_{VP}$ . . .]]. This "special purpose VP" is unavailable for VPs with a [+special] head, i.e. *be, have* and modals.

From a purely empirical view point, the "core grammar" analysis of the previous section and Baker's analysis sharply contrast in a number of domains. The most important difference is the following: under Baker's analysis *do, be, have* and *can* in sentences like (38) stand in their D-structure position, i.e. have not undergone any movement:

(38) a. John probably DID prefer pecan pie
b. John probably is unhappy
c. John probably has enjoyed making a fool of himself
d. John probably will get something to eat in that restaurant

In their negative counterparts in (39), however, they have undergone the "special" rule in (36).

(39) a. John probably did not prefer pecan pie
b. John probably is not unhappy
c. John probably has not enjoyed making a fool of himself
d. John probably will not get anything to eat in that restaurant

That (38) and (39) should have two different S-structures is the most striking empirical claim in C. L. Baker's work. In that it crucially differs from Pollock (1989), Chomsky (1989) and all their predecessors, e.g. Chomsky (1955/1957), Emonds (1978).

I will make use of (the basic intuition behind) this feature of Baker's analysis in section 5.3.2. From a more theoretical point of view, let me point out here that C. L. Baker (1991) only deals with an extremely limited subset of the facts covered in Pollock (1989). If its data base was widened, a number of questions would have to be faced, among which the following:

(40) a. What is the structure of the clause in English (e.g. does it have a head or not?)
b. Are there specific constraints on head to head movement?
c. How should one analyze question formation?
d. How should one analyze infinitives?
e. How should one analyze the OE, ME, Modern English diachronic evolution with respect to Verb movement?
f. How should one analyze Verb movement in French?
g. How should one analyze the restrictions on Verb movement in French infinitives?

Because of the lack of any concrete proposals concerning (40) Baker (1991) does not have to take a stand with respect to the generalizations under A, B, C, D in the previous section. So for example, since it does not deal with the syntax of Verb movement in French infinitives, (40g) does not have to be answered. Consequently the question of how to best capture the parallelism between (41) (= (6) above) and (42) (= (7)) simply does not arise:

(41) a.* John ownsn't a car
b. John doesn't own a car
c.* John likesn't Mary
d. John doesn't like Mary
e. John hasn't a car
f. John isn't happy
g.* John seemsn't happy

(42) a.* Ne posséder pas voiture en banlieue rend la vie difficile
b. Ne pas posséder de voiture en banlieue rend la vie difficile
c.* N'aimer pas Marie
d. Ne pas aimer Marie
e. N'avoir pas de voiture en banlieue rend la vie dificile
f. N'être pas heureux, . . .
g.* Ne sembler pas heureux

But of course the question does arise, even though the article does not address it. We know how it deals with (41): only [+special] tensed verbs (i.e. tensed auxiliaries) undergo (36), and only [–special] tensed verbs take a special purpose VP variant. How could it account for (42)? There are only two logical possibilities: (42) could be taken to be a core grammar phenomenon and analyzed as such. If so there can be no direct relationship between that UG account and the language particular one offered for (41). (42) could also be considered language particular, i.e. specific to French and formulated accordingly. But then again the two analyses would be necessarily unrelated. In short, Baker (1991) implicitly denies the generalizations under A and B.

The rejection of the parametrized UG analyses of Pollock (1989) and Chomsky (1989) is based on the idea that a core grammar account of Verb movement in English is too "costly" because it has to posit two base positions for adverbs in English and a special ("exotic") analysis of *être/be* and *avoir/have* in French and British English. In a similar vein, it is argued that it's more difficult to state the selectional restrictions of negation if *not* is a head rather than an adverb. Baker's (1991) general claim, then, is that economy considerations favor a language particular approach because Pollock (1989) and Chomsky (1989) have to posit the existence of entities and processes not needed in (36)–(37), for example Pollock's null *do* or Chomsky's (1989) assumptions that AGR traces are freely deletable at LF and that there is covert LF Verb movement in English that erases the offending trace of (syntactic) affix lowering. The following quotation gives the gist of Baker's (1991) approach:

"We can attempt to bring a process within the domain of core grammar, at the cost of being forced to introduce ad-hoc complications elsewhere in the grammar, most notably in the base component. Or we can accept a small degree of irreducible language particularity in this process, and as a result retain the possibility of an uncomplicated base component"

I do not believe that this is a legitimate criticism. Even if it were the argument would remain without force for the simple reason that the idea that verb syntax in English should be considered an "irreducible language particularity" has the inevitable consequence of making the "transformational component" of English more costly (cf. (36)). But Baker (1991) never says why it is fine to complicate that component and why it is wrong to complicate what he calls the base.[10] Without an argument to this effect the chief consequence of Baker's program is that linguists cannot capture cross linguistic generalizations: they cannot – perhaps should not try to – offer a uniform account of the identical lexical restrictions on V to COMP in Italian, V-movement in French infinitives and V-mvt in English negative and interrogative tensed sentences. If this were true linguistics would be set apart any other domain of empirical inquiry known to me.

Furthermore Baker's observations concerning the greater complexity of a core-grammar approach to English verb syntax are debatable. He is correct in observing that Pollock's (1989: note 8) idea that English (also Italian and Spanish) but not French allowed for a pre-F_1 adverbial position was not satisfactory. However, it is not inherent to a UG approach to English verb syntax or the SIH: Kayne (1989) and Belletti (1990) have each provided an account of the puzzle that remains safely within the core grammar account and the SIH. The same is true of the approach developed below in section 5.

That *have* and *be* are very special verbs in many respects has been known in linguistics for many centuries (for recent developments see Freeze (1992), Kayne (1992), Postma (1993)). Pollock's (1989) idea that the lexical entry of British English *have* was "exotic" was only capitalising informally on ideas that are independently justified by empirical properties that all linguists have to deal with.

Similarly the existence of a non lexical counterpart to *do* is not inherent to a core grammar account of verb movement syntax in English: null *do*'s were repeatedly introduced in descriptive work in the 1960's and 1970's. Arguing against such entities on grounds of *a priori* simplicity is thus questionable: it is on empirical grounds only that their fate should be settled.

Summarizing, I believe that the two "radical" attempts by S. Iatridou and L. Baker to question (the core grammar account of) the generalizations under A and B are inconclusive, although both contain interesting insights. I will therefore continue to consider A and B correct and will rely on the SIH as a crucial ingredient in the analyses that aim at capturing them.[11] I now turn to real inadequacies in Pollock's (1989) and to ways of remedying them.

4. INCORPORATION AND/OR CHECKING

4.1. *On Some Real Conceptual and/or Empirical Problems of Pollock (1989)*

As has been noted many times since 1989, postulating $F_2 = AGR_S$ in (11), repeated below,

(11) $[_S$ NP F_1 pas F_2 $[_{VP}$ (adv) VP]]

leads to a violation of Baker's (1985) Mirror principle on the "classical" view that verbs move to functional heads to pick up their inflectional morphology (e.g. tense, person, mood affixes).

This was recognized from the very start (cf. Pollock (1989: note 19)) but brushed aside because of the necessity to capture the link between "strong" suject agreement and (short) main verb movement (to F_2) to F_1. A less flippant view of morphology led Belletti (1990)) to turn (43) upside-down, which yields (44):

(43) $[_{TP}$ NP T $[_{NegP}$ Neg $[_{AgrP}$ AGR $[_{VP}$ (adv) VP]]]]

(44) $[_{AGRP}$ NP AGR $[_{NegP}$ Neg $[_{TP}$ T $[_{VP}$ (adv) VP]]]]

(44) solves the most obvious morphological inadequacy of Pollock (1989), at a rather serious cost, unfortunately: (44) cannot link the [±opaque] finite inflection parameter to any overt (i.e. learnable) morphological property of F_2.[12]

Although Pollock (1989) was willing to throw morphological plausibility overboard in its attempt to interpret the restrictions on ("short" hence – because of the HMC – "long") verb movement as a consequence of the poverty or strength of (person) agreement, it failed to express the correlation in a (fully) satisfactory way for at least three reasons.

Firstly, the link it established between verb syntax and morphology was extremely indirect since the treatment summed up in section 2 above required that F_2 in French infinitives – covert AGR_S – be "transparent" (vs F_2 in English) since all main verbs can (though need not, unlike Italian main verbs, see Belletti (1990)) move to it in French. If [±opaque] is the thematic reflex of the [±strong] person agreement parameter, as was claimed for both tensed sentences and infinitives, we have to say that covert AGR_S in French is [+strong]. But if this is so the learnability problem rears its head again: how can the French child associate the right value of the parameter with a functional head it has at best very indirect evidence for? A possible solution would be to claim that there is such a thing as "covert morphological richness" in infinitives and maintain that it somehow reflects the overt morphological richness in person agreement of French tensed clauses. Unfortunately this implicit theory of paradigmatic richness remained in limbo in Pollock (1989).

Although it is perhaps less acute, identifying F_2 with AGR_S raises another problem since it obviously commits one to the far from obvious view that French, Italian and Spanish infinitives *necessarily* have an AGR_S(P) despite the fact that AGR_S(P) *never* has any overt manifestation in infinitives in those languages. Because of European Portuguese where it has, we know that AGR_S and the inflection of infinitives are not incompatible in general. Still, the evidence for it in French, Italian and Spanish is so tenuous that one might wish to take a more cautious – i.e. less divorced from overt morphology – view of F_2, if at all possible.

Be that as it may, the effort to link the [±opaque] parameter to a [±strong] person agreement feature was in any case insufficiently general since, short of saying that Italian and Portuguese infinitival C and French gerundial *-ant* are covertly [±strong] despite the fact that they never show any trace of person agreement, it did not have anything to say about the fact that infinitival C was opaque in Aux-to-comp constructions or about the fact that French gerundial morphology is transparent (though that of English is not, compare OK *ne chantant pas* vs **singing not*) while F_1 in infinitives is opaque. All Pollock (1989) did concerning this unpleasant state of affairs was give a list of [–opaque] vs [+opaque] functional positions, clearly an unsatisfactory result since it merely restates the facts instead of explaining them.[13]

Finally, as Manuela Ambar was one of the first to observe, Pollock (1989) had nothing to say concerning the rather basic question of why morphological "richness" in person agreement was associated with the [+transparent] value of the parameter rather than the other way round.

Aside from these basic problems concerning the proper characterisation of F_1, F_2 and their associated parameters, Pollock's (1989) analysis of comparative French vs English (ad)verb syntax ought to be improved upon in at least three different areas:

Firstly, the article tried to account for the obligatory Verb movement of tensed clauses by stipulating that finite Tense is an operator-like element binding an event variable (identified with the verb trace). The major empirical problem with this is that if finite Tense is an operator it ought to interfere with (A-bar) movement in the same way better-known sentential operators do. Unfortunately it does not. To give just one example, observe that while (the (null) negative operator in the specifier position of[14]) *not* creates well-known opacity effects in questions like (45),

(45) *How$_i$ didn't he say John would repair the car t$_i$?

finite Tense does not, as the acceptability of (46) shows

(46) How$_i$ did he say John would repair the car t$_i$?

This is unexpected. On a more conceptual level it might be said that allowing such an unusual analysis of Tense to play a major part in the overall explanation of the "raison d'être" of (obligatory) Verb movement in tensed clauses might be considered at the very least a little rash.

Secondly, as Kayne (1989) was the first to point out, the comparative syntax of English and French adverbs was not dealt with optimally in Pollock (1989) because of pairs like (47) and (48):

(47) a. John is never satisfied
b. John never is satisfied

(48) a. Jean (n')est jamais content
b.*Jean jamais (n')est content

According to Pollock (1989) in both (47a) and (48a) the auxiliaries have moved to the topmost functional position F_1. The contrast between (47b) and (48b) cannot therefore be dealt with in the same way as (49a) vs (49b) since only in the latter pair can it be claimed to result from the (un)availability of main verb movement to F_1.

(49) a. John never seems happy
b.*Jean jamais (ne) semble heureux

Surely, as Kayne (1989) observed, we need a unique account of (48) *and* (49). However, Pollock (1989: note 8) uninterestingly had to fall back on two unrelated differences between the two languages.[15] I will come back to this at length in section 5 below.

Thirdly, Pollock (1989) crucially relied on obligatory inflection lowering (= Chomsky's (1957) "affix hopping") in English tensed clauses and French infinitives.[16] The tension with the ban on lowering rules in general was thus a conspicuous problem which the paper discussed briefly (cf. Pollock (1989: 394))) but did not explicitly address. It only assumed that it could be solved and sketched a number of possible options without taking a specific stand.

In brief, it seems fair to say that the conceptual framework of Pollock (1989) made it possible to relate a complex set of comparative properties of (ad)verb syntax in Modern, Elizabethan, Middle and Old English and Modern French in a way that shed revealing light on the data. However, it didn't capture all the descriptive generalizations that it ought to have captured. Furthermore it also left a number of important theoretical problems unsolved and failed to reach (full) explanatory adequacy since the parameters of UG it conjectured are not based on (morphological) properties that could make them plausible candidates for learning on the basis of primary linguistic data. Section 5 will attempt to move in that direction.

4.2. *Case, Checking and the SIH*

4.2.1. *Case and the SIH*

Chomsky (1989) expressed explicit or implicit agreement on the descriptive generalizations summed up under A, B, C and D in section 2.1 above. It suggested a number of alternative executions for some of those ideas, provided answers to some of the conceptual problems discussed in the previous section and further expanded on the split inflection hypothesis by positing an extra functional position AGR_O(P).

Since it too is formulated within the "standard" incorporation framework in which verbs move to "pick up" their inflectional morphology, it adopted Belletti's view that if AGR_S and Tense are to be distinguished, their order of embedding should be AGR_S(P) > Tense(P), not only because of morphological plausibility, but also because nominative Case assignment should always be analyzed as an instance of Specifier-Head agreement with AGR_S standing in the topmost functional position (cf. Chomsky (1989: 57)).

However, the article also agrees with Pollock (1989) that the (un)availability of main verb movement to the functional position below *pas* (identified by the short verb movement phenomenology in French) should be linked to properties of agreement, as originally suggested in Roberts. In order to solve the obvious paradox, Chomsky (1989: 58) suggests that Pollock's F_2 is really AGR_O. On that view Pollock's and Belletti's apparently conflicting structures, repeated under (50), neatly combine to yield (51), which captures the best of both worlds, so to speak.[17]

(50) a. $[_{TP}$ NP T $[_{NegP}$ Neg $[_{AgrP}$ AGR $[_{VP}$ (adv) VP]]]]
b. $[_{AGRP}$ NP AGR $[_{NegP}$ Neg T $[_{VP}$ (adv) VP]]]]

(51) $[_{AGR_SP}$ NP AGR_S $[_{TP}$ Tense $[_{NegP}$ Neg $[_{AGR_OP}$ AGR_O $[_{VP}$ (adv) VP]]]]]

Chomsky (1989) and (1992), despite many important differences in other domains, share the view that AGR_O is responsible for objective Case assignment (or checking) via Spec-head agreement. Put another way, one fundamental motivation for the SIH in Chomsky's view is that it makes it possible to give a uniform characterization of (structural) Case assignment/checking: Nominative and Objective case are each an instance of

Spec-Head agreement, with AGR_S and AGR_O, respectively.[18] This conceptually very elegant idea was entirely missing from Pollock (1989). On the other hand Roberts' (1985) and Pollock's (1989) idea that the [±strong] person morphology of AGR, as interpreted above, was at least in part responsible for the [±opaque] parameter is not taken up in Chomsky (1989)[19] where no attempt is made to provide a general account of the [±opaque] functional position parameter.

The other fundamental problem that Chomsky tackles in both papers is the violation of the ECP inherent in the existence of Inflection lowering. In Chomsky (1989) that was done via an elaborate combination of LF Verb movement "undoing" Affix-hopping and trace erasure of meaningless AGR. The somewhat surprising "yo-yo" movement inherent in that approach was obviously a consequence of the existence of syntactic Inflection lowering.

4.2.2. *Checking Theory*

Among many other things, one particularly important result of Chomsky's (1992) minimalist program is precisely the elegant elimination of Inflection lowering and its replacement by a "checking theory", also advocated in different form in e.g. Kitagawa (1986) and Speas (1991: section 5).

Under such a theory, in line with work ascribing to the strong lexicalist theory (see e.g. Selkirk (1982), Di Sciullo and Williams (1987) and the references therein), verbs enter the computational component in their fully inflected morphological form α, analyzed as in (52):

(52) $\alpha = [\text{Root} + \text{Infl}_1 + \ldots + \text{Infl}_n]$

α further adjoins to some inflectional head I, forming (53):

(53) $[_I\ \alpha, \text{I}]$

Under Chomsky's (1992) particular execution of the checking theory, I must delete if the derivation is to "converge" (be accepted) at LF. Deletion of I is possible in Chomsky's (1992) system if and only if Infl_i of α "agrees" (shares all relevant features) with I. Within a system of this type the French-type languages are languages where α adjoins to I before "spell-out" (that is, where Verb raising is a D-structure/S-structure operation in a GB-type theory) while in English type languages it does so after spell-out, that is, covertly at LF.[20]

In short, the idea that raising can apply by phonological spell-out point or after solves the problem posed by lowering rules in a particularly elegant way and yields the desired result that some languages or constructions give the appearence of having their V+inflection complex realized outside of VP or inside it.

4.2.3. *Checking Theory, the SIH and Clause Structure*

It has not often been noted that the checking theory of Verb movement just sketched and fairly standard conceptions of morphological structure combine to yield interesting, if somewhat unexpected, ideas concerning clause structure.

Observe first that under fairly standard ideas concerning morphology (cf. Williams (1981)), (52) is really the simplified version of (53), where each $Infl_i$ is the head of the constituent to its left:

(53) $\alpha = [_{Infl_n} \ldots [_{Infl_1} Root\ -_{Infl_1}]- \ldots\ _{Infl_n}]$

So for example a future form like *parlerons* (we will speak) in French would be analyzed in simplified fashion as in (54):[21]

(54) $[[[_{Root}\ parl]\ \text{-er}\ _{Tense/mood}]\text{-ons}\ _{AGRS}]$

Under this interpretation notice that the syntactic structure in (55),

(55) $[_{TP}\ NP\ T\ [_{AgrP}\ AGR\ [_{VP}\ \alpha]]]$

provides the most adequate input structure for the "checking" of the various inflectional affixes under the natural view that the outer "shells" of a morphologically complex item are to be checked first. On that view (54) should first move to AGR_S to get the 1person pl. marker *-ons* "checked" (i.e. "peeled off" in Chomsky's theory), then to T to get the Tense-mood marker *-er* checked.[22] Thus (55), which is the functional structure suggested in Pollock (1989), is the required input for checking and Belletti's (56), because of the HMC, cannot provide the input for checking first the *-ons* AGR_S head, then the Tense/mood *-er*.

(56) $[_{AGRSP}\ NP\ AGR_S\ [_{TP}\ T\ [_{VP}\ VP]]]$

More generally Chomsky's (1992) checking theory would seem to require that the syntactic embedding of functional projections in syntax be the *mirror image* of the morphological make-up of a verb, at least under the prevalent view of where morphological heads stand in languages like French and English.[23]

Under this approach, we can reconcile the traditional conception of the respective syntactic "scope" of the various inflectional elements – where AGR_O is closer to V than AGR_S for example, as in Chomsky (1989, 1992) – and their morphological ordering in languages like Navajo in which the affixes closest to the verb stem surprisingly take widest scope (cf. Speas (1991)). If the morphological make-up of a Navajo verb is as in (57) (= Speas (1991, (37)),[24] then the corresponding functional syntactic structure should be as in (58) under the view of checking just sketched and also advocated in Speas (1991):

(57) $V° = [AGR_O\ [Asp\ [T\ [AGR_S + Root]]]]$

(58) $[[[[[V°\ _{VP}]\ AGR_O°\ _{AGROP}]\ ASP°\ _{ASPP}]\ T°\ _{TP}]\ AGR_S°\ _{AGRSP}]$

We would then claim that languages like Japanese and Korean, in which, contrary to Navajo, the morphological ordering of affixes does seem to directly mirror their syntactic scope, have "real" head-to-head incorporation, à la Baker, *not* checking, as argued for Korean for example in Bak (1991) and Hong (1992). If so, one might go one step further and claim that checking and real head-to-head incorporation can coexist in certain languages. We would then predict that in such languages verbal morphology should exhibit variations in the ordering of (certain) inflectional affixes and interpret this variation as the reflex of the checking vs incorporation strategies. It is extremely tempting to reinterpret along such lines the (admittedly delicate) data that led Campbell (1991) to suggest that German verbs in the present have a morphosyntactic representation where AGR precedes Tense but one where Tense precedes AGR in the past. Under such an approach the underlying hierarchy of syntactic functional projections in both tenses would be $[_{TP}[_{AGRSP}$ AGR] T] – perhaps universally, linear order apart (but see Kayne (1994)) – but the present tense forms would be derived via V to AGR to T incorporation whereas the past tense ones would be derived via checking of the morphologically complex $[[[_{root}$ V] T] AGR] lexical input.

Let me put an end to these speculations here[25] and tentatively conclude that Chomsky's (1992) checking theory, as (re)interpreted in this section, elegantly solves the lowering problem raised by main verbs in English tensed clauses and French infinitives[26] and, in conjunction with fairly standard views of derivational morphology, strongly suggests that the hierachy of functional projections in the two languages is in the spirit of that suggested in Pollock (1989). We now turn to an independent characterization of what it is that makes an inflectional head "strong" or "weak" in French and English.

5. ON THE [±STRONG] INFLECTION PARAMETER

Before we can address the question we must determine what counts as a legitimate inflectional head. Let us start with English, relying mostly on adverb syntax, as in Pollock (1989).

5.1. *On the Functional Projections of English Tensed Clauses*

As pointed out above, the analysis of Pollock (1989) was incapable of providing a uniform account of the pairs in (59) and (60):

(59) a.* Jean probablement aime la linguistique
 b. John probably likes linguistics

(60) a.* Jean probablement (n') a (pas) fait beaucoup d' erreurs
b. John probably has(n't) made many mistakes

(59) was accounted for by claiming that main verbs move to the F_1 functional position of (61) in French but not in English.

(61) $[_{F_1P}$ NP F_1 Adv (not) $[_{F_2P}$ F_2 $[_{VP}$ V . . .]]]

In that framework, however, the two auxiliaries *avoir* and *have* in (60) *have* moved to F_1 and, everything else being equal, (60b) should be as unacceptable as (60a), an incorrect prediction. The account for this offered in Pollock (1989: note 8) was unsatisfactory, as pointed out in Kayne (1989) who suggested instead that English auxiliary verbs only move up to F_2, never to F_1.[27] If so Kayne claims that in (62) the auxiliaries are adjoined to the functional projection headed by *not/so/too* (cf. Laka (1990), Pollock (1989: 421n), Kayne (1989: section V)).

(62) a. John has not understood
b. John is not/so/too in a hurry
c. John didn't understand
d. John isn't in a hurry
e. John should/will/can not be in a hurry

Although it does deal with (59)–(60) in a uniform fashion I will not adopt this analysis because it seems to have a number of rather unnatural consequences,[28] and will for the time being tentatively adopt the approach to such pairs advocated by Belletti (1990, section 2.2) which has the advantage of shedding light on similar contrasts between French and Italian – also Spanish – illustrated in (63):

(63) a.* Jean probablement a fait plusieurs erreurs
b. Gianni probabilmente ha sbagliato

Kayne's account of (59) and (60) cannot readily extend to (63) since there are many good reasons to believe that all Italian verbs do move up to F_1 (cf. Belletti (1990)). Belletti's analysis rests on the generalization in (64), illustrated in (65):

(64) Italian and English allow NP focalization freely but French typically does not.[29]

(65) a.* Jean j'ai vu
b. Gianni ho visto
c. John I have seen

Let us suppose like her that (63b) is derived by adjoining (i.e. "focalizing") the subject NP to the left of the sentence initial adverb *probabilmente*. Since no such focalization process exists productively[30] in French (cf. (65a)) the derivation in question is unavailable and (63a) is therefore ungrammatical. On this analysis, the occurrence of sentence adverbs in pre-Infl position in Italian, Spanish and English is not a reflex of the failure to apply V to F_1 syntactic incorporation or checking, but follows from an orthogonal difference between French and other Romance languages and English, namely their (in)ability to productively use "move α" for focalization purposes.[31]

This analysis thus removes the major obstacle to the (standard) idea that those auxiliary verbs that stand to the left of *not* in negative sentences and in sentence initial position in questions stand in, or have been moved along with, a functional head position F_1.[32]

5.2. *On the "Weakness" of Modern English Inflectional Heads*

As we saw above, Pollock (1989) took its clue to the "raison d'être" of the opacity of F_1 from the diachronic change affecting richness of person agreement – more precisely from the loss of 1, 2, 3 singular vs plural agreement distinctions, as in Roberts (1985) and (1993) – and analyzed the concomitant demise of main verb movement to F_1 or C° as a consequence of it. I now believe that this is insufficiently general and that the diachronic facts are the reflex of the more fundamental loss of morphologically encoded mood distinctions between indicative, subjunctive and imperative, as proposed in my Seoul and UQAM 1991 lectures and as Pollock (1992) and Murakami (1992) independently argued. As for the opacity of the remaining Modern English inflectional heads, we shall see that it follows in part from the absence of a morphologically identified category of mood on the one hand, and the morphologically defective nature of agreement morphology on the other.

To support my first claim I shall consider the diachronic change affecting subjunctive and imperative sentences in English. Although their respective paradigms *never* showed any 1, 2 and 3 person singular vs plural distinctions, the syntax of their verb movement has undergone essentially the same change as in indicative sentences which did have morphologically overt person distinctions. This clearly demonstrates that the opacity of F_1 cannot be (directly) related to loss of singular vs plural agreement distinctions.

The indicative, subjunctive and imperative forms of Old English strong verbs and class one weak verbs (cf. Mossé 1945, volume 1, chapter 10) are given in (66), (67) and (68) for a representative verb like *niman* (to-take):

(66) Indicative:
Sg 1: nime
sg 2: nim(e)st
sg 3: nim(e)ð
Pl: nimað

(67) Subjunctive:[33]
Sg: nime
Pl: nimen

(68) Imperative:
Sg: 2 nim
Pl: 2 nimað

Even the present subjunctive of *be* did not distinguish first from second or third person singular or plural since the singular was *beo* for all three and the common plural form was *beon*.

In Middle English the *-e* and *-en* endings of the subjunctive lost ground and were often altogether dropped – in the North – or optionally survived as [ə] and syllabic [n] in the Midlands and the South (cf. Mossé 1945: volume II, 111sq). Similarly the plural imperative ending was reduced to [əð]. In short, as Traugott (1972: 148–149) puts it:

"[. . .] the inflectional distinctions between indicative and subjunctive [and imperatives J.-Y. P] came, like other inflectional distinctions, to be obscured by the tendency of unstressed vowels to be pronounced [ə]. [. . .] Despite the recessiveness of subjunctive inflections they are nevertheless found throughout the ME and ENE periods"

Finally these inflectional distinctions were altogether lost in late ENE, as noted by many scholars. How does this morphological, ultimately phonetic, change relate to verb syntax? Up until the ENE all verbs could move to the pre-negative functional position in the subjunctive and (from there to some higher position) in the imperative, just as they did in the indicative. (69) and (70) are a few representative examples, borrowed from Murakami (1992: 124, 131):

(69) Subjunctive:
a. ðe cardinals ordeyned and demed ðat ðe pope be not buried in holy chirche
b. Beware thou that thou bring not my son thither (Bible 1611, Genesis)
c. God send we be all better this day three months (Goldsmith 1792)
d. I am not to advertise my reader that he impute not to them the faultes of their ancestours (1571, Campion, *The History of Ireland*)

(70) Imperatives:
a. Be not inconsistant, careless of your fame (Marlow, *Tamberlain the great*)
b. I charge thee, be not thou more grived than I am (Shakespeare, *As you like it*)

c. Buy thou the cottage, pasture and the flock (Shakespeare, *As you like it*)
d. Fear you not my part of the dialogue (Shakespeare, *Much ado about nothing*)

All these are ungrammatical in Modern English, with the exception of a few residual set phrases and expressions.

Clearly, it would be most desirable to account for the acceptability of (69a,d) and (79c,d) in OE, ME and ENE the same way we would account for examples like (71) – from Roberts (1993: section 3.1, examples (19b), (20b), (25a,b) respectively:

(71) a. What menythe this prieste?
b. Why come dogges so often to the churche?
c. Weepyng and teres counforteth not dissolute laughers
d. Because they come not up and offre

But if so, their acceptability cannot be dependent on (residual) "strong" person agreement since the verb forms of (69) and (70) never had any. Instead the following descriptive generalizations suggest themselves:

(72) Overt main verb raising to the pre-negative functional position was allowed in English when the indicative, subjunctive and imperative paradigms were kept at least residually distinct morphologically.

(73) Loss of overt main verb raising to the pre-negative functional position is a consequence of the loss of morphologically manifested mood distinctions between the indicative and the subjunctive.

We shall now attempt to deduce (73) from deeper principles of grammar, in particular a general morphological constraint on checking.

5.3. *MoodP, TenseP, AGRP and Checking Theory*

5.3.1. *Mood and Main Verbs*

Suppose, in line with the "mirror image" idea sketched in section 4 above, that the order of embedding of functional categories in English and French is as in (74):

(74) $[_{MoodP}$ Mood $([_{NegP}$ neg$)$ $[_{TP}$ T $[_{AgrP}$ AGR $[_{VP}$ $\alpha]](])]$

We may for the time being analyze the (main) verb morphology of Modern English as (75):

(75) $[[[_{Root}$ V$]$ $-\{ø,$ ed$\}_{Tense}]]\{-$s, $ø\}_{AGRS}]$

Note that, in line with the morphological findings of the previous section, (75) is *not* characterized for mood.

Let us now adopt the following principle :

(76) Only morphologically identified ("strong") functional heads can be checked overtly.[34]

It follows that no main verb can raise to F_1 = Mood (overtly) in Modern English, though that was possible untill the late ENE period because the lexical entry of verbs still had at least residually identifiable mood morphology contrasting indicative, subjunctive (and imperative).

As promised, (73) follows directly from the combination of (76) and the functional structure (74).

5.3.2. *Mood,* Be, Have, Do *and Modals*

Whatever theory of lexical structure one adopts, it seems clear that *be*, *have* and modal verbs should be distinguished from ordinary "main" verbs. They fail to have a thematic structure of their own, an intuition shared, though expressed in various forms, by Pollock (1989), Chomsky (1989, 1992) and many other articles. Perhaps because of this, they also fail to denote events in and of themselves.[35] As a consequence, the tense morphology with which they are associated does not play the normal "anchoring" role it plays with lexical verbs. This is best shown by so-called modal verbs. Clearly, the semantic import of the present vs past tense contrast in pairs like (78) is very different from that in (79).

(78) a. I may/can/will/shall sing
b. I might/could/would/should sing

(79) a. I sing/talk/speak
b. I sang/talked/spoke

I will take my clue from these informal considerations and suggest that the present and past tense morphology associated with "light" verbs like modals, *be*, *have* and *do* are reanalysed as indicative mood markers,[36] along the lines of the informal characterizations (80):

(80) [[[{do, be, have, M}]+ [±past] $_{\text{Tense/Mood}}$] (AGR)]

Observe further that if (80) is allowed to alternate with the "normal" form in (81),

(81) [[[{do, be, have, M}]+ [±past] $_{\text{Tense}}$] (AGR)]

we may capture part of the interesting intuition shared by C. L. Baker (1991) and Kayne (1989) that even auxiliaries do not have to move up to the highest (i.e. Mood) functional head in a clause in English. In short, we can maintain that pairs like (82) vs (83),

(82) John probably {is making/has made} a fool of himself

(83) John {is, has} probably {making, made} a fool of himself

follow from (76) and the morphological/lexical analyses in (81) and (80), respectively.

If functional negation *not* and its reduced allomorph *n't* were always generated in between tense and Mood, as implicitely assumed in structure (74) above, examples like (84) would show that there is still need for a Belletti-like analysis in English:

(84) John probably {isn't, has't} {making, made} a fool of himself

That assumption is not justified, however, as convincingly shown by Zanuttini (1991). Like her, let us allow *not/n't* – also *so*, *too*, the possible heads of Pollock's (1989), Laka's (1990) ΣP under Kayne's (1989) analysis – to (optionally) appear below tense.[37]

We can now advantageously preserve the spirit of Kayne's analysis for English without many of its more problematic aspects (cf. footnote 28) and claim that in (84) *is/has* – also *do* and modals – stand in Tense rather than in the highest functional position, the Mood position. On the contrary, it is in the Mood position that the same auxiliairies are standing in the minimally contrasting (85):

(85) John {isn't, has't} probably {making, made} a fool of himself

Given the fact that French has overt mood distinctions, we can now explain the French vs English contrast of (86) vs (87)[38] if we strengthen (76) by assuming that everything else being equal, in the absence of independent blocking factors, those functional heads that *can* be checked overtly *must* be so checked.

(86) John never {is, has} (not) {happy, uncerstood}

(87) *Jean jamais (n') est/a (pas) heureux, compris

It now also follows that Belletti's analysis of French vs Italian contrasts like (63), repeated here under (88), is vindicated since both *a* and *ha* have overtly moved to Mood. Observe too that the problematic aspects of her analysis when extended to English summed up in footnote 31 are also now advantageously avoided.[39]

(88) a.* Jean probablement a fait plusieurs erreurs
b. Gianni probabilmente ha sbagliato

5.3.3. *On the [± strong] Nature of English Tense and AGR*

Accepting the conclusions of the previous section, we must find principled reasons for blocking (89) and the like, on an analysis where *not* is generated below Tense, since nothing in what precedes prevents main verbs from moving to AGR and from there to Tense for overt checking:

(89) a.* {I, you, we, they} (probably) talk n't
b.* John (probably) talks n't
c.* {I, you, (s)he, we, they} (probably) talked n't

Independently of this glaring problem, we must also prevent English verbs from reaching these two functional positions if we are to continue giving formal execution to generalizations A and B of section one, i.e. account for the fact that no adverb, whether it be adjoined to the left of VP – *completely*, *very much* etc. – or to the left of AGRP – perhaps subject oriented adverbs like *willingly* – can end up in between a main verb and its NP complement. In short, having shown that F_1 = Mood cannot be checked before spell-out because it no longer is morphologically identified in Modern English, is only one element in the overall analysis of Modern English (ad)verb syntax.

Given the fact that the tense and AGR morphology of examples like (89a) is non lexical, (76), which I repeat under (90) for convenience,

(90) Only morphologically identified ("strong") functional heads can be checked overtly

would suffice to block overt movement to AGR and to Tense, if the so far implicit notion "morphologically identified" was equated with "lexical".

This however would not permit a much needed extension to (89b,c). Furthermore, it would be inconsistent for me to claim that "strong" simply means "lexical" since on the analysis of the Fench present indicative *parlons*, adopted above and repeated in (91), both tense and mood are non lexical and yet require checking before spell-out.

(91) $[[[[_{Root}$ parl$]$ –ø $_{Mood}]$–ø $_{T}]$-ons $_{AGR}]$

Instead, I would like to claim that the non lexical indicative and present tense morphemes in examples like these are "morphologically identified" because they unambiguously alternate in regular, productive paradigms with lexical [-*er*] and [-*i*], as in the future *parlerons*, the conditional *parlerions* etc.

Let us start from there and suggest (92) :

(92) An inflectional morpheme $[_{I}\ \alpha]$ is morphologically identified (i.e. "strong") in Language L with respect to paradigm P if it alternates unambiguously in P with at least one distinct morpheme of the same inflectional category.

With this definition in mind consider (89) again. The promised conclusion is that the null morpheme(s) in (89a) and either *-ed* or *-s* in (89b,c) – or both – fail to be "morphologically identified" in Modern English.

We have in fact already implicitly adopted the idea that Tense is "strong" in Modern English in section 5.3.2. In this we were implicitely relying on the traditional analysis of the English Tense system as consisting of alternating $[_{Past}$-ed] and $[_{Present}$ ø] morphemes.[40]

The only logically consistent conclusion, therefore, is that it is the agreement morphemes of Modern English that are "weak" (i.e. not morphologically identified). To give support to this idea I will adopt the conclusion of Kayne's (1989: section 3) demonstration that *-s* stands for [singular] and that the "bare forms" of (89a) are indeed absolutely bare, that is, are not even associated with a null agreement affix, contrary to the standard morphological description in (75) above which ought therefore to be replaced by the more perspicuous (93):[41]

(93) $[[[_{Root}$ V] {ø, ed} $_{Tense}$]](-s) $_{Numb}$]

On Kayne's analysis the lexical *-s* morpheme is therefore not "morphologically identified". It follows that checking of AGR in (89b) cannot be overt. The checking of the totally empty AGR of the bare forms of (89a) cannot be either. Finally the overt checking of lexical $[_{past}$-*ed*] in (89c) – and of non lexical $[_{present}$ ø] in (89a) – is impossible, despite the fact that [±past] is morphologically identified, on the (natural) assumption that overt checking of a head H_o is made impossible by an intervening "opaque" (non overtly checkable) head H_p.[42]

To summarize, let me stress that the conclusion that it is the presence of the morphologically defective agreement morphology of Modern English that is responsible for many of the distinguishing features of contemporary (ad)verb syntax is evidently very much in the spirit of Roberts' (1985), (1993) and Pollock's (1989) idea concerning the loss of "strong" (subject) agreement. What I have added to this idea here is the claim that the loss of morphologically identifiable mood morphemes should be seen in the same light and has comparable, though not identical, effects on (ad)verb syntax. Granted this, the correct formulation of the required notion of morphological "strength" cannot be made to depend on the specifics of (subject) agreement too closely. (92) is my attempt at formulating the required general definition, applicable to both mood and agreement.

5.3.4. *More on English Auxiliaries*

Granted the above, we must obviously comment on the fact that modals, *do*, *have* and *be* can end up in the Mood and Tense positions of the functional structure (94):

(94) $[_{MoodP}$ Mood $[_{TP}$ T $[_{AgrP}$ AGR $[_{VP}$ α]]]]

In much the same spirit as Pollock (1989, sections 5.5.3 and 5.5.4) I will take advantage of the fact that Modals and *do* are "pure" auxiliaries – that is, verbs that *never* project a VP – and assume that, as a consequence, they can be generated in the AGR position and the Tense position, respectively, independently of checking.

Be and *have* do project a VP, however. I shall consequently rely on the striking fact that *be* is the only verb of English that has morphologically identified tense *and* person agreement to explain that its agreement (hence tense) morpholoy can – therefore must on the interpretation of (76)–(90) adopted above – be checked overtly. Although the same is less transparently true of *have*, I shall assume that its agreement too is "strong" in the sense of (92). This will ensure possible, therefore obligatory, overt checking for both verbs, as required.

5.4. *Checking and French Infinitives*

The facts that must be accounted for are repeated in (95):

(95) a. A peine/mal comprendre l'Italien . . .
b. Comprendre à peine/mal l'italien
c. Ne pas comprendre l'italien . . .
d. Ne pas être/avoir . . .
e. N'être/avoir pas . . .
f.* Ne comprendre/*sembler/*parler/. . ./pas

Because French infinitives never show any person agreement I shall adopt the conservative view that the morphological decomposition of a French verb in the infinitive does not include an agreement slot at all. Correspondingly, I shall suppose that the inflectional structure of infinitival clauses does not have a functional AGRP projection either. Put another way, I am now rejecting the extremely strong "uniformity thesis" adopted in Pollock (1989) and formulated as D in section 2:

D. The D-structures of finite clauses, infinitives and gerunds are identical and only differ with respect to the feature composition of functional projections and/or Comp.

Instead I would like to suggest that the finite vs non-finite distinction in French – indeed Romance except European Portuguese – correlates significantly with the presence vs absence of an AGR(P) in morphological/functional structure. Aside from that difference, I will continue to assume that the functional projections of infinitives and tensed clauses are identical, i.e. that a sentence in the infinitive has the functional structure in (96); of course, (96) *is* the functional structure of French tensed clauses except for the absence of AGRP:

(96) $[_{MoodP}$ Mood (neg) $[_{TP}$ T $[_{VP}$(Adv) $[_{VP}\ \alpha]]]]$

Seen from the perspective of (92), now, it is clear that the corresponding mood and tense suffixes of infinitives cannot both be "strong". In the non-finite paradigms of French the *-er*, *-ir*, *-oir* endings can presumably be said to alternate with the *-ant* ending of present participles (*chant+{ant*, vs *er}*), but no further decomposition in non-finite paradigms[43] can isolate any further morpheme with which the null suffix could alternate. Furthermore the status of the infinitival suffixes with respect to the tense vs mood distinction is unclear since there exists no alternation of the type *chanterons* vs *chanterions* operative in tensed sentences to help disambiguate the structure.

This, then, yields an indeterminate situation where two possible analyses for the infinitival suffix would seem to coexist:

(97) $[[[_{Root}]\ \{\text{-er, –ir, oir}\}_{mood}]\ ø\ _{tense}]$

(98) $[[[_{Root}]\ ø\ _{mood}]\ \{\text{-er, –ir, oir}\}_{tense}]$

In (97) the null tense suffix is "weak", for the reasons just stated. In (98) the null mood suffix is. Let us assume that ambiguity to be real, i.e. a true characteristic of the linguistic knowledge of French speakers which, because of the relative poverty of French infinitival morphology, can only remain indeterminate.[44]

Notice now that the analytical framework developed in 4.3.3 predicts that no overt checking can take place in (97) since the "strong" mood suffixes are separated from their functional head by "weak" tense. This, I take it, is how one should analyze examples like (95a) where the inflected verbs obligatorily stand in their VP.

In (98), on the other hand, the tense head is "strong", therefore can, hence must, be checked overtly. Because the mood suffix is weak, however, further overt checking of the (null) mood suffix is impossible (see notes 41 and 23). This will account both for the grammaticality of (95b) and the ungrammaticality of (95f).

In order to account for the exceptional behavior of *être/avoir* – and modals like *vouloir*, *devoir* and *falloir* – in examples like (95d) and (95e) I will extend to French infinitives the analysis developed for English finite sentences like (99),

(99) John {isn't, has't} probably {making, made} a fool of himself

by suggesting that the infinitive tense morphemes associated with "light" verbs – i.e. verbs without thematic structure – are optionally reanalyzed as mood markers, along the lines of the informal (100)

(100) $[[[\{\text{Root}\}]+\ [ø\ _{Mood}][\{\text{-er, -ir, -oir}\}]\ _{Tense/Mood}]$

(100) will then permit overt checking of the "strong" lexical tense/mood morphemes in French infinitives like (96) exactly for the same reason that

overt checking of the "strong" tense/Mood suffixes was possible in English finite sentences like (99).

As promised, then, we do deal with the similarities and differences in French-English paradigms like (101) and (102) in uniform fashion, using essentially the same analytic tools.

(101) a.* John ownsn't a car
b. John doesn't own a car
c.* John likesn't Mary
d. John doesn't like Mary
e. John hasn't a car
f. John isn't happy
g.* John seemsn't happy

(102) a.* Ne posséder pas voiture en banlieue rend la vie difficile
b. Ne pas posséder de voiture en banlieue rend la vie difficile
c.* N'aimer pas Marie . . .
d. Ne pas aimer Marie . . .
e. N'avoir pas de voiture en banlieue rend la vie dificile
f. N'être pas heureux, . . .
g.* Ne sembler pas heureux . . .

Recall that this is a prerequisite on any analysis of French and/or English. I am aware of no alternative analysis reaching this goal.[45]

6. CONCLUSION

In this article I have used the (ad)verb syntax of French and English, studied both comparatively and diachronically, as a testing ground for developing a more articulated theory of the "strength" of inflectional heads and of checking. The analyses developed here rest importantly on (103),

(103) An inflectional morpheme $[_I \alpha]$ is morphologically identified (i.e. "strong") in Language L with respect to paradigm P if it alternates unambiguously in P with at least one distinct morpheme of the same inflectional category

and on the idea that overt checking – i.e. checking before spell-out – is constrained by (104):

(104) Only morphologically identified ("strong") functional heads can be checked overtly.

I have also suggested that overt checking is favored over covert LF checking in that it applies obligatorily whenever all relevant conditions are met. In this I differ rather sharply from Chomsky (1992) since in my account of verb movement I have in effect replaced his "procrastinate" by its antonym "haste".

I have also tentatively tried to develop the rather heterodox idea that under a plausible interpretation of checking the functional structure of a clause should be what I have called "the mirror image" of the verb's inflectional morphology: assuming the structure of an inflected verb to be represented as in (105),

(105) $\alpha = [\ldots[[\text{Root} + a] + b] + \ldots] + n]$

the functional structure that corresponds to it under the purely "local" conception of checking advocated here should be (106),

(106) $[_{a''}\ a\ [_{b''}\ b\ [\ldots [_{n''}\ n]\ [_{VP}\ \alpha]].\ .\ .]]]$

in which the functional head closest to the verb stem is topmost in the functional hierarchy, not lowest, as in the "standard" incorporation framework of Baker (1988).

This idea leads to the conclusion that the highest functional projection in Modern French, Modern English and many other languages is MoodP.[46] I have also tried to show that this idea and the fact that Mood is morphologically weak in Modern English – though not in Old, Middle and ENE English – have revealing consequences for the comparative treatment of (ad)verb syntax in the two languages.

Assuming (some of) these controversial ideas to be on the right track, it must be emphasized that they have done little more than scratch the surface of a fully articulated theory of clause structure and much remains to be done both in the general theory of functional projections and in the theory of checking proper.[47]

Université de Picardie
Amiens

NOTES

[1] This article was written in 1992. I had planned to revise it for publication in this volume by including comments on, and alternatives to, the relevant literature published between 1987 and 1995. (Un)fortunately the amount of work on clause structure and functional projections done over the last five years is so staggering that it has forced me to take a more realistic view of what ground I could cover in an introductory article. I have therefore pretty much stuck to the original text. Had I tried to integrate the more recent developments of the Minimialist program, in particuler the views on funtional structure put forward in Chomsky (1995: chapter 4) I would have had to rewrite the article entirely and the points it does make would have been lost. For some suggestions see Pollock (1997, Chapter 13). The text of this article is based on my notes for a class on funtional structure I taught in Montreal in June and July 1991 and Seoul, Korea, in July 1991. I would like to thank all the participants of the UQAM seminar, in particular Monique Lemieux, and all the participants of the Seoul summer school, in particular professor Dong-Whee Yang and the two other guest speakers, Kyle Johnson and Ian Roberts. Naturally, the usual disclaimers about the responsibility of the persons cited hold of the present work. Finally I would like to dedicate

this article to the memory of C. L. Baker: the great respect in which I hold his work should not be masked by the disagreement I voice here with some of his views on the functional structure of English sentences.

[2] For discussion see section 3 and note 11.

[3] On Chomsky's (1992) "checking" alternative to lowering, see section 4.

[4] On the usual assumption, considered as self-evident in better established domains of rational empirical inquiry, though sometimes not in linguistics, that generalizations that *can* be expressed *must* be expressed.

[5] Cf. Pollock (1989: 2.4.2). As pointed out there, the English infinitive data are rather murky and in themselves could only provide a depressingly shaky foundation for B, hence also for the SIH which is crucially based on "short verb movement" data. Indeed, the (somewhat marginal) acceptability of cases like *I believe John to be often sarcastic* (Pollock's (1989, (39c)) probably requires a more complex analysis than I originally suggested, as argued by Iatridou (1990). Fortunately the French counterparts to all such (see e.g. (10) below) are perfectly clear-cut and reliable and they suffice to vindicate B, once certain misconceptions about adverb placement have been corrected. See section 3.1.

[6] In contrast, Chomsky (1989, 50) suggested that the SIH might simply follow from a rigid X-bar-theoretic condition of single-headedness. The *Barriers*-type Inflection contains both tense-mood features and AGR features. Therefore, under the single-headedness condition appealed to by Chomsky, it would simply have to be "split" into an AGR_SP and a TenseP.

[7] At least for tensed sentences. On Pollock's (1989) [±opaque] parameter in infinitives (and Aux-to-Comp constructions) see the critical remarks in section 4.1. For a more satisfactory account see section 5.4. The short-lived existence of well-formed negative sentences of the type in (i) – on which see Roberts (1993: 3.1) –

(i) S + *not* + tensed verb + O

follows from the orthogonal fact that *not* remained a non functional negative adverb comparable to *never* for a short while at a time when main verbs had already ceased to (have to) raise to F_1. The ungrammaticality of (i) in Modern English follows from the loss of lexical *not* with the presence of the resulting functional NegP interfering with (a suitable reinterpretation of) affix hopping.

[8] Pollock (1989: footnote 12) suggests another argument, not mentioned by Iatridou (1990), based on the *to not V* vs *not to V* alternation of English infinitives. I come back to this in section 5.4. See (text to) note 44.

[9] Among which the ECP, as in Baker (1988), if those "adverbs" that do incorporate are really argument-like, maybe comparable to atomic "adverbs" like *hard, loud, dur, fort* in English and French sentences like *John works hard, sings loud, Jean travaille dur, chante fort* etc.

[10] In fact, contray to what C. L. Baker states, his analysis does complicate the "base component" of English since it posits a "special purpose VP" for which there is no need in core-grammar accounts.

[11] Ouhalla (1990) and Johnson (1992) offer other explicit challenges to generalizations A and B above. Unlike Iatridou and Baker, neither of them argue against the SIH or the core grammar interpretation of the comparative data in Pollock (1989). Their criticisms are thus very different in spirit from those of the two articles just reviewed.

Johnson's mainly relies on Icelandic in which (main) verbs move to C° in questions and end up to the left of negation in embedded tensed clauses, as (i) and (ii) show, but cannot move to the left of adverbs in infinitives and participial clauses, as demonstrated by the unacceptability of (iii) ((i), (ii), (ii) and (iv) = Johnson's (1992, (8), (9) and (10)):

(i) Keypti Jón bókina?
(bought John book-the?)

(ii) . . . að Jón keypti ekki bókina
(that John bought not book-the)

(iii) a. *Jón virđist lesa hægt bókina
(John seems to-read slowly book-the)

b. *Jón hefur lesiđ hægt bókina
(John has read slowly book-the)

So Icelandic main verbs pattern like their English counterparts in infinitives and participle clauses. Yet they do move to the left of adverbs in (embedded) simple tensed clauses, as (iv) shows:

(iv) . . . ađ Jón keypti hægt bókina
(that John bought slowly book-the)

Although the facts are a little murky, for reasons discussed by Johnson, let us assume that (i) . . . (iv) provide adequate characterization of the data. Accepting the SIH for Icelandic, what these data show is that V moves to F_2 (then to F_1) in (i), (ii) and (iv) but cannot in (iii). Although this is unexpected when compared to the situation in French where F_2 in structure (v),

(v) $[_S$ NP F_1 F_2 $[_{VP}$ . . . V . . .]]

appears to be [–opaque] in participial clauses, I do not believe that (i) . . . (iv) should lead us to give up generalizations A and B: all we have to assume descriptively is that F_2 is [+opaque] in infinitives and participial clauses in Icelandic though [–opaque] in tensed sentences. In fact this is true of French infinitives as well. Everything else being equal, only a language in which in a given sentence type (the counterparts of) (i)–(ii) and (iv) differed in acceptability would successfully establish that generalizations A and B are spurious. I am not aware of any such case and Icelandic does not show that, clearly. I cannot do justice here to Johnson's (1991) and (1992) extremely interesting analysis of particle constructions in English in which he claims that English main verbs do move to what he and Pesetsky (1989) call a "μ-position". Again, this would be compatible with A and B if that μ-position stood below F_2 to the right of (functional) negation and (most) adverbs. On this see Pollock (1996).

Along partly similar lines, Ouhalla (1990) develops the idea that even English can move verbs to the left of adverbs, as in the following sentences (= Ouhalla's (57)):

(vi) a. Bill knocked recently on it
b. Sue looked carefully at him
c. Harry relies frequently on it

I do not think that the leftward V-movement analysis of such examples is correct; observe that (vii) are considerably worse than (vi):

(vii) a. *Bill knocked hardly on it
b. *Sue looked hardly at him
c. *Harry relies sure on it

Adverbs like *merely, barely, hardly, sure,* unlike *recently, carefully* and *frequently,* cannot be VP final. This will suffice to make such pairs understandable if we interpret (vi) either as involving PP extraposition to the right of VP final adverbs (but see Kayne (1994) on right adjunction) or as involving base generation of adverbs inside a Larsonian VP shell. The same will never yield (vii) assuming the adverbs there are always generated outside of VP, whence the noted unacceptability. On the fact that careful choice of adverbs is essential when arguing in favor of (short) verb movement see Pollock (1989: 380–381). See Pollock (1996).

12 Since Belletti (1990) was mainly concerned with a comparative analysis of French vs Italian (ad)verb syntax in infinitives there was no need for her to raise the question of how

the [±opaque] parameter of Pollock (1989) could be acquired or that of the "raison d'être" of the diachronic evolution of English. On the few informal suggestions Belletti did make see Pollock (1992). For an analysis see section 5.

[13] The problem would be compounded if we were to offer a uniform account for all the cases of downgrading vs raising documented in the literature over the last few years, for example, the Serbo-Croatian vs Bulgarian *-li* raising vs *-li* hopping of Rivero (forthcoming) or the copula inversion constructions of Modern Hebrew which Borer (1993) claims arise either as a result of participial/adjective (Head to head) raising or of lowering of the copula to the participle/adjective. I will not attempt to offer such a uniform account here.

[14] See for example Haegeman and Zanuttini (1991), Belletti (1990) and the references therein.

[15] Pollock (1989: note 8) suggested that there was an additional adverb position in English, absent in French, between the subject NP position and F_1. To further account for the fact that *not* cannot occupy that extra position an informal principle requesting *not* to always be in the (c-command) domain of tense (at S-structure) was offered that was taken up and considerably extended by Laka (1990) who suggested that it could in fact account for all restrictions on English *not*, including those that were dealt with in terms of violations of the Head to Head contraint on Affix-lowering and/or (LF) Verb movement in Pollock (1989) and Chomsky (1989), like, say, **John not sings*. Laka's analysis does not appear to jibe well with Chomsky's minimalist program since it specifically relies on an S-structure constraint.

[16] F_1 must lower to the main verb in (ia) (cf. (ib), can lower to the auxiliary in (iia) (cf. (iib)); F_1 and F_2 lower to the verbs in (iiia) while only F_1 need lower in (iiib):

(i) a. Ne pas chanter
b. *Ne chanter pas

(ii) a. Ne pas être heureux
b. N'être pas heureux

(iii) a. Ne pas souvent chanter
b. Ne pas chanter souvent

The simultaneous existence of (iia, b) and (iiia, b) thus shows that French may use either a lowering or a raising strategy in otherwise identical contexts (see note 26 for some consequences and section 4.4 for an analysis). Hebrew copular inversion constructions show the same thing if Borer (1992) is right. It is therefore a rather misleading oversimplification to talk of languages as being either French-style or English-style in their verbal syntax: most are both. The fact that Modern English isn't is probably quite atypical.

[17] The growing body of work that accepts (51) for languages like French and English has offered little independent empirical argument showing that finite Tense and subject (person) agreement are seperate functional projections, aside from the general, so far non empirical, claim that each distinguishable inflectional affix should head its own separate functional projection. One argument is provided by Finnish where person agreement can be affixed to negation while the tense and mood suffix is attached to the verbal element below negation, as illustrated by (i) (= (2) in Holmberg et al. (1991)).

(i) (Minä) e+n osta + isi sitä kirjaa
I neg+1SG buy + COND that book
(I wouldn't buy that book)

As far as (Modern) English is concerned, the fact that finite Tense and AGR_S are in complementary distribution has led some to revert to the "standard" non-split view of inflection in which the (subject) agreement morphology simply reflects feature sharing under Spec-Head agreement with finite tense (see e.g. Iatridou (1990)). Recall that the "short verb movement" adverbial data that served to motivate the SIH only concerns F_2 in (i), identified as AGR_O by Chomsky (1989) and (1992):

(i) $[_S$ NP F_1 pas F_2 $[_{VP}$ (adv) VP]]

No independent empirical argument kown to me shows that the functional position that precedes negation – F_1 in (i) – must be further split in French or English. The lack of specific empirical arguments in favour of this further distinction obviously does not show that it cannot exist. It should however encourage one to take a cautious view and be on the look-out for some independent support one way or the other.

[18] For criticisms concerning the uniform Spec-Head view of Nominative Case-assignment see e.g. Hulk and Van Kemenade (1993). The other motivation offered by Chomsky is past-participle agreement with pre-participial clitics and *Wh*-phrase, as in Kayne (1987). It is not entirely clear to me that the AGR_O postulated on the basis of past-participle agreement should be identified with the AGR_O in Romance and Germanic non participial clauses; in particular the former has no Case-theoretic motivation, unlike the latter.

[19] For good reasons given the insufficient generality Pollock's (1989) approach pointed out above. Even if the link between [±opaque] and [±strong] AGR was correct there is no obvious reason why (overt) "richness" in AGR_S should be correlated with (covert) "richness" in AGR_O. But only if there were such a link could Roberts's and Pollock's original correlation be expressed on a structure like (51).

[20] Chomsky's checking theory thus makes the intricate ups and downs of Chomsky (1989) unnecessary on principled grounds.

[21] The fully articulated analysis should in fact be as shown in (i) where Mood and (present) Tense are dissociated:

(i) $[[[[_{Root}$ parl] -er $_{Mood}]$-ø $_T]$-ons $_{AGR}]$

That *-er* is a [-realis] mood marker is justified by the fact that it is also the marker of conditionals (and infinitives). Analyzing it as the mere future form of French (and Italian) would miss the obvious generalization. The embedding chosen in (i) is justified by conditionals and imperfect forms like *parl+er+i+ons* ((we) would speak) and *parl+i+ons* (we were speaking), where *i* vs *ø* can be plausibly analyzed as past vs present markers. If this is correct, then *parlions* should in turn be further analyzed as in (ii) where ø is the null marker of [+realis] mood. For the same reason, *parlons* (we speak) should be analyzed as in (iii) which has an additional null present tense affix.

(ii) $[[[[_{Root}$ parl] -ø $_{Mood}]$-i $_T]$-ons $_{AGR}]$

(iii) $[[[[_{Root}$ parl] -ø $_{Mood}]$-ø $_T]$-ons $_{AGR}]$

Observe that the V + Mood + Tense morphological ordering of French in such examples is the mirror image of the syntactic Modal + Tense + V ordering of English examples like (iv) under the traditional analysis of *have* as a past tense marker in those contexts (cf. Hofman (1969)), perhaps for reasons discussed speculatively in the text below.

(iv) John would have spoken

[22] I am ignoring the AGR_O layer here since its motivations do not lie in verb morphology proper – in languages like English – my main concern here.

[23] This follows only, as Speas (1991: section 5) notes, if there is no feature percolation from one morphological head to the next. This seems to be independently true: an adverb like, say, *constitutionally* is derived from a verb root by the derivation shown in (i):

(i) [[[[constitut $_V]$+ion $_N]$+al $_{Adj}]$+ly $_{Adv}]$

Surely, *-al* does not inherit "noun status" from *-ion*, anymore than *-ly* inherits adjectival status from *-al*. In short I am suggesting that "checking" is a strictly local process which can only "see" the features of the head of the outermost shell of a morphologically complex item.

[24] An alternative would be to consider AGR_O in (57) as an incorporated clitic. On that interpretation Navajo provides no direct support for the mirror image idea developed in the text.

[25] They are obviously incompatible with the literal formulation of Chomsky's (1992) "procrastinate". See also next note.

[26] In view of (i)–(ii) vs (iii)–(iv) and the like, and the simplified morphological/functional structures in (v)–(vi)

(i) *ne parler pas
(ii) ne pas parler
(iii) Il ne parlera pas
(iv) *Il ne pas parlera

(v) $\alpha = [[[_{Root}\ \text{parl}]\ \text{-er}\ _{Mood}]\text{-}\emptyset\ _T]$
(vi) $[_{MoodP}\ \text{NP Mood}\ [_{TP}\ \text{T}\ [_{VP}\ \alpha]]]$

we have to assume that checking of the Mood features is before spell-out in tensed clauses but after spell-out in infinitives. The simultaneous existence of (vii) and (viii):

(vii) Ne pas très bien parler l'italien, c'est dommage
(*ne* not very well to-speak Italian is a pity)

(viii) Ne pas parler très bien l'italien, c'est dommage
(*ne* not to-speak very well Italian is a pity)

means that in infinitives the checking of the lowest functional catagory, (null) tense under the analysis in (vi), can either take place in overt syntax or at LF. Such free variation would seem to be incompatible with Chomsky's (1992) version of "procrastinate". The free variation in (ix) and (x),

(ix) Ne pas être content
(x) N'être pas content

can be described along the lines of (viii) but is incompatible both with procrastinate and Chomsky's (1992) account of the obligatoriness of *have/be* raising in tensed clauses in English since that account would seem to incorrectly predict (ix) to be ungrammatical.

Specifying piecemeal the level at which checking takes place, as we have just done, is reminiscent of the extrinsic orderings of earlier versions of generative grammar and is just as uninteresting. This is not specific to analyses formulated within Chomsky's checking theory since the ad-hoc character of these stipulations had a direct counterpart in Pollock's (1989) quasi arbitrary association of [±opaque] or [±strong] features with specific inflectional endings (see above). What we need, as pointed out earlier, is a theory of what counts as [±strong] features (see section 5.3). For a more articulated analysis of checking in French infinitives see section 5.4.

[27] This is in the same spirit as, though technically different from, L. Baker's idea that in, say, *John probably has understood* the auxiliary has failed to move (see section 2.2.2).

[28] Especially with respect to questions like (i),

(i) a. Is John not in a hurry?
b. {Did/Should/Has/Is} John {not say anything/not gone/not singing}?

in which *be/have/do* and Modals presumably moved from the adjoined position to Laka's (1990) ΣP to C°, a movement usually held to be prohibited by some version of structure preservation. The idea that *so*, *not* and *too*, the possible heads of ΣP under Kayne's (1989) analysis, are clitics even in their non reduced forms is somewhat counterintuitive. The question of what forces adjunction to ΣP in a system of this type is also left unsolved in Kayne (1989). For a reformulation of the gist of Kayne's analysis which, believe, solves these problems see section 5.3.2 and section 5.3.3.

[29] The process at work in (65b) is to be carefully distinguished from clitic left dislocation as in *Jean, je l'ai vu* (Jean, I him+have seen).

[30] The qualification is meant to allow for the sporadic existence in French of sentences like, say, *Fruit d'or, j'adore!* (Fruit d'or, I love) which are very common in advertisments but which are restricted to a very small set of verbs (essentially *aimer* (like), *détester* (hate) and their synonyms) and which seem to depend on rhymes for perfect acceptability, as in the example just given.

[31] Belletti's account, though elegant and fairly straightforward in its analysis of the Italian vs French data, leaves at least three prominent properties of sentences like (59b) unsolved when it is extended to English. Firstly, untressed subject pronouns can precede the pre-F_1 adverbs, as in (i), an unexpected property under Belletti's NP focalization analysis – compare (ii):

(i) He probably has made many mistakes
(ii) HER/*her I will kiss

As pointed out to me by Richard Kayne (p.c.), this problem is reminiscent of a similar problem in the "classical" Verb Second analysis of SVO main clauses in German or Dutch, which has led some (e.g. Travis (1986)) to suggest an analysis where the subject NP does not move to Spec C.

Secondly, there are adverbs that appear (very) unnaturally in sentence initial position but which sit very comfortably in pre-Aux position, an unexpected contrast under Belletti's account

(iii) ??I wonder if ever John was a rational man
(iv) I wonder if John ever was a rational man

Thirdly, while focalizing indefinite quantifiers like *nessuno* requires contrastive stress in Italian, as in (v) (cf. Belletti (1990: (35), 43)), no such requirement exists in English (but see also Belletti (1990: 132n) on the marginality of (vi) for some):

(v) NESSUNO probabilmente telefonerà alle 5
(vi) (??) Noone probably will phone at 5

For a solution to these puzzles see sections 5.3.2 and 5.3.3.

[32] But see sections 5.3.2. and 5.3.3 for another execution of Kayne's – also in part Baker's – idea that English sentences of the form *NP Adv Aux (not) main V* show that even auxiliaries do not move as far up as main verbs and auxiliaries do in Romance.

[33] I am neglecting the past subjunctive forms here.

[34] I come back to the definition of "morphologically identified" in section 5.3.3.

[35] This will follow as an automatic consequence if alongside ordinary thematic roles the entries of lexical verbs include an event variable, in the spirit of recent proposals by Higginbotham (1985) and others.

[36] A finer-grained study should have something principled to say about the further modal distinctions associated with [±past]. It is plausible for example to view (78a) vs (79b) as a [+realis] vs [–realis] opposition, also at work in the *-er* vs *ø* opposition of Romance indicative pairs like [[[[*parl*]*er*]*i*]*ons*] (would speak) vs [[[[*parl*]*ø*]*i*]*ons*] (were speaking). On the other hand, it seems clear that no such opposition manifests itself in the case of *do, is, have* vs *did, was, had* which are all to be analyzed as ([+realis]) indicative.

[37] That negation can vary in position cross-linguistically has been demonstrated at length in Zanuttini (1991). I am following her here in assuming that English *not* can function either as Italian *non* and French *ne* or like French *pas* and Piedmontese *nen*. On this and much else, see Zanuttini (1991).

[38] As pointed out in Pollock (1989), there are irrelevant cases of acceptable sequences like (86b) if the adverb is set off from the rest of the sentence by a heavy pause. I am not concerned with such parenthetical structures here.

[39] On the morphologically highly plausible assumption that in Modern English verbs in the imperative and subjunctive have neither mood nor tense – nor agreement – morphology, the fact that sentences like (i) and (ii),

(i) *Be not afraid
(ii) *I suggest that he be not disturbed

are impossible simply follows from the unavailability of the Tense to Mood reanalysis in (80), which makes overt checking impossible. The fact that such sentences were acceptable untill the ENE period, together with *Main verb + not* sequences, follows from the (residual) existence of "strong" (morphologically identified) mood morphology at these earlier stages.

[40] In this we differ from Johnson (1990), Campbell (1991), Enç (1991)) and others who have tried to develop the intuition that English finite verbs are best characterized on the assumption that the so-called present tense is just Agr, while the past tense is just tense. If this were correct, neither *-ed* nor Agr would enter in the sort of paradigmatic alternation that would make them "strong". This is incompatible with the views on overt tense, hence – derivatively – mood checking of the preceding section.

[41] For independent support of Kayne's idea see Pollock (1994)

[42] This could in fact be made to follow from the strictly "local" character of checking. See note 23.

[43] I have implicitely assumed that the notion of "morphological identifiability" developed above should be relativized to "comparable" paradigms. I am unfortunately not in a position to offer independent rigorous characterization of that intuitive notion at present.

[44] It would be extremely tempting to reinterpret the *to not* vs *not to* alternation of English infinitives like (i) and (ii):

(i) To not go now would be a mistake
(ii) Not to go now would be a mistake

along similar lines. If so the French morphological ambiguity of (97)–(98) would have a direct counterpart in the functional ambiguity of (iii) and (iv):

(iii) $[_{MoodP}\ [\text{to}\ _{Mood}]\ \text{not}\ [_{TP}\ [\text{ø}\ _{T}]\ [_{VP}\ _{go}]]]]$
(iv) $[_{MoodP}\ [\text{ø}\ _{Mood}]\ \text{not}\ [_{TP}\ [\text{to}\ _{T}]\ [_{VP}\ _{go}]]]]$

[45] See in particular note 26. A complete study, unfortunately beyond the scope of the present article, would have to shed light on the diachronic changes that have affected French infinitival (ad)verb syntax (on which see e.g. Martineau (1992), Hirschbühler and Labelle (1994)). It is tempting to interpret these changes as arising as a conseqence of the loss of the general Verb movement to (= overt checking of) the highest functional position still characteristic of contemporary Italian (see Belletti (1990)). This in turn could be seen as a consequence of the loss of the "nominal" properties of the mood head of infinitival functional structures which "attracted" the otherwise weak Mood morphology of Old, Middle and Classical French verbs in the infinitive. On this view Modern Italian's functional mood in infinitives would still be nominal, a property showing up I believe in the fact that infinitives in Italian can still be preceded by determiners productively and in the fact that Italian, but not (Modern) French, allows for passives of *faire*+infinitive constructions (compare: √*La macchina sarà fatta riparare* vs **La voiture sera faite réparer* (the car will be made repair). A similar line could perhaps be taken for Modern French present participles in *-ant*. See Pollock (1994), (1997, chapter 13).

[46] To which various agreement-like morphemes might be cliticized, irrelevantly for my present purposes.

[47] (92) is at best a very modest contribution to what could be called the "morphological side" of the theory of checking. Concerning the "functional side" of that theory I have added nothing to Chomsky (1992). For some (wild) speculations see note 45, Pollock (1994), (1997, chapter 13).

REFERENCES

Bak, Jung-Sup (1990) *Accord Casuel et sujets multiples en coreén*, unpublished thèse de doctorat, Université de Paris VIII.

Baker, C. L. (1991) 'The syntax of English *not*: The limits of core grammar', *LI* **22**(3), 387–429.

Baker, M. (1988) *Incorporation.* University of Chicago Press, Chicago, Illinois.

Battistella, E. and A. Lobeck (1991) 'On verb fronting, inflection movement and aux support', *Canadian Journal of Linguistics, revue candienne de linguistique* **36**(3), 255–267.

Belletti, A. (1990) *Generalized Verb Movement.* Rosenberg & Sellier, Torino.

Borer, H. (1993) 'The ups and downs of Hebrew berb movement', Unpublished article, UMass Amherst.

Campbell, R. (1991) 'Tense and agreement in different tenses', *The Linguistic Review* **8**, 159–183.

Chomsky, N. (1955) *The Logical Structure of Linguistic Theory*, Plenum.

Chomsky, N. (1957) *Syntactic Structures*, Mouton

Chomsky, N. (1981) *Lectures on Government and Binding*, Foris

Chomsky, N. (1986), *Barriers*, MIT Press.

Chomsky, N. (1989) 'Some notes on economy of derivation and representation', MIT working Papers in Linguistics, vol. 10, 43–75 (also in *Principles and Parameters in Comparative Grammar* (Freidin (ed), MIT Press).

Chomsky, N. (1992) 'A minimalist program for linguistic theory', MIT Occasional Papers in Linguistics No. 1, MIT.

Chomsky, N. (1995) *The Minimalist Program*, MIT press.

Di Sciullo, A.-M. and E. Williams (1987) *On the Definition of Word*, MIT Press.

Emonds, J. (1978) 'The verbal complex V′-V in French', *LI* **9**, 151–175.

Enç, M. (1991) 'On the absence of present tense in English', unpublished manuscript, University of Wisconsin.

Fassi-Fehri, A. (forthcoming) 'Temporal reference, finiteness, and the inflectional structure of S in Arabic', to appear as a (revised) chapter in (interim title) *Issues in the Structure of Arabic Clauses*, Reidel.

Freeze, R. (1992) 'Existentials and other locatives', *Language* **68**, 553–595.

Hægeman, L. and R. Zanuttini (1991) 'Negative heads and the Neg criterion', *The Linguistic Review* **8**, 233–251

Higginbotham, J. (1985) 'On semantics', *LI* **16**, 547–593.

Hirschbühler, P. and M. Labelle (1994) 'Changes in verb position in French negative infinitival clauses', *Language Variation and Change* **6**, 149–178.

Hofman, T. R. (1969) 'La transformation de remplacement du constituant "passé" et ses rapports avec le système modal de l'anglais', in *Languages* **14**, 28–43. Larousse, Paris.

Holmberg, A. (1991) 'The structure of INFL and the finite clause in Finnish', unpublished paper, University of Upsala, Sueden.

Hong, Yong-Tcheol (1992) *Théorie de l'incorporation et théorie du cas: leurs implications sur la structure phrastique de la structure du groupe nominal en coréen*, unpublished thèse de doctorat, Université de Paris VIII.

Hulk, A. and A. van Kemenade (1993) 'Subjects, nominative case, agreement and functional heads', *Lingua* **89**, 181–215

Iatridou, S. (1990) 'About AGR(P)', in *LI* **21**(4), 551–577.

Jackendoff, R. (1972) *Semantic Interpretation in Generative Grammar*, MIT Press, Cambridge.

Johnson, K. (1991) 'Object Positions', *NNLT* **9**, 577–637.

Johnson, K. (1992) 'On the typology of the V+Adverb+NP word order', unpublished article, University of Wisconsin-Madison.

Kayne, R. (1984) *Connectedness and Binary Brancing*, Foris.

Kayne, R. (1985) 'L'accord du participe passé en français et en italien', *Modèles Linguistiques* **VII**, 73–91.

Kayne, R. (1987) 'Null subjects and clitic climbing', in: O. Jaeggli and K. Safir (eds.), *The Null Subject Parameter*, Kluwer.

Kayne, R. (1989) 'Notes on English Agreement', *CIEFL Bulletin* **1**(2).

Kayne, R. (1992) 'Toward a modular theory of auxiliary selection'. unpublished article, the Graduate Center, CUNY.

Kayne, R. (1994) *The Antisymmetry of Syntax*, MIT Press.

Kitagawa, Y. (1986) *Subjects in Japanese and English*, unpublished dissertation, UMass, Amherst.

Kroch, A. (1990) 'Reflexes of grammar in patterns of language change', *Journal of Language Variation and Change* **1**(3).

Laka, I. (1990) *Negation in Syntax: On the Nature of Functional Categories and Projections*, unpublished MIT Dissertation.

Lonzi, L. (1991) 'Which adverbs in Spec VP?', *Rivista di grammatica Generativa* **15**, 141–160.

Martineau, F. (1993) 'Movement of negative adverbs in French infinitival clauses', unpublished article, University of Ottawa, to appear in *Journal of French Language Studies*.

Murakami, Tomita. M. (1992) 'From Infl features to V movement: The subjunctive in English', unpublished MA thesis, University of Hawaii at Manoa.

Ouhalla, J. (1990) 'Sentential negation, relativised minimality and the aspectual status of auxiliarioes', *The Linguistic Review* **7**(2), 183–231.

Pesetsky, D. (1989) 'Language-particular processes and the earliness principle', unpublished article, MIT.

Pollock, J.-Y. (1989) 'Verb movement, universal grammar and the structure of IP', *LI* **20**(3), 365–425.

Pollock, J.-Y. (1992) 'A review of A. Belletti's generalized verb movement', *Language* **68**(4), 836–840.

Pollock, J.-Y. (1994) 'Checking theory and bare verbs', in: *Paths Towards Universal Grammar*, studies in honor of Richard Kayne, Cinque et al. (eds.), Georgetown University Press.

Pollock, J.-Y. (1996) 'Case checking and particle constructions', unpublished article, Harvard University.

Pollock, J.-Y. (1997) *Langage et cognition, introduction au programme minimaliste de la grammaire générative*, Presses Universitaires de France, Paris.

Potsma, G. (1993) 'The syntax of the morphological defectivity of be', unpublished article, University of Leiden.

Rivero, M. L. (1990) 'Adverb incorporation and the syntax of adverbs in modern Greek', unpublished paper, University of Ottawa.

Rivero, M. L. (1994) 'Clause structure and V-Movement in the languages of the Balkans', *Natural Language and Linguistic Theory* **1**(1), 63–120.

Rivero, M. L. (forthcoming) 'Bulgarian and Serbo-Croatian yes-no questions: V°-raising to *-li* vs *Li*-Hopping', to appear in *LI* **24**(3).

Roberts, I.(1985) 'Agreement parameters and the development of English modal auxiliaries', *NLLT* **3**, 21–58.

Roberts, I. (1993) *Verbs and Diachronic Syntax*, Reidel

Selkirk, E. (1982) *The Syntax of Words*, LI Monograph 3.

Speas, M. (1991) 'Inflectional heads and inflectional morphemes', *The Linguistic Review* **8**, 389–417.

Traugott, E. C. (1972) *A History of English Syntax*, New York, Rinehart & Winston.

Travis, L. (1984) *Parameters and Effects of Word Order Variation*, unpublished MIT Dissertation.

Williams, E. (1981) 'On the notions "lexically related" and "head of a word"', *LI* **12**, 245–274.

Zanuttini, R. (1991), *Syntactic Properties of Sentential Negation. A Comparative Study in Romance Languages*, unpublished dissertation, University of Pennsylvania.

LUIGI RIZZI

THE FINE STRUCTURE OF THE LEFT PERIPHERY

1. INTRODUCTION[1]

Under current assumptions, the structural representation of a clause consists of three kinds of structural layers, each layer an instantiation of the X-bar schema:

1. The lexical layer, headed by the verb, the structural layer in which theta assignment takes place.
2. The inflectional layer, headed by functional heads corresponding to concrete or abstract morphological specifications on the verb, and responsible for the licensing of argumental features such as case and agreement.
3. The complementizer layer, typically headed by a free functional morpheme, and hosting topics and various operator-like elements such as interrogative and relative pronouns, focalized elements, etc.

In the mid eighties, each layer was identified with a single X-bar projection (VP, IP, CP), but this assumption quickly turned out to be too simplistic. Under the impact of Pollock's (1989) influential analysis of verb movement, IP dissolved into a series of functional projections, each corresponding to a single feature specification overtly or abstractly expressed on the verbal system (Agr, T, Asp, . . .). Kayne's (1984) binary branching hypothesis naturally led to the postulation of multiple VP layers for multi-argument verbs, e.g. along the lines of Larson (1988) and much related work.

Various proposals in the recent literature indicate that the complementizer layer should share the same fate: much more than a single X-bar schema seems to constitute the left (pre-IP) periphery of the clause.[2]

In this article, I would like to explore some aspects of the fine structure of the left periphery. The first part (sections 2–6) is devoted to the identification of the basic configurational structure. Four kinds of elements typically occurring in the left periphery will be taken into account: interrogative and relative pronouns, topics and focalized elements. Studying the interactions between these elements, we will be led to postulate an articulated array of X-bar projections which will be assumed to constitute the complementizer system. The second part (sections 7–12) concerns a number of adjacency and anti-adjacency effects involving elements of the C system and different kinds of fillers of the subject position (overt DP, PRO, trace) which are amenable to an explanation in terms of the assumed structure of the C system. The core of the empirical material to be discussed is drawn from Italian, French and English, with occasional comparative extensions to other Romance and Germanic languages.

Liliane Haegeman (ed.), Elements of Grammar, 281–337.

A preliminary word on the theoretical framework adopted in this work is necessary. An idea borrowed from the system presented in Chomsky (1993) will play a crucial role: syntactic movement (or, more neutrally, the formation of non-trivial chains in syntax) is "last resort" in the precise sense that it must be triggered by the satisfaction of certain quasi-morphological requirements of heads. As I will be concerned with the A′ system, I will phrase such requirements in the style of the Criteria (Rizzi 1991, Haegeman 1995 and much related work), rather than as feature checking, the main reason for this choice being that such features have an interpretive import (Wh, Neg, Top, Foc, . . .): they determine the interpretation of the category bearing them and of its immediate constituents (e.g., see section 3), function as scope markers for phrases with the relevant quantificational force in a local configuration, etc. so that their role cannot simply be to trigger movement and disappear from representations. Independently from the particular style of presentation, the "last resort" intuition provides the conceptual justification for postulating a rich and articulated structure to host the different kinds of phrases moved to the left periphery: no free preposing and adjunction to IP is permissible, all kinds of movements to the left periphery must be motivated by the satisfaction of some criterion, hence by the presence of a head entering into the required Spec-head configuration with the preposed phrase. So, the "last resort" guideline will be critical for drawing the map of the left periphery; the presence and action of the system of heads involved will be independently detected by the various adjacency and anti-adjacency effects that we will focus on in the second part. A restrictive theory of adjunction (à la Kayne (1994) and related work) is also instrumental for this endeavor.

On the other hand, in the following discussion I will continue to assume that Relativized Minimality (RM) is a representational principle, and that one of the core structural relations allowed by UG is head government, as in Rizzi (1990) and contra Chomsky (1993). As for the second point, head government continues to be needed, as far as I can see, for optimally simple accounts of various familiar subject-object asymmetries of the *that*-t kind, as well as for many cases in which a head enters into some kind of "action at a distance" with the specifier of its complement (for Case assignment/checking or the licensing of different kinds of ec's). A number of examples of this sort are analyzed in what follows; we will adopt approaches based on head government and will occasionally allude to properties of possible alternatives not referring to head government, even though no systematic comparison will be attempted.

As for the representational view of RM, it is not the goal of the present article to argue for this theoretical option, and I intend to address the issue in independent work (see also Manzini (1992, 1995), Brody (1995) for relevant discussion). It should be clear though that there is a significant (even though not a necessary) connection between the two conservative assumptions I am making. One consequence of the representational view of RM is that head government comes for free as the local environment within which a head can "act at a distance" upon a maximal projection. The action at a distance between a head and a maximal projection and the different kinds of chains obey the same fundamental locality principle under the representational view of RM, a unification that is missed if locality on chains is expressed derivationally.

2. THE FORCE-FINITENESS SYSTEM

One important question to be asked at the outset of a study on the complementizer system is: what is the role of the complementizer in the clausal structure?

We can think of the complementizer system as the interface between a propositional content (expressed by the IP) and the superordinate structure (a higher clause or, possibly, the articulation of discourse, if we consider a root clause). As such, we expect the C system to express at least two kinds of information, one facing the outside and the other facing the inside.

Consider first the information looking at the higher structure. Complementizers express the fact that a sentence is a question, a declarative, an exclamative, a relative, a comparative, an adverbial of a certain kind, etc., and can be selected as such by a higher selector. This information is sometimes called the clausal Type (Cheng 1991), or the specification of Force (Chomsky 1995). Here we will adopt the latter terminology. Force is expressed sometimes by overt morphological encoding on the head (special C morphology for declaratives, questions, relatives, etc.), sometimes by simply providing the structure to host an operator of the required kind, sometimes by both means (this is the rare case, presumably due to an economy of representation type principle favoring overt expression of a certain substantive specification on the head or on the specifier, but not simultaneously on both: see Cheng (1991), Sportiche (1992)).

The second kind of information expressed by the C system faces the inside, the content of the IP embedded under it. It is a traditional observation that the choice of the complementizer reflects certain properties of the verbal system of the clause, an observation formalized, e.g., by "agreement" rules between C and I, responsible for the co-occurrence of *that* and a tensed verb, of *for* and an infinitive in English (Chomsky and Lasnik 1977), etc. A straightforward manner to account for these dependencies would be to assume that C contains a tense specification which matches the one expressed on the lower inflectional system (an idea which goes back at least to Den Besten (1977)). On the other hand, the "temporal" properties encoded by C are very rudimentary. For instance, in Italian the form *che* co-occurs with present, past and future indicative, with present and past subjunctive and present and past conditional, thus distinguishing these forms from infinitival, gerundival and participial clauses, a situation which is quite general in Romance and Germanic. So, it appears that, at least in these language families, C expresses a distinction related to tense but more rudimentary than tense and other inflectional specifications on the verbal system: finiteness.

I will assume here that the finiteness distinction is a valid linguistic one, even though its morphological realization can vary somewhat from language to language. Languages tend to split verbal paradigms into two classes of forms. Finite forms can manifest mood distinctions (indicative, subjunctive, conditional and/or other distinctions of the realis/irrealis type), manifest tense and subject (person) agreement, cooccur with overt nominative subjects. Non-finite forms do not manifest mood distinctions, in the core case they do not express person agreement, and do not co-occur with nominative subjects, they have a more rudimentary system of tense distinctions (e.g., in many languages non-finite forms do not have a morphological present/future distinction, can express past only through the periphrastic form aux + past participle, etc.). The first class of forms co-occurs with complementizers of the *that* kind, the second does not. Various dissociations from these core clusters are apparently tolerated,[3] but a split along these lines is robustly attested cross-linguistically.

Following much recent work (e.g., Holmberg and Platzack 1988), I will then assume that the C system expresses a specification of finiteness, which in turn selects an IP system with the familiar characteristics of finiteness: mood distinctions, subject agreement licensing nominative case, overt tense distinctions (these specifications being subjected to some cross-linguistic variation, as we have seen).

Again, we should think of finiteness as the core IP-related characteristics that the complementizer system expresses; languages can vary in the extent to which additional IP information is replicated in the complementizer system: some languages replicate mood distinctions (special subjunctive complementizers in Polish, etc.), some replicate subject agreement (different Germanic varieties; Haegeman 1992, Bayer 1984, Shlonsky 1994), some seem to express genuine tense distinctions (Irish, Cottell 1994), negation (Latin, Celtic), etc.[4]

How does the CP system relate to the rest of the clausal structure? Recent proposals consider the IP system an extension of the V system: the different inflectional heads are V-related in that they attract the verb (overtly or covertly) to check its morphological specification (Chomsky 1993), so that the whole IP system can be seen as an extension of the verbal projection (an "extended projection", in Grimshaw's (1991) sense). Should the CP system be considered an analogous extension of the IP system, hence ultimately of the VP? I believe there is a substantial difference between the two cases. Whatever "inflectional" properties C reflects, they are not encoded in the form of verbal morphology, in the general case: they are expressed on free functional morphemes (*that*, *que*, etc.) which, if anything, look nominal more than verb-like, as they often resemble demonstrative pronouns, *wh* elements, certain kinds of nouns ("fact", etc.), etc. So, I will continue to assume that the C system is fundamentally distinct from the I system, the latter but not the former being V-related in the general case.[5,6]

3. THE TOPIC-FOCUS SYSTEM

If the force-finiteness system expresses the selectional relations between a C system and the immediately higher and lower structural systems, the C system can have other functions which are by and large independent from selectional constraints.

A traditional articulation of the clause that typically involves the left periphery is the articulation in topic and comment, as expressed by the English construction referred to as Topicalization:

(1) Your book, you should give t to Paul (not to Bill)

The topic is a preposed element characteristically set off from the rest of the clause by "comma intonation" and normally expressing old information, somehow available and salient in previous discourse; the comment is a kind of complex predicate, an open sentence predicated of the topic and introducing new information.

Formally similar but interpretively very different is the focus-presupposition articulation:

(2) YOUR BOOK you should give t to Paul (not mine)

Here the preposed element, bearing focal stress, introduces new information, whereas the open sentence expresses contextually given information, knowledge that the speaker presupposes to be shared with the hearer (see below for further refinements). If the interpretive relation of the preposed element to the open sentence is very different, virtually the opposite in the two cases, the form of the two articulations appears to be constant in English (even though significant differences emerge at a more refined analysis: see Culicover's (1992) discussion, based in part on Gundel's (1974) earlier analysis, and, on focus, Rochemont and Culicover (1990)).

Other languages sharply distinguish the form of the two articulations as well. We will briefly analyze here two Italian constructions which illustrate the point. In Italian, and more generally in Romance, the topic-comment articulation is typically expressed by the construction that Cinque (1990) has called Clitic Left Dislocation (CLLD), involving a resumptive clitic coreferential to the topic (this construction differs from left dislocation in languages which do not possess clitic forms in a number of respects, so that the English gloss, involving a non-clitic resumptive pronoun, is somewhat misleading: see Cinque (1990: 57–60) for relevant discussion; see also Cecchetto (1994), Iatridou (1991)):

(3) Il tuo libro, lo ho letto
"Your book, I have read it"

The focus-presupposition articulation can be expressed in Italian by preposing the focal element (focalization) and assigning it special focal stress:

(4) IL TUO LIBRO ho letto (, non il suo)
"Your book I read (, not his)"

In Italian this structural option is restricted to contrastive focus, i.e., (4) presupposes that you believe that I have read something different from your book, and corrects this belief. It could not be felicitously uttered as conveying non-contrastive new information, i.e. as an answer to the question "What did you read?". Other languages use the clause initial focus position for non-contrastive focus as well (Hungarian: Kiss (1987), Horvath (1985), Brody (1990, 1995b), Puskas (1992) and references quoted there; Albanian: Turano (1995), Greek: Tsimpli (1990)). Some other languages (e.g. French) do not seem to use a structural focus position, at least in the overt syntax (Spanish seems to have a focus construction similar to the Italian one: Laka (1990)).

I will assume here that these two articulations are expressed by the usual building block of syntactic representations: the X-bar schema (whether the schema is a primitive, or can be derived from more elementary principles (Kayne 1994, Chomsky 1995) is irrelevent for our purposes). I.e., topic-comment has the following structure:

(5)
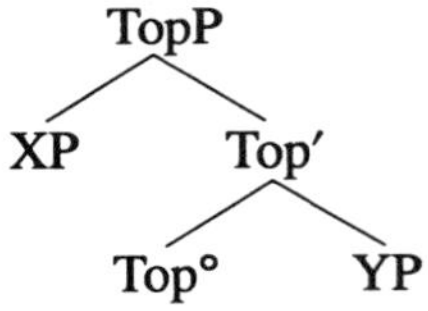

XP = topic
YP = comment

A Top° head, a functional head belonging to the complementizer system, projects its own X-bar schema with the following functional interpretation: its specifier is the topic, its complement is the comment. Top° defines a kind of "higher predication", a predication within the Comp system; its function is thus analogous to the function of AgrS within the IP system, which also configurationally connects a subject and a predicate. The most basic difference between higher and lower predication is that the former involves a specifier which is an A′ position.

Analogously, a Foc° head takes the focus as its specifier and the presupposition as its complement:

(6)

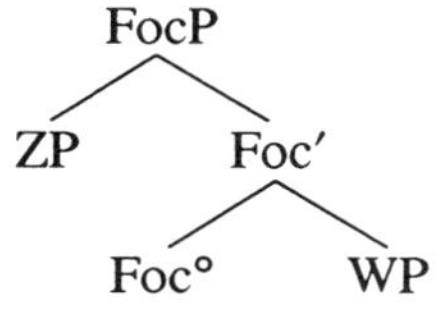

ZP = Focus
WP = Presupposition

Here too Italian seems to possess a lower focalization, involving focal stress (possibly contrastive, but not necessarily so) on an element *in situ* (see Antinucci and Cinque (1977), Belletti and Shlonsky (1995), Calabrese (1982), Cinque (1993)):

(7) Ho letto IL TUO LIBRO (, non il suo)
"I read YOUR BOOK, not his"

But it is conceivable that at LF (7) will have a representation involving (6) if the focal element must be moved to a peripheral position, as Chomsky's (1976) classical analysis of Weak Cross-over implies.

While Top° and Foc° are phonetically null in Italian, they may be pronounced in other languages. For instance, Aboh (1995) argues that the focus particle *wè* in Gungbe should be analyzed as Foc°, an analysis immediately plausible for many other cases of such markers found across languages (we will not analyze here other constructions involving focalization such as clefts and inverse copular sentences (Moro 1995)).

As for the topic or focus interpretations of the specifiers in (6) and (7), we will assume that a constituent endowed with topic or focus features must end up in a Spec/head configuration with Top or Foc, respectively; in other words, there are Topic and Focus Criteria, reminiscent of the Wh and Neg Criteria (Rizzi 1991, Haegeman 1995). Focus and Topic movement are then brought to line to the view that movement (or, in more neutral terms, the construction of non-trivial chains) is "last resort", and must be triggered by the satisfaction of a criterion (or feature checking, in Chomsky's (1993) terminology). In fact, under such a restrictive theory we expect that no kind of (syntactic) movement to the left periphery may involve free, optional adjunction to IP (LF movement may still involve IP adjunction if it is triggered by the necessity of properly interpreting certain expressions, as in May (1985)); we will see later on that there are strong empirical reasons against this rather usual analysis of different kinds of preposing, and in favor of a uniform X-bar analysis involving (5) and (6).

How is the topic-focus system integrated into the force-finiteness system? We think of the latter as the essential part of the C system, so we assume it to be present in all non-truncated clausal structures (i.e., except in ECM and other "S′ deletion" contexts). On the other hand, it is reasonable to assume that the topic-focus system is present in a structure only if "needed", i.e. when a constituent bears topic or focus features to be sanctioned by a Spec-head criterion. If the topic-focus field is activated, it will inevitably be "sandwiched" in between force and finiteness, as these two specifications must terminate the C system upward and downward, in order to meet the different selectional requirements and properly insert the C system in the structure. So, we should have:

(8) . . . Force . . . (Topic) . . . (Focus) . . . Fin IP

We will see later on that this positional property of the topic-focus system is instrumental for the explanation of several adjacency and anti-adjacency effects. For the time being we can simply observe two straightforward empirical reflexes of the theory of C that is taking shape.

In Italian, and more generally in Romance, prepositional elements introducing infinitives such as *di* in (9)b are generally considered the non-finite counterparts of the finite complementizer *che* of (9)a (see Kayne 1984, Rizzi 1982 for relevant evidence); still *che* always precedes and *di* always follows a left-dislocated phrase (examples like (11)b are slightly marked if compared to the corresponding cases of CLLD with finite embedded sentences, but the contrast with (11)a is very sharp):

(9) a. Credo che loro apprezzerebbero molto il tuo libro
"I believe that they would appreciate your book very much"

b. Credo di apprezzare molto il tuo libro
"I believe 'of' to appreciate your book very much"

(10) a. Credo che il tuo libro, loro lo apprezzerebbero molto
"I believe that your book, they would appreciate it a lot"

b.*Credo, il tuo libro, che loro lo apprezzerebbero molto
"I believe, your book, that they would appreciate it a lot"

(11) a.*Credo di il tuo libro, apprezzarlo molto
"I believe 'of' your book to appreciate it a lot"

b. Credo, il tuo libro, di apprezzarlo molto
"I believe, your book, 'of' to appreciate it a lot"

This distribution is hardly consistent with a theory assuming a unique C position, while it can be immediately expressed within the current articulated theory of C by assuming that *che* manifests the force position, while *di* manifests the finiteness position, hence they show up on opposite sides of the topic. We will come back to this peculiar distribution in section 6.[7]

A similar type of argument is provided by the distribution of different kinds of operators hosted by the C-system. In Italian, relative operators must precede topics, while question operators must follow topics in main questions and can follow or (slightly marginally) precede them in embedded questions:[8]

(12) a. Un uomo a cui, il premio Nobel, lo daranno senz'altro
"A man to whom, the Nobel Prize, they will give it undoubtedly"

b.*Un uomo, il premio Nobel, a cui lo daranno senz'altro
"A man, the Nobel Prize, to whom they will give it undoubtedly"

(13) a.*A chi, il premio Nobel, lo daranno?
"To whom, the Nobel prize, will they give it?"

b. Il premio Nobel, a chi lo daranno?
"The Nobel prize, to whom will they give it?"

(14) a. Mi domando, il premio Nobel, a chi lo potrebbero dare
"I wonder, the Nobel Prize, to whom they could give it"

b.?Mi domando a chi, il premio Nobel, lo potrebbero dare
"I wonder to whom, the Nobel Prize, they could give it"

This distribution suggests that relative operators occupy the highest specifier position, the Spec of Force, while question operators can occupy a lower position within the Topic/Focus field (the ordering in (13)a being blocked by the fact that I to C movement is compulsory in main questions (Rizzi 1991)). See below for more detailed discussion of these positional properties. The crucial point here is again that a theory involving a unique C head and projection does not seem equipped to deal with such simple distributional constraints.

4. ON SOME DIFFERENCES BETWEEN TOPIC AND FOCUS

Topic and focus constructions are similar in several respects as A′ constructions involving the left periphery of the clause, and their structural similarities are further stressed by the assumption that the same configurational schema is involved. Nevertheless, they differ in a number of respects, which highlight a fundamentally different nature. A detailed analysis of these two constructions is beyond the scope of this article. Drawing on Cinque's (1990) analysis, we will concentrate on five salient differences, which are directly relevant for our main topic.[9]

1. *Resumptive Clitic.* A topic can involve a resumptive clitic within the comment. If the topicalized constituent is the direct object, the clitic is obligatory. On the other hand, a focalized constituent is inconsistent with a resumptive clitic (Cinque 1990: 63):

(15) a. Il tuo libro, lo ho comprato
"Your book, I bought it"

b.*Il tuo libro, ho comprato t
"Your book, I bought"

(16) a.*IL TUO LIBRO lo ho comprato (non il suo)
"YOUR BOOK I bought it (not his)"

b. IL TUO LIBRO ho comprato t (non il suo)
"YOUR BOOK I bought (not his)"

2. *Weak Cross-Over.* A topic never gives rise to any Weak-cross- over effect. Such effects are detectable with focus, even if the judgment is somewhat difficult (Culicover (1992) has observed an analogous distinction between topic and focus in English):

(17) Gianni_i, sua_i madre lo_i ha sempre apprezzato
"Gianni, his mother always appeciated him"

(18) ??GIANNI_i sua_i madre ha sempre apprezzato t_i (non Piero)
"GIANNI his mother always appreciated, not Piero"

3. *Bare Quantificational Elements.* Quantificational elements (*noone*, *all*, etc.) which are not associated to a lexical restriction within the DP cannot be topics in CLLD constructions, while they easily allow focalization (Rizzi 1986; on the special behavior of *qualcosa*, *qualcuno* (something, someone) see Cinque 1990: 74ff.):

(19) a.*Nessuno, lo ho visto
"Noone, I saw him"

b.*Tutto, lo ho fatto
"Everything, I did it"

(20) a. NESSUNO ho visto t
"NOONE I saw"

b. TUTTO ho fatto t
"Everything I did"

4. *Uniqueness.* A clause can contain as many topics as are consistent with its (topicalizable) arguments and adjunts; on the other hand, there is a unique structural focus position, focalization of two elements as in (22) is excluded (Benincà 1988: 144):

(21) Il libro, a Gianni, domani, glielo darò senz'altro
"The book, to John, tomorrow, I'll give it to him for sure"

(22) *A GIANNI IL LIBRO darò (non a Piero, l'articolo)
"TO JOHN THE BOOK I'll give, not to Piero, the article"

A focus and one or more topics can be combined in the same structure.

In that case, the focal constituent can be both preceded and followed by topics:

(23) A Gianni, QUESTO, domani, gli dovrete dire
"To Gianni, THIS, tomorrow, you should tell him"

5. *Compatibility with Wh.* A Wh operator in main questions is compatible with a Topic in a fixed order (Top Wh), whereas it is incompatible with a Focus:

(24) a A Gianni, che cosa gli hai detto?
"To Gianni, what did you tell him?"

b.*Che cosa, a Gianni, gli hai detto?
"What, to Gianni, did you tell him?"

(25) a.* A GIANNI che cosa hai detto (, non a Piero)?
"TO GIANNI what did you tell (, not to Piero)?"

b.*Che cosa A GIANNI hai detto (, non a Piero)?
"What TO GIANNI did you tell (, not to Piero)?"

On the other hand, both Top and Foc are compatible with a preceding relative operator (see (12)a and (44) below).

The next section is devoted to showing that, in terms of a slight updating of Cinque's (1990) approach, the first three differences can be traced back to one basic distinction: focus is quantificational, topic is not. In section 6 we will tentatively suggest that also the fourth difference is directly linked to an interpretive distinction between the two constructions, and then we will address the fifth difference in the context of an articulated theory of the C system.

5. FOCUS IS QUANTIFICATIONAL, TOPIC IS NOT

Let us concentrate on the first three differences. Starting from the second property, we follow Lasnik and Stowell (1991) and assume that WCO is a distinctive caracteristic of A′ relations involving genuine quantification. So, A′ dependencies must be split into those involving a quantifier which binds a variable and those that involve non-quantificational A′ binding, binding of a null epithet or a null constant (*nc*, as in Rizzi 1994). The two cases are illustrated by questions and appositive relatives:

(26) a.?*Who does his mother really like t (=vbl)?
b. John, who his mother really likes t (=nc) . . .

Chomsky (1986a) had proposed that the principle of Full Interpretation requires that variables be strongly bound, where strong binding means either assignment of a range or assignment of a value from an antecedent. We can rephrase Lasnik and Stowell's (1991) proposal as distinguishing these two cases more sharply: A′ dependencies, all sensitive to Strong Cross-Over (principle C), split into variable binding by a quantificational operator (assigning a range to the variable, as in (26)a) and binding of a null constant by an anaphoric operator (whose role is to connect the null constant to an antecedent, as in (26)b). The former, but not the latter, is sensitive to Weak Cross-Over.

Assuming WCO to be a diagnostic, the contrast in (17)–(18) leads us to conclude that Focus involves quantificational A′ binding while Topic does not, as the interpretation of the two constructions suggests.

If Focus is quantificational and Topic is not, the first difference also follows: the focalized element in (16) must bind a syntactic variable (a non-pronominal empty Xmax category in an A-position). This happens in (16)b, but not in (16)a, in which potential bindees are the clitic and its trace, neither of which qualifies as a syntactic variable: the clitic is an overt pronominal head, its trace is an X° trace (if clitic movement involves an initial step qua Xmax to SpecAgrO, the initial trace is a DP-trace and the one in Spec/AgrO is an X° trace, neither of which qualifies as a variable). So, the structure is ruled out by the component of the principle of Full Interpretation which requires that quantifiers bind variables (Cinque 1990: 180, fn. 10).

Under classical assumptions on the typology of empty categories, (15)b is ruled out in a symmetric way: the topicalized element is not quantificational, as the lack of WCO shows; therefore, the empty category in object position has no legitimate status: it cannot be a variable, as there is no quantifier to bind it, nor can it fulfill the conditions of any other type of ec (PRO, pro or DP-trace). (15)a is fine, as the ec in object position has the legitimate status of a clitic trace (Cinque 1990: 71–72).[10]

If we accept Lasnik and Stowell's split within A′ dependencies, the argument excluding (15b) should be sharpened. We must exclude the possibility that the *ec* in (15)b be a null constant, A′ bound (hence identified) by the topic phrase. Consider some typical cases of A′ chains not giving rise to WCO

(27) a. John is easy [Op to please t]

b. John has Mary [Op to talk to t]

c. John is too stubborn [Op to talk to t]

d. John, who I just met t

e. Gianni, Op che ho appena incontrato t
"Gianni, that I just met"

f. Op habe ich schon t gesehen
"(it) have I already seen"

(27)abc are familiar English constructions involving null operators; (29)d–e are appositive relatives in English and Italian, involving an overt and a null operator, respectively; f instanciates the discourse bound null operator construction of colloquial German and many other languages. Suppose then that the licensing of null constants is not freely available, but is restricted to a designated kind of A′ binder, the anaphoric operator (en element inherently characterized as an operator but different from quantificational operators in that it does not assign a range to its bindee; rather, the anaphoric operator seeks for an antecedent, to which it connects its bindee); anaphoric operators are typically but not necessarily null (for instance, as we have just seen, relative pronouns involved in appositive relatives are anaphoric operators in general; still, they may – or must – be overt, depending on language specific conditions):

(28) A null constant is licensed by an anaphoric operator

So, (15)b continues to be excluded: it involves no genuine quantification, hence no licit variable, and no anaphoric operator, hence no licit null constant, under principle (28).

Why is the English gloss of (15)b well formed? Again, I will basically follow Cinque's (1990) updating of Chomsky's (1977) analysis of English topicalization and assume that it involves a null operator identified by the topic:

(29) Your book, [OP [I bought t]]

The null operator (a non-quantificational anaphoric operator) licenses the null constant under principle (28). The null constant status of the trace is further confirmed by the Lasnik and Stowell's diagnostic, the lack of WCO effects:

(30) $John_i$, his_i mother really likes t_i

So, I am assuming that the parameter differentiating English and Romance topic-comment structures resides in the non-availability of the null anaphoric operator in Romance topic-comment. Null operators and clitics are functionally equivalent here in that they establish the connection between the topic and the open position in the comment; Romance has the second device freely available while English, which lacks clitics in general, reverts to the first device.[11]

Languages may choose whether the anaphoric operator in a given construction is overt or null; we have already seen that appositive relative operators are null in Italian and overt in English (this may in turn be the consequence of a more abstract structural difference, see Cinque (1982) and the recent discussion of the issue in Bianchi (1995)). Analogously, other Germanic languages differ from English in allowing the overt realization (as a so-called D-pronoun) of the anaphoric operator involved in topic-comment structures:[12]

(31) Den Hans, den kenne ich t seit langem
"The Hans, whom I have known for a long time"

Let us now turn to the fact that the resumptive clitic becomes optional if the topic is a pronominalizable PP (as in (32)) and it is, of course, absent if the PP cannot be pronominalized as the benefactive in (33):

(32) A Gianni, Maria (gli) ha parlato recentemente
"To Gianni, Maria spoke to him recently"

(33) Per Gianni, Maria lavora da molto tempo
"For Gianni, Maria has worked for a long time"

Later on we will provide evidence suggesting that the clitic is not really optional in (32) and the two cases instantiate two distinct constructions. The question still remains why the PP topic can directly licence an empty category in these cases. Here again, we can follow Cinque and assume that the classification of null elements into anaphors, pronominals and variables determined by the feature system $\pm$a, $\pm$p is a unique characteristic of DP's in A-position; it does not extend to PP's, either because they are not DP's, or they do not constitute A-positions. In fact, we do not have anaphoric or pronominal PP's; cases of clitic PP's such as *ne* and *ci* in Italian, for which pronominal status is often assumed, have been shown to behave like non-pronominal (and, of course, non-anaphoric) elements with respect to the binding principles (Belletti 1994).

So, the *ec* left in the VP in (32)–(33) must be chain connected to an antecedent in order to fulfill the identification requirement of the ECP, exactly as any other trace (see, e.g., Rizzi 1990, 1994 for discussion), but no further requirement is put on the nature of the antecedent, and the non-quantificational topic can fulfill this role.[13]

Consider now the third difference, i.e. the fact that quantified expressions cannot be topics, as in (19), whereas they can be focus, as in (20). These quantified expressions must bind a variable at LF, but they can't in (19): neither the clitic nor the clitic trace qualify and, if the quantified expressions are further moved by QR leaving a trace in Topic position, this trace does not qualify as a variable because it is an A′ position; on the other hand, a well-formed variable is available at S-structure and at LF in (20), so these structures are fine. This is, in essence, the analysis in Rizzi (1986).

Things are complicated somewhat if we observe that CLLD of quantified expressions is significantly improved, sometimes to full acceptability, if the quantified expression includes a lexical restriction:

(34) a.? Ciascun (ogni) membro della commissione, lo devi contattare personalmente
"Each member of the committee, you should contact him personally"

b. Tutti i tuoi libri, li ho rimessi a posto
"All your books, I put them back"

c. Molti libri, li ho buttati via
"Many books, I threw them away"

Why is (34) different from (19)? I will assume that QR can further extract the quantifier from the DP, yielding such LF's as

(35) Molti [ec libri] TOP°, [li ho buttati via]

Here the structure is fine: the quantifier binds the variable within the Spec of Top°, which in turn is connected to the pronoun. No principle is violated here. On the other hand, the same structure involving a bare quantifier is ill-formed, as before:

(36) *Molto ec TOP°, [lo ho capito]
"Much, I understood it"

If the bare quantifier does not move at LF, it will have no variable to bind, thus violating Full Interpretation. If it moves yielding (36), the structure will be ill formed: the *ec* is not in an A (or functional) position, hence it does not qualify as a variable and FI is violated again.[14]

6. SOME INCOMPATIBILITIES AND ORDERING CONSTRAINTS

The fourth difference between Topic and Focus is that there can be an indefinite number of Topics but only one structural Focus position per clause in Italian (see (22)). At first sight, this would seem to support more diverging structural analyses for the two articulations than we have proposed. An idea that immediately comes to mind would be to exploit the X-bar schema for Focus, thus deriving the uniqueness of Focus from the general uniqueness of specifiers under binary branching X-bar theory, and assume an adjunction analysis for Topic, under usual assumptions on the reiterability of adjunction (but see Kayne (1994) for a more restrictive view on adjunction). So, consider the following possible permutations of Topic and Focus:

(37) a. Credo che a Gianni, QUESTO, domani, gli dovremmo dire

Credo	che	a Gianni,	QUESTO,	domani,	gli dovremmo dire
	C	Top	Foc	Top	IP

"I believe that to Gianni, THIS, tomorrow we should say"

b. Credo che domani, QUESTO, a Gianni, gli dovremmo dire

Credo	che	domani,	QUESTO,	a Gianni,	gli dovremmo dire
	C	Top	Foc	Top	IP

c.	Credo	che	domani, a	Gianni,	QUESTO gli	dovremmo dire
		C	Top	Top	Foc	IP
d.	Credo	che	a Gianni,	domani,	QUESTO gli	dovremmo dire
		C	Top	Top	Foc	IP
e.	Credo	che	QUESTO,	a Gianni,	domani, gli	dovremmo dire
		C	Foc	Top	Top	IP
f.	Credo	che	QUESTO,	domani,	a Gianni, gli	dovremmo dire
		C	Foc	Top	Top	IP

In between the phonetically realized complementizer *che* and the IP, we can have a sequence of Topics followed by a Focus, followed by another sequence of Topics:

(38) . . . C° (Top*) (Foc) (Top*) . . .

One could then assume that a unique focal head can project its X-bar schema (FocP) in between C and IP and that topics can be freely adjoined to IP (or, in the terms of the structure proposed in section 3, to FinP immediately above IP) and FocP.

In spite of its appeal, I will not adopt this analysis. There is empirical evidence in favor of the more symmetric theory of Topic and Focus presented in section 3. In short, the intervention of Topics induces certain locality effects which are best treated under the assumption that a whole X-bar projection is involved, rather than a simple adjunction structure. This argument is developed in the following sections. For the moment, let us just concentrate on the observed asymmetry: if both topic and focus involve an X-bar schema, the obvious way to express the asymmetry is to assume that the Top Phrase is recursive, while the Foc Phrase is not. But why should it be so? A simple inspection of the interpretive properties of the two constructions may provide an adequate answer.

Let us go back to the proposed interpretation of the projection of Foc, reproduced here for convenience:

(39)

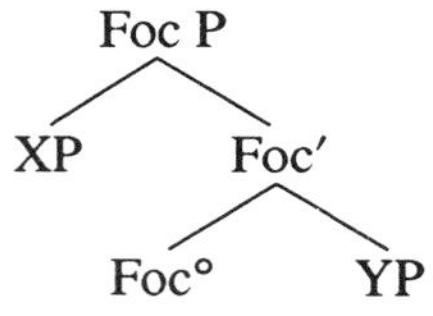

The specifier is the focal element, while the complement of Foc is the presupposition, the given information. Consider now a recursion of FocP, i.e., the option of realizing YP itself as a FocP.

(40)

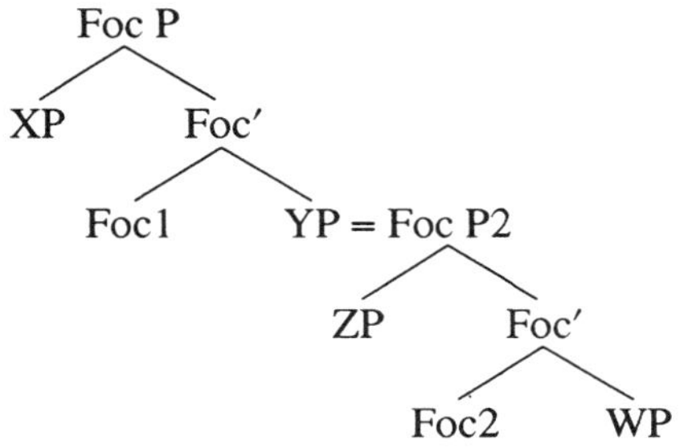

Such a structure would contain a focus position ZP, the specifier of the lower focal head, Foc2. But this would be inconsistent with the proposed interpretation: YP is the presupposition of the higher focal head Foc1, and as such it can only specify given information. So, recursion of FocP is banned by the interpretive clash that would arise. No such interpretive problem arises in the case of a recursion of Top: nothing excludes that a comment (the complement of the topic head) may be articulated in turn as a topic-comment structure, so that the topic phrases can undergo free recursion. If this speculative proposal is correct, we can continue to assume a structurally uniform analysis for Top and Foc, and derive the observed difference with respect to recursion from an interpretive peculiarity of Foc.[15]

Based on the arguments of the preceding sections, we have proposed the following articulated structure for the complementizer system:

(41)

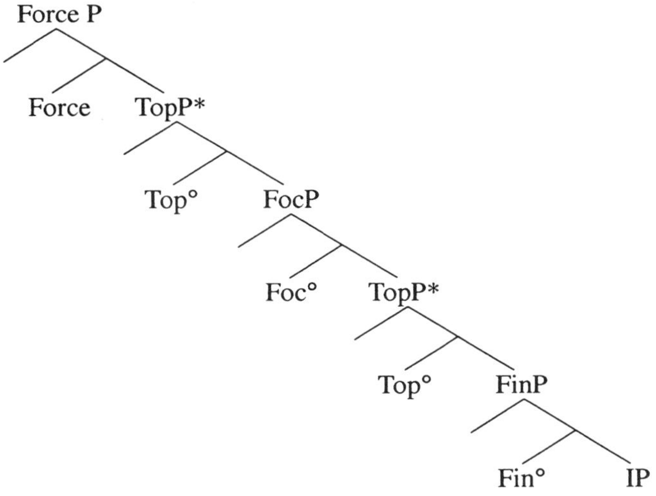

This structure can now be immediately used to account for a number of ordering constraints involving elements of the C system.

We have already seen that relatives sharply contrast with main questions in Italian in that relative and question operators must respectively precede and follow a topic:

(42) a. Un uomo a cui, il premio Nobel, lo daranno senz'altro
"A man to whom, the Nobel Prize, they will give it undoubtedly"

b.*Un uomo, il premio Nobel, a cui lo daranno senz'altro
"A man, the Nobel Prize, to whom they will give it undoubtedly"

(43) a.* A chi, il premio Nobel, lo daranno?
"To whom, the Nobel prize, will they give it?"

b. Il premio Nobel, a chi lo daranno?
"The Nobel prize, to whom will they give it?"

On the basis of (41) we are immediately led to conclude that relative operators occupy the specifier of Force, the one position which cannot be preceded by topics, while question operators occupy a lower position.[16]

Things get more precise as soon as we observe that relative pronouns are compatible with a focalized constituent in a fixed order, while question operators in main questions are not, regardless of the ordering (the contrast between (44) and (45) was referred to as the fifth difference between Top and Foc in section 4):

(44) a. Ecco un uomo a cui IL PREMIO NOBEL dovrebbero dare (non il premio X)
"Here is a man to whom THE NOBEL PRIZE they should give (not prize X)"

b.*Ecco un uomo IL PREMIO NOBEL a cui dovrebbero dare (non il premio X)
"Here is a man THE NOBEL PRIZE to whom they should give (not prize X)"

(45) a.* A chi IL PREMIO NOBEL dovrebbero dare?
"To whom THE NOBEL PRIZE should they give?"

b.*IL PREMIO NOBEL a chi dovrebbero dare?
"THE NOBEL PRIZE to whom should they give?"

If the relative pronoun is in the Spec of Force in (41), it is expected to be compatible with a lower focus, as in (44)a. As for the incompatibility of the question operator and a focalized constituent illustrated by (45), the possibility that immediately comes to mind is that the question operator sits in the Spec of Foc in main questions, hence focalized constituents and question operators compete for the same position and cannot co-occur. An apparent problem for this analysis is raised by the fact that there seems to be a positional asymmetry between question operators and focus: a focalized constituent can be followed by a topic, but a main question operator cannot:

(46) (Domani,) QUESTO (a Gianni,) gli dovreste dire
"(Tomorrow,) THIS (to Gianni,) we should say"

(47) (Domani,) che cosa (*a Gianni,) gli dovremmo dire?
"(Tomorrow,) what (to Gianni,) we should say?"

At first sight, this asymmetry seems to suggest that question operators do not move as far as Foc in (41) and fill a lower position, one that cannot be followed by a Top, such as the Spec of Fin in (41). But if this were correct, question operators would not be competing with focalized constituents for the same position; so, why should the incompatibility shown by (45) arise?

In fact, there are good reasons to think that the asymmetry in (46)–(47) is not due to a positional difference but follows from an independent factor: even a normal preverbal subject cannot intervene between the question operator and the verb, while it can intervene between a focalized constituent and the verb:

(48) QUESTO Gianni ti dirà (, non quello che pensavi)
"THIS Gianni will say to you (, not what you thought)"

(49) *Che cosa Gianni ti dirà?
"What will Gianni say to you?"

In Rizzi (1991) the impossibility of (49) is derived from the Wh Criterion: a Wh operator and a head endowed with the Wh feature must be in a Spec/head configuration at S-structure (or before Spell-out, if one opts for a formalization of things à la Chomsky (1993); for a reformulation of the Criterion approach within the guidelines of Chomsky (1993) see Friedemann (1995); see also Guasti (1994)); if the Wh feature is generated under T in main questions, I to C movement must apply to bring the feature to the C system, where the Criterion is satisfied. In (49) I to C has not applied, as the word order shows, hence the Criterion is violated. This analysis can now be immediately transposed to the more articulated C structure of (41). The question operator ends up in the Spec of Foc in main questions, where it competes with a focalized constituent, whence the incompatibility of (45). If that position is filled by a Wh element, the inflected verb, carrying the feature Wh, must move all the way up to Foc° to permit satisfaction of the Wh Criterion. Both (47) and (49) (when the lower Top is present) are excluded as violations of the Wh Criterion: in (49) the inflected verb has not moved out of the IP, as the intervening subject shows; in (47) it may have moved to FinP but not further, as the intervening Top shows; in neither case is the required Spec/head configuration created, so that the structures are ruled out by the Wh Criterion (I cannot move past the lower Top either, yielding the order Wh V+I Top IP, as Top blocks I movement: see section 7 below).

On the other hand, I to C movement is not triggered by focalization in Italian: if there is a Focus Criterion (as I am assuming here), the Focus feature is inherently possessed by the Foc° head and no movement of an inflectional head is required.[17]

So, when the Spec/Foc of (41) is filled by a non-Wh focal element, both a preverbal subject and one or more Topics can occur. In this way, the apparent asymmetry between questions and Focus of (47) can be reconciled with the natural hypothesis that they occupy the same position in main questions.[18]

7. ADJACENCY EFFECTS ON CASE

In this section we will discuss the following descriptive generalization: whenever the case properties of the subject depend on an element of the complementizer system, no preposed phrase of any sort can intervene between this element and the subject.

In order to explain this generalization, we must first extend our analysis of topic-comment structures from simple argumental topicalization to all sorts of cases of preposing, adverb preposing in particular (*Yesterday, John came back*, etc.).

A rather common analysis of adverb preposing in English assumes adjunction of the preposed element to IP (or S); sometimes this analysis is assumed for argumental topicalization as well: Baltin (1982), Rochemont (1989) Lasnik and Saito (1992). The approach we have adopted for argumental topicalization is, in essence, an updating of Chomsky (1977), Cinque (1990): the topicalized element is in the Spec of a Top head, with a null anaphoric operator in the immediately lower Spec to ensure connection with the open position in the sentence. Now, it is not plausible that adverb preposing may involve the anaphoric null operator, which appears to be restricted to argumental material; apart from that, the analysis of argumental topicalization can be extended. So, we can hold constant the assumption that adverb preposing involves a TopP, but we must assume that the adverb itself moves from its base position to the TopP, without the mediation of Op (alternatively, if the "preposed" adverb is a sentential adverb, it could be base-generated in the Top system: cf. Cinque (1990), Longobardi (1980), Rizzi (1990)). We will see later on that there are reasons to assume that the adverb is adjoined to the TopP, rather than moving to its Spec, but this refinement is unnecessary at the moment.

A straightforward conceptual motivation for the involvement of TopP in adverb preposing, and against the simple adjunction to IP is offered again by Chomsky's (1993) approach to movement (/formation of non-trivial chains): if movement is a last resort operation, and (at least syntactic) movement is always triggered by the satisfaction of some (concrete or abstract) morphological requirement, there can be no free adjunction to IP (or to any other category) in the overt syntax; adverb preposing, on a par with argumental topicalization, must be triggered by the satisfaction of a Topic Criterion; this naturally leads, under usual assumptions, to the postulation of a Top head and phrase also for simple adverb preposing.

An immediate empirical counterpart of this conceptual argument has to do with the selectivity of the landing site of preposing. The preposed element must land in an IP-peripheral position; but if the process involved simple adjunction to IP, what would prevent movement to other potential adjunction sites, i.e. in between the modal and the VP, a position which can host various kinds of adverbials (and, under May's (1985) analysis, is a possible landing site of QR), but not a topicalized constituent, as in (50)b? And what would prevent adjunction to the whole CP, as in (50)c?

(50) a. Around Christmas, John will come home
b.*John will, around Christmas, come home
c.*I think, around Christmas, that John will come home

Standard accounts of (50)b involve the assumption that adjunction cannot apply to arguments (Chomsky 1986b, McCloskey 1992), while the problem raised by (50)b is hardly even mentioned (but see McCloskey (1992: 2)). Both problems disappear at once under the criterial approach to adverb preposing: movement is to an IP-peripheral position because the TopP is a component of the C system; it cannot be external to the Force marker *that* because the higher verb selects the specification of Force, not the TopP: verbs select for declaratives or questions, not for clauses with or without topic (or focus).[19]

If preposed phrases of all kinds (not just topicalized arguments) always detect a TopP projection in the C system, many adjacency effects discussed in the literature are amenable to a straightforward explanation. Consider first the fact that a preposed adverb can intervene between a tensed complementizer and the subject, but not between *for* and the subject in English:

(51) a. . . . that John will leave tomorrow
b. . . . that, tomorrow, John will leave

(52) a. . . . for John to leave tomorrow
b.*. . . for, tomorrow, John to leave

Case theory provides a natural explanation in conjunction with our assumptions on preposing of the adverbial phrases. In order to be able to determine case on the subject, *for* must be in a sufficiently local configuration with it, hence it must be in the lowest head of the C system, finiteness. Therefore, there is no room for a TopP in between *for* and the IP (see structure (41)), hence the order in (52)b cannot arise. If we were to assume that *for* could be generated under a higher head of the C system, the occurrence of a lower TopP would give rise to the following structure:

(53) [for [tomorrow Top° . . . [John . . .

in which *for* would be too far away from *John* to determine its case, under

Relativized Minimality (that UG must allow for the possibility of a prepositional complementizer higher than Fin is shown below).[20]

The same explanation can extend to the adjacency constraint between absolutive *with* and the subject of the small clause:

(54) a. With John unavailable in the week-end, . . .
b.*With, in the week-end, John unavailable, . . .

(cf. ". . . that, in the week-end, John is unavailable"). If the small clause has no C system (see note 3), then there cannot be any TopP to host the preposed phrase. Even if the TopP could be present, it would disrupt the local relation between *with* and *John* which is necessary for case assignment.

That case is crucial for determining the ill-formedness of (52)b (and (54)b) is suggested by the contrast with (51)b, in which the overt complementizer *that* is not involved in case assignment to the subject (which is determined by the T-Agr complex), hence it can occur in a higher head of the C system, Force, compatible with a lower TopP.

The contrast between (51) and (52) is not minimal, though, as we are comparing a finite and a non-finite structure. A more minimal pair with (52) would be provided by a construction with the following characteristics: an infinitival complement involving a lexical subject and a prepositional complementizer, but with the case of the subject not determined by the preposition. The relevant construction exists in West Flemish (Liliane Haegeman, p.c.; see Haegeman (1986) for discussion):

(55) Mee (?gisteren) zie nie te kommen, . . .
"With yesterday she not to come, . . ."

These infinitives introduced by *mee* (with) have the lexical subject marked with nominative case, which is presumably determined by abstract Agr, not by the prepositional complementizer (which would be expected to govern accusative or oblique). So, under the case approach it comes as no surprise that adverb interpolation is possible (if somewhat marginal): the prepositional complementizer is not involved in case assignment to the subject, so it can occur on a higher head of the C system, and it is consistent with the occurrence of a lower TopP. The contrast between English and West Flemish then strongly suggests that the adjacency effect observed in (52)b should be closely tied to the case properties, rather than to some general distinction between finite and non-finite clauses.

Even more straightforward evidence for the role of case is provided by Brazilian Portuguese. The infinitive introduced by preposition *pra* (for) has its subject marked nominative or, in colloqual registers, oblique; in the former case, but not in the latter, an adverb can interpolate (Cristina Figueiredo-Silva, Lucienne Rasetti, p.c.; see Figueiredo-Silva (1994) for further discussion):

(56) a. Ela me deu o livro pra (amanha) eu ler
"She gave me the book for tomorrow I to read"

b. Ela me deu o livro pra (*amanha) mim ler
"She gave me the book for tomorrow me to read"

While in (56)a nominative case is determined by Agr in the infinitival structure, oblique case is plausibly determined by the preposition *pra* in (56)b. So, under a Case approach, it is expected that adverb interpolation will be excluded in (56)b and possible in (56)a.

If nominative case is assigned by the auxiliary in C in the Italian Aux-to-Comp construction (Rizzi 1982), the fact that an adverb cannot intervene is amenable to the same explanation:

(57) a. Essendo egli improvvisamente tornato a casa, . . .
"Having he suddenly come back home, . . ."

b.*Essendo improvvisamente egli tornato a casa, . . .
"Having suddenly he come back home, . . ."

(cf. ". . . poiché improvvisamente egli è tornato a casa" = Because suddenly he has come back home).[21]

This case is apparently akin to the well-known fact that in Aux inversion structures in English nothing can intervene between the inflection moved to C and the overt subject, even though the role of Case is not obvious here (but see Rizzi and Roberts (1989)):

(58) a. . . . that yesterday John came
b.*Did yesterday John come?

If I to C movement involves movement to Fin, then there is no intervening TopP to host the preposed adverb in between I and the subject, under structure (41). On the other hand, in some cases it is plausible that I moves to a higher head of the C system, e.g. in conditionals:

(59) a. If (yesterday) John had done that, . . .
b. Had (*yesterday) John done that, . . .

Here the preposed auxiliary alternates with *if*, which can precede a preposed adverb, hence must be higher than Fin. If the auxiliary actually replaces *if*, as is plausible here, then at least this instance of I to C may be able to move higher than Fin.

So, what rules out the following representation?

(60) Had [yesterday Top° [John I° done that]] . . .

We are lead to assume that Top° in English is not a suitable host for I movement, so that (60) is excluded by the Head Movement Constraint (the ECP under RM): I cannot move to Top° by assumption, and the higher head of the C° system normally filled by *if* is too far away for the required antecedent government relation to hold.[22]

8. ADJACENCY EFFECTS ON PRO

An apparently different kind of adjacency effect exists in control structures between a head of the C system and PRO in subject position. As was briefly discussed in section 3, in Italian, *di* is often considered the infinitival counterpart of the finite complementizer *che*; but the distribution of topics is the opposite in the two cases: a topic must follow *che*:

(61) a.*Penso, a Gianni, che gli dovrei parlare
"I think, to Gianni, that I should speak to him"

b. Penso che, a Gianni, gli dovrei parlare
"I think that, to Gianni, I should speak to him"

On the other hand, a topic is strongly disallowed in between the prepositional complementizer *di* and the infinitival IP, while it can precede *di*:

(62) a. Penso, a Gianni, di dovergli parlare
"I think, to Gianni, 'of' to have to speak to him"

b.*Penso di, a Gianni, dovergli parlare
"I think 'of', to Gianni, to have to speak to him"

The contrast (61)a–(62)a clearly shows that *che* and *di* do not occupy the same position: at S-structure, *che* occupies the highest position of the C system, the Force head, preceding the topic string, while *di* occupies a lower position, presumably the finiteness head. Why should it be so? and, in particular, why should *di* be forced to occur on the lowest head of the C system?

It is a remarkable fact that control infinitives pattern with infinitival (and finite) clauses in which the case of the lexical subject is determined by some element of the C system in that they both require adjacency between this element and the subject position:

(63) *C° [XP Top° . . . [PRO . . .

The traditional approach to the distribution of PRO in terms of the PRO Theorem does not seem to be well equipped to capture this constraint: it is not clear why the intervening TopP should determine a violation of the PRO Theorem (particularly in cases of CLLD, in which, as the subject/object asymmetries discussed in section 9 show, Top° clearly does not have the capacity to govern a lower Spec position). The null case approach to PRO of Chomsky and Lasnik (1991) looks more promising in this respect, if properly adapted.

The null case approach captures the distribution of PRO by stipulating that PRO requires a null case, sanctioned by the minimal inflection, the inflection of infinitives; its occurrence is then restricted to the subject position of non-finite clauses.

As such, the null case approach has nothing to say on the descriptive constraint (52).

On the other hand, as Watanabe (1993) has observed, this variant of the null case approach has the weakness of not expressing one of the fundamental distributional constraints on PRO, i.e., the fact that it cannot occur in non-finite structures not protected by a CP layer:

(64) a.* It seems [PRO to be happy]
b.* John believes [PRO to be happy]
c.* John considers [PRO happy]

These predicates select IP complements or small clauses in the non-finite paradigm. The non-occurrence of PRO here immediately follows from the PRO theorem (PRO is governed by the higher predicate), but not from the null case approach: why should these non-finite inflections not license the null case? In order to deal with this problem, Watanabe stipulates that null case checking in AgrS creates a new feature [+F] which in turn must be checked by movement of AgrS to the C system. But this follow up operation and the feature involved have no independent status or justification, apart from the fact of expressing a dependency C° – PRO in a system which disallows head government.

As we are admitting head government for other reasons (cf. introduction), we can directly rephrase the null case approach in a way consistent with Watanabe's observation by stipulating the following principle:[23]

(65) Null Case is sanctioned by [-fin] under government

So, the different cases of (64) can be excluded, under (65), because of the lack of the C system (implying the lack of the required -fin specification). The adjacency effects summarized in (63) can now be treated on a par with the adjacency effects in cases in which the lexical subject has its case sanctioned by a non-finite complementizer ((52)b, (54)b, (56)b, etc.). The similarity of the adjacency effects in the two cases thus seems to lend straightforward support to the null case approach to PRO (with the proposed revision).

9. ADJACENCY EFFECTS ON TRACES

If Topicalized elements involve an independent X-bar projection in the C system, we expect that the presence of a topicalized element will interfere with subject extraction, under standard assumptions on the licensing of traces. In fact, we find two opposite, almost contradictory, kinds of interactions: some preposed elements block subject extraction; other preposed elements alleviate *that*-trace violations and make subject extraction possible. We shall call these two effects adjacency and anti-adjacency effects on traces, respectively. Let us concentrate on the former in this section.

First of all, intervening CLLD phrases induce subject-object asymmetries in French:

(66) a. ? Je ne sais pas à qui, ton livre, je pourrais le donner t
"I don't know to whom, your book, I could give it t"

b.*?Je ne sais pas qui, ton livre, t pourrait l'acheter
"I don't know who, your book, t could buy it"

(67) a. ? Un homme à qui, ton livre, je pourrais le donner t
"A man to whom, your book, I could give it t"

b.*?Un homme qui, ton livre, t pourrait l'acheter
"A man who, your book, t could buy it"

A verbal complement can be moved across a Topic with slightly marginal results in questions and relatives; movement of a subject across a Topic determines a clear decrease of acceptability. These asymmetries are obviously reminiscent of the familiar subject-complement extraction asymmetries (*that*-trace effects, which produce somewhat sharper contrasts; on this, see below):

(68) a. A qui crois-tu que Marie va parler t?
"To whom do you believe that Marie is going to speak t?"

b.*Qui crois-tu que t va parler à Marie?
"Who do you believe that t is going to speak to Marie?"

Comparative evidence supports the hypothesis that (66)–(67) are parallel to (68). Italian, a language which does not show subject-complement asymmetries of the kind illustrated in (68) (ultimately as a function of the positive fixation of the Null Subject Parameter, see Rizzi 1982, ch. 4, 1990: 62–65 for discussion), also allows subject and complement extraction across a Topic at the same level of acceptability:

(69) a. Un uomo a cui, il tuo libro, lo potremmo dare
"A man to whom, your book, we could give it"

b. Un uomo che, il tuo libro, lo potrebbe comprare
"A man who, your book, could buy it"

As for English, a language which typically shows *that*-trace effects, Lasnik and Saito (1992) observe that topicalization also determines detectable asymmetries, in spite of the fact that even complement extraction across a topic is quite degraded:

(70) a.??The man to whom [that book [I gave t t]]

b. *The man who [that book [t gave t to me]]
(adapted from Lasnik and Saito 1992)

Some cases of complement extraction across a topic are more natural (Baltin 1982); this produces sharper asymmetries (on the effect of stress on the acceptability of such cases see below):

(71) a.? A man to whom [liberty [we should never grant t t]]
b.* A man who [liberty [t should never grant t to us]]

Let us first consider the French paradigm. In Rizzi (1990, ch. 2) the following analysis of standard subject-complement asymmetries is proposed: the ECP requires that traces must be properly head-governed (governed by a head within its immediate projection); a trace in complement position is properly head governed (by the verb), but a trace in subject position normally is not, as C is inert for government; so, (68)b is excluded as an ECP violation. Movement of the subject may be well-formed in cases like (72):

(72) Je ne sais pas [qui C° [t pourrait l'acheter]]
"I dont know who could buy it"

Here the analysis, expressed within a traditional theory of C, assumed that the Wh element in the Spec of C could trigger abstract agreement on C (sometimes with audible morphological effects) which turned C into a proper head-governor for the trace in subject position. Under the current assumptions on a structured C system, it must be the case that finiteness, the lowest C head interfacing the IP system and structurally adjacent to the subject, can be endowed with Agr features to ensure well-formedness of the subject trace (if the Wh elements end up in a Spec higher than Spec/Fin in (72), there must be a higher head endowed with Agr features to license the subject trace in Spec/Fin; a more precise characterization of the possible occurrence of Agr features on a given head is proposed in section 12). Consider now the structural representation of such examples as (66)b, etc. under the X-bar analysis of Topics (C here is whatever head of the complementizer system has the Wh element in its Spec in indirect questions):

(73) Je ne sais pas [qui C° [ton livre Top° . . . [t pourrait . . .]]]

Here, even if C is turned into a governor via agreement, it is too far away to license the subject trace, due to the intervening head Top°, a standard case of Relativized Minimality effect. If Fin, lower than Top, is endowed with Agr features, things do not change: the trace in subject position t would be well-formed, but the subject should move through the Spec of Fin to license the Agr features on this head, and the trace in the Spec of Fin, t′, would now be the offending trace:

(74) Je ne sais pas [qui C° [ton livre Top° [t′ Fin+Agr [t pourrait . . .]]]]

(66)b with representation (74) is close enough to (68)b to make it possible to appeal to the same structural explanation for both cases of subject/non-subject asymmetries; on the other hand, it is different enough to leave room for an account of the different strength of the effect with respect to ordinary *that*-trace effects. Assuming uniform strength for all ECP violations, the somewhat weaker deviance of (66)b could be due to the possibility of resorting to a deviant device of a different kind to avoid the ECP violation. For instance, if t′ is omitted from representation (74), no ECP violation would arise, and the source of the deviance would be the fact that Agr in Fin is not locally licensed by its specifier (alternatively, it could be that the structure resorts to an unlicensed occurrence of the null operator Op, a null element which does not fall under the ECP, to support the Agr features in Fin; or that the structure makes an improper use of the "bypassing" device to be introduced in section 12). None of these (deviant) devices is available for the subject position, so that (68)b can only produce a straight ECP violation.

If we had assumed that Topics in the CLLD construction are adjoined to IP, such contrasts as (66)a–b would be unexpected. One could deal with them through the stipulation that adjunction creates a barrier for government (Lasnik and Saito 1992). Since, under the X-bar analysis of the topic-comment articulation, the result follows straightforwardly from core principles of locality, I take these asymmetries to provide evidence for the X-bar analysis.

The same analysis accounts for the ill-formedness of English examples such as (70)b and (71)b (modulo the independent differences between Romance CLLD and English Topicalization). Under the null operator analysis of English topicalization, the complete representation of (71)b would be, for the relevant part:

(75) A man [who C° [liberty Top° [Op [t should never grant to us]]]]

Suppose that the null Op sits in the Spec of the Fin head. Then, no Agr features can occur in Fin to satisfy the ECP on t: among other things, such features would have to agree with Op, hence disagree with t, and we continue to assume that Agr features have their governing capacity restricted to elements coindexed with them. If Agr features were specified on some higher head of the C system (say, under Force), they would be too far away from t to have any beneficial effect, under RM (see the following sections for additional discussion of this case). Again, an analysis of English topicalization based on simple IP-adjunction would not offer an equally principled analysis of the asymmetries.

Moreover, a generalized adjunction analysis is not selective enough to lead one to expect the following asymmetry. Adverb preposing contrasts sharply with argument topicalization in that it does not affect subject extraction:

(76) a.*I wonder who, this book, would buy around Christmas
b. I wonder who, around Christmas, would buy this book

In the face of this contrast, and restricting one's attention to adjacency effects on traces, one could be tempted to assume that adverb preposing differs from argumental topicalization in that it does involve simple adjunction to IP, a structure which is transparent to government relations, so that the well-formedness of the subject trace is not affected:

(77) I wonder who C+Agr [around Christmas [t would buy this book]]

On the other hand, this analysis is inconsistent with the conceptual argument for assuming the involvement of a TopP also with adverb preposing, and the supporting empirical evidence provided by the adjacency effects on Case, with respect to which argument topicalization and adverb preposing pattern alike. We are then left with the question why adverb preposing involves a structure which triggers adjacency effects on case but is transparent for adjacency effects on traces. This point is addressed in the next section in the context of the anti-adjacency effects.

In order to conclude the survey on the adjacency effects on traces, I will now take a brief look at some such effects involving traces in A-chains. We have seen in (69) that Italian differs from French in that CLLD does not induce subject-object asymmetries in A′-chains, a fact that is amenable to other similar contrasts between the two languages as a consequence of the different fixation of the Null Subject Parameter. On the other hand, adjacency effects are detectable in Italian if we look at A-chains. Here the relevant contrast is between raising and control: control infinitives are compatible with CLLD (with the dislocated element preceding the infinitival complementizer, as we have seen), while raising infinitives are not: compare, in particular, the different behavior of the control and raising use of *sembrare* (seem):

(78) a. Gianni pensa, il tuo libro, di PRO conoscerlo bene
"Gianni thinks, you book, of to+know it well"

b. Mi sembra, il tuo libro, di PRO conoscerlo bene
"It seems to me, your book, of to+know it well"

c.*?Gianni sembra, il tuo libro, t conoscerlo bene
"Gianni seems, your book, to know it well"

If raising infinitives must involve a bare IP in order to allow the subject trace to be properly governed by the main V, there is no room for a TopP to occur in such structures; on the other hand, control infinitives can (and must) involve a CP system, so that they are compatible with a TopP.[24]

A more subtle case of incompatibility with a dislocated phrase is provided by the special Romance construction involving Wh extraction of the subject from the infinitival complement of an epistemic verb, a complement which does not allow an overt subject *in situ* (Kayne 1984, Rizzi 1982, 1990):

(79) Un uomo che ritengo (*a Gianni,) potergli parlare
"A man whom I believe (to Gianni) to be able to talk to him"

Here a C structure (say, minimally, a -Fin head) is needed to ensure, on the one hand, the fact that the subject trace satisfies the ECP, and, on the other hand, the case-licensing of the chain of the subject by the higher verb:

(80) Un uomo che ritengo [t′ -Fin [t potergli parlare]]

But then, if a TopP occurs, it will make t′ inaccessible to V for case licensing and satisfaction of the ECP, so that the structure will be ill-formed. Again, no such effect is found with the control structure, normally possible with epistemic verbs in Italian:

(81) Ritengo, a Gianni, di potergli parlare
"I believe, to Gianni, to be able to speak to him"

Here, no special relation must be established between the main V and (the chain of) PRO, hence a TopP can occur in the C system.

10. ANTI-ADJACENCY EFFECTS

In the previous sections the intervening head of the TopP was detected through a negative effect, the blocking of a locality relation that was required to hold between a higher head and a lower subject position. Interesting complementary evidence for the postulation of such a head is the positive effect to be discussed here: in a nutshell, in some cases an otherwise ill formed occurrence of a subject trace is made possible by the presence and action of an intervening Top layer (in an indirect way, as we shall see in a moment).

Consider a typical *that*-t effect, as in (82)a below. In this context, argument topicalization and adverb preposing differ sharply. If embedded argument topicalization applies (with comma intonation and the pragmatics of topic-comment), as in (82)b, the effect is not alleviated (on the other hand, if the preposed element bears focal stress, the acceptability improves; see below on this effect):

(82) a.* A man who I think that t knows this book very well
b.* A man who I think that, this book, t knows t very well

On the other hand, Bresnan (1977: 194) observed that an adverb interpolating between *that* and the subject trace renders the structure clearly more acceptable (thanks to Kinsuke Hasegawa for bringing Bresnan's observation to my attention in the context of his comment paper to Rizzi (1993), Tokyo, November 1992); these facts have been analyzed independently in

Culicover (1992, 1993), Fukui (1993)). Consider the following examples from Bresnan's article:

(83) a.* An amendment which they say that t will be law next year
b. An amendment which they say that, next year, t will be law

(84) a.* Which doctor did you tell me that t had had a heart attack during an operation?
b. Which doctor did you tell me that, during an operation, t had had a heart attack?

Bresnan considers such examples "mildly awkward". Culicover appears to consider them fully grammatical. In any event, there seems to be a consensus that a clear contrast exists between the two cases.

We will call this improvement effect an "anti-adjacency effect", in that it arises when an intervening adverb or adverbial PP makes the subject trace non-adjacent to *that*. That the adverb must be higher than the subject trace is shown by the fact that a lower (IP internal) adverb does not give rise to the effect, Hasegawa points out:

(85) *Who did she say that t hardly speaks to her?

And the effect is selective enough to distinguish between argument topicalization (82)b and adverb preposing ((83)b, etc.).

Here I will develop an analysis along the lines of the approach proposed by Culicover (1992) (but rejected in Culicover (1993) for reasons that we will come back to) and, more directly, of the independent proposal sketched out in Rizzi (1993: fn. 6) in response to Hasegawa's point. As a first approximation, we can think that the preposed adverb or PP has the effect of licensing a head of the C system (in an indirect way, as we shall see in a moment) which in turn licenses the subject trace, thus alleviating the ECP violation.

(86) . . . that . . . next year . . . X° [t will be law

Various questions arise at this point: What is X°? Why is its presence contingent on the preposed adverbial? Why does it license the subject trace?

As for the first and third questions, we clearly want to unify this case as much as possible with other successful cases of subject extraction. If in such cases subject extraction is made possible by an agreeing Fin specification, this should be the device involved in (86) as well. But why should an agreeing Fin be allowed to cooccur with *that* just in case an adverb has been preposed?

So far we have not taken a position as to the question whether force and finiteness must be specified on distinct heads of the complementizer system or can be specified syncretically, on a single head. We have only observed that these two specifications must be structurally adjacent, respectively, to the lower IP and higher VP structure in order to meet selectional constraints. Suppose that the force-finiteness system can be expressed by a single item drawn from the functional lexicon. In English, for embedded finite declaratives we have the alternation *that/0*; I will continue to assume that the latter, but not the former, is consistent with Agr:

(87) That = +Decl, +fin
0 = +Decl, +fin, (+Agr)

The analysis of the simple cases of subject extraction then proceeds as in Rizzi (1990). If the form *that* is selected, the trace in subject position remains non properly governed and ECP is violated. If *0* is selected, it is turned into a governor by the Agr specification (which, in turn, is sanctioned by the passage of the subject through its specifier, where it leaves t′), and it properly governs the subject trace t (in turn, t′ is properly governed by the higher verb):

(88) a.* Who do you think [t′ that [t will win the prize]]?
b. Who do you think [t′ 0 [t will win the prize]]?

Suppose now that the Topic-Focus field is activated in the C system. Then, the force-finiteness system cannot be realized on a single C head any more because either one or the other specification would not be adjacent to its selecting or selected domain. The force-finiteness system must then split into two heads which sandwich the topic-focus field. So, in examples like the following:

(89) a. I think that next year John will win the prize
b. Bill said that your book, he really liked

the force specification, which interfaces the C system (and the whole clause) with its selector (the higher V) must be manifested by *that* above the topic; on the other hand, finiteness, which interfaces the C system with the IP, must be manifested by a zero C head (Fin) under the topic. So, we should revise (87) in the following way:

(90) That = +decl, (+fin)
0 = (+decl), +fin, (+Agr)

That expresses declarative force and may optionally express finiteness; *0* expresses finiteness, and may optionally express declarative force (as well as agreement). In simple cases, in which the force-finiteness system can be expressed on a single head, *that* and *0* are functionally equivalent and alternate (there are further restrictions on the occurrence of *0* that we will come back to in section 12); in complex cases in which force and finiteness must split because the topic-focus system is activated, the higher head, expressing pure force, must be realized as *that* and the lower head, expressing pure finiteness, must be realized as *0*:

(91) . . . [that [next year Top° [0 [John will win the prize]]

As expected under this analysis, the two specifications do not alternate in the "splitting" case: the lower specification cannot be realized as *that* and, more importantly, the higher specification cannot be realized as *0* (Rochemont (1989), Nakajima (1993), Grimshaw (1995)):

(92) I think *(that) next year, (*that) John will win the prize

We are now in a position to explain the anti-adjacency effect. When the Topic-Focus field is activated by a preposed adverbial, force and finiteness must split, and we get a representation like (91). If the subject is extracted, as the lower *0* expressing Fin can be associated with Agr, we get (93)a; t is properly governed by Fin with the Agr specification; what about t′, whose presence in the Spec of Fin is needed to license the Agr specification? I will assume here that Fin can move head to head to the next available head, here Top, yielding representation (93)b, and from that position it can properly govern t′, thus satisfying the ECP.[25]

(93) a. . . . that [next year Top° [t′ Fin° +Agr [t will be law]]]
b. . . . that [next year [Fin° +Agr [Top°]] [t′ Fin° +Agr [t will be law]]]

According to this analysis, whether or not the moved subject ultimately passes through the Spec of *that* is immaterial for the anti-adjacency effect, as the critical actions (licensing of Agr in Fin and of the two traces of the subject) take place under *that* in these complex structures. This predicts that we should find anti-adjacency effects also in indirect questions (abstracting away from the independent subjacency effects), in which the Spec of Force, filled by the Wh operator, would not be available for movement of the subject. In fact, Culicover (1993) detects an anti-adjacency effect in such cases as well (his example (20)b is adapted here):

(94) It is this person that you might well wonder whether for all intents and purposes dislikes you

Here the structure would be

(95) . . . whether [for all intents . . . Top° [t′ Fin+Agr [t . . .

and the analysis would proceed exactly as in the case of the declarative (Fin° endowed with Agr moves to Top°, from where it can license t′; its trace licenses t).

We should now make sure that the analysis is selective enough to account for the difference between adverb preposing and argument topicalization. Remember that the latter in English must involve a null operator, which we have assumed to be sitting in the Spec of Fin. So, a relevant representation with subject extraction across a topicalized phrase would be:

(96) . . . that [this book Top° [Op Fin° [t knows . . .

Here the Fin head is not available to salvage t (if it hosted Agr features, they should agree with Op in its Spec, hence they would disagree with t, and t could not be licensed).[26]

The question which remains to be answered is: why is this technique contingent on the presence of the preposed adverbial? i.e., why couldn't one always violate the *that*-t constraint by separating force and finiteness, hence have a lower agreeing *0* finiteness head licensing the subject trace and cooccurring with a higher *that* (with t' licensed by head movement of Fin°+Agr to *that*)?

(97) Who do you think [that [t' Fin°+Agr [t will win the prize]]]

This representation must be barred, otherwise we would have free violations of *that*-t. So, the descriptive generalization appears to be that we can have the split between Force and Finiteness (and the consequent salvaging of the subject trace) only if the split is forced by the activation of the topic-focus field. This state of affairs has an obvious "last resort" flavor, and as such is reminiscent of much discussed economy constraints (Chomsky 1991, 1993, 1995, etc.). I will assume the following economy principle to constrain the structure-building process:

(98) Avoid structure

much in the line of analogous proposals by Safir (1992), Grimshaw (1993), Speas (1994), Giorgi and Pianesi (1994), Crisma (1992) and other recent work (the principle has no exact equivalent in Chomsky's system, but is akin to his Economy of representations).

The effect of principle (98) in the case at issue is intuitively clear: as the grammar of English has the option of expressing Force and Finiteness in a single head, this option wins over the option of selecting two separate heads (which would imply two X-bar projections); the latter becomes permissible only if the former is not available because of the activation of the topic-focus field, which forces the split (otherwise, selectional constraints would be violated). This happens in (93), (94), but not in (97), which is barred by principle (98). So, (98) is operative up to the satisfaction of selectional constaints, as is obvious: a principle of structural parsimony cannot win over the fundamental structure building principles. On the other hand, the ECP is weaker than (98): a structural layer cannot be added to a representation just to salvage an ECP violation.[27]

This is rather straightforward intuitively, but the question arises as to how (98) may work formally. Let us assume the basic idea of Chomsky's (1995) approach: economy is computed by comparing derivations within a given reference set, and selecting the simplest. The question then reduces to how the reference set is defined. Chomsky's proposal is that it is fixed on the basis of the numeration, the set of items picked from the lexicon to act as heads in the syntactic representation to be formed. But this definition does not help in our case: (97) and (88) would have different numerations (the latter with a syncretic Force-Fin head, the former with two separate heads for force and finiteness, a permissible option in English, as the well-formedness of (93) shows), so there could not be any blocking effect of (88) over (97) if the reference set is defined on the basis of the numeration.

On the other hand, it may be desirable to consider less strict definitions of the reference set. Consider, for instance, the basic distributional constraint on *do* support: *do* can occur only when it is needed (Grimshaw 1993). It is natural to try to express this constraint in terms of an economy principle like (98) (Rizzi 1995), but this is not possible if the reference set is restricted by the numeration: structures with and without *do* would always have distinct numerations. The same problem may be raised, e.g., by the distributional constraints on certain kinds of expletives (in German, Icelandic, etc.), which are limited to positions in which they are needed to satisfy the V-2 constraint. So, our case seems to belong to a larger family of cases having this structure: functional element X can occur only if it is needed to satisfy some structure-building principle. It is natural to try to explain these constraints through principle (98), but this requires a less strict definition of the reference set. A simple modification which achieves the desired result here is that we define the reference set exclusively on the basis of the *lexical* elements of the numeration: functional elements do not define the reference set, rather their occurrence is limited by principle (98) (this is very similar to the approach, expressed within Optimality Theory, by Grimshaw (1995)).[28]

11. ANTI-ADJACENCY EFFECTS WITH NEGATIVE PREPOSING

Culicover (1993) discusses a problem for his own (1992) analysis of what we have called the anti-adjacency effect: the effect is triggered by preposed negative elements as well:

(99) Leslie is the person who I said that at no time would run for any public office

Even though in such cases the linear order cannot show whether I to C has applied or not, the negative element has clausal scope here (with licensing of a phrase-external polarity item), a state of affairs in which inversion is normally required

(100) a. At no time would Leslie run for any public office
b.*At no time Leslie would run for any public office

Culicover concludes that inversion must have applied in (99) as well, so that the representation must be

(102) . . . that at no time would [t I run . . .

On the other hand, it is well-known that in other contexts in English I to C does not licence a subject trace. For instance, Hiberno English embedded interrogatives, which allow I to C movement, strongly disallow subject extraction, as McCloskey (1992) points out (see also Henry (1995)):

(103) a. I wonder would she do that
b.*Who do you wonder would t do that

So, Culicover's conclusion is that cases like (99) raise an intractable paradox: on the one hand we observe the anti-adjacency effect, with the preposed negative element able to license an otherwise ill-formed subject trace; on the other hand the preposing should have triggered I to C movement, a context which in general precludes the occurrence of a subject trace. This problem leads Culicover to abandon his own analysis of anti-adjacency, and the whole underlying approach to the licencing of subject traces.

I would like to show that the above facts can be integrated into the analysis of anti-adjacency developed in section 10, which shares the background and many elements with Culicover's original analysis; in fact the phenomenon provides important (if intricate) evidence for that family of approaches.

The key empirical observation is provided by Culicover himself (fn. 4): if we take a structure like (99) but involving no modal or auxiliary, the variant with (unstressed) *do* is deviant and the variant without is fine:

(104) a.??Leslie is the person who I said that only in that election did run for public office
b. Leslie is the person who I said that only in that election ran for public office

If subject extraction does not apply, the judgment is reversed, with *do* insertion and inversion obligatorily applying:

(105) a. I think that only in that election did Leslie run for public office
b.*I think that only in that election Leslie ran for public office

If we take, as seems reasonable, the ill-formedness of the structure with *do* and, even more clearly, the well-formedness of the structure without *do* as evidence that inversion has not applied in (104), we reach a rather surprising conclusion: inversion with a preposed negative element must apply except in case the subject has been extracted, as in (104) (and, by analogy, (99)). Why should it be so?

In fact, there is another familiar case in which I to C movement, otherwise obligatory, does not apply in connection with movement of the subject. This happens with main questions on the subject:

(106) a. Who did you see t?
b.*Who you saw t?

(107) a.*Who did see you?
b. Who saw you?

I will reproduce here the basic elements of the analysis of Rizzi (1991): I to C movement is compulsory in (106) in order to carry the Wh feature, generated under T, to C, as is required to fulfill the Wh Criterion at S-structure (or before Spell-out); in fact, if I to C does not apply, as in (106)b, the structure is ill-formed; on the other hand, I to C movement cannot apply in the case of a subject question (107)a because the subject trace does not satisfy the ECP in that environment (see the discussion of (103)b above); nevertheless, the Wh Criterion is satisfied: as the subject has been moved from its base position in the VP to the Spec of C through the Specs of T and AgrS, we obtain the following representation:

(108) [Who_i $C°_i$ [t_i $AgrS°_i$ [t_i $T°_i$ [t V° . . .]]]]
+wh

C, AgrS and T have specifiers belonging to the same chain, so that, assuming Spec-head coindexation, they share the same index. As they are in the appropriate local relation (no other head intervenes), they can form a representational chain which possesses the Wh feature (still sitting under T); if we define the Wh criterion on chains (a Wh operator must be in a Spec head configuration with a head whose chain possesses the Wh feature), we achieve the desired result: I to C is not required to fulfill the Wh Criterion just in case the questioned element is the subject. This device is not available in (106)b: the specifiers of C and AgrS (and T) are contra-indexed, so that the heads are contra-indexed, too, and no representational chain connecting C to T can be built. The only option to satisfy the Wh criterion with non-subject main questions then is to move I (T) to C, as in (106)a.

Going back to negative preposing, I will assume that I to C movement in this case is triggered by the Negative Criterion (Rizzi 1991: 11–12, Haegeman and Zanuttini (1991), Haegeman (1995)): the Neg feature, which I assume to be generated under T on a par with the Wh feature, must be brought up to the C system if a negative element is preposed in order to create the required Spec/Head configuration. So, for instance, (105)a is fine and (105)b is ruled out as a violation of the Neg Criterion because the Neg feature has not reached the C system. Consider now the representation associated to (104)b (and (99)). I will assume for concreteness that the preposed negative element is moved to a Foc phrase, but labels don't matter much here. Assuming the technique adopted for ordinary anti-adjacency effects, we would have the subject passing through Spec/Fin (leaving trace t‴), from which it can license agreement features in Fin, which in turn license the subject trace t″ in Spec/AgrS; Fin° then moves to Foc°, from where it licenses t‴:

(109) . . . [only in that election Foc° [t'''_i Fin°+Agr_i [t''_i $AgrS°_i$ [t'_i $T°_i$ [t ran . . .]]]]]
+neg

Remember that the Neg feature is under T. Now, T is coindexed with the subject trace in its Spec t′ and both AgrS and Fin are coindexed with other traces of the subject chain, t″ and t‴. So, exactly as in the case of a subject question, there is a representational chain connecting Fin, AgrS and T through the transitivity of indexation. As Fin further moves to Foc°, we end up with a representational chain connecting Foc° (to Fin to AgrS) to T, the head endowed with the negative feature. Hence, the Neg Criterion can be fulfilled without I to C movement, in parallel with the satisfaction of the Wh Criterion with subject questions. If the subject had not been extracted, the option of the representational chain would not arise:

(110) . . . [only in that election Foc° [Fin° [Bill AgrS° [t′ T° [t ran . . .]]]]]

Here Agr in Fin cannot be activated, as it would not be supported by a specifier, hence there is no way to build a representational chain connecting Foc° to the negative feature under T, so that the only option to satisfy the Neg Criterion is to apply I to C movement (in fact, T to AgrS to Fin to Foc). In conclusion, the system deals with Culicover's observation that anti-adjacency effects are determined by negative preposing without raising any paradox. At the same time, it offers an explanation for the surprising observation that I to C movement, generally obligatory with negative preposing, does not apply when the subject is extracted; it does so by drawing a close parallel with the other major gap in the application of I to C movement: main questions on the subject.

12. SOME DIFFERENCES BETWEEN ENGLISH AND FRENCH

French does not show anti-adjacency effects of the English kind. Remember that in cases of successful subject extraction in French the agreeing complementizer is not *0*, but the overt form *qui*; if the agreeing form does not occur and C is in the unmarked form *que*, an ECP violation is produced, as in (111)a:

(111) a.* Voici l'homme que je crois t que t pourra nous aider l'année prochaine
"Here is the man who I believe that will be able to help us next year"

b. Voici l'homme que je crois qui t pourra nous aider l'année prochaine
"Here is the man who I think 'qui' will be able to help us next year"

The paradigm remains essentially unchanged if an adverbial interpolates between C and the subject trace; the ECP violation is not alleviated and the agreeing form of C must occur:

(112) a.* Voici l'homme que je crois que, l'année prochaine, t pourra nous aider
"Here is the man who I believe that, next year, will be able to help us"

b. Voici l'homme que je crois qui, l'année prochaine, t pourra nous aider
"Here is the man who I think 'qui', next year, will be able to help us"

Some speakers do not find any improvement in (112)a in comparison to (111)a; other speakers find a very slight improvement (say ?* vs *) which does not seem comparable to the robust effect found in English, which appears to hold systematically across speakers. We will come back to this nuance in a moment after giving an analysis of the core comparative fact, the essential lack of anti-adjacency in French. Consider the structure of (111)a–b under our analysis, assuming maximal uniformity with what was proposed for English:

(113) . . . je crois [que [l'annee prochaine Top° [t′ Fin° [t . . .]]]]

Assume that Fin can also be endowed with Agr features in French, an option which is presumably what permits simple subject questions such as *Quel garçon t est venu?* (Which boy came?). Then, the offending trace could not be t, and should be t′ here. Remember that t′ is licensed in the English equivalent (93), under the proposed analysis, by the option of having Fin jump by head movement to Top, from where it can properly govern t′. We are then led to locate the difference between the two languages in this device: if Fin cannot jump to Top in French, t′ would remain in violation of the ECP, and the lack of anti-adjacency effects would be expected. But why should this instance of head to head movement be permissible in English and barred in French? I would like to speculate that this subtle contrast is related to a more conspicuous difference between the two grammatical systems.[29]

English has null complementizers for subordinate declarative clauses, whereas French does not.

(114) a. I think (that) John will come
b. Je crois * (que) Jean viendra

The zero finite complementizer of English has the characteristic distribution of traces, as Kayne (1984: ch. 3), Stowell (1981) pointed out; it is possible in clauses that are internal arguments, but not in subject or preposed clauses:

(115) a. I didn't expect [0 [John could come]]
b.*[0 [John will come]] is likely
c.*[0 [John could come]], I didn't expect

A natural way to express this distribution is to assume that a trace is actually involved. Pesetsky (1995: 8) proposes that the null finite complementizer is affixal, and incorporates onto the higher V. The observed distribution then follows from the ECP. Our analysis of subject extraction in cases like *Who do you think came?* remains unchanged, except that it is now *the trace* of the agreeing Fin which properly governs the subject trace. In anti-adjacency configurations, things continue to work essentially in the same way, with the affixal (and agreeing) Fin moving to the next higher head, except that here the target is not the higher V, but another head of the C system, Top (or perhaps Foc in cases like (104)b, and possibly the cases mentioned in the last paragraph of note 26).

In the corresponding French structure (112)a, as French complementizers are not affixal, the agreeing Fin head cannot jump further, and t′ continues to violate the ECP. So, if our speculation is on the right track here, the English-French contrast (103)–(113) may be reduced to the more conspicuous and familiar contrast (114)a–b.

We still have to account for the well-formedness of (112)b in French: if the higher C element is in the agreeing form *qui*, subject extraction is fine across a preposed adverbial. This is not expected on the basis of what we have been assuming so far. The structure would be

(116) . . . t″ qui [l'année prochaine Top° [t′ Fin°+Agr [t pourra . . .]]]

Here t is properly governed by Fin, but t′ violates the ECP: Fin cannot jump to Top, Top itself is unable to license t′ (otherwise (112)a would be well-formed too), and the agreeing form *qui* is too far away from t′ to have a beneficial effect on it, under RM.

In short, paradigm (112) shows that adverb preposing is transparent to subject extraction in French, which is not affected either positively or negatively, and this transparency is not fully expressed by our analysis. In order to account for the well-formedness of (112)b within our frame of assumptions there are two basic possibilities. Either structure (116) is made more impoverished, to the effect that t′ becomes close enough to *qui* to be licensed by it;[30] or the structure is made richer than (116), and there is a device which allows the subject chain to bypass the Top layer without damage, and to benefit from the presence of *qui*. As the second possibility seems to involve a less radical departure from assumptions that we have adopted so far, I will pursue it here.

Let us then focus on the second possibility. How can the subject chain successfully bypass the TopP in (112)b? Clearly, Top should have the quality of licensing t′ here, but in such a way that the higher agreeing C *qui* should continue to be relevant for the global well-formedness of the chain. So, we can try to use the same method, and ascribe to Top the same governing device that we attributed to Fin: Agr. This gives us the opportunity of rethinking the distribution of Agr in somewhat more general terms.

What makes an abstract (sometimes concrete) Agr specification available to the C system and, more generally, to any structural system? Following Shlonsky (forthcoming), I will assume that Agr specifications are available to heads containing certain substantive specifications: tense (AgrS), aspect (Agr of Past Participle), perhaps V (AgrO), and so on. In the C system, a natural substantive specification that Agr can occur with is finiteness. So, the AgrFin technique to allow subject extraction just is a particular case of the general distributional property of Agr.

Going back to (116), suppose that also the null Top head is among the substantive heads (with finiteness, tense, aspect, etc.) which can combine in a similar way with an Agr specification. At first sight, this does not seem to help for our problem: in general, Agr is able to govern an element it agrees with, but an Agr specification in Top would not be in an agreement configuration with any member of the chain of t′ (if anything, it could agree with the topicalized adverb, not what we need here). On the other hand more structure may be involved here. A fairly standard assumption on the structure of the IP system is that, when a substantive head X is endowed with Agr features, an independent Agr projection can crop up on top of it:

(117)

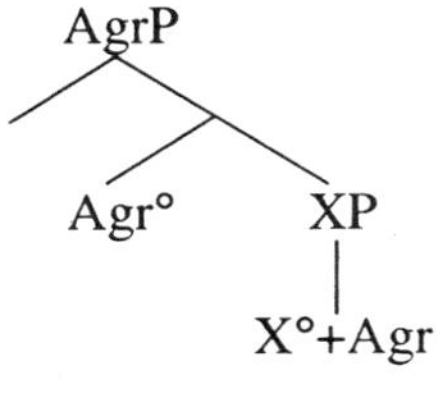

This extra projection has the function, among others, of making a specifier available for checking the Agr features with a phrase in the required local configuration. For instance, in Romance past participle agreement the aspectual head hosting the participial morphology (with its Spec possibly filled by an aspectual adverbial) is assumed to license an Agr projection where agreement is checked with the object (with clitics and in other constructions preposing the object). Suppose this possibility exists for the C system as well.[31]

The structure of (112)b could then be:

(118) . . . t‴ qui [t″ Agr° [l'année prochaine Top°+Agr [t′ Fin+Agr [t pourra . . .]]]]

here t′ is licensed by the Agr features in Top, these features in turn are licensed in a configuration like (117) by the passage of the subject through the Spec of the Agr (Top) projection; t″ is licensed in turn by agreeing *qui*, etc. In this way, the Top phrase is successfully bypassed and the crucial effect of *qui* made compatible with our analysis of Adverb preposing. (112)a remains excluded because we still have an offending trace, t″ in the equivalent of (118) with the non-agreeing form *que*.

We should now make sure that the proposed device does not overgenerate. In particular, we do not want to lose the important fact that CLLD blocks subject extraction in French (see section 9): how can this fact be reconciled with the device that we have just introduced to allow the subject chain to bypass a TopP with adverb preposing? Clearly, adverb preposing and CLLD differ in that the latter but not the former blocks extraction of the subject; so, there must be at least one structural property distinguishing the two cases, and making the "bypassing" device unavailable with CLLD.

A further facet of the problem is added by an observation due to Christopher Laenzlinger. In section 5 we have discussed the fact that the resumptive clitic, obligatory when the dislocated element is the direct object, becomes optional when the dislocated element is a PP:

(119) Au Pape, personne n'oserait (lui) parler ainsi
"To the Pope, nobody would dare to talk to him like that"

Now, Laenzlinger has observed that the two cases pattern differently with respect to the licensing of a subject trace:

(120) a.?* Je me demande qui, au Pape, t oserait lui parler ainsi
"I wonder who, to the Pope, would dare to talk to him like that"

b. ? Je me demande qui, au Pape, t oserait parler ainsi
"I wonder who, to the Pope, would dare to talk like that"

Movement of the subject across a preposed PP is slightly marginal, but the presence of the resumptive clitic makes the structure detectably more degraded. The contrast in (120) immediately invites the conclusion that it is not appropriate to analyze these structures as involving an optional clitic; rather, we should postulate two distinct structural representations: simple PP preposing, which does not affect subject extraction (except a weak subjacency-like effect), and CLLD of the PP, which does. The first construction is the only device available to create a topic-comment configuration with a non-cliticizable PP (an adverbial PP, for instance), and it is not available with the object DP for the reason discussed in section 5. Cliticizable PP's allow both devices, CLLD and simple preposing, and this gives rise to the apparent optionality of the clitic. In sum, argumental PP preposing in French patterns by and large with adverb preposing in not blocking subject extraction, and contrasts with CLLD (but see note 32).

How can we express this contrast? The structural difference between Spec and adjoined position suggests itself again: we continue to assume that the Topic in CLLD is in the Spec of a TopP, a structural layer that interferes with subject extraction in the way that we have discussed. It could be that the preposed PP is adjoined, hence in a configuration transparent to government relations. On the other hand, we do not want to lose the conceptual and empirical arguments which have led us to postulate a TopP for every kind of preposing involving a Topic-comment interpretation. But we can use the Specifier/Adjunct distinction in a more subtle manner.

Suppose that the Top projection may optionally have a specifier (I assume this option to be the general case, unless special principles hold such as the extended clause of the EPP for AgrS). If Spec is not projected, the topicalized element is adjoined to TopP; I will assume that the adjunction configuration is adequate to satisfy the Top Criterion (Chomsky 1993 explicitly assumes that the adjoined position is a part of the checking environment of a head). So, a topic XP can be in one of the two following configurations, both sufficient to satisfy the Top Criterion:

(121)

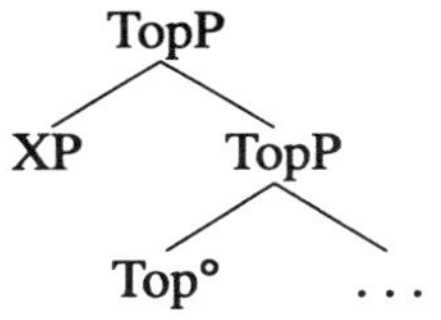

(122)

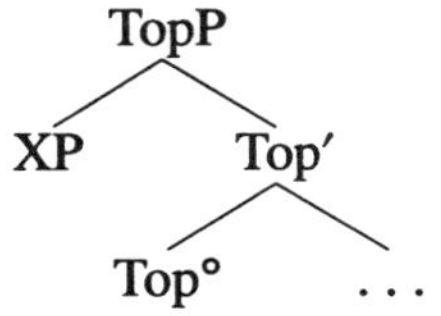

The analysis to be proposed will have the following form: Simple preposing may involve structure (121), a configuration which can be bypassed by the subject chain. On the other hand, CLLD must involve configuration (122), which blocks the subject chain by determining an ECP violation on the subject trace.

Let us consider how this idea can be implemented. As for configuration (121), we continue to assume that it can be bypassed by the subject chain in the way suggested for (118): Top° may be endowed with Agr features, hence license a higher AgrP through whose specifier the subject can be moved.

(123)

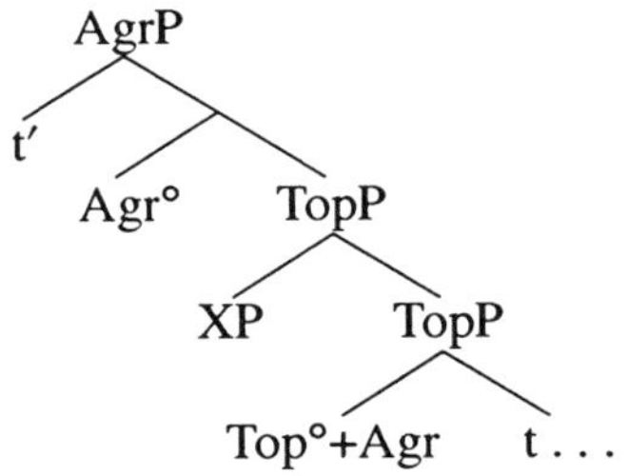

Now, suppose that this option is not available in case the topic phrase occupies the Spec of TopP, as in (122). A natural motivation for this may be that if an agreeing head has a specifier, it can't refrain from agreeing with it (see Chomsky (1995) for relevant discussion expressed in slightly different terms); so, in the equivalent of (123) but containing substructure (122) instead of (121)

(124)

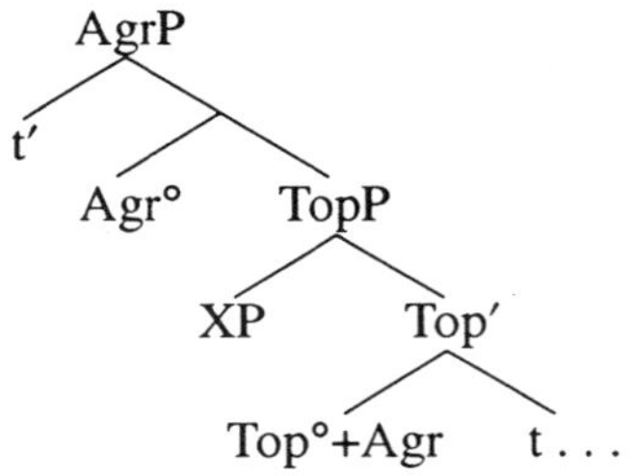

the presence of Agr features on Top could not have any beneficial effects on the subject trace, as the Agr specification would be taken up by the topic XP. On the other hand, if the agreeing head does not have a Spec, as in (123), the Agr features on Top are not taken up by XP and can be related to a licensing specifier (t′) through the mediation of the independent Agr projection, thus bypassing the adjoined topic XP; the Agr features in Top° can then be construed with t′ in (123), hence fulfil the proper government requirement on t.

Then, in order to account for Laenzlinger's contrast, we have to make the assumption that CLLD must necessarily involve configuration (122), while (121) is restricted to simple preposing. Again, there seems to be a natural motivation for this. Simple preposing plausibly involves a single chain, from the position in which the PP is selected to the position in which it satisfies the Top Criterion (possibly through a number of intermediate steps). CLLD, on the other hand, appears to involve two arguments, the topic phrase and the clitic pronoun, hence two chains; as only one theta role is available for them, the construction must then involve some kind of chain composition (Chomsky 1986b) forming a single composed chain at LF. In other cases of chain composition (the *easy to please* construction for instance), both chains entering the composition operation must meet certain conditions, must be independently licensed in some sense. Suppose that a minimal licensing requirement is that each chain must be selected, must have one member in a selection configuration (specifier or complement) with a selecting head. So, the dislocated phrase must be in configuration (122), in the Spec of Top, in order to be available for composition with the clitic chain. But so, the dislocated phrase is incompatible with an agreement specification which could license a subject trace, hence CLLD, contrary to simple PP preposing, always blocks subject extraction.[32]

13. CONCLUSIONS

1. The complementizer system minimally consists of a specification of force, accessible to higher selection, and a specification of finiteness, selecting a finite (or non-finite) IP.

2. It may also consist of a topic and a focus field, expressing the topic-comment and focus-presupposition articulations, respectively. Within "movement as last resort" guidelines, there is no free optional preposing and IP adjunction: all instances of preposing to the left periphery must be triggered by the satisfaction of a Criterion. Topic-comment and focus-presupposition articulations involve two instances of the larger family of A′ Criteria. These guidelines naturally lead one to assume special Top and Foc heads and projections for topic and focus constructions.

3. In English topic-comment structures, the topic sits in the Spec of TopP and is locally construed with a null operator mediating the topic and the comment; in Romance, topic-comment is typically expressed by the CLLD construction. A number of properties differentiating topic and focus (compatibility with a resumptive clitic, sensitivity to WCO, . . .) follow from the assumption that only the latter involves genuine quantification, the former involving a non-quantificational A′ dependency.

4. The global articulation of the topic-focus field in Italian involves a FocP surrounded by recursive TopP's, this configuration being in turn sandwiched in between the Force-Finiteness system, as in tree (41). The non-recursiveness of FocP may be a consequence of its own interpretive characteristics. Different types of elements fill different positions in (41). Straightforward distributional evidence suggests that relative pronouns are in the Spec of Force, while interrogative pronouns in main questions compete with focussed phrases for the Spec of Focus. Complementizers such as *that*, *que*, etc. are in Force° (when the topic-focus field is activated), while prepositional complementizers in Romance are in Fin°.

5. In non-finite structures in which the Case properties of the subject are determined by an element of the C system, this element must be under Fin; if it was on a different head (and a lower head of the C system was activated), the required local configuration (head government) would not hold, under Relativized Minimality. So, many well-known adjacency effects are immediately explainable. The adjacency effect between a prepositional complementizer and PRO in Romance is amenable to the same explanation under a slight revision of the null case approach to PRO.

6. Extraction across French CLLD gives rise to subject-object asymmetries, as is expected under the X-bar analysis of Top: in this construction, at least one trace member of the chain of the extracted subject inevitably violates the head government requirement of the ECP under Relativized Minimality, hence subject extraction is blocked.

7. Argumental topicalization in English also blocks subject extraction, as is expected. On the other hand, adverb preposing gives rise to an apparently opposite effect: a *that*-t violation is alleviated by the intervention of a preposed adverbial (an anti-adjacency effect). Under our interpretation, the preposed adverbial licenses enough C structure to ensure the survival of the subject trace. More precisely, force and finiteness, normally expressed as a syncretic head, must split when the topic field is activated by a preposed adverbial. The lower Fin, endowed with Agr features, properly governs the subject trace, as in all successful cases of subject extraction. In the absence of the preposed adverbial, a principle of structural economy enforces the choice of a minimal C structure with the syncretic force-finiteness head, which gives rise to an ECP violation if the subject is extracted across *that*. The fact that negative preposing gives rise to anti-adjacency effects, as well as the surprising fact that I to C movement with negative preposing ceases to be obligatory exactly when the subject is extracted, receive a unitary analysis under the proposed framework.

8. The lack of anti-adjacency effects in French is related to the lack of affixal complementizers in this language. The fact that (the structure associated to) a preposed adverbial is nevertheless transparent to subject extraction is interpreted by sharpening the assumptions on the possible occurrence of Agr features: they can be associated to every substantive head, and an independent AgrP can be projected; this makes it possible for the subject chain to "bypass" the TopP associated to the preposed adverbial. The apparently optional occurrence of the clitic in certain cases of CLLD is shown to determine the blocking of subject extraction, thus suggesting that two distinct constructions with different structural properties are signalled by the presence or absence of the clitic.

Università di Siena

NOTES

[1] Preliminary versions of this paper were presented in class lectures at the University of Geneva (1993–94, 1994–95), at the 3ème Cycle Romand on Syntax and Pragmatics, Neuchâtel, January 1994, and in talks at the University of Florence, June 1994, April 1995 and at DIPSCO, Istituto San Raffaele, Milan, February 1995. This research is part of the FNRS project n. 11-33542.93. Thanks are due to Adriana Belletti, Guglielmo Cinque, Brent De Chenes, Grant Goodall, Maria Teresa Guasti, Liliane Haegeman, Ur Shlonsky, Michal Starke for helpful comments.

[2] One class of attempts to integrate into the CP system more material than a single X-bar schema can contain involves the assumption that CP may undergo a limited recursion (Rizzi and Roberts 1989, Rizzi 1991, McCloskey 1992); other attempts directly involve the postulation of heads of the C system distinct from the lexical complementizers (Culicover's (1992) Polarity head, Shlonsky's (1994) agreement in C (a development of Cardinaletti and Roberts' (1991), Roberts' (1993) idea of AgrS recursion), as well as much recent literature on focus (see below)). See also Nakajima's (1993) explicit reference to a Split-C hypothesis. Work on V-2 languages has also envisaged the possibility of a structured C-system (e.g. Muller and Sternefeld (1993)). Reinhart's (1981) earlier proposal for a multiple C structure was motivated by bounding theoretic considerations.

[3] As for agreement, certain paradigms do not manifest any overt morphological form of subject agreement (English past and future, English subjunctive, the normal verbal paradigms in Mainland Scandinavian) and still cooccur with *that* type complementizers; conversely, inflected infinitives in Portuguese possess morphological marking for subject person agreement, and still do not cooccur with *that* type complementizers. As for tense, Latin infinitives express the present/past (and periphrastic future) distinction, and still we do not want to consider such forms finite (no nominative case assigned to subjects, etc.). In spite of these and many other cases of dissociation, the generalization still holds that finite forms are more richly specified for features of the Tense-Person Agreement-Mood complex (the latter presumably being a unique characteristic of finiteness). See also George and Kornfilt (1981) for an earlier discussion of this notion.

[4] If a finite verbal form must be selected by a C system bearing the feature [+fin], we account for the fact that direct selection of IP from a higher verb is limited to non-finite verbal forms. This is shown by the absence of exceptional case marking with finite structures, as well as by the impossibility of Heavy NP Shift (under the analysis of Rizzi 1990: 34–35)

(i) a. *I believe [him is smart]
b. *I believe [t is smart] every student who. . . .

cf.

(ii) a. I believe [him to be smart]
b. I believe [t to be smart] every student who. . . .

ECM-like constructions appear to be possible with subjunctive complements in languages with missing or highly restricted non-finite verbal forms: see Guasti (1993), Turano (1993) on the Albanian causative construction, Rivero (1991) on Rumanian. Perhaps V can directly select IP's with the minimal specification of finiteness that the language allows, which is subjunctive in languages basically lacking infinitives.

One should also observe that indirect questions can be finite or infinitival clauses, but not small clauses:

(iii) a. John does not know of what he can be proud
b. John does not know of what to be proud
c. *John does not know of what proud

Presumably, if the C system always starts from ± fin, it must select an IP on which the feature can be defined; as finiteness is a verbal feature, non-verbal small clauses cannot have a C system, hence they offer no structural slot in which a Wh element could be hosted, so that small clause questions are predicted not to exist. Another consequence of the lack of C system for small clauses is that there are no control argumental small clauses (**John wants PRO rich*), if PRO is licensed by -fin, as is argued in section 8 (the ill-formedness of (iii) could then also fall under this larger class of cases). Control small clauses appear to be possible in adverbial position in such expressions as *while PRO at home, if PRO in doubt*, etc., in which presumably the adverbial subordinator is different enough from the ordinary clausal C system to be consistent with a propositional content not specifiable for finiteness, and still capable of licensing PRO. The C-like particles introducing certain small clauses analyzed in Starke (1994) could perhaps be treated as subordinators (in the sense of note 6) rather than as markers of -fin.

[5] Things may be different in full V-2 languages, in which the inflected verb typically moves to C in certain tensed clauses; presumably in such cases one particular choice of +fin attracts the finite verb to have its finiteness feature checked by the tense specification on V; even this case differs from verb movement to an inflectional head, though, in that, V movement is not sanctioned by any special affix on the verb.

[6] As for the assumption that the force head closes off the C system upwards, it should be noticed that operators do not always fill the highest Spec of the C system, e.g. interrogative operators are placed in a lower Spec position in Italian, see section 6. I will continue to assume that also in such cases the highest head of the C system expresses Force, as is required if selection takes place in a strictly local configuration; the actual position of the operator is determined by the relevant A′ Criterion (on which see the next section), and may or may not coincide with the Spec/Force. An alternative is suggested by Bhatt and Yoon's (1991) distinction between type markers (our Force heads) and simple subordinators, heads which make a clause available for (categorial) selection independently of its force. If this proposal is combined with ours, a tripartite system would result (subordinator, Force, Finiteness). This possible refinement will not be developed here.

[7] Additional straightforward evidence for an articulated C system is provided by the existence, in some languages, of strings of complementizers occurring in a fixed order, e.g. the Danish case discussed in Vikner (1991).

[8] (13)a becomes more acceptable if the Wh element is stressed; in that case, the structure receives a kind of echo interpretation (e.g., to express surprise or disbelief in reaction to somebody else's statement). The contrast (12)–(13) was already noticed and discussed by Cinque (1979: 113–114), who argued on this basis for a different position of relative and interrogative pronouns (thanks to Guglielmo Cinque for drawing my attention to this reference); see also Grosu (1975) for an early discussion of the topic.

[9] It should be noted here that my terminology is slightly different from Cinque's: he follows the traditional terminology in using the term "Topicalization" to refer to the English constructions (1) and (2); he then extends this term to cover the Italian construction (4). I try to avoid the term Topicalization, and refer to (1) and (3) as Topic (Comment) structures and to (2) and (4) as Focus (Presupposition) structures.

[10] The possibility of a topic-comment structures of the following kind in French:

(i) Les gâteaux, j'adore
"The cakes, I love"

is presumably related to the capacity that a restricted class of verbs (*aimer, adorer, connaître, . . .*) has of licensing *pro* in object position with a referential interpretation, a capacity shared by certain French prepositions (see Zribi-Hertz 1984 for discussion). With most verbs the French paradigm is like the Italian one, with the clitic obligatorily present:

(ii) Les gâteaux, je *(les) ai mangés à midi
"The cakes, I ate (them) at lunch"

[11] As for the focus construction in English (as in (2)), it could have the same syntax as the topic construction and involve a null operator, sitting in the Spec of the complement of Foc° (much as a cleft construction); on the other hand, the mediation of the null operator is not needed in this case under our assumptions, as the focal element should be able to directly bind a variable in (2), on a par with the Italian equivalent (16)b. So, a priori we would expect a possible structural difference between Top and Foc in English as well. In fact, Culicover (1992) observes that Top induces subjacency-like effects (on which see also Rochemont (1989), Lasnik and Saito (1992) and references quoted there), while Foc does not (at least, not to the same extent), a contrast which suggests the existence of a structural difference between the two constructions. See also note 26 for the different behavior of the two constructions with respect to anti-adjacency.

[12] See Koster (1978: 199ff.) for an analysis of this construction in Germanic. As for the possibility of non-focal topicalization in V-2 Germanic, we should either follow the reference quoted (see also Cardinaletti (1984)) and assume that a null operator identified by a topic is always involved in such cases, or assume that V-2 endows the specifier of the head attracting the inflected verb of the capacity to license a null constant.

[13] Of course, we want to be able to admit that the preposing of a PP can determine a genuine operator variable structure in some cases, e.g. in questions like *To whom did you talk?*, or a genuine null constant interpretation, e.g. in appositive relatives like *A man to whom I talked*, but here we could invoke a reconstruction process à la Chomsky (1993) and maintain that variable and null constant interpretation are restricted to DP's.

[14] Moreover, the entire Spec of Top is moved out in (36), but this does not seem to be a well formed option: in general, A′ criteria cannot be satisfied "in passing", e.g., a Wh element cannot satisfy the Wh Criterion in an embedded C and then be moved to the main C system.

[15] Other functional categories like T, Asp, D, Agr do not admit recursion, under economy of representations, because one specification is sufficient, hence maximal. This does not apply to Top or Foc though, as there can be n constituents involved.

The proposed analysis of the impossibility of FocP recursion also correctly predicts that a FocP can be activated in a main clause (i), in an embedded clause (ii), but not in both simultaneously (iii):

(i) A GIANNI ho detto t che dovremmo leggere il tuo libro
"TO GIANNI I said that we should read your book"

(ii) Ho detto a Gianni che IL TUO LIBRO dovremmo leggere
"I said to Gianni that YOUR BOOK we should read"

(iii) * A GIANNI ho detto che IL TUO LIBRO dovremmo leggere
"TO GIANNI I said that YOUR BOOK we should read"

(iii) is excluded because the embedded clause is part of the presupposition of the main Foc, hence it cannot contain a Foc position. Predictably, Topic-comment structures of the CLLD kind are possible in main and embedded clauses simultaneously:

(iv) A Gianni, gli ho detto che il tuo libro, lo dovremmo leggere
"To Gianni, I said to him that your book, we should read it"

[16] This is only a first approximation: on the position of relative operators, see the detailed discussion of Bianchi (1995), conducted within the guidelines of Kayne (1994) and based in part on a previous version of the present article, an analysis which I will not be able to discuss here.

[17] The location of the Foc feature may vary across languages, as many languages (Hungarian, . . .) require I to C movement with left-peripheral focalization. In this case, the lower Top position of (41) is not activated (its presence would block I to Foc movement), exactly as in main questions in Italian. Perhaps a reflex of this UG option is found in the fact that

some speakers of Italian find the activation of the lower TopP (e.g., in (37)b) marginal if compared to the activation of the higher TopP (as in (37)d). For such speakers the Foc feature may preferentially be located in the inflectional system, whence the preferred application of I to C with Focus (alternatively, these speakers may be (more) sensitive to a weak subjacency-like effect induced by the lower TopP on the movement of the focal element: cf. the marginality detected by speakers of French in examples like (66)a).

[18] As we have already seen (ex (4), repeated here) a topic preceding the Wh element is fully acceptable, and a topic following the Wh element is marginal in embedded questions:

(i) a. Mi domando, il premio Nobel, a chi lo potrebbero dare
"I wonder, the Nobel Prize, to whom they could give it"

b. ?Mi domando a chi, il premio Nobel, lo potrebbero dare
"I wonder to whom, the Nobel Prize, they could give it"

The marginal acceptability of the latter is not surprising, as the obligatoriness of I to C movement is weakened in embedded questions (Rizzi 1991: 17). The fact that the Wh element is marginally compatible with an embedded focalized element in embedded questions, in clear contrast with main questions,

(ii) a. ?Mi domando A GIANNI che cosa abbiano detto (, non a Piero)
"I wonder TO GIANNI what they said (, not to Piero)"

b. *A GIANNI che cosa hanno detto (, non a Piero)?
"TO GIANNI what did they say (, not to Piero)?"

may suggest that the Wh element can sit in an independent position distinct from Spec/Foc in embedded questions. The properties of this position, as well of the other special positions filled by certain Wh elements (*perché* (why) and Wh with lexical restriction: Rizzi (1991, fn. 16), exclamative Wh elements: Benincà (1995)) or of the other kinds of C elements in different Romance varieties discussed in Poletto (1993), Bianchi (1995) and references cited there, could lead to further extensions of the maximal structure of C along lines that will not be investigated here.

[19] McCloskey (1992: 15) points out that "external" preposing of a whole adverbial clause is marginally possible in some cases:

(i) ?He promised, when he got home, that he would cook dinner for the children

Here one could assume, with McCloskey, that this case involves genuine CP recursion, as is particularly plausible for cases in which *that* occurs twice (McCloskey 1992, fn. 12):

(ii) She maintained that when they arrived that they should be welcomed

I will leave open here the question of why this option seems to be restricted to full adverbial clauses.

[20] If Case Theory does not appeal to the notion of head government, as in the system of Chomsky (1993), some other notion of locality will be needed to express the fact that the intervening X-bar structure in (53) disrupts the required case configuration. For instance, in a move feature analysis à la Chomsky (1995), one could assume that the case features on *John* cannot reach *for* at LF because of the intervention of Top.

On the other hand, the environment for a potential violation of Case Theory of the kind illustrated in (53) may simply not arise here: in fact, preposing of an element to a position external to *for* does not seem to give rise to an acceptable structure either (* *I would very much prefer, this book, for you to read immediately*), so one seems to be led to conclude that *for* always expresses force and finiteness syncretically (in the sense of section 10), and therefore no topic-focus field can be activated with this choice of C. In this respect, *for* is different from the infinitival complementizer *di* in Italian, which is compatible with an external topic (see section 8).

[21] The impossibility of (57)b is sharper than in the corresponding structure with a lexical subject NP presumably because *egli*, as a weak pronoun (Cardinaletti and Starke 1994), strongly disallows being left in a position lower than the highest subject position.

[22] Actually, a weaker assumption is sufficient: Top does not allow I to move through it to Force, i.e., there is no Top to Force movement (direct movement of I to Force being barred by RM in (60)).

It should be noticed that, even in main questions like (58)b, it is not obvious that I to C movement stops at Fin: if it is the case in general that the Wh element sits in the Spec of Focus in main questions (see section 6), then the auxiliary should reach Foc° in order to satisfy the Wh Criterion, a position that may be followed by a TopP if structure (41) is transposed to English. So, the HMC analysis seems to be needed to exclude (58)b on a par with (59)b.

[23] This analysis can be straightforwardly expressed within Chomsky's (1995) move features approach, which comes very close to reintroducing the head government relation in Case Theory. Alternatively, if one assumes that C systems can be normally endowed with concrete or abstract Agr features (Rizzi 1990, Haegeman 1992, Shlonsky 1994, etc.) one could think that it is the non finite Agr in the C system which licenses PRO in a Spec-head configuration.

[24] Speakers of French are reluctant to accept CLLD with infinitives. Nevertheless, a detectable contrast exists between control and raising (Ch. Laenzlinger, p.c.):

(i) ?? Je pense, ton livre, pouvoir le comprendre
"I think, your book, to be able to understand it"

(ii) *Marie semble, ton livre, pouvoir le comprendre
"Marie seems, your book, to be able to understand it"

[25] This way of satisfying the ECP on t′ by moving the head agreeing with it to the next higher head position seems to be in contrast with the fact that, in an analogous configuration, I to C movement does not license a subject trace (Rizzi 1990: 40, 1991, and the following section). Still, we can express the difference between the two cases by observing that with I to C a governing head (I) moves to a head of a different categorial type (C), whereas in the structure derived from (93) a head of the C system (Fin) moves to another head of the C system (Top) from where it can properly govern t′, if we intend proper government as government within a projection of the same categorial type (slightly modifying Rizzi (1990: 32). In order to express this distinction we must now crucially appeal to the assumption (section 2) that the I and the C systems are distinct.

Postulating head movement of Fin° solves the technical problem raised by Culicover (1993) on the status of the trace licensing agreement in C. The assumed head movement is not simply a "local" technical solution, as it crucially contributes to the explanation of the difference between English and French with respect to the anti-adjacency effect (section 12).

The assumption that Fin can move to Top is not inconsistent with the assumption that an intervening Top blocks (further) movement of a lower head to Force (section 7): Top may be able to host a lower head without being itself movable to a higher head position (see note 22).

[26] Here it becomes crucial to assume that Op goes to Fin; this hypothesis is in fact supported by the fact that if argument topicalisation and adverb preposing take place in the same structure, the preferred order is with the topicalized argument internal ((i) is more acceptable than (ii)):

(i) Around Christmas, this book, you should buy

(ii) This book, around Christmas, you should buy

This order is expected if Op goes to Spec of Fin, and if only argument topicalization, not adverbial PP preposing, involves the null operator. On the other hand, (ii) is not totally excluded; moreover, if the argumental topic and the preposed adverbial appear in that order, there seems to be a detectable anti-adjacency effect (even though the judgment is difficult):

(iii) This is the man who I think that, this book, around Christmas, should buy

All this then suggests the following interpretation: the null Op involved in argumental topicalization normally goes to Spec/Fin; this explains the preferred order of (i) over (ii) and the lack of anti-adjacency effects with argumental topicalization (as per the discussion in the text); on the other hand, Op can survive in a higher position as a marked possibility if the Top position immediately higher than Fin is taken up, as is shown by the marginal possibility of the order in (ii); in this case, if the subject is extracted an anti-adjacency effect is expected, and indeed it seems to exist in structures like (iii) (with all the caveats justified by the complexity of this kind of judgment).

The idea that the null operator is responsible for the lack of anti-adjacency effects with argumental topicalization in English has one additional interesting consequence. Ian Roberts (p.c.) observes that structures like (96), excluded with the topic intonation on the preposed object, improve if the preposed object bears focal stress. Culicover (1993, fn. 1), observes the same improvement effect of focal stress with preposed argumental PP's. The existence of anti-adjacency effects with English focalisation is expected, under our analysis, if focalization, contrary to (English) topicalisation, does not involve a null operator, as suggested in note 11 (if no null operator is involved in the equivalent of (96), Fin can be endowed with Agr features licensed by the passage of the subject in its spec, and capable of licensing the subject trace, etc.). So, there are two significant, if subtle, differences between English topicalization and focalization with respect to subjacency (see note 11) and anti-adjacency effects which may both be related to the absence of a null operator in the second construction. See also de Chenes (1995) for discussion of other factors alleviating *that*-t violations.

[27] I remain agnostic here as to the question whether the theory should contain an explicit statement of relative strength, or this selective interaction just follows intrinsically from the fact that selectional constraints are directly invoked in the structure building process, where (98) is operative, while ECP applies on representations that are already formed.

[28] The proposed analysis assumes that force and finiteness can be expressed in a single head, and that this option is enforced by economy unless the activation of the topic-focus field makes it non viable. Alternatively, one could consider the possibility that the force-finiteness is "agglutinative" as many other syntactic subsystems seem to be, hence it always involves two distinct heads

(i)

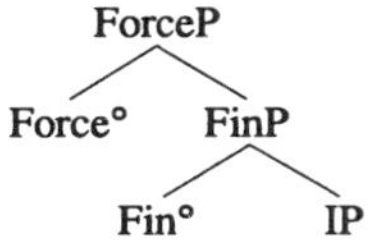

The analysis can then be rephrased in the following form: in (i) the representation can involve a single item from the functional lexicon (*that* or *0*, one of the two options (90)a–b), generated under Fin and moved to Force to check the force features. If the Top-Foc field is activated (assuming that Fin° would not be allowed to move through the heads of the Top-Foc field all the way up to Force), two distinct items from the functional lexicon are needed (both (90)a and b, *that* for force and *0* for finiteness), a possibility which gives rise to the anti-adjacency effects in the way we have discussed. This possibility is not freely available due to Economy, whence the lack of free *that*-t violations.

[29] The slight improvement that some speakers find in (112)a, compared to (111)a, could be related to the possibility of not leaving a trace in the Spec of an agreeing Fin. Then there would be no ECP violation, at the price of leaving in the structure a non-licensed occurrence of Agr features, a violation which may be felt by these speakers as slightly less severe than an ECP violation.

[30] E.g., it could be that adverb preposing, contrary to our assumptions so far, does not necessarily involve an independent TopP: one could consider the possibility that Fin itself can be endowed with Top features, and a preposed adverbial can satisfy the Top Criterion by adjoining to the FinP. If this alternative is adopted, the analysis of anti-adjacency would become less straightforward than in section 10: it should express the fact that a syncretic force+fin head cannot bear the required Top features, so that the split is required when a preposed adverb is to be integrated, with the consequence of determining anti-adjacency effects in English along the lines indicated in section 10. See note 32 below for potential empirical support for the alternative proposed in this footnote.

[31] We do not take a position here on whether the double structure (117) is compulsory whenever a substantive head is endowed with Agr features, or it is simply an option, which is taken just in case an extra specifier is needed to license the Agr features. In the latter case, everything that has been said so far can be left unchanged; in the former, all the structures involving Agr features associated to a substantive head should involve the extra Agr layer, with no significant additional modification of the analysis.

[32] Adverbial PP preposing in French still differs from argument PP preposing in a subtle way: the latter, but not the former, determines a weak subjacency-like effect (see (120)b) when something is extracted; this suggests that the two cases should not be fully assimilated. One possibility is to restrict the adjunction analysis proposed in the text (adjunction to the TopP) to argumental PP preposing, and go back to the proposal of note 30 for adverbial PP preposing (direct adjunction to a FinP endowed with Top features); so, both adverbial and argumental preposed PP's can be bypassed by the subject chain (as in both cases the preposed element can sit in an adjoined position, to FinP and TopP, respectively), but only the latter involves an autonomous TopP, which may be deemed responsible for the weak subjacency effect. CLLD cannot be bypassed by the subject chain for the reason discussed in the text, and determines a weak subjacency effect on non-subject extraction (cf. (66)a, etc.) because a TopP is involved.

The tripartite system of Romance (CLLD, argument PP preposing, adjunct PP preposing) appears to reduce, in English, to the bifurcation between argument topicalisation (of both DP's and PP's) and adverbial PP preposing, the first blocking subject chains and determining subjacency-like effects on non-subject extraction, the second not blocking subject chains (in fact, determining anti-adjacency effects) nor determining subjacency-like effects for non-subject extraction. For the first case, we continue to assume the null operator construction, which is inconsistent with the "bypassing" device, as we have seen. For the second, we may also adopt the proposal of note 30. What appears to be missing in English is the option of adjoining a preposed argumental PP to TopP, an option apparently blocked by the generalized availability of the null operator structure for all cases of argumental topicalisation in this language.

REFERENCES

Aboh, E. (1995) 'Notes sur la focalisation en Gungbe', manuscript, University of Geneva.

Antinucci, F. and G. Cinque (1977) 'Sull'ordine delle parole in italiano: l'emarginazione', *Studi di grammatica italiana* **6**, 121–146.

Baltin, M. (1982) 'A landing site for movement rules', *Linguistic Inquiry* **13**, 1–38.

Bayer, J. (1984) 'COMP in Bavarian', *The Linguistic Review* **3**, 209–274.

Belletti, A. (1994) 'Case checking and clitic placement: Three issues in (Italian/Romance) clitics', *GenGenP* **1.2**, 101–118.

Belletti, A. and U. Shlonsky (1995) 'The order of verbal complements: A comparative study', *NLLT* **13**, 489–526.

Benincà, P. (1988) "Costruzioni con ordine marcato degli elementi', in: L. Renzi (ed.), *Grande grammatica italiana di consultazione*, Volume I, il Mulino, Bologna, pp. 129–145.

Benincà, P. (1995) 'La struttura della frase esclamativa alla luce del dialetto padovano', manuscript, University of Padua.

den Besten, H. (1977/1983) 'On the interaction of root transformations and lexical deletive rules', in: W. Abraham (ed.), *On the Formal Syntax of Westgermania*. Benjamins, Amsterdam, pp. 47–131.

Bhatt, R. and J. Yoon (1991) 'On the composition of comp and parameters of V-2', *WCCFL* **10**, 41–52.

Bianchi, V. (1995) *Consequences of Antisymmetry for the Syntax of Headed Relative Clauses*, doctoral dissertation, Scuola Normale Superiore, Pisa.

Bresnan, J. (1977) 'Variables in the theory of transformations', in: P. Culicover et al. (eds.), *Formal Syntax*, Academic Press, New York.

Brody, M. (1990) 'Some remarks on the focus field in Hungarian', *UCL Working Papers*, Vol. 2, University College of London.

Brody, M. (1995a) *Lexico-Logical Form: A Radically Minimalist Theory*, MIT Press, Cambridge, Mass.

Brody, M. (1995b) 'Focus and checking theory', in: I. Kenesei (ed.), *Levels and Structures* (Approaches to Hungarian, Vol. 5), JATE, Szeged, pp. 30–43

Calabrese, A. (1982) 'Alcune ipotesi sulla struttura informazionale delle frase in italiano e sul suo rapporto con la struttura fonologica', *Rivista di Grammatica Generativa* **7**, 3–78.

Cardinaletti, A. (1983) 'Lo status dei pronomi d- e la ricostruzione nella dislocazione a sinistra in tedesco', *Rivista di Grammatica Generativa* **8**, 111–125.

Cardinaletti, A. and I. Roberts (1991) 'Clause structure and X-second', manuscript, University of Venice, University of Geneva.

Cardinaletti, A. and M. Starke (1994) 'The typology of structural deficiency', manuscript, University of Venice, University of Geneva.

Cecchetto, C. (1994) 'Clitic left dislocation and scrambling: Towards a unified analysis', manuscript, DIPSCO, Fondazione San Raffaele, Milano.

Cheng, L. (1991) *On the Typology of Wh Questions*, doctoral dissertation, MIT.

Chomsky, N. (1976) 'Conditions on rules of grammar', *Linguistic Analysis* **2**, 303–351.

Chomsky, N. (1977) 'On Wh movement', in: A. Akmajian, P. Culicover and T. Wasow (eds.), *Formal Syntax*. Academic Press, New York, pp. 71–132.

Chomsky, N. (1986a) *Knowledge of Language*. Praeger, New York.

Chomsky, N. (1986b) *Barriers*. MIT Press, Cambridge, Mass.

Chomsky, N. (1991) 'Some notes on the economy of derivations and representations', in: R. Freidin (ed.), *Principles and Parameters in Comparative Grammar*. MIT Press, Cambridge, Mass., pp. 417–454.

Chomsky, N. (1993) 'A minimalist program for linguistic theory', in: K. Hale and S. J. Keyser, (eds.), *The View From Building 20*. MIT Press, Cambridge, Mass.

Chomsky, N. (1995) *The Minimalist Program*. MIT Press, Cambridge, Mass.

Chomsky, N. and H. Lasnik (1977) 'Filters and control', *Linguistic Inquiry* **8**, 425–504.

Chomsky, N. and H. Lasnik (1991) 'Principles and parameters theory', in: J. Jacobs, A. von Stechow, W. Sternefeld and T. Vennemann (eds.), *Syntax: an International Handbook of Contemporary Research*. Berlin, De Gruyter.

Cinque, G. (1979) *Studi di sintassi e pragmatica*, CLESP, Padova.

Cinque, G. (1982) 'On the theory of relative clauses and markedness', *The Linguistic Review* **1**, 247–296.

Cinque, G. (1990) *Types of A' Dependencies*. MIT Press, Cambridge, Mass.

Cinque, G. (1993) 'A null theory of phrase and compound stress", *Linguistic Inquiry* **24**, 239–298.

Cottell, S. (1994) 'The representation of tense in modern Irish', manuscript, University of Geneva.

Crisma, P. (1992) 'On the acquisition of Wh questions in French', *GenGenP* **0**(1-2), 115–122.

Culicover, P. (1992) 'Topicalisation, inversion and complementizers in English', OTS Working Papers, D. Delfitto et al. (eds.), *Going Romance and Beyond*, University of Utrecht, Utrecht.
Culicover, P. (1993) 'The adverb effect: Evidence against ECP accounts of the that-t effects", *NELS* 1993, pp. 97–110.
de Chenes, B. (1995) 'Towards and explanatory account of the that-trace effect', manuscript, University of Geneva.
Figueiredo-Silva, M. C. (1994) *La position sujet en portugais brésilien*, doctoral dissertation, University of Geneva.
Friedemann, M.-A. (1995) *Sujets syntaxiques: positions, inversions et pro*, doctoral dissertation, University of Geneva.
Fukui, N. (1993) 'A note on improper movement', *The Linguistic Review* **10**(2), 111–126.
George, L. and J. Kornfilt (1981) 'Finiteness and boundedness in Turkish', in: F. Heny (ed.), *Binding and Filtering*. Croom Helm, London, pp. 105–127.
Giorgi, A. and F. Pianesi (1994) 'Extraction from subjunctive clauses and clausal architecture', talk presented at the University of Geneva, November 1994.
Grimshaw, J. (1991) 'Extended projections', manuscript, Rutgers University.
Grimshaw, J. (1993) 'Minimal projections, heads and optimality', manuscript, Rutgers University.
Grimshaw, J. (1995) 'Projection, heads and optimality', manuscript, Rutgers University.
Grosu, A. (1975) "The position of fronted Wh phrases', *Linguistic Inquiry* **6**, 588–599.
Guasti, T. (1993) *Causative and Perception Verbs*, Rosenberg & Sellier, Turin.
Guasti, T. (1994) 'On the controversial status of romance interrogatives', manuscript, DIPSCO, Fondazione San Raffaele, Milano.
Gundel, J. (1974) *The Role of Topic and Comment in Linguistic Theory*, Indiana University Linguistic Club, Bloomington, Indiana.
Haegeman, L. (1986) 'INFL, COMP and nominative case assignment in Flemish infinitivals', in: H. van Riemsdijk and P. Muysken (eds.), *Features and Projections*. Foris, Dordrecht, pp. 123–137.
Haegeman, L. (1992) *Theory and Description in Generative Syntax*, Cambridge University Press.
Haegeman, L. (1995) *The Syntax of Negation*, Cambridge University Press.
Haegeman, L. and R. Zanuttini (1991) 'Negative heads and the negative criterion', *The Linguistic Review* **8**, 233–251.
Henry, A. (1995) *Belfast English and Standard English: Dialect Variation and Parameter Setting*, Oxford University Press, Oxford.
Holmberg, H. and Ch. Platzack (1988) 'The role of inflection is Scandinavian syntax', *Working Papers in Scandinavian Syntax* **42**, 25-43.
Horvath, J. (1985) *Focus in the Theory of Grammar and the Syntax of Hungarian*, Foris, Dordrecht.
Iatridou, S. (1991) 'Clitics and island effects", manuscript, MIT.
Kayne, R. (1984) *Connectedness and Binary Branching*, Foris Publications, Dordrecht.
Kayne, R. (1994) *The Antisymmetry of Syntax*, MIT Press, Cambridge, Mass.
Kiss, K. (1987) *Configurationality in Hungarian*, Reidel, Dordrecht.
Koster, J. (1978) *Locality Principles in Syntax*, Foris Publications, Dordrecht, 2nd printing: 1981.
Laka, I. (1990) *Negation in Syntax: On the Nature of Functional Categories and Projections*, PhD Dissertation, MIT.
Larson, R. (1988) 'On the double object construction', *Linguistic Inquiry* **19**, 335–391.
Lasnik, H. and M. Saito (1992) *Move Alpha*. MIT Press, Cambridge, MA.
Lasnik, H. and T. Stowell (1991) 'Weakest cross-over', *Linguistic Inquiry* **22**, 687–720.
Longobardi, G. (1980) 'Connectedness, complementi circostanziali e soggiacenza', *Rivista di Grammatica Generativa* **5**, 141–185.

Manzini, R. (1992) *Locality*. MIT Press, Cambridge, Mass.
Manzini, R. (1995) 'From "merge and move" to "form dependency"', *University College London Working Papers in Linguistics* 7, 205–227.
May, R. (1985) *Logical Form: Its Structure and Derivation*. MIT Press, Cambridge, Mass.
McCloskey, J. (1992) 'Adjunction, selection and embedded verb second', *Working Paper LRC-92-07*, Linguistics Research Center, University of California, Santa Cruz.
Moro, A. (1995) *The Raising of Predicates*. Cambridge University Press.
Motapanyane, V. (1995) *Theoretical Implications of Complementation in Romanian*. Unipress, Padua.
Muller, G. and W. Sternefeld (1993) 'Improper movement and unambiguous binding', *Linguistic Inquiry* **24**, 461–507.
Nakajima, H. (1993) 'Topic phrases and complementizers', manuscript, Tokyo Metropolitan University.
Pesetsky, D. (1995) *Zero Syntax*. MIT Press, Cambridge, Mass.
Poletto, C. (1993) 'Subject clitic – verb inversion in north-Eastern Italian dialects', in: A. Belletti (ed.), *Syntactic Theory and the Dialects of Italy*, Rosenberg & Sellier, Turin, pp. 204–251
Pollock, J.-Y. (1989) 'Verb movement, universal grammar and the structure of IP', *Linguistic Inquiry* **20**, 365–424.
Puskas, G. (1992) 'The Wh criterion in Hungarian', *Rivista di Grammatica Generativa* **17**, 141–186.
Reinhart, T. (1981) 'Two comp positions', in: A. Belletti, L, Brandi and L. Rizzi (eds.), *Theory of Markedness in Generative Grammar*. Scuola Normale Superiore, Pisa.
Rivero, M.-L. (1991) 'Exceptional case marking effects in Rumanian subjunctive complements', in: D. Wanner and D. A. Kibbee (eds.), *New Analyses in Romance Linguistics*. Benjamins, Amsterdam, pp. 273–298.
Rizzi, L. (1982) *Issues in Italian Syntax*. Foris Publications, Dordrecht.
Rizzi, L. (1986) 'On the status of subject clitics in Romance', in: O. Jaeggli and C. Silva-Corvalan (eds.), *Studies in Romance Linguistics*. Foris Publications, Dordrecht, pp. 391–419.
Rizzi, L. (1990) *Relativized Minimality*. MIT Press, Cambridge, Mass.
Rizzi, L. (1991) 'Residual verb second and the Wh criterion', *Technical Reports in Formal and Computational Linguistics* **2**, University of Geneva.
Rizzi, L. (1993) 'A parametric approach to comparative syntax: Properties of the pronominal system', *English Linguistics* **10**, Tokyo, 1–27.
Rizzi, L. (1994) 'Early null subjects and root null subjects', in: T. Hoekstra and B. Schwartz (eds.), *Language Acquisition in Generative Grammar*. Benjamins, Amsterdam/ Philadelphia.
Rizzi, L. (1995) 'A note on do support', manuscript, University of Geneva.
Rizzi, L. and I. Roberts (1989) 'Complex inversion in French', *Probus* **1**, 1–30.
Roberts, I. (1993) *Verbs and Diachronic Syntax*. Kluwer, Dordrecht.
Rochemont, M. (1989) 'Topic islands and the subjacency parameter', *Canadian Journal of Linguistics* **34**, 145–170.
Rochemont, M & P. Culicover (1990) *English Focus Constructions and the Theory of Grammar*, Cambridge University Press, Cambridge.
Safir, K. (1992) 'Structural economy', manuscript, Rutgers University.
Shlonsky, U. (1994) 'Agreement in comp', *The Linguistic Review* **11**, 351–375.
Shlonsky, U. (forthcoming) *Clause Structure and Word Order in Hebrew: An Essay in Comparative Semitic Syntax*, to appear, Oxford University Press.
Speas, P. (1994) 'Null arguments in a theory of economy of projections', in: E. Benedicto and J. Runner (eds.), *Functional Projections*, UMOP 17.
Sportiche, D. (1992) 'Clitic constructions', manuscript, UCLA.

Starke, M. (1994) 'On the format for small clauses', *GenGenP* **2**, 79–97.
Stowell, T. (1981) *Origins of Phrase Structure*, PhD Dissertation, MIT.
Tsimpli, I. M. (1994) 'Focussing in modern Greek', in: K. Kiss (ed.), *Discourse-configurational Languages*, Oxford University Press.
Turano, G. (1993) 'Subjunctive constructions in arberesh and standard Albanian', *Rivista di Grammatica Generativa* **18**, 101–133.
Turano, G. (1995) *Dipendenze sintattiche in albanese*, Unipress, Padua.
Vikner, S. (1991) 'Relative der and other C elements in Danish', *Lingua* **84**, 109–136.
Watanabe, A. (1993) 'The notion of finite clauses in Agr-based case theory', *Papers on Case and Agreement I: MIT Working Papers* **18**, 243–296.
Zribi-Hertz, A. (1984) 'Prépositions orphélines et pronoms nuls', *Recherches Linguistiques* **12**, 46–91.

INDEX

Kluwer International Handbooks of Linguistics

1. L. Haegeman (ed.): *Elements of Grammar.* Handbook in Generative Syntax. 1997
ISBN 0-7923-4297-6; Pb 0-7923-4298-4

Kluwer Academic Publishers – Dordrecht / Boston / London